D0857718

# Midcentury Quartet

# Midcentury Quartet

## Bishop, Lowell, Jarrell, Berryman, and the Making of a Postmodern Aesthetic

Thomas Travisano

University Press of Virginia
Charlottesville and London

The University Press of Virginia

Printed in the United States of America

*First published 1999*

∞ The paper used in this publication meets the minimum requirements of the American National Standard for Information Sciences—Permanence of Paper for Printed Library Materials, ANSI Z39.48-1984.

Library of Congress Cataloging-in-Publication Data

Travisano, Thomas J., 1951–
Midcentury quartet : Bishop, Lowell, Jarrell, Berryman, and the making of a postmodern aesthetic / Thomas Travisano.
p. cm.
Includes bibliographical references (p. ) and index.
ISBN 0-8139-1887-1 (cloth : alk. paper)
1. American poetry—20th century—History and criticism. 2. Postmodern (Literature)—United States. 3. Bishop, Elizabeth, 1911–1979—Criticism and interpretation. 4. Jarrell, Randall, 1914–1965—Criticism and interpretation. 5. Berryman, John, 1914–1972—Criticism and interpretation. 6. Lowell, Robert, 1917–1977—Criticism and interpretation. I. Title.
PS310.P63T73 1999
811'.509113—dc21 99-16426
CIP

For Elsa Kathryn, Michael Coulliette, and Emily Claire,
and for Paul, Carol, Richard, Gary, Sandra, Steven, and Camille,
and in memory of Margaret Dickie

# Contents

# Preface

Over the course of a decade's research, while sifting through the massive published and archival record left by this most writerly quartet of poets, I grew ever more impressed by the depth, scope, dynamism, and sheer duration of this midcentury quartet's personal and literary relations.[1] And I grappled with the problem of conveying in readable form some sense of their complex and ongoing process of artistic interchange, parallel development, and mutual influence. The challenge lay partly in the sheer abundance and heterogeneity of the materials and partly in the length and complexity of their ongoing, interweaving relationships over more than forty years, as their four-way conversation increasingly intersected. It would be instructive for readers to see at close range the painfully lived experience, the conflicting and harmonizing ideas and aspirations, the often staggering psychic burdens, the emotional courage, and the frequently obsessional artistic dedication—Lowell said to Berryman in an elegy, "We asked to be obsessed with writing / and we were" (*DBD* 27)—that these poets inscribed on so many leaves of their multilayered cultural palimpsest. Like poets, critics can learn much if they set themselves specific formal problems, and perhaps this unique critical problem called for a unique formal solution.

As an illustration of the problem, while I was beginning a final draft of this study, a fellow scholar with experience in the field asked me what set of issues would be appearing "in your Berryman chapter?" I was forced to confess, to my colleague's surprise, that I had no "Berryman chapter." My friend's question alluded to the practice common to group studies of treating each individual figure in a discrete formal unit. Hence, one might well expect to see in this book's contents page a "Berryman chapter," a "Lowell chapter," a "Bishop chapter," and so forth.[2] Another practice, nearly as common, pairs a single "central" figure with a succession of secondary authors.[3] But I felt early on in the ten-year process of researching and writing this book that to do justice both to the individual integrity and to the developing interrelations of the four poets in this midcentury quartet, I must attempt to recreate for the reader at least a partial experience of the unfolding process of "conversation" and "responsiveness"—of alternating discipleship, companionship, and confrontation—that characterized their mutual interchange over more than forty years.

Elliott Carter observes in his notes to a composer-supervised recording of his String Quartet No. 2 that "In a certain sense each instrument is like a character in an opera made up primarily of 'quartets.' The separation of the instrumental character is kept quite distinct throughout the first half of the work but becomes increasingly homogenized up to the *Conclusion*, at which point the separation reemerges."[4] Such a process of moving from nearly total distinctness of voicing to increasingly dialogic interaction appears, historically, in the parallel development of these poets (though their voices never became "homogenized"). Carter adds, of his recording, "The musical contrasts of behavior and material associated with each instrument can be brought to the listener's attention by a special stereophonic placement which helps to sort them out." Restricted to the printed page, this study seeks to emulate Carter's "stereophonic placement" of his voices by drawing on techniques of literary juxtaposition and counterpoint developed by such nonfiction writers as John McPhee (a former Princeton University student of both Berryman and Jarrell). The aim has been to produce an unfolding critical narrative that counterpoints the parallel development of these poets over four decades while keeping alive at least a partial experience of their simultaneous four-way dialogue. Thus, this book is structured as a series of interwoven, thesis-centered, chronologically sequenced chapters that give each poet roughly equal time while exploring key issues in their aesthetic and personal development. This apparently unique narrative-argumentative structure evolved slowly out of the demands of the material. In a sense, the structure seems to have chosen me. What follows, then, is the product of a decade-long effort: an essay in interpretation, a reading of human and cultural history, a set of polyphonic variations on a melancholy theme, a sequence of intensive studies in parallel artistic development.

# Acknowledgments

This book, a study of conversation and collaboration between four mid-century poets, is itself a product of intensive scholarly conversation and collaboration. I first encountered the work of Robert Lowell, Randall Jarrell, Elizabeth Bishop, and John Berryman in the graduate classroom of poet and critic Alan Williamson. Later, my doctoral dissertation committee at the University of Virginia, including J. C. Levenson, Steven Railton, and Victor Cabas, advised that my thesis more specifically "place" Bishop in literary history—an assignment that, in the long run, led to this extensive sequel. Levenson and Paul Breslin provided invaluable encouragement and counsel as the project took shape. Colleagues at Hartwick College, including Thomas Beattie, Robert Bensen, David Cody, Peter Wallace, and Marilyn Wesley, provided support and editorial commentary as the book evolved through a series of outlines and partial drafts. Another Hartwick colleague, poet Carol Frost, deserves particular mention for her penetrating commentary on the manuscript, for her excellent essays on Berryman, which led me to look at all four poets in the context of an emerging aesthetic while focusing on crucial slices of time, and for her encouragement to present my work-in-progress as a series of lectures at the Catskill Poetry Workshop. Another invaluable by-product of my participation in the workshop was the chance it offered to observe, over several seasons, the interchange between literary peers and between established poets and their students.

As the book approached its final form, colleagues in the United States and Canada unselfishly contributed their time and expertise. Richard Flynn's insights into Randall Jarrell and the literature of childhood has been invaluable. The late Margaret Dickie served as my trusted guide into the complexities of gender studies. Sandra Barry knows more about Bishop's childhood experience and family background in Nova Scotia than anyone living and has generously shared that knowledge. Charles Thornbury, a profound student of Berryman, has shared his extensive knowledge of the Berryman archive, located at the University of Minnesota. Steven Gould Axelrod, an equally profound student of Lowell, read a late draft of the entire manuscript and suggested many substantive improvements. Gary

Fountain and Camille Roman read still later drafts, and the book's final shape and tone owes much to their wide-ranging knowledge and critical acumen.

Other colleagues who have offered invaluable commentary and encouragement include: Jacqueline Vaught Brogan, Bonnie Costello, Suzanne Ferguson, Laurie Goldensohn, Donald Justice, Richard J. Kelly, Marilyn May Lombardi, Paul Mariani, Laura Jehn Menides, Brett C. Millier, Barbara Page, and Cheryl Walker. I owe a debt of gratitude to the many knowledgeable and cooperative librarians and curators of special collections who have supported my research. Among these I particularly wish to acknowledge the able assistance of researcher Vivian Newbould at the Manuscripts Division, University of Minnesota Library and Nancy MacKechnie, Curator of the Rare Books and Manuscripts Collection, Vassar College Library.

Alfred Bendixen and the American Literature Association kindly provided numerous forums in which sections of this book were informally presented—leading directly or indirectly to much of the collegial interchange already cited. This book is indebted to Eileen Simpson, for the luminous example she provided in *Poets in their Youth: A Memoir*, and to Mary Jarrell. I am grateful for her insightful writings about her husband Randall, for her enthusiastic encouragement of this project, and for her patiently answering my many questions about Jarrell in letters, telephone calls, and during the course of a memorable day in Greensboro as her guest.

This book might never have been completed without the help of the National Endowment of the Humanities. A 1988 Summer Stipend from the Endowment helped begin the research in earnest, and a Fellowship for College Teachers in 1994–95 enabled me to finish a preliminary draft. I am indebted to Hartwick College for two sabbatical leaves during the course of the writing, for several Trustee Research Grants providing funds to visit manuscript collections, and for the timely award of an endowed chair that provided further release time as I was putting the book through its final drafts. I would also like to thank my students in four Hartwick College seminars for their many challenging questions about these poets.

I would like to acknowledge the encouragement and forbearance of my editors at the University Press of Virginia for permitting this book to evolve according to its own inner logic. And, finally, I wish to praise the patience and generosity of my family, especially my wife, Elsa. She has lived with this project as long, and almost as intimately, as its author.

The following are reprinted by permission of Farrar, Straus & Giroux, Inc.: Excerpts from *Collected Poems: 1937–1971* by John Berryman. Copyright © 1989 by Kate Donahue Berryman; excerpts from *The Dream Songs* by John Berryman. Copyright © 1969 by John Berryman; excerpts from *The Freedom of the Poet* by John Berryman. Copyright © 1976 by Kate Berryman; excerpts from *The Collected Prose* by Elizabeth Bishop. Copyright © 1984 by Alice Helen Methfessel; excerpts from *The Complete Poems 1927–1979* by Elizabeth Bishop. Copyright © 1979, 1983 by Alice Helen Methfessel; excerpts from *One Art: Letters* by Elizabeth Bishop. Copyright © 1994 by Alice Methfessel. Introduction and compilation copyright © 1994 by Robert Giroux; excerpts from previously unpublished writings of Elizabeth Bishop used with permission of Farrar, Straus & Giroux, Inc. on behalf of the Estate of Elizabeth Bishop. Copyright © 1998 by Alice Helen Methfessel; excerpts from *The Complete Poems* by Randall Jarrell. Copyright © 1969 by Mrs. Randall Jarrell; excerpts from *Kipling, Auden & Co.* by Randall Jarrell. Copyright © 1980 by Mrs. Randall Jarrell; excerpts from *Collected Prose* by Robert Lowell. Copyright © 1987 by Caroline Lowell; excerpts from *Day by Day* by Robert Lowell. Copyright © 1977 by Robert Lowell; excerpts from *For the Union Dead* by Robert Lowell. Copyright © 1959 by Robert Lowell. Copyright renewed © 1987 by Harriet Lowell, Caroline Lowell, and Sheridan Lowell; excerpts from *History* by Robert Lowell. Copyright © 1973 by Robert Lowell; excerpts from *Life Studies* by Robert Lowell. Copyright © 1959 by Robert Lowell. Copyright renewed © 1987 by Harriet Lowell, Sheridan Lowell, and Caroline Lowell; and excerpts from *Near the Ocean* by Robert Lowell, drawings by Sidney Nolan. Copyright © 1967 by Robert Lowell. Drawings copyright © 1967 by Sidney Nolan.

Excerpts from *The Dream Songs* and *Collected Poems* by John Berryman, excerpts from *Life Studies* and *Collected Prose* by Robert Lowell, and excerpts from Randall Jarrell's *Complete Poems* in the United Kingdom and British Commonwealth by permission of Faber & Faber, Ltd.

Excerpts from Randall Jarrell's *Kipling, Auden & Co.* (1980 ed.) in the United Kingdom and British Commonwealth by permission of Carcanet Press, Ltd.

Excerpts from previously unpublished writings of Randall Jarrell, *Poetry and the Age*, and *The Third Book of Criticism* by permission of Mary Jarrell.

Excerpts from previously unpublished writings of John Berryman by permission of Kate Donahue and by the John Berryman Papers, Manuscripts Division, University of Minnesota Libraries, St. Paul, MN.

Excerpts from previously unpublished writings of Robert Lowell by permission of Frank Bidart, Literary Executor for the Estate of Robert Lowell.

Excerpts from previously unpublished writings of Allen Tate are used with permission of Helen H. Tate.

Excerpts from previously unpublished writings by Elizabeth Bishop, Robert Lowell, and John Berryman by permission of Special Collections of Vassar College Libraries.

Excerpts from previously unpublished writings by Allen Tate and John Berryman. Allen Tate Papers, Manuscripts Division, Department of Rare Books and Special Collections, Princeton University Library. Published with permission of the Princeton University Library.

Excerpts from letters by Elizabeth Bishop to Robert Lowell and letters by John Berryman to Robert Lowell by permission of the Houghton Library, Harvard University.

Portions of chapter 5 appeared, in altered form, as "Randall Jarrell's Poetics: A Rediscovered Milestone" in the *Georgia Review* L(4) (winter 1996).

Excerpts from previously unpublished writings by Elizabeth Bishop by permission of the Elizabeth Bishop Papers, Special Collections, Washington University Libraries.

# Abbreviations

John Berryman:

| | |
|---|---|
| *DS* | *The Dream Songs.* New York: Farrar, Straus & Giroux, 1969. |
| *JBPoems* | *Collected Poems: 1937–1971*, ed. Charles Thornbury. New York: Farrar, Straus & Giroux, 1989. |
| *JBProse* | *The Freedom of the Poet.* New York: Farrar, Straus & Giroux, 1976. |

Elizabeth Bishop:

| | |
|---|---|
| *EBPoems* | *The Complete Poems: 1927–1979.* New York: Farrar, Straus & Giroux, 1983. |
| *EBProse* | *The Collected Prose*, ed. Robert Giroux. New York: Farrar, Straus & Giroux, 1984. |
| *EBLet* | *One Art: Letters*, ed. Robert Giroux. New York: Farrar, Straus & Giroux, 1994. |

Randall Jarrell:

| | |
|---|---|
| *RJPoems* | *The Complete Poems.* New York: Farrar, Straus & Giroux, 1969. |
| *P&A* | *Poetry and the Age.* New York: Farrar, Straus & Giroux, 1953. |
| *TBC* | *The Third Book of Criticism.* New York: Farrar, Straus & Giroux, 1969. |
| *KA&Co* | *Kipling, Auden & Co.* New York: Farrar, Straus & Giroux, 1980. |
| *RJLet* | *Randall Jarrell's Letters*, ed. Mary Jarrell. Boston: Houghton Mifflin, 1985. |

Robert Lowell:

| | |
|---|---|
| *LWC/MK* | *Lord Weary's Castle* and *The Mills of the Kavanaugh's*. New York: Harcourt, Brace, 1951. |
| *LS/FUD* | *Life Studies* and *For the Union Dead*. New York: Farrar, Straus & Giroux, 1964. |
| *Notebook 1967–68* | *Notebook 1967–68*. New York: Farrar, Straus and Giroux, 1969. |
| *RJ1914* | *Randall Jarrell: 1914–1965*, edited with Peter Taylor and Robert Penn Warren. New York: Farrar, Straus & Giroux, 1967. |
| *NTO* | *Near the Ocean*. New York: Farrar, Straus & Giroux, 1967. |
| *History* | *History*. New York: Farrar, Straus & Giroux, 1973. |
| *DBD* | *Day by Day*. New York: Farrar, Straus & Giroux, 1973. |
| *RLProse* | *Collected Prose*, ed. Robert Giroux. New York: Farrar, Straus & Giroux, 1987. |

# Midcentury Quartet

# Part 1

# DRAWING THE CIRCLE

# 1 Midcentury Quartet

## *Bishop, Lowell, Jarrell, Berryman*

I think it was extremely sweet of you to give me a witticism in a dream—it shows real subconscious generosity.

Letter from Elizabeth Bishop to Robert Lowell, 28 July 1953

I enjoyed your dream and felt extremely complimented to be mixed up with your own conscience and judgment in such a way.

Letter from Randall Jarrell to John Berryman [1963]

### Drawing the Circle

In February 1966, following the sudden, tragic death the previous October of their close mutual friend Randall Jarrell, Elizabeth Bishop wrote to her intimate correspondent and long-standing artistic ally Robert Lowell, "I read my class your wonderful piece on Randall one day—I had missed that copy in Brazil, of the NY Review—and they were very moved by it, obviously. I have also read them a lot of Randall's poems. . . . He doesn't seem very well known here, so I am bringing him in—and Berryman—and a few others every chance I get."[1] Bishop, always cautious about being labeled and thus reluctant to identify her favorite contemporaries publicly, here draws a circle quite casually around an intriguing quartet of midcentury American poets who are not commonly seen as a coherent group: Lowell, Jarrell, Berryman, and Bishop herself.

This book explores the underlying network of literary relations linking the quartet Robert Lowell (1917–1977), Randall Jarrell (1914–1965), Elizabeth Bishop (1911–1979), and John Berryman (1914–1972). This network grew, persisted, and thrived for forty years just a layer below the journalistically constructed map of contemporary American poetry, and its influence abides to this day. Yet its operations remain, at best, a semi-open secret two decades after the death of Elizabeth Bishop, the quartet's last surviving member. Operating along the margins of or even in flat contradiction to those categories most commonly applied by conventional literary histories, this midcentury quartet left a compelling record of their interchange scattered across a wide range of published and unpublished sources. This book seeks to combine the best elements of aesthetic and cultural criticism as it uncovers and retraces across the middle decades of the twentieth century the making of their flexible, influential, artistically compelling, and surprisingly coherent postmodern aesthetic. What follows is a reading of the interconnecting life-texts and literary texts of four of America's most brilliant, complex, and elusive postmodern poets as they engage in an ongoing four-way public and private dialogue about what poetry was and could be.

The aesthetic and the many inventive techniques this quartet evolved in its pursuit gradually took shape as an incompletely formulated but coherent and powerful set of intuitions: intuitions about which these brilliantly educated and articulate poets did not choose to be entirely forthcoming, nor even, perhaps, entirely conscious. The authors of this aesthetic were remarkably consistent in their refusal to voice a formalized doctrine, despite persistent demands by interviewers, editors, and anthologists. One searches in vain for a single published manifesto outlining their individual or group intentions. And the flexible, practice-centered, intuitive aesthetic that they exercised resists explicit articulation. Until she became a recent focus of intensive critical attention, Bishop had remained the most elusive of the four. Literary historians have found these four poets "hard to 'place'"[2] and their aesthetic principles hard to characterize—both because their artistic strategies were flexible and complex and because each so consistently avoided stating a systematic poetic doctrine.

As early as 1940, Bishop, Berryman, and Jarrell found different ways to frustrate publisher James Laughlin's demand for a prefatory essay defining one's artistic principles for the anthology *Five Young American Poets.* Berryman was acknowledging a shared disposition when he praised Jarrell's famous essay collection *Poetry and the Age* (1953) in a review for *New Republic* for "his neglect to theorize about poetry," which Berryman found "one of the most agreeable features of a prepossessing and engaging book. . . . The point is to deal with the stuff itself, and Jarrell does, nobody better" (*RJ1914* 13). In 1967, Lowell cut through the ongoing and already ritualized formalism-versus-open-forms debate quite commonsensically with the remark that "I can't understand how any poet, who has written both metered and unmetered poems, would be willing to settle for one and give up the other." Lowell adds, significantly, that "I have never worked my intuitions on this subject into a theory. When I drop one style of writing, it is usually a surprise to me."[3] Bishop's enigmatic yet powerfully inclusive response to a midcentury questionnaire about poetic theory and practice—"*it all depends*"—might serve as a motto for each member of this circle, as would her continuation: "It all depends on the particular poem one happens to be trying to write, and the range of possibilities is, one trusts, infinite. After all, the poet's concern is not consistency."[4] Yet, if one reads with sufficient care their published poems, essays, and interviews in the context of the unpublished documentary record—if one deals "with the stuff itself"—then the active principles of a flexible but surprisingly coherent and specifically postmodern aesthetic begin to emerge.

The unusually extensive manuscript record these poets left behind now resides in library archives scattered across North (and South) America. These sources include a diverse array of letters, journals, project lists, class notes, workbooks, grant proposals, autobiographical fragments, juvenilia, and multiversion drafts of published and unpublished poems, as well as unpublished or fugitive lectures and critical essays—and the extraordinary memoranda of their remembered dreams of one another—material that provides invaluable insights into their ongoing dialogue. These poets cared intensely about what their fellow quartet members said and thought, involving both art and life and extending even into the unconscious. Bishop would write to Lowell in 1951, as she sailed on the freighter *Bowplate* toward her long, unexpected sojourn in Brazil, "With me on the boat I brought your review of Randall['s *Seven League Crutches*] and Randall's review of you[r *The Mills of the Kavanaughs*] . . . & I've been brooding over them both" (*EBLet* 225). Ten years later Bishop would write to Lowell, "I have had you on my mind all this time and yesterday morning when I woke up I had been having a long dream about you."[5] And when Berryman had an intense dream, a few years later, centering on Jarrell's fancied appraisal of Berryman's recent work, the latter wrote to Jarrell that "the judgment was delivered w[ith] all the tender but great authority of the author of 'I find no fault in this just man' (wh[ich] is certainly one of y[ou]r masterpieces)."[6] Here Berryman alludes to the clinching yet profoundly ambiguous final line of Jarrell's "Eighth Air Force," a study of the intertwinings of human innocence and guilt in the postmodern world. Moreover, Berryman acknowledges the extraordinary authority, for him, of Jarrell's critical judgment.

After Jarrell's death, Berryman would write to his friend's widow that

Randall's taste was "impeccable if anyone's may be said to be."[7] Lowell agreed, acknowledging Jarrell as "a critic of genius, a poet-critic of genius" who was "so often right that sometimes we said he was always right" (*RLProse* 91, 93). In 1957 Lowell wrote excitedly to Bishop—whose own example helped Lowell find the style of *Life Studies* (1959)—announcing that several poems from his new sequence-in-the-making had been praised in manuscript by Jarrell and by Philip Rahv, the influential editor of *Partisan Review*. Bishop replied, "I am so pleased Randall liked the poems—also Philip [Rahv], but Randall's liking them really means infinitely more" (*EBLet* 348). These poets were lifelong learners about their art who studied and learned in particular from one another in a process of flexible, ongoing mutual interchange. Each evolved a personal voice and style, a personal sense of scale, but in the process each looked steadily at the others as they engaged in an extensive, devious, and multifaceted process of literary exploration.

## The Problem of Selfhood in the Postmodern World

Applying the term "postmodern" to the aesthetic of this quartet of poets may, just as the grouping itself, surprise some readers—but this epithet is not chosen lightly. One aspect of this quartet's postmodern claim is historical priority. As we shall see, the term "post-modernist" was first used extensively in a published and private dialogue between Jarrell, Lowell, and Berryman as early as 1947, as they were reviewing one another's early books, and responding to the postwar cultural and poetic scene. Paul Hoover notes that "Charles Olson used the word 'postmodern' as early as an October 20, 1951, letter to Creeley from Black Mountain," offering this as a founding date for the postmodern canon enshrined in his 1994 anthology *Postmodern American Poetry*.[8] Hoover adds that "as used here, 'postmodern' means the historical period following World War II," and he insists that "Postmodernist poetry is the avant-garde poetry of our time."[9] Donald Allen and George F. Butterick assert in the introduction to the 1982 anthology *The Postmoderns: The New American Poetry Revised* (whose canon of first generation "postmoderns" Hoover replicates without deviation) that "Postmodernism is not simply after, in time, the modernism of Pound and Eliot, Auden and Stevens, and their younger successors such as Berryman and Lowell, Bishop and Sexton."[10]

For Allen, Butterick, and Hoover such poets as Bishop, Lowell, Berryman—and by extension Jarrell—are mere "successors" to modernism and must be excluded by name from any account of a postmodernist canon. However, an extensive, and largely neglected, published dialogue in which Jarrell, Lowell, and Berryman apply the term "post-modernist" to one another occurred in 1947–48. This dialogue *immediately* followed the end of World War II (one of Hoover's criteria) and appeared in print several years prior to Olson's letter. Their poetry and criticism before, during, and after World War II—including an important, long-lost, and now newly published 1942 essay by Jarrell on "Structure in Poetry"—explicitly explores the problem of writing "the poetry that replaces modernism." Moreover, their poetry written during this period deals ever more decisively and powerfully with themes now widely considered postmodern.

Despite their constant, subtle innovation in subject matter and form, the label "avant-garde" does not fit this midcentury quartet. Interestingly, John Ashbery once noted of Bishop that she is "somehow an establishment poet herself, and the establishment ought to give thanks; she is proof it can't be all bad"[11]—a remark that might well be extended to the other members of her quartet. Hoover acknowledges "The risk . . . that the avant-garde will become an institution with its own self-protective rituals."[12] And LANGUAGE poet Michael Palmer acknowledges that "Each time one replaces a given model with another model, a theoretical model, whatever, you are inscribing yourself in the larger myth of innovation (and/or myths of recovery, renascence, et al.)." Poets such as Lowell, Jarrell, Bishop, and Berryman, though persistently innovative in matters of form and content, resisted inscribing themselves within particular theoretical models or popular myths of innovation or recovery—myths that remain fundamental to a theory of the avant-garde—and in doing so each remained at the service of the particular poem he or she was then trying to write. They also resisted what Palmer describes as the tendency of "avant-gardism" to become "so clearly commodified now, so clearly and simply a matter of what perfume or what soap you're selling."[13] This book makes the case that the literature of postmodernism has produced a range of equally valid, yet often contradictory, postmodern aesthetics too dynamic and too various to be limited to a single protectively canonized and commodified "avant-garde."[14] Further, it can be argued that the particular aesthetic embodied in the poems of Lowell, Jarrell, Bishop, and Berryman is one of the earliest, most flexible, most powerful, and most influential of postmodernism's diverse aesthetics.

Their postwar dialogue suggests that by the mid-1940s poets such as Lowell, Jarrell, and Berryman had already begun to recognize in one another—and were already attempting tentatively to characterize—a shared, complex, and still emerging aesthetic agenda that they saw as significantly different from "the modernism of Pound and Eliot, Auden and Stevens." Moreover, this new aesthetic, especially when articulated in prose, encountered significant resistance from their own immediate modernist mentors Allen Tate, John Crowe Ransom, and Marianne Moore. Jarrell, encountering significant resistance from the same mentors, recognized Lowell's *Lord Weary's Castle* in his famous January 1947 review "From the Kingdom of Necessity" as poems embodying "a dramatic, dialectical organization" offering "a unique fusion of modernist and traditional poetry, and there exist side by side in it certain effects that one would have thought mutually exclusive; but it is essentially a post- or anti-modernist poetry, and as such certain to be influential" (*P&A* 216). The "well-nigh universal practice today of what might be called pastiche" identified by Fredric Jameson in 1984 as a key postmodern trait is already present in Jarrell's 1947 reading of Lowell, particularly in Jarrell's stress on "certain effects that one would have thought mutually exclusive," though Lowell's work exhibits its resistance to modernism by offering a significantly greater emphasis on "the individual subject" and a "personal style" than Jameson's definition of a postmodern aesthetic might allow.[15] Bishop, in the recently rediscovered 1962 essay "Some Notes on Robert Lowell," found similar elements of pastiche in early Lowell through the work's "subtle, involved" texture, "full of linguistic associations," and its "astonishing mixture of demotic and formal language."[16]

The resistance to this generation by the modernists themselves, precisely on the grounds of its deployment of pastiche, combined with renewed attention to "the individual subject," and the search for a "personal style," was already in evidence well before 1947. In 1941, still earlier than their just-cited postwar dialogue—in what appears to be the first use, ever, of the term in a literary context—the word "post-modernist" was applied to one of this quartet's young members in a review by a famous, powerful (and disgruntled) modernist mentor. The young poet under review, Randall Jarrell, had dared to acknowledge, in his reluctant self-introduction for James Laughlin's 1940 New Directions anthology *Five Young American Poets,* his as yet unrealized dream to write "the sort of poetry that replaces modernism" (*KA&Co* 51). This confession provoked an early and irritated recognition of his incipient postmodernism by reviewer John Crowe Ransom, Jarrell's former teacher and the powerful editor of *Kenyon Review.* Ransom wrote that "In the prose conclusion, as in the poetic sequel, Jarrell forbids us to say yet that he is a post-modernist. But probably he will be. It is self-consciousness which stops the young poets from their own graces; too much thinking about all the technical possibilities at once, as well as too much attention to changes in fashion."[17]

It was this and similar lessons, in part, that taught these poets to embody their innovations in their poetry and avoid explicit theoretical formulations. Jarrell, Bishop, Berryman, and Lowell were drawn so magnetically and lastingly to one another's work (despite obvious differences in temperament, artistic manner, gender, sexual orientation, and so forth) because each consciously or unconsciously recognized in the others a shared determination to bypass or unmake modernism's impersonal aesthetic and to create amongst themselves a new aesthetic that would empower them to address the problem of selfhood in the postmodern world.

In their recent survey of the theoretical discourse of postmodernism, Stephen Best and Douglas Kellner assert that "there is no unified postmodern theory, or even a coherent set of positions. Rather, one is struck by the diversities between theories often lumped together as 'postmodern' and the plurality—often conflictual—of postmodern positions."[18] Perhaps the single facet of postmodernism on which some of its current commentators shrewdly agree is that this phenomenon is, by its nature, multivalent. Mutlu Konuk Blasing recently argued for a "resilient" model of "poetic change" that can "accommodate the variousness of twentieth-century American poetry," for "With such a flexible approach, we can account for the fact that, in the postmodern period, closure (metaphysical, moral, or political) can occur within open forms, which have become only one more 'tradition,' and openness is possible within conventional, closed forms."[19] Lowell, Jarrell, Bishop, and Berryman tended toward metaphysical, moral, and political "openness" while working in the context of semi-open forms (such as Berryman's elaborately flexible *Dream Song* structure) or within revisionary versions of closed forms (such as Bishop's innovative use of the double sonnet, the villanelle, and the sestina). And certainly, despite their own significant claims to historical priority, what this quartet of poets eventually created was not "the" postmodern aesthetic but "a" postmodern aesthetic. Theirs is one of the earliest and most persistent of the several distinctive, powerful, and often contradictory aesthetics that has striven to "replace modernism." Their particular postmodern aesthetic concerns itself principally with exploring the vicissitudes and displacements of the individual human self—the denied or threatened child, the embattled adolescent, the bereaved, imperiled, or disordered adult—dramatizing that individual's problems of knowledge, identity, traumatic loss, and repressed or otherwise unresolved feelings of isolation, confusion, anger, and grief.

In his influential characterization of the postmodern self, Fredric Jameson wrote in 1984 of "the 'death' of the subject itself—the end of the autonomous bourgeois monad or ego or individual—and the accompanying stress, whether as some new moral ideal or as empirical description, on the *decentering* of that formerly centered subject or psyche." And Jameson adds, by way of explanation, "Of the two possible formulations of this notion—the historicist one, that a once-existing centered subject, has today in the world of organizational bureaucracy dissolved; and the more radical poststructuralist position, for which such a subject never existed in the first place but constituted something like an ideological mirage—I obviously incline toward the former; the latter must in any case take into account something like a 'reality of appearance.'"[20] Curiously, Jameson neglects to entertain a third possibility: that the embattled, decentered ego, the threatened and possibly traumatized individual human self—of whatever social class, gender, race, age, ethnicity, nationality, or sexual orientation—lives on in the postmodern world, in the midst of what Bishop called "our worst century so far,"[21] struggling toward survival, toward self-knowledge, and even toward tentative or contingent forms of recovery.

Jameson's insistence on an "impersonal" postmodern aesthetic would sound curiously "modernist" to this particular foursome, who, long before Jameson's characterization, created their own aesthetic field of action in that neglected—but vitally important—third realm, the realm of the embattled self. Lowell, for example, noted that for him, "So much of the effort of the poem is to arrive at something essentially human. . . . A poem needs to include a man's contradictions."[22] Asked why he called *The Dream Songs* "one poem rather than a group of poems in the same form?" Berryman replied, "Ah—it's personality—it's Henry. . . . The reason I call it one poem is the result of my strong disagreement with Eliot's line, 'the impersonality of poetry. . . . It seems to me on the contrary that poetry comes out of personality'"[23]

The aesthetic that Lowell, Jarrell, Bishop, and Berryman worked throughout the middle decades of the twentieth century to create, which explores what Lowell calls "the confusion and sadness and incoherence of the human condition,"[24] has emerged as one of the most artistically successful and pervasively influential of postmodernism's many lines of development. But given the refusal of its authors to write manifestos or to indulge their editors and readers in extended discursive commentary on their intentions, this complex, flexible, and elusive aesthetic remains perhaps the least explicitly theorized of any of America's poetic postmodernisms. Therefore, in order to articulate the key operating features of this quartet's aesthetic, one must identify and explore the basic emotional, intellectual, and cultural issues of the poems, while piecing together, from their extensive running commentary in letters, interviews, reviews, and prefaces, an understanding of the aesthetic's distinguishing literary techniques and characteristics.

Mature poems engaging in an original way with such core issues as the individual's problems of knowledge, identity, grief, and loss—subtly yet dramatically placed in a detailed yet conflicted landscape of social and cultural history—include Bishop's "The Man-Moth," "At the Fishhouses," and "One Art"; Jarrell's "Losses," "Protocols," and "The House in the Wood"; Berryman's "Homage to Mistress Bradstreet" and his "Opus Posthumous" and final Dream Songs; and Lowell's "Falling Asleep over the Aeneid," "Skunk Hour," and "For the Union Dead."

These poems span the middle decades of the twentieth century, but even such early examples as Berryman's "The Ball Poem" (1942) dramatize the intersection of these concerns of self-knowledge. In "The Ball Poem" an adult observer contemplates a boy who, facing an early crisis of loss

> is learning, well behind his desperate eyes,
> The epistemology of loss, how to stand up
> Knowing what every man must one day know.

*Epistemology*—the study of the nature and grounds of human knowledge, with particular reference to its limits and validity—is generally considered among the more recondite branches of metaphysics. So one might not casually think of a boy facing his first loss from an epistemologist's viewpoint. But Berryman suggests that any thinking and feeling human being must learn to be a practicing epistemologist. And he suggests further that to begin, as a child, to question the limits and validity of one's knowledge sources—particularly in the context of an apparently unaccountable but symptomatic experience of "ultimate shaking grief" (*JBPoems* 11)—is to take a critical first step toward understanding both the problem of loss and the problem of identity. "The Ball Poem" engages quite early with the core problems—all of which were a concern for this quartet—of knowledge, identity, loss, and emotional disorder. The poem suggests that to survive and be fully human in the postmodern world—fraught as this world is with veiled and conflicting messages and with complex emotional burdens, distractions, and displacements—one must be, in effect, an epistemologist, weighing the relative validity of different vital but uncertain knowledge sources and extracting the knowledge needed to survive.

Berryman's colleagues Bishop, Jarrell, and Lowell shared his preoccupation with loss and with the uncertain process of coming to know the traumatic past. In their poems and stories, it will be suggested, these four epistemologists of loss, even those, such as Lowell and Berryman, most commonly labeled "confessional poets," are not primarily engaged in a process of revealing the self. Rather they are engaged in a process of exploring the self, of reaching back through a consideration of surviving artifacts, documentary records, lingering memory traces, dreamlike recurrences, symptomatic behaviors, and verbal slippages—that is, through tangible cultural markers and through the intangible and unreliable but powerful messages of the unconscious—toward the elusive junctures of the traumatic past. Their poetry places a sensitized individual amongst these elusive, ambiguous, but naggingly insistent correlatives of past losses and traumas as it probes for insight into the causation of present dismays and disorders. In short, these four poets are exploring as well as coming to terms with lost worlds.

Jarrell reveals his own intense interest in the mysterious process of artistic growth, and his own understanding of the problems of selfhood engaging a valued colleague, when he concludes his study of "Fifty Years of American Poetry" with praise for such Lowell poems as the recently published "For the Union Dead." Speaking at the National Poetry Conference in Washington in October 1962 under the nuclear shadow of the Cuban Missile Crisis, Jarrell interprets this poem in the context of Cold War realities. He suggests that for his close friend Lowell "his own existence seems to him in some sense as terrible as the public world—his private world hangs over him as the public world hangs over others—he does not forsake the headlined world for the refuge of one's private joys and decencies, the shaky garden of the heart; instead, as in his wonderful poem about Boston Common, he sees all these as the lost paradise of the childish past, the past that knew so much, but still didn't know" (*TBC* 333). Lowell similarly sought a psychologically revealing thematic thread when he reviewed Bishop's first book in 1947, stressing the presence of a single elusive "symbolic pattern" involving "two opposing factors. . . . The first is something in motion, weary but persisting, almost always failing and on the point of disintegrating, and yet, for the most part, stoically maintained. . . . The second factor is a terminus: rest, sleep, fulfillment or death" (*RLProse* 76–77).

Each of these four midcentury poets came to recognize in "the shaky garden of the heart" a last, uncertain refuge in a dangerously decentered world—a refuge that was itself unsettling, permeable, and fragmentary. This refuge could not be counted on as much of a shield, but it preserved the vital remains of the troubled and yearning human spirit, a spirit that, in their work, remains in constant, uncanny motion, "weary but persisting."

In poem after poem, hemmed round by the temptations of terminus, of "rest, sleep, fulfillment or death," their work persistently attempts to recover and explore "the lost paradise of the childish past" and other lost worlds or worlds of loss, worlds that remain forever outside the range of one's certainties and that may only be recreated through the painful and elusive processes of memory and art. Their explorations within, and their wide-ranging sallies beyond, the shaky garden of the individual human heart lead them to inquire into history, culture, politics, and gender, as well as into books, retrospection, observation, and dreams, and into childhood, parenthood, adolescence, aging, and death. And throughout these inquiries their work, at its exploratory best, loses neither its emotional acuteness, nor its piercing insight and unlikely compassion. It loses neither its dry, witty, and curiously unbridled respect for human frailty and courage, nor its faculty for surprise. Jarrell, who recognized that Lowell "bullied his early work" into existence, noted that, despite the vigor of his friend's intelligence and will, Lowell's "own vulnerable humanity has been forced in on him." It is the "vulnerable humanity" in the work of each of these four poets, emerging sometimes with delicacy, sometimes with wit, sometimes with pathos, sometimes with "barbarous immediacy," that provides the common ground across which they observed one another and frequently met. And this remains, in no small measure, the source and basis of their continuing relevance and value.

## Lowell, Jarrell, Bishop, Berryman and Literary History

Because of their predominately behind-the-scenes interchange, literary historians who attend chiefly to the published record do not readily place these poets together. David Perkins's respected *History of Modern Poetry: Modernism and After* (1987), for example, treats them in three separate chapters. Lowell and Berryman, celebrated after 1960 for the autobiographical dimension of their work, were promptly labeled "confessional poets," a label that has stuck. Even the recent *Columbia History of American Poetry* (1993), a collection of historical essays edited by Jay Parini and Brett C. Millier generally marked by its critical freshness, continues to separate this midcentury quartet along conventional lines.[25] *The Columbia History* pairs Bishop with Marianne Moore, places Lowell in his standard role as the fountainhead of confessional poetry, and sweeps Berryman into a chapter with Theodore Roethke. Jarrell appears only in passing and chiefly as a critic. Jarrell—a close friend and artistic associate of Lowell's since 1937 and a friend of Berryman's since the mid-1940s—proved hard to categorize as confessional, since his work is rarely self-referential in any *direct* way. This difficulty of classifying Jarrell has hurt his reputation as a poet.

Bishop, once widely termed "delicate," "reticent," or "impersonal," is still often placed in an aesthetic position more or less diametrically opposed to the "confessional" Lowell's. This peculiarly persistent critical construct ignores three major points: first, Lowell was Bishop's closest friend in the arts; second, their mutual admiration was keen and lifelong, as Bishop suggested when she drew her circle in 1966; and third, Lowell acknowledged Bishop as one of the three greatest direct influences on his work, and the most influential among his immediate contemporaries.[26]

Historical studies that accept the "confessional" model as a defining principle—including those by Bruce Bawer, James Breslin, Karl Malkoff, Stephen Matterson, and Jeffrey Meyers—consistently omit Bishop. Such studies also typically omit Jarrell—despite his three-decades-long artistic intimacy with Lowell—or strain to force his work into the confessional mold. The circle these four poetic peers created amongst themselves was private, informal, unofficial; it was never fully recognized, even by the poets themselves. Perhaps its very privacy and informality served to keep this casual but long-lasting alliance of literary talents so productive and durable: without a public front to defend, without apportioned cultural turf to be maintained, their relations could remain elastic enough to cope with one another's ongoing growth and change.

David Kalstone's posthumously published *Becoming a Poet: Elizabeth Bishop with Marianne Moore and Robert Lowell* (1989) moved the understanding of two of these poets decisively forward, making extensive use of documentary sources to provide a nuanced reading of Bishop's relationships with Lowell (and with her mentor Marianne Moore). Still, Kalstone's largely biographical inquiry does not attempt that "more general study" of her aesthetic relations with her contemporaries which Kalstone acknowledges, in an unfinished preface, that he had once begun but which he forsook in favor of his eventual concentration on "the anomalies of Bishop's experience, her intense difference as a poet."[27] Kalstone understood those degrees of separation—based on differences of gender, sexual orientation, temperament, and literary recognition—that complicated Bishop's relationship with Lowell. This more general study, which should be read as complementary rather than contradictory to Kalstone's work, stresses those painfully acute differences that isolated each of these poets from the emotional centers of home, family, and national culture. This shared outlook formed the basis for a common artistic enterprise that cut across those popularly perceived barriers—including gender, sexual orientation, temperament, region, social class, or canonized artistic "school"—that might appear to separate this quartet. United by a commitment to a demanding art, what anxieties, animosities, and affinities did each of these poets feel as they eyed one another across lines partly defined by gender? Such cross-genderal studies offer a promising new direction to the historian who proposes to study a more fully gendered postmodernism.

Bishop and Lowell, just as Berryman and Jarrell, shared a sense of estrangement from many of the run-of-the-mill assumptions, consolations, myths, and illusions that served as pillars of that midcentury American society through which they so uncomfortably moved. This awareness of being different from an established norm extended even to acutely felt differences with their galaxy of modernist mentors, whose often avowedly "reactionary" critical and political dictums served as a confining blanket from under which these poets struggled—quietly but strenuously—to emerge. These four poets were drawn to one another on the basis of elective affinities that encouraged them, despite their own real differences, to gravitate into this private, unofficial circle of literary peers. Theirs was a circle that drew on tacitly understood commonalties in their lives and work rather than on publicly announced and agreed-upon aesthetic or political agendas. In a 1957 letter Jarrell tried to define his own sense of affinity for Bishop, a poet many have considered elusive. Jarrell explains that "I always have a queer feeling when I talk to you. . . . It's as if what you said—even when it's uncongenial to me, something I'd never think or say—were in another way always congenial, direct, easy for me to see and feel; as if we were very different but *did* come from the same planet. . . . It's a feeling I never have with anybody else: I'm not saying this as a vague intensive but as a precise observation. It's as if you were a color I see so easily I hardly have to look" (*RJLet* 420). In a posthumous prose tribute for Jarrell, Bishop notes that "Sometimes we quarreled, silently, in infrequent letters"—a not infrequent experience with Jarrell. His close friend Peter Taylor noted that if Jarrell "liked your effort, [he] would write you a long letter about it, and if he didn't he wouldn't speak to you. Cal [Lowell] had exactly that experience, too, and we would laugh about it."[28] Bishop adds, however, that "each time we met we would tell each other that it had meant nothing at all; we really were in agreement about everything that mattered" (*RJ1914* 20).

When Elizabeth Bishop heard of Jarrell's death, she was living in Brazil, coping as best she could with the deteriorating emotional condition of her friend and lover of fourteen years, Lota de Macedo Soares. Four months later Bishop found herself back in the States for her first extended sojourn, after fifteen years in Brazil, teaching—for the first time in her life, at the age of fifty-five. Holding the position of poet in residence at the University of Washington in Seattle, Bishop was covering courses previously taught by the late Theodore Roethke. In his prose elegy on Jarrell, Lowell noted that "Randall had once said, 'If I were a rich man, I would pay money for the privilege of being able to teach" (*RJ1914* 105). Bishop, on the other hand, through a combination of shyness, impatience, and confirmed habits of independence, was finding her belated first attempt at teaching more than a little challenging. Her letter to Lowell laments of her Seattle students, "They are so wrapped up in Roethke, still." Roethke has sometimes been configured alongside the poets of this study, but Bishop makes it clear that she is bringing the work of Lowell, Jarrell, and Berryman into her class in part as an antidote to the powerful, lingering influence of the intensely romantic Roethke.

Uncomfortable with her new role as teacher, and half-wanting to return to her temporarily abandoned life in Brazil, Bishop declared to Lowell, "For a while I felt if I really wanted to get away all I'd have to do would be to stand up and pull my hair one day and scream I HATE ROETHKE. . . . I don't really, anyway—but one hates feeling like his ghost—and I think *some* of his influence has been very bad—although at the same time he attracted a lot of good potential poets here—and I am still getting some of those."[29] In her letter Bishop aligned herself with the work of Lowell, Jarrell, and Berryman, who represented a standard she wanted her students to share.

Roethke, born in 1908, was three years older than Bishop and is generally recognized as an artistic peer of the poets in this midcentury quartet. Moreover, in several ways his development paralleled theirs. Roethke was similarly preoccupied with selfhood, loss, the wonder and darkness of childhood, and a long-term experiment with dreamlike textures. Still, Lowell, Jarrell, Bishop, and Berryman each felt that Roethke's work, even as they admired it, evinced a markedly different sensibility. Put simply, they found Roethke's work significantly more romantic. Roethke, they believed, was more deliberately lyric and sensuous, more emotionally expansive, and also, they appear to have felt, less searchingly self-critical and self-ironic.

Jarrell, a tough judge, liked Roethke's work on balance, characterizing him in 1962 as "a forceful, delicate and original poet whose poetry is still changing" (*TBC* 327). But Jarrell found his longer poems "not perhaps as thoroughly satisfying as the best small ones. . . . Don't such poems have impressive 'positive' endings of a certain rhetorical insincerity?" For Jarrell, Roethke's presentation of the unconscious was more "marshlike," more preoccupied with "continually celebrating its marriage to the whole dark wet underside of things" than one finds in the sharper, more distinct outlines drawn by the poets in this quartet, whose poems commonly set the unconscious against a foreground or background (which Jarrell found "entirely lacking" in Roethke) of "hydrogen bombs, world wars, Christianity, money, ordinary social observations . . . , everyday moral doubts" (*TBC* 326). The poetry of these four introspective yet socially observant travelers, employing a technique that Bishop described in a letter to Anne Stevenson as "the always-more-successful surrealism of everyday life,"[30] continuously interweaves the unconscious with a past or historical present that balances larger cultural concerns against the historical or the domestic quotidian. The taut, self-ironic sharpness shared by the work of Berryman, Bishop, Jarrell, and Lowell is foreign to Roethke's lyrical exuberance.

Roethke liked to speak in what he called "the wild disordered language of the natural heart,"[31] leading him to create lines such as the following characteristic passage from "The Shape of the Fire," "A low mouth laps water. Weeds, weeds how I love you. / The arbor is cooler. Farewell, farewell, fond worm."[32] For Bishop, Jarrell, Lowell, and Berryman, the "wild, disordered language of the natural heart" was a speech heard all too frequently, perhaps, and one that they did not entirely trust. Berryman, who admired both Lowell and Roethke, characterized them in a 1959 discussion as two "powerful and original talents," but he concluded of their differences, "The contrast is so deep that one would almost be justified in adopting the terms 'Eastern' and 'Western' style. . . . Lowell's work is Latinate, formal, rhetorical, massive, historical, religious, impersonal; Roethke's Teutonic, irregular, delicate, botanical, and psychological, irreligious, personal. . . . Both are witty, savage, and willing to astonish, but the fundamental unlikeness is great. If both are authoritative, the nature of their authorities differs. . . . One gets an impression, in their work, of the American spirit advancing on different fronts rather than on different parts of the same front" (*JBProse* 310).

In *Life Studies*, published just after Berryman's article appeared, Lowell's work, drawing—as Berryman acutely noticed—on Bishop's example, relaxed from the "Latinate, formal, rhetorical, massive, religious, [and] impersonal," into a more casual and personal style relying on what Lowell called "drifting description" (*RLProse* 227). Still, a backbone of the earlier characteristics remained beneath this more casual surface. Lowell would never be Teutonic or botanical and rarely delicate nor, despite his lapse from the Church, irreligious. Ian Hamilton's assessment of the Lowell-Roethke relationship is well taken: "Roethke had not been a close friend. . . . Lowell . . . was never wholly converted to Roethke's work, although he would politely name him in any list of his favorite contemporaries."[33] This uneasy balance of distance and kinship is implicit in a late letter from Lowell to Roethke, "We couldn't be more different, and yet how weirdly our lives have often gone the same way. Let's say we are brothers, have gone the same journey and know far more about each other than we have ever said or will say."[34] The caution and ambivalence in Lowell's tone, the mention, even as he acknowledges kinship, of their necessary silences, strikes a note uncharacteristic of his intimate letters to Bishop, Jarrell, and Berryman. With them—despite their own many differences, and even their occasional silences—Lowell's spirit is "advancing on . . . the same front."

Delmore Schwartz's sensibility reveals a much closer affinity to two key members of our midcentury quartet. Schwartz was an intimate friend of Berryman's, especially during the early 1940s, when these poets were young instructors at Harvard and shared, as well, the neighborhood of Boston's Beacon Hill. Berryman dedicated a sequence of eloquent elegies to Schwartz in the *Dream Songs*, after the latter's tragic and lonely death by a heart attack in a sordid Manhattan hotel. In one of these, Berryman declared that

> I don't suppose
> in all them years a day went ever by
> without a loving thought for him. Welladay.
> In the brightness of his promise,
>
> unstained, I saw him thro' the mist of the actual
> blazing with insight, warm with gossip
> thro' all our Harvard years
> when both of us were just becoming known
> (*DS* 149).

Lowell, too, was close to Schwartz, sharing a flat with him at Harvard after Berryman's departure. Bishop and Jarrell, however, knew Schwartz far less well, and felt, it would seem, less affinity either with him or with his work.

At its best, Schwartz's work projects a similar preoccupation with loss, with exploring painful childhood experience, and with uncovering unsettling psychological depths. And just as this midcentury quartet, Schwartz was carrying out a complex dialogue with literary tradition. Berryman could cite his departed friend's wittily impromptu pseudo-Vergilian parodic couplet: "I am the Brooklyn poet Delmore Schwartz / Harms & the child I sing, two parents' torts" (*DS* 149), and Lowell, in his poem "To Delmore Schwartz," chose his friend's similarly mordant twist on Wordsworth, "You said: / 'We poets in our youth begin in sadness; / thereof in the end come despondency and madness'" (*LS* 54). Both Lowell's and Berryman's remembrance and preservation of their friend's witty turns of phrase suggest that they recognized in Schwartz's vision of childhood a parallel to their own dark, ironic vision. Schwartz emerged in the 1930s with a highly successful first book, the poem and story collection *In Dreams Begin Responsibilities* (1938). It was a time when, as Berryman later put it, "he was young & gift-strong" (*DS* 149). However, Schwartz had trouble following up on his early success, suffering in later years an artistic decline connected to worsening episodes of schizophrenia. Berryman would later acknowledge that "I'd bleed to say his lovely work improved / but it is not so" (*DS* 150).

Bishop's assessment of Schwartz' work tallied with the opinion of her literary circle. In an April 1960 letter to Lowell, she asked, "Tell me: what do you think of Delmore S's new book? All the new poems by him I've seen I thought were really bad, I'm sorry to say. Have you seen anything new by Randall?"[35] As early as 1942, Jarrell felt compelled to describe

Schwartz's verse drama *Paris and Helen* as "self-conscious, self-indulgent, a literary and embarrassing failure. . . . It is a real grief to see so good a writer (the most promising extensive poet of the time) wasted on this" (*KA&Co* 84–85). Jarrell wrote to Lowell from his Army Air Corps post in 1945, "Give me a little précis of Delmore Schwartz in private life." And he continued, bluntly, "That a person of his taste and intelligence should write the stories he does—half the sentences would serve as textbook models of banal and ingenuous vulgarity—is extraordinary, and must be symptomatic of some queer segmentation of his personal being into an objective part with taste and another part with nothing but adolescent self-absorption" (*RJLet* 132). This hard-nosed statement of Jarrell's appears as do so many of his critical observations as uncannily predictive. It anticipates not just the eventual judgment of posterity on the bulk of Schwartz's later work, but, more to the point, the tragic path Schwartz's life would eventually follow, as the "queer segmentation of his personal being" took stronger and stronger hold.

Roethke was romantic enough to ask, without apparent irony, "What's madness but nobility of soul / At odds with circumstance?"[36] Berryman's characterization of Delmore Schwartz's decline in one of his Dream Song elegies offers a different and significantly less romantic view of madness:

> He had followers but they could not find him;
> friends but they could not find him. He hid his gift
> in the center of Manhattan,
> without a girl, in cheap hotels,
> so disturbed on the street friends avoided him
>
> (*DS* 150)

Sadly, one cannot trace in Schwartz's work the pattern of sustained artistic growth one finds among his friends in this midcentury quartet. Bruce Bawer defined Schwartz as the central figure of his *The Middle Generation*, finding in Schwartz's personal breakdowns a paradigm of the emotional breakdowns Bawer argues were the chief characteristic of this generation.[37] The present study, on the other hand, focuses on the themes of survival, persistent artistic growth, and the successful making of a still-influential aesthetic. From this perspective Schwartz serves not as paradigm but as painful counterpoint. If for Lowell, Jarrell, Bishop, or Berryman "art" never quite served as "a way to get well" (*DBD* 124)—which is, after all, not art's function—these poets nonetheless displayed in their lives and work a resiliency of persistence, recuperation, and imaginative growth. Such inner strength allowed them to survive and return from severe personal difficulties and disorders en route to realizing their own early artistic promise in compelling, unforeseen, and original ways. So, whereas Berryman may have been right to say of Schwartz, "the young will read his young verse / for as long as such things go" (*DS* 156), with Schwartz remaining a pivotal figure in Berryman's own early career, Schwartz does not find a place in the present study. Still, many conclusions drawn here readily extend to Schwartz's work at its best.

## A Four-Way Conversation: Discipleship, Companionship, and Confrontation

Borrowing the title of an anthology published in 1950 by John Ciardi, *Mid-Century American Poets*, this study refers to these four poets as a "midcentury quartet." The term "midcentury" neatly indicates the long period, from 1933–1979, during which this foursome flourished as publishing poets. The term "quartet" suggests a special degree of dialogue and ongoing artistic interchange between these poets, resembling the polyphonic interchange within a string quartet as first one instrumental voice and then another takes the lead, shifts into an accompanying role, or injects a surprising chromaticism into the harmonic texture, tilting the conversation toward a dramatic modulation into a contrasting key. Describing the texture of his own midcentury string quartets, the contemporary American composer Elliott Carter (who based the orchestral song sequence "A Mirror on Which to Dwell" on poems by Elizabeth Bishop) said that each instrument "fairly consistently invents its material out of its own special expressive attitude and its own repertory of musical speeds and intervals." As in one of Carter's string quartets, each literary voice of this particular quartet resonated with its own feelings, ideas, and stylistic devices, being engaged in inventing "material out of its own special expressive attitude and its own repertory."

Speaking of the musical structure of his quartets as a "four-way conversation," Carter adds that "The individuals of this group are related to each other in what might be metaphorically termed three forms of responsiveness: discipleship, companionship, and confrontation."[38] These three forms of responsiveness recur as well throughout the lifelong four-way conversation of Lowell, Jarrell, Bishop, and Berryman. Carter's model suggests a way of understanding their artistic circle as neither moving in necessary orbit around a central, dominant voice, nor uniting in a solid phalanx behind a specific manifesto or dramatic act of protest, nor even grouped around a particular geographical center or identifiable set of stylistic traits. This quartet of poets engaged, over time, in a complex, ongoing conversation of multiple voices, representing varied expressive attitudes and encompassing multiple forms of responsiveness—including shifting modes of discipleship, companionship, and confrontation.

One tangible artifact of their ongoing interchange, an intimate, and highly developed form of colloquy which Bakhtin would have termed "dialogical," may suffice as an example: Lowell's *Notebook 1967–68*. In form *Notebook* is a diary-like, book-length sequence linking hundreds of brief, fact-filled, history-laden, yet frequently surreal or dream-like semiformal lyrics—a structure clearly inspired by Berryman's recently published *77 Dream Songs* (1964). The inner-and-back dust jacket flaps of *Notebook* are entirely covered by reprints of the verbatim texts of rather lengthy, recent, and incisive prose analyses (and endorsements) of Lowell by the remaining members of this quartet: Jarrell and Bishop. Adding another layer of conversation, several poems about these three friends appear within *Notebook*'s covers. Nuances of companionship, discipleship, and confrontation run through each of the quartet's voices as they appear in this volume. And the dialogue explicit and implicit in this particular volume had a long foreground. For example, Lowell had suggested that Berryman shape those first seventy-seven Dream Songs into a book, a book that would win the Pulitzer Prize. And Berryman was quick to admit that in the writing of his earlier masterpiece *Homage to Mistress Bradstreet*, "I sort of seized inspiration from Lowell."[39]

## Making a Postmodern Aesthetic

This quartet produced great verse throughout the mid-twentieth century. Besides its many advantages, the term "midcentury" avoids two problems that beset the more common conception of a "middle generation." One obvious problem is that of temporal and generational ambiguity. As generation follows generation, the question "middle of what?" becomes ever more pressing. A second problem is the subtly pejorative connotation "middle generation" has acquired, suggesting a merely miscellaneous gaggle of transitional poets, awkwardly maintaining a liminal status between the modern and the postmodern—and thus enjoying no independent historical or artistic standing. Both problems perplex the analysis of the late James E. B. Breslin in *From Modern to Contemporary*. In the course of asserting "the apparent defeat—the absence—of the middle generation of poets, including such figures as John Berryman, Elizabeth Bishop, Randall Jarrell," Breslin claims that "As early as 1948, John Berryman, in a survey of the work of this 'middle generation,' concluded that 'it has gone to pieces.'"[40] Breslin's reading of Berryman's essay has the unfortunate effect of actually inverting Berryman's intention. For the "middle generation" that Berryman referred to his 1948 essay "Waiting for the End, Boys" was by no means his own generation, but a cadre of poets, including several of his own mentors, whom Berryman saw as existing in a liminal status between the great modernists and the emerging circle that included our midcentury quartet. In this essay, Berryman praises Bishop, and Jarrell, and—explicitly responding to Jarrell's 1947 essay "From the Kingdom of Necessity"—praises Lowell, and concurs with Jarrell in naming him a "postmodernist."

In the passage on which Breslin draws, Berryman, then a young poet of thirty-three, was commenting on the recent near-silence of an *older* generation of modernist poets such as Eliot, Pound, and Ransom. These older poets constituted the oldest tier, as he saw it, of three distinctive groups of writers. He then adds "As for the middle generation, it has gone to pieces. Tate has published one booklet in a decade, Crane died, MacLeish evaporated. Léonie Adams and Putnam fell silent, Louise Bogan nearly so, Van Doren and Warren developed no following. . . . The young poets lately, in short, have had not fathers but grandfathers" (*JBProse* 299). Though already the term suggests a secondary status, Berryman's "middle generation" that has "gone to pieces" is obviously *not* his own age-mates Lowell, Bishop, or Jarrell, or their contemporaries but such absent or nearly silent "fathers" (and mothers) as Crane, Warren, MacLeish, and Adams, as well as Berryman's own closest mentors, Tate and Van Doren. One must question why the young Berryman would see his own immediate contemporaries as "going to pieces." How could he? For this was the period when he and his friends had begun to emerge as powerful and distinctive voices in such brilliant books as Jarrell's *Little Friend, Little Friend* (1944) and *Losses* (1948), Bishop's *North & South* (1946), Lowell's Pulitzer-Prize-winning *Lord Weary's Castle* (1946), and, perhaps more tentatively, in Berryman's own *The Dispossessed* (1948). Rather, it is the artistic silence of Berryman's immediate elders, a "middle generation" including mentors Tate and Van Doren, that troubles (and perhaps encourages) him.

Significantly, at the start of his essay "Waiting for the End, Boys," Berryman asserts, "The word 'modern' now seems less important. It is not easy now to imagine a poet attempting to be modern. In fact, one sensitive and experienced critic—Randall Jarrell—has described Lowell's poetry as 'post-modernist'; and one certainly has a sense that some period is drawing to a close. I want to document this sense, explaining why it seems to me a very good thing that the period is closing." Thus, in 1948, the young Berryman, far from proclaiming the defeat of his own generation, is doing precisely the opposite: endorsing his friend Jarrell's discovery, in his recent review of Lowell's first important book, of "post-modernist" directions in Lowell; noting a loss of momentum in the revolutionary work of modernist grandfathers; and citing evidence of the peculiar silence of a "middle-generation" of "fathers." Berryman's words reveal an articulate, confident, historically-aware young poet and critic, already intensely in dialogue with such peers as Lowell and Jarrell and eager to make common cause with these members of his emerging generation as they work, in the presence of institutionally powerful and already-canonical competition, to place their distinctive stamp on literary history.

"The End" that Berryman is waiting for, in his essay's title, is plainly the end of modernism. Other members of the quartet were also cognizant of imminent change they sensed, like autumn, in the air. Six years earlier, in his 1942 position paper "The End of the Line," Jarrell had similarly declared that "Modernism As We Knew It—the most successful and influential body of poetry of this century—is dead" (*KA&Co* 81). Of course, since Pound's *Pisan Cantos*, Eliot's *Four Quartets*, most of Williams's *Paterson* and all his late lyrics, as well as the later poems of Moore and Stevens, still lay ahead in 1942, hindsight makes it clear that Jarrell's (and, later, Berryman's) anticipation of the "end" of modernism was premature. But the impulse to get on with the making of what Berryman and Jarrell agreed on terming a "post-modern" aesthetic was an urgent reality for these poets in the 1940s. Their concern with creating this postmodern aesthetic places them well ahead of preemptive but belated claims by more recent theorists and anthologists.

As it turned out, a range of parallel and conflicting postmodern aesthetics would develop and elaborate side by side throughout the 1940s and 1950s, competing with the continuing and powerful presence of such leading modernists as Williams, Pound, Eliot, Stevens, and Moore.[41] The ongoing and discordant colloquy that arose among these conflicting voices in the 1950s marks that under-appreciated middle decade—with its explosive literary politics and vigorously fought "anthology wars"—as among the most diverse and vital epochs of American poetry. The problematic but indispensable term "postmodernism" is defined here as denoting an *historical* phenomenon of the middle and latter decades of the twentieth century. After more than fifty years of postmodernism, it seems necessary to address the problem of where postmodern came from and how it developed. Moreover, one might wonder whether "postmodernism-as-we-knew-it" will survive the turn of the millennium. In any case, this study explores the emergence of a specific postmodern aesthetic, as it grew from tentative beginnings in the mid-1930s, developed into early articulations in the early 1940s, and achieved its mature manifestations in the late 1940s and beyond.

In *The Postmodern Condition* Jean-François Lyotard asserts, "We no longer have recourse to the grand narratives. . . . But . . . the little narrative [*petit rècit*] remains the quintessential form of imaginative invention."[42] Madan Sarup responds that "Lyotard rejects totalizing social theories, the master narratives, because he believes they are reductionist and simplistic. Yet he himself is offering a theory of the postmodern condition which presupposes a dramatic break from modernity. But surely the concept of postmodernism presupposes a master narrative, a totalizing perspective? While Lyotard resists grand narratives, it is impossible to discern how one can have a theory of postmodernism without one."[43] But if one understands postmodernism not as unitary but as a pluralistic or multivalent phenomenon of long historical standing, it is by no means necessary to base "a theory of postmodernism" on a single "master narrative," nor on any single "totalizing perspective." Placing the search for a "theory" of postmodernism in temporary abeyance, it may be more prudent to begin by constructing a history and taxonomy of postmodernism. Postmodernism is a long, broad river with almost as many tributaries as the Amazon, and its students remain at an early stage of studying that river's elaborate sourcings and devious branchings. This critical narrative follows just one of that river's important tributaries back to its headwaters. It would be a good thing if other important lines of American and international literary postmodernism were similarly retraced and mapped. Such an accumulation of "little narratives" would enable the construction of a more fully historicized and contextualized understanding of the postmodern condition and its diverse and conflicting array of artistic products.

Fredric Jameson claims that "any conveniently coherent thumbnail meaning" cannot be applied to postmodernism "for the concept is not merely contested, it is also internally conflicted and contradictory." Jameson asserts "that every time it [the term postmodernism] is used, we are under the obligation to rehearse those inner contradictions and to stage those representational inconsistencies and dilemmas; we have to work all that through every time around."[44] However, if scholars were to produce a detailed matrix of cogent "little narratives" exploring the diverse lines of development that together create the complex web of mid-to-late-twentieth-century postmodernism, these narratives might enable us to construct a more adequate, and less inconsistent, account of the origins, development, and future directions of literary postmodernisms than those that currently stand. This multivalent, historically grounded reading would avoid oversimplifications derived from thumbnail formulations while making better sense of postmodernisms' apparent "inner contradictions, inconsistencies and dilemmas." Relieved of the unique and daunting task of perpetually rehearsing these inconsistencies, scholars could more effectively do their work. Such an accumulation of little narratives, like any truly collaborative project, might serve to sustain a discourse on these postmodernisms, even as this varied from interpreter to interpreter, beyond the abstract realm of mere definition and into the more concrete, if still conflicted, realm of event and artifact and history.

This particular quartet's contribution to the literature of postmodernism is challenging to trace, since, as we have seen, these poets were particularly reluctant to make master statements of aesthetic doctrine—one mark of their abiding suspicion of and resistance to "totalizing" ideologies of every stripe. Yet, an analysis of the ongoing interchange of these poets leads to several key questions raised by cultural criticism. Hence, as we explore their developing careers and look at the ways they have been read—and at times misread—we will be studying, first hand, the development of various literary-historical and critical paradigms. We will be observing how canons and paradigms are formed, and how they persist, mutate, elaborate, or wither away, as they shape or misshape readings and careers. At the same time, a fascinating human story will be revealed, a story in which these poets' lives are so intimately interwoven with their work that the life-texts of the poets, and their cultural positionings and problems, interweave inextricably with a reading of the work and with important theoretical questions. Throughout this study, key moments in the process will be viewed whereby these friends and colleagues were laboring to create, moment by moment and in poem after poem, a sequence of works that became what Jarrell referred to, as early as 1940, as "the sort of poetry that replaces modernism" (*KA&Co* 51).

When Jarrell spotted Berryman's "Waiting for the End, Boys" in the February 1948 *Partisan Review*, he wrote to Berryman with words of exultant praise: "I was crazy about it—I haven't read a long poetry review I enjoyed as much in years and years and years. I thought the general picture of the poetic situation or scene or whatever you'd call it was best of all. I don't like [Henry] Reed nearly as much as you do, but this is a small point."[45] Reviewing the same volume of Henry Reed's that Berryman had cited in "Waiting for the End, Boys," Jarrell would soon declare, "Compared to our bad young poets Mr. Reed is a controlled, civilized, attractive affair; but compared to the good ones—Robert Lowell and Elizabeth Bishop, say—he is a nap after dinner" (*KA&Co* 147).

The first widely recognized link in the complex web of connections joining these four poets is the attachment that formed between Jarrell and Lowell in 1937. These young poets, one in his early twenties, one not yet out of his teens, formed an instant and lasting friendship when they met as John Crowe Ransom's protégés that autumn at Kenyon College.

But documentation contains traces of still earlier connections, such as letters from Berryman that show him reading Jarrell and Bishop closely and appreciatively as early as 1935, while he was still an undergraduate at Columbia University. Although the travels, teaching careers, and in Jarrell's case, military service, of these poets barred frequent meetings throughout the war years, Jarrell and Lowell continued to correspond intensely, and each of these four poets was assiduously reading the others. When World War II ended and Jarrell arrived in New York City in 1946 for a year as literary editor of *The Nation*, the circle really began to take shape. Just after the war, Berryman forged enduring friendships with both Lowell and Jarrell. And in January 1947, Jarrell hosted a dinner party in New York City at which he introduced Bishop to Lowell. Bishop would later recall that evening, in an unfinished memoir, as "one of the pleasantest I can remember," and she, always diffident when it came to talking about her own writing, added, "I remember thinking that it was the first time I had ever actually talked with someone about how one writes poetry —and thinking that . . . it could be strangely easy 'Like exchanging recipes for making a cake.'"[46] Bishop acknowledged "feeling very much at home" on this occasion, an important feeling for an intensely shy poet who had suffered through a virtually homeless childhood. Lowell and Jarrell, from that day forward, would remain Bishop's most important friends and contemporaries in the world of poetry. The web of personal connections was completed when a belated but emphatic link was forged between Bishop and Berryman, following a fan letter Bishop wrote to Berryman praising *His Toy, His Dream, His Rest* in 1968. In the course of the warm exchange of letters that followed, Bishop and Berryman, separated throughout their careers by physical distance, as well as by mutual awe and shyness, quickly closed the gap separating them. In these late letters, Bishop, in Brazil, and Berryman, in Minnesota, declared themselves one another's friends and confirmed their status as life-long admirers.

Though they never formed a publicly recognized movement, the private sense of connection these poets felt was reinforced by frequent public and private endorsement. As early as 1953, Lowell was listing Bishop and Jarrell as his favorite contemporaries.[47] When Lowell was asked in 1961, "What poets among your contemporaries do you most admire?" He replied "The two I've been closest to are Elizabeth Bishop . . . and Jarrell." In 1965 he repeated, "Of poets alive now my favorites are Elizabeth Bishop and Randall Jarrell."[48] When Berryman, already admired by Lowell and Jarrell for his quick intelligence, wide reading, and critical acumen, belatedly emerged as a powerful poet—after years of comparative obscurity and frustration—first with *Homage to Mistress Bradstreet* (1953) and more decisively with the critical and popular success of his 77 *Dream Songs* (1964), he too entered this charmed circle as an artistic peer: a fellow master to be admired, studied, and learned from. As extracts from what became his 77 *Dream Songs*, which won the Pulitzer Prize for 1965, were making their first appearances in magazines in the early sixties—and in the process making waves—Bishop wrote to Lowell from Brazil admitting that she found Berryman difficult. But, she continued, "One has the feeling 100 years from now *he* may be all the rage—or a 'discovery'—*hasn't one*?"[49] Bishop's own discovery of Berryman led her to feature his work in her 1966 class in Seattle, alongside the work of Lowell and Jarrell, and later to introduce it to Brazil.

Although all four never met under the same roof, the taut and fragile web of friendship, artistic affinity, and mutual influence that linked these individual talents would endure for decades in a state of continuing evolution and adjusting tension. Despite the personal difficulties in their lives of emotional breakdowns, divorce, patterns of dislocation and travel that converged only fleetingly, the rigors of alcoholism (which seriously afflicted Lowell, Bishop, and Berryman), pangs of jealousy and literary rivalry, and even their more-than-occasional quarrels and misunderstandings, none of the strands linking these poets would ever be severed—except by death. These poets, having strong personalities, could disagree sharply. They not infrequently disapproved of or misunderstood a specific poem—or at times even a particular turn a friend's career had taken. Yet despite their differences—or rather because even these differences mattered so much—Lowell, Jarrell, Bishop, and Berryman continued to look to one another for support and comprehension as they grew in expressive power and individuality.

This brilliant midcentury quartet came to view one another as indispensable and as irreplaceable colleagues, friends, and artistic peers. When one of them was lost, the loss was keenly felt by the survivors, and the feeling of loss never healed. The loyalty of the living persisted beyond the death of one of its members, as one sees in the extensive elegiac writings, in prose and verse, that the survivors devoted to their departed friends and colleagues, as first Jarrell (in 1965), then Berryman (in 1972), and then Lowell (in 1977) passed abruptly and painfully from the scene. Lowell, like Bishop, could never quite accept the death of his friend Randall. In his prose memoir for Berryman, written seven years later, in 1972, Lowell was still brooding on the might-have-beens. If this avoidable tragedy had been avoided, Jarrell "would be with me now, in full power, as far as one may at fifty. This might-have-been (it's a frequent thought) stings my eyes" (*RLProse* 114).

Despite Lowell's and Bishop's confrontations late in their lives, they craved one another's companionship. Dana Gioia notes that in 1975, when he and his fellow Harvard students were engaged in the formal study of Lowell's poetry in Bishop's classroom, "occasionally we would see them casually walking together near Harvard Square."[50] When distance precluded their walking together, they wrote letters—hundreds of long letters—letters that, even after Kalstone's groundbreaking *Becoming a Poet* and the recent published selection of Bishop's letters *One Art*, have yet to be comprehensively represented or explored. Neither book, for example, cites Bishop's 1968 letter to Berryman, in which she defines the nature and intensity of her admiration with the remark: "There is really not much more I can say than this: I like your poetry and Cal's [Lowell's] better than any of my contemporaries"[51]—praise that, not surprisingly, touched Berryman to the quick.

Bishop, who defined the circle in her 1966 Seattle letter to Lowell, was born first and died last, at the age of sixty-eight, on 6 October 1979. Her death occurred just a few months after completing "North Haven," her elegy to Lowell, who died suddenly of a heart attack in 1977. Lloyd Schwartz, a student and mutual friend of Bishop's and Lowell's at Harvard, recalled that "Elizabeth was terribly upset when Lowell died, partly because they really hadn't resolved the increasing tension in their friendship. Elizabeth didn't care for his last poems all that much." Ilse Barker, a visitor who was present on the island of North Haven when Bishop finished her farewell to Lowell, added that, "She read it to us and walked about with it in her hand. I found it very moving that she felt she could hardly bear to put it down, that it was part of her."[52] Twenty years earlier Lowell had showed a similar attachment to one of Bishop's poems, "The Armadillo." He acknowledged it as not only "a much better poem" than his own "Skunk Hour" but also a poem "I had heard her read and later carried around with me" (*RLProse* 227).

## A Road Map

The book's eight chapters center on a series of turning points in the personal and artistic development of these four poets, beginning in the 1920s and 1930s and extending through the 1960s and 1970s. Chapters 1 and 2 explore the origins and persistence of canonical literary paradigms—especially postmodernism and confessionalism. Because, at this writing, the confessional paradigm stands as the largest and most visible roadblock to a full understanding of the literary relations of this unofficial circle, the second chapter is devoted to a reconsideration of the conceptual limitations and historical inadequacies that have placed this influential critical paradigm squarely in the way of a more integrated understanding of midcentury American poetry.

The remaining chapters center on a series of turning points in the personal and artistic development of these four poets, beginning in the 1920s and 1930s and extending through the 1960s and 1970s. These six chapters may be read as a further sequence of paired formal units that look closely at key issues of this quartet's evolving aesthetic. Chapter 3, "Expulsion from Paradise," centers on the year 1927, showing how parallels in the extremely painful and traumatic childhoods of these four poets, which left each with permanent feelings of abandonment and loss, profoundly shaped their later work and provided the foundation for their ongoing affinity. The issues of youth, powerlessness, and the search for personal and artistic maturity outlined in "Expulsion from Paradise" are developed in Chapter 4, "Points of the Compass." Centered on the year 1936, this chapter examines the varied rewards and challenges this quartet experienced during their parallel apprenticeship under a famous and overlapping circle of mentors, as they attempted to cope with the conflicting and at times nearly debilitating demands of self, home, and family. This chapter outlines the beginnings of the process by which they sought artistic maturity and independence at a moment when they were just beginning to recognize one another as literary peers.

Chapter 5, "The Problem of Selfhood in the Postmodern World" launches a pair of chapters studying the mature phase of their work, centering on the emergence of their particular postmodern aesthetic. Chapter 5 examines the process by which, in the mid-to-late 1930s and early 1940s, these poets began to piece together their specific response to the postmodern condition, whose emerging outlines they were among the first to descry. Chapter 6, "Exploring Lost Worlds," develops this thesis, examining a sequence of postmodern narratives composed in the mid-1950s, as this quartet was defining and elaborating their new aesthetic.

The final two chapters focus on last things, on the problems of unresolved grief and loss so pervasive in their work. Chapter 7, "Displacing Sorrow," explores the unsettling mode of postmodern elegy that these poets pioneered and developed into one of the most pervasive and powerful modes of contemporary poetic discourse. The book concludes with "A Cycle of Elegies," which explores the elegies these poets produced as one by one—first Jarrell in 1965, then Berryman in 1972, then Lowell in 1977—the members of this circle died and the survivors mourned their passing. Bishop was the final survivor of this quartet, and thus a consideration of "North Haven," her eloquent lament for the death of her friend Lowell, closes this study of their shared poetic circle.

# 2 The Confessional Paradigm Revisited

> A name is adequate or it is not. If it is adequate then why go on calling it, if it is not then calling it by its name does no good.
>
> Gertrude Stein, *Lectures in America*

## Origins of the Confessional Paradigm

One prevailing model for assessing the poetry of the 1960s and 1970s is the confessional paradigm. The late M. L. Rosenthal explained in 1967 that "The term 'confessional poetry' came naturally to my mind when I reviewed Robert Lowell's *Life Studies* in 1959, and perhaps it came to the minds of others just as naturally. Whoever invented it, it was a term both helpful and too limited, and very possibly the conception of a confessional school has by now done a certain amount of damage."[1] One measure of the damage done so far is that "the conception of a confessional school" has done much to obscure the career-long conversation about poetry and poetics that engaged Robert Lowell, Randall Jarrell, John Berryman, and Elizabeth Bishop. Indeed, this invention of the critics has been far from universally popular with the poets. When an interviewer asked Berryman how he reacted to being termed a "confessional poet," he replied, "With rage and contempt! Next question."[2] Joel Conarroe, the author of a 1977 book on Berryman, suggested as recently as 1994 that Berryman's riposte amounts to an "obvious contradiction," just one more eccentric move in what Conarroe terms "a life . . . filled with inconsistencies."[3] But Berryman's scornful rejection of the confessional label was anything but inconsistent with the way this resourceful and self-aware poet understood his own artistic practice. Defining the protagonist of the *Dream Songs*, Berryman insisted that his poem is "essentially about an imaginary character (not the poet, not me), named Henry" (*DS* vi), even though, as he lamented, "nobody believes me."[4] Berryman acknowledged the obvious parallels between himself and Henry, but he could not accept reductive readings of the relation between an author and that author's fictive things. As Berryman put it regarding Henry, "We touch at certain points. But I am an actual human being; he is nothing but a series of conceptions—my conceptions. . . . He only does what I make him do. If I have succeeded in making him believable, he performs all kinds of other actions besides those named in the poem, but the reader has to make them up."[5]

Berryman said of the young protagonist of his earlier "Ball Poem," a "boy . . . who has lost his ball" (*JBPoems* 11), that "The poet himself is both left out and put in; the boy does and does not become him and we are confronted with a process which is at once a process of life and a process of art" (*JBProse* 326–27).[6] Recognizing the curious relation between mask and maker in the *Dream Songs*, Lowell referred to Henry, with droll precision, as "John's love-child and ventriloquist's doll" (*RLProse* 117). Adrienne Rich spoke with like precision when she observed in a 1964 review of *77 Dream Songs* for the *Nation* that: "Through a device too integral to seem devised, [Berryman] manages private history without self-photography."[7] Rich read the *Dream Songs* as a triumph of artistic perspective and representation, observing that Berryman "is in a position to use—and does—any conceivable tone of voice and manner to needle, wheedle, singe, disarm and scarify the reader. He is a bruised, raging and fiendishly intelligent man, and he has found a way to be all three simultaneously." Rich observed that "his book owes much of its beauty and flair to a kind of unfakable courage, which spills out in comedy as well as in rage, in thrusts of tenderness as well as defiance."[8]

Berryman was so heartened by her reading that he thanked Rich in a letter, calling her review "the most remarkable American verse-review (I may be wrong about this) since Jarrell's study of Lord Weary's Castle 17 y[ear]rs ago." He added, that "it is your accuracy that most moves me and girds me up for the awful stuff ahead—hundreds of them [i.e. Dream Songs], in all stages, to be composed together, in a second volume."[9] The complex interweaving of "a process of life" with "a process of art" that Berryman began with early achievements such as "The Ball Poem"—and that he raised to an extraordinary pitch in *The Dream Songs*—remained a dynamic feature, not just of his own poetic program, but of the work of the contemporaries he most admired, including Robert Lowell, Randall Jarrell, and Elizabeth Bishop.

Rosenthal claimed in his review of Lowell's *Life Studies* that the poems involved the "most naked kind of confession,"[10] and he asserted in 1967 that, "Because of the way Lowell brought his private humiliations, sufferings, and psychological problems into the poems of *Life Studies*, the word 'confessional' seemed appropriate enough."[11] Rosenthal himself employed the term with a sensitivity to artistic values and a tact not always evident in the readers who followed him.

Throughout the 1960s, 1970s, and well into the 1980s, the confessional model remained influential with academic critics and literary historians across a wide spectrum, perhaps because it offered a humanly compelling and rather clear-cut way of evaluating poetry. Poems involving daring self-revelation could be assumed to be bold and sincere. However, poets whose work appeared *not* to conform to the confessional mode were often viewed condescendingly by critics. For example, Elizabeth Bishop's poetry, widely viewed as "impersonal" or "reticent," was often dismissed as artificial and too polite. Bishop received condescending treatment even from such early feminist critics as Alicia Ostriker. In her influential 1986 feminist history of women's poetry *Stealing the Language*, Ostriker called "Roosters"—which the conspicuously unrestrained Berryman, for one, felt was Bishop's boldest and best—a "capsule representation of the restraints inhibiting poets who would be ladies."[12] Women poets such as Sylvia Plath and Anne Sexton, two erstwhile disciples of Lowell, seemed to mark out a bolder style, as did the poetics of feminist protest forged by Adrienne Rich and others. As Betsy Erkkila has observed, "feminist critics tended to dismiss Bishop's work in favor of more explicitly personal and confessional women poets."[13]

Male critics have had similar problems placing Bishop in literary history. In 1984 James E. B. Breslin's historical survey *From Modern to Contemporary* dismissed Bishop, in a passing phrase, as a poet who had suffered the "apparent defeat" of "the middle generation of poets." She was a poet who "worked steadily and independently, but the cost was isolation and critical neglect."[14] Alan Williamson acknowledges the exclusion of Bishop from his *Introspection and Contemporary Poetry* (also 1984) with the remark: "This turning inward has, of course, not been universal; good poets (Bishop and Wilbur, to name two) have ignored or resisted it."[15]

Such readiness to dismiss Bishop from the central account reaches back at least to Rosenthal's own *The Modern Poets* (1960), where he, too, pairs Bishop with Richard Wilbur. Rosenthal there asserted that while these poets have "done exquisite and richly suggestive work," they have "touched the imagination of their generation very little. The reason seems to be that they remind us only of what we have already been taught to value: elegance, grace, precision, quiet intensity of phrasing."[16]

Of course, Bishop's defeat, taken for granted by Breslin little more than a decade ago, really was only "apparent," and today her work is certainly not suffering from either isolation or critical neglect. The recent reevaluation of Bishop's achievement, which has firmly established her as a major figure in American poetry, rests in part on the discovery of underlying emotional complexities and intensities in her work. Critics have begun to recognize the ways in which Bishop's deeply introspective and subtly encoded writing engages with problems of gender, love, sexuality, nature, poverty, and culture, as well as with experiences of grief and loss, of moral, emotional, and perceptual uncertainty and insecurity.

This new phase in the reading of Bishop's work has expanded rapidly, encouraged both by shifts in the cultural perspectives of the readership, and by the new availability of a vastly extended biographical and documentary record. Including the recent appearance in print of previously unpublished poems and a substantial, though still far from complete, selection of her letters, these sources give a far more complex and compelling picture of Bishop than was available while she lived.[17] This new understanding of Bishop—unavailable to all but the most percipient even a decade ago—also clarifies the nature of her affinity for poets such as Lowell and Berryman.

Bishop studies have been particularly stimulated by fresh and provocative critical approaches, such as one first suggested by Adrienne Rich herself in a 1983 review of *The Complete Poems 1927–1979*. Rich was an eventual, though at times conflicted, admirer of all four of these poets. But she came last to appreciate the indirect style of Elizabeth Bishop. Rich underwent this conversion by understanding Bishop's work as having been written with the "eye of the outsider." Rich observed in a 1983 review, "In particular I am concerned with her experience of outsiderhood, closely—though not exclusively—linked with the essential outsiderhood of a lesbian identity; and with how the outsider's eye enables Bishop to perceive other kinds of outsiders and to identify, or try to identify, with them."[18] In the years since Rich's review, critics have become ever more practiced and adept at reading the many texts by women that meet Rich's criteria, understated texts observed with an outsider's eye and encoded with the perceptions, identifications, and quiet protests of outsiderhood. Rich is particularly acute in directing attention toward Bishop's subtle rendering of acts of attempted identification, attempts that often remain imperfect and incomplete in Bishop's poems but that in the process achieve quiet miracles of authenticity, surprise, and humor. Rich was perhaps the first to read Bishop as a poet "who was critically and consciously trying to explore marginality, power and powerlessness, often in poetry of great beauty."[19]

David Kalstone's posthumously published *Becoming a Poet* (1989), Brett Millier's recent document-based and Gary Fountain's recent interview-based biographies, and recent critical studies by Lorrie Goldensohn, Bonnie Costello, Victoria Harrison, Joanne Feit Diehl, Marilyn May Lombardi, and Susan McCabe have further delineated the public Bishop, while also taking us deeper into Bishop's once all-but-inaccessible private world. These and other studies have demonstrated convincingly how a life marked by traumatic childhood losses, by alcoholism, by a lifelong battle with asthma and other auto-immune disorders, and by what Rich terms "the essential outsiderhood of a lesbian identity," became intimately intertwined, in Bishop's *oeuvre*, with the processes of an art that at once disguises and discloses. Bishop told her student Wesley Wehr, in 1966, "I *hate* confessional poetry" (*EBLet* 45). But as we have seen, she also stated in a 1968 letter to Berryman, "I like your poetry and Cal's [Lowell's] better than any of my contemporaries."[20]

When Berryman rejects the confessional label with "rage and contempt" he is accused of perpetrating an "obvious contradiction." Is Bishop's statement to Berryman an equally obvious contradiction? Or can it be that there is no contradiction? The best way to approach these questions is historically. While the term "confessional poetry" had been around for only six years (since Rosenthal's review) when Bishop declared that she hated "confessional poetry" in 1966, she had known and admired Berryman's and Lowell's work since the 1940s. Moreover, Bishop (like their mutual friend Jarrell) had read and praised Lowell's *Life Studies* poems in manuscript in 1957 as the poems were being written, three years before Rosenthal named her old friend and colleague a confessional poet. When Bishop praised *Life Studies* in glowing terms on the book's original dust jacket, or when she praised Berryman's "extraordinary performance" in *77 Dream Songs* in a 1964 letter to Anne Stevenson,[21] she was not thinking of these long-term colleagues as "confessional poets" but simply as poets. And she was responding to their work not as "confessional poetry" but simply as poetry.

Bishop, in fact, insisted on the measurable distance between what she found in Lowell's work and the writing of some of his disciples. In a 1960 letter to Lowell, Bishop disparaged Lowell's student, Anne Sexton, in comparison to him: "She *is* good, in spots,—but there's all the difference in the world, I'm afraid, between her kind of simplicity and that of *Life Studies*, her kind of egocentricity that is simply that, and yours that has been—what would be the reverse of *sub*limated, I wonder—anyway, made intensely *interesting*, and painfully applicable to every reader. I feel I know too much about her—whereas, although I know much more about you, I'd like to know a great deal more."[22] A year later Bishop insisted, in another letter to Lowell, on what she felt was "the vast vast difference between you and one of your better imitators." She asserts, for example, that "Snodgrass is really saying—'I do all these awful things—but don't you really think I'm awfully *nice* . . . ? You tell things—but never wind up with your own darling gestures, the way he does (he'd be giving Lepke home-made cookies or something). I went right through Life Studies again and there is not a trace of it." Instead, she praised the book as "courageous and honest."[23]

Of course, the confessional paradigm has prompted several constructors of historical schema to present Bishop and Lowell—in life the most intimate of colleagues and friends—on opposite poles of some artistic antipodes. Hence, an integrated reading of their poetic development has remained elusive. Many critics and historians, mesmerized by the "process of life" represented in the work of Berryman and Lowell, have turned a blind eye to how the "process of art," in the same work, imparts an aura of both tangible reality and epistemological uncertainty. These poets labeled "confessional," like their colleagues Bishop and Jarrell, compose poems that are significantly fictive. Their work involves a process of selection, borrowing, voicing, of invention or recasting of incident, of arrangement, rearrangement, and reinterpretation of fact, that goes far beyond "self-photography." Yet, even so sensitive a reader as David Kalstone, when he stresses Bishop's "intense difference" from Lowell (and in the process omits from his account many of Bishop's most approving statements about Lowell's work, and many of her most supportive and appreciative statements about him as a poet and person) seems to be accepting, implicitly, the distinction implied by the confessional paradigm.

Critics more committed to the confessional paradigm than Kalstone have been, as a group, less than ideally sensitive to the varied triumphs of imaginative re-creation embodied in the work of Lowell and Berryman. They have overlooked—with uncanny consistency—the wide range of aesthetic features that link Lowell's and Berryman's work to Bishop's (or Jarrell's). In the process they have either bypassed altogether, or dismissed in puzzlement, the poets' own public declarations of their mutual influence and affinity. To cite one example of this tacit dismissal, Terri Witek's 1993 book *Robert Lowell and Life Studies: Revising the Self* does not include a single reference to Bishop. This omission is difficult to explain, considering the fact that the volume's pivotal poem, "Skunk Hour," is dedicated to Bishop, that *Life Studies* included her glowing dust jacket blurb, which for Lowell had truly talismanic value, and that there is mounting evidence of Bishop's decisive involvement in the book's creation. Imagine never mentioning Ezra Pound in a book about *The Waste Land.*

The same critics who have portrayed Bishop as the antithesis of Lowell have often, as we shall see, either ignored Lowell's profound relation to his close colleague Jarrell, or have pressed Jarrell, very awkwardly indeed, into service under the confessional banner. In short, critics following the confessional paradigm have either ignored or minimized the means by which—in the poems of Lowell and Berryman, as in the poems of Bishop and Jarrell—the characteristically devious tactics of art have made the processes of life seem real. And they have also seriously misread, or overlooked altogether, the accumulating evidence that points to an underlying network of literary relations between these four poets. The popular success of the term "confessional poetry" in the face of its many limitations has sadly compounded the "damage" that worried Rosenthal in 1967, in part by encouraging a good deal of bad history.

Indeed, the confessional model is of little use, and is often a downright hindrance, to a conscientious analyst faced with a massive array of published and unpublished data—letters, annotated manuscripts, workbooks, reviews, memoirs, interviews, and so forth. These sources confirm the presence and extraordinary persistence of that intricate and unofficial, yet powerful and enduring, web of links that joined Bishop and Jarrell to Lowell and Berryman in a private literary circle. Indeed, evidence of this matrix of connectives—emerging from the documentary record with much of the organic particularity and complexity of a skein of living tissue—is what initially prompted this researcher to seek specific alternatives to the confessional paradigm. Any paradigm that persistently discourages alertness in the face of anomalies deserves to be questioned as an analytical tool.

The most decisive piece of evidence undermining the use of the confessional paradigm as a means of distinguishing Lowell from Bishop may be the connection between Bishop's poem "The Armadillo" and Lowell's "Skunk Hour." Lowell underlined his strong affinity for Bishop and his gratitude for her example by dedicating "Skunk Hour" to her. It is worth stressing here that this was the poem with which Lowell broke through to the *Life Studies* style and in consequence inspired Rosenthal to coin the term "confessional poetry." Lowell stated categorically that "rereading

[Bishop] suggested a way of breaking through the shell of my old manner. Her rhythms, idiom, images, and stanza structure seemed to belong to a later century" (*RLProse* 227). "The Armadillo," which Bishop dedicated to Lowell, is the poem that catalyzed his breakthrough in "Skunk Hour."

The "Armadillo" also inspired Lowell to take up the prose autobiographical sketches that had recently been accumulating on his desk and to recreate the same material in crisply imaged poetic versions. Richard Wilbur has said, "I can remember Cal's carrying Elizabeth's 'Armadillo' poem around in his wallet everywhere, not the way you'd carry the picture of a grandson, but as you'd carry something to brace you and make you sure of how a poem ought to be. [Cal talked] eternally about her merits as a poet. I have a feeling that finally she was the poet he most respected, which was quite apart from his feelings of affection for her. . . . I think he regarded her as a perfect judge and a splendid model."[24] Writing to Bishop on 10 June 1957, before the completion of "Skunk Hour," Lowell noted "Maybe I'll do my poem, sad, resonant, ferocious, as a counterpiece to yours."[25]

Given Bishop's and Lowell's mutually acknowledged affinity, for which the evidence keeps piling up, and given, as well, Bishop's decisive influence on the technique (the "rhythms, idiom, images, and stanza structure") of the seminal poem ("Skunk Hour") in what is generally posited as the seminal book in the confessional mode[26]—just where is one to draw the line between Bishop's and Lowell's supposedly antithetical practices? Just how is one to define "confessional poetry"?

## Defining Confessional Poetry?

The title of a 1993 essay by Diane Middlebrook for the *Columbia History of American Poetry* asks the appropriate question, "What Was Confessional Poetry?" Middlebrook advocates the continuing usefulness of the confessional paradigm as long as its scope is limited quite narrowly. She asserts that "confessional poetry" is "a term more properly applied to a handful of books that appeared between 1959–1966." Moreover, Middlebrook limits her canon of genuine confessional poets to just four—Lowell and three of his students: W. D. Snodgrass, Anne Sexton, and Sylvia Plath. Middlebrook insists on the importance of the "close personal affiliations" of these poets with Lowell. Along with these affiliations, she identifies as confessional poetry's chief characteristics that it "investigates the pressures on the family as an institution regulating middle-class private life, primarily through the mother. Its principle themes are divorce, sexual infidelity, childhood neglect, and the mental disorders that follow from deep emotional wounds received in early life. A confessional poem contains a first-person speaker, 'I,' and always seems to refer to a real person in whose actual life real episodes have occurred that cause actual pain, all represented in the poem."[27]

But by Middlebrook's definition Bishop, whose "impersonal" practice was long considered the opposite of confessional, and whom Middlebrook neglects to mention, had been writing something hard to distinguish from confessional poetry (and prose) since the early 1950s. Six years before Middlebrook's starting date of 1959, Bishop had already begun to explore, in the context of a familial network of moderate means, the impact that "childhood neglect" had on her own life. In Bishop's case, this neglect was prompted by the death of her father when she was eight months old, and by her mother Gertrude's "mental disorders," which led to Gertrude's permanent placement in a Dartmouth, Nova Scotia mental hospital when Bishop was five. After the loss of her mother, and Bishop's own shocking removal from Nova Scotia by her paternal grandparents a year later, Bishop suffered a series of physical and emotional disorders of her own. Bishop's exploration of the "actual pain" caused by these "episodes" taken from "actual life" appeared in stories such as "In the Village"(1953) and "Gwendolyn" (1953), as well as in poems like "Sestina" (1956). Lowell, seeking a new style for himself, was reading these texts assiduously and often in typescript as Bishop finished them.

Bishop's experiences of loss, emotional violence, and involuntary abandonment "primarily through the mother" left "deep emotional wounds" that profoundly shaped Bishop's development as person and artist. Bishop's influential poems and stories—though comparatively discreet in their handling of the first person speaker, sometimes referring instead to "the child"—consistently "seem to refer to a real person in whose actual life real episodes have occurred that cause actual pain, all represented in the poem." In the poem "Sestina," as in the stories "In the Village" and "Gwendolyn," the reader is meant to understand that the narrator and central observer represents a version of the author. Lowell not only read and praised these writings as they appeared, he even composed his own verse "imitation" of "In the Village," which he titled "The Scream." Importantly, as Lowell pursued his own development of the self-exploratory theme, he followed Bishop's progression from prose into verse.

Lowell's prose autobiographical sketch "91 Revere St." appeared in the

*Partisan Review* in December 1956, three years after Bishop's "In the Village." At this point, Lowell had not begun any of the self-exploratory poems in *Life Studies*. However, he had drafted more than a dozen further autobiographical prose fragments, including two—"Antebellum Boston" and "Near the Unbalanced Aquarium"—that now appear in Lowell's *Collected Prose*. In the ensuing months, after Bishop sent Lowell a typescript of "The Armadillo," Lowell was to render several of these prose sketches into the poems of *Life Studies*. As Lowell completed these poems, he sent them first in manuscript to Bishop in Brazil, who read and praised them. Thereafter, as Lowell's book was being published in 1959 and greeted by its first reviews, Bishop was continuing her own simultaneous explorations of traumatic childhood experience. During this time she wrote such poems as "First Death in Nova Scotia" (1959) and such prose as the then-unpublished story "The Country Mouse" (1960)—a crucial memoir which did not appear in print until the posthumous publication of Bishop's *Collected Prose* in 1984.

We can see, then, that Bishop's and Lowell's explorations in the 1950s and early 1960s of the traumatic character of early childhood experience were significantly parallel—and for the most part contemporaneous. As the years passed, these parallel explorations would continue in the collegial spirit that had marked the poets' interaction from the beginning. Yet Bishop's work anticipated Lowell's, both in technique and in subject matter, and showed him a way to convert his own accumulating material into effective verse. As Lowell freely acknowledged, both in public and in private, it was he who considered himself *Bishop's* pupil when it came to the language, the tonal balance, and even much of the subject matter of *Life Studies*. Indeed, Lowell stated in a letter to Bishop that, "I used your Armadillo in class as a parallel to my Skunks and ended up feeling a petty plagiarist."[28]

For the moment, however, let me emphasize another point: Bishop meets or exceeds every one of the stated criteria by which Middlebrook defines the "confessional poet." As we have seen, Bishop not only investigates "the pressures on the family" working "primarily through the mother" but also explores "disorders that follow from deep emotional wounds received in early life." Moreover, Bishop's "close personal affiliation" with Lowell began in January 1947 and lasted until Lowell's death thirty years later. Thus, it predates Lowell's relations with Snodgrass, Sexton, and Plath by many years. And of course the Bishop-Lowell connection was more lasting, more intense on both sides, and more profound in terms of its personal and literary importance for both poets. Hence, by Middlebrook's stated criteria, Bishop would seem to qualify, not merely as a confessional poet, but as, perhaps, the school's most decisive progenitor. But it is not my purpose here to argue for Bishop as originating confessional poet, despite the surprisingly strong case that can be constructed along these lines. Instead, I want to suggest just how amorphous the term "confessional poet" was from the start, and how amorphous it remains after more than thirty years of hard use—even if one attempts to define the term quite narrowly.

If this term cannot be defined in its most restrictive form to exclude a poet who declared, point-blank, "I *hate* confessional poetry," its value as a tool for naming, for categorizing, or for cogent historical analysis remains unproven. But I think we can go even further in a critique of the term on definitional grounds, and in this I am encouraged by the poets themselves. In another interview, for example, Bishop termed the paradigm "nonsense."[29] For his part, John Berryman, deeply schooled in the arcana of Shakespearean textual editing and an exceptionally precise linguist, protested in 1972 that "The word [confessional] doesn't mean anything."[30] This chapter will show just why the term has been so hard to define, just why it has been of so little demonstrable value as a literary-historical paradigm, and just why it has met with such resistance—even downright hostility and contempt—from poet-friends on both sides of its putative divide. These difficulties grow in definable ways out of the paradigm's basic assumptions—assumptions that rest in part on misreadings of the complex and at times deceptive historical background out of which the poetry emerged. They also rest in part on specific misconceptions about the techniques operating in the poetry of Berryman or Bishop, Lowell or Jarrell. And they rest in part on the paradigm's inherent ethical and epistemological contradictions. It will be necessary to clarify the nature of these problems more specifically before moving on to a fresh, positive, and integrated reconsideration of the poetry itself.

Of course, I am not the first to voice discomfort with the implications of the confessional paradigm. Earlier critics and historians, even as they placed poets like Lowell or Berryman in the confessional category, have tended to express a lingering uneasiness with the term. For example, in 1982, Berryman's first biographer, John Haffenden, who groups his subject with "Delmore Schwartz, Robert Lowell, Randall Jarrell and Theodore Roethke," remarks that it might be a "critical convenience to call much of their work 'Confessional,'" yet he finds this "sweet theory . . .

limp in application."[31] And in 1984, Alan Williamson in *Introspection and Contemporary Poetry* speaks of the "problems and triumphs of intimately self-revelatory ('confessional') poetry." Here Williamson compounds Haffenden's quotation marks with parentheses in an attempt to distance himself from the word "confessional."

Williamson, in search of an alternative, acknowledges that "Valid objections have been raised to the implications latent in the phrase 'confessional poetry'—artlessness, theatricality, shame—almost from the moment it was first employed. I allow myself the term when referring to specific literary conventions of the 1960s, or to a thematic concern with disclosure or shock. Under other circumstances, I prefer the expression 'personal poetry.'"[32] As Williamson implies, the word "confessional" does carry with it both a series of pejorative implications and a certain raw descriptive force. Adopted almost instantaneously, despite the worries voiced even by its coiner, Rosenthal, about potential "damage" from "a term both helpful and too limited," the term has by now entered the mythic background of literary studies.

One should not expect to see it soon, if ever, dislodged from this background. Given the extraordinary durability, once attached, of any handy label, even if misleading or reductive (think of Mozart's so-called "Elvira Madigan" piano concerto), Lowell's poetry will surely be called "confessional" as long as it is read. The concern here is not with the term's ongoing mythic or stereotypic presence, but the validity of the term's continuing use as a critical paradigm. Is this term still worth using as an analytical tool or a literary-historical category? However one chooses to answer that question, the confusions fostered by the confessional paradigm must be cleared away before a cogent discussion of the poetry of this generation, and of these four poets in particular, can proceed.

After examining in some detail the specific problems imposed by the confessional paradigm, an alternative paradigm will be proposed that attempts to specify those features of Lowell, Bishop, Berryman, and Jarrell that distinguishes their work from the personal poetry of the past. Of course, any alternative conception will have to encourage clearer, more cogent analysis than the term it is replacing.

The grip of the confessional paradigm has proven so strong, and its influence so lasting and pervasive, that before embarking on a reconsideration of the term we would do well to consider the most significant barriers the paradigm has imposed between the reader and the poetry. It will also be vital to delineate the assumptions about poetry and poets on which these barriers rest. In particular we shall consider: 1) how the confessional paradigm has prejudiced, and is still prejudicing, artistic evaluation; 2) how the paradigm's treatment of the poem as a reliable source of factual disclosure slights the epistemological complexity of the work while downplaying its fictive character; 3) how the paradigm's assumption of authorial stasis ignores the poetry's perceptual mobility and moral relativism; 4) how the paradigm promotes assumptions of the reader's moral authority over the author; and, 5) how the paradigm promotes assumptions of the author's creative passivity.

## First Problem: The Confessional Paradigm Prejudices Evaluation

Ironically enough, as the problems imposed by the confessional paradigm have grown more obvious and critical discomfort with the category has increased, the main target has not been the paradigm itself, but the poets forced to live under it. Hence, the brusque dismissal many critics once accorded Bishop because she appeared too "reticent" is now being meted out to the putative "confessional poets," as if they had themselves invented the label pasted on them by literary journalists.

Harold Bloom, for example, praises Bishop for functioning "so securely" within a tradition of "rhetorical control, overt moral authority, and sometimes . . . fairly strict economy of means" (which he traces through Emerson, Dickinson, Frost, Moore, and Stevens) that she can deploy her "superb art" to "profoundly play at trope."[33] But Bloom condemns Robert Lowell, identifying him with "the trope of vulnerability. The trope, once influential and fashionable, has become the mark of a school of poets who now seem writers of period pieces: the 'Confessional' school of Anne Sexton, Sylvia Plath, the earlier W. D. Snodgrass, the later work of John Berryman. 'Confessional' verse, intended to be revelatory, soon seemed opaque."[34]

Of course, as I have suggested, the best work of Lowell, Berryman, and their students is not "intended to be revelatory" but to be exploratory. And its degree of opacity is not inconsistent with an exploratory spirit nor with traditional standards of literary excellence, as readers of Shakespeare, Milton, or Elizabeth Bishop might agree. Speaking of Lowell's last book, *Day by Day*, Bloom observes, "I am left uncertain as to whether I am not being moved by a record of human suffering, rather than by a making of any kind."[35] Alluding as he does to the word *poet*'s Greek root—*maker*—Bloom is accusing Lowell of being no poet at all. Here, Bloom appears to be reading Lowell's poems as exemplars of the confessional paradigm, rather than reading the poems as they stand on the page. As such, Bloom attacks the victim of the paradigm (Lowell), when he might be critiquing the paradigm itself. Asserting that "Elizabeth Bishop is now firmly established as the enduring artist of Lowell's generation,"[36] Bloom uses Bishop as a club to beat Lowell, just as earlier critics had used Lowell as a club to beat Bishop.

In fact, the pastime of using one of the four poets in this unofficial circle as a club to beat another has become a favorite critical practice that, unfortunately, shows no sign of abating. Some of the most respected critics cannot seem to resist this pastime's allures. Recently, for example, Richard Flynn declared Jarrell's verse "morally superior" to Berryman's or Lowell's, asserting that "the cult of personality that is preeminent in Lowell's later work" presents more of the "egotistical ridiculous" than "the egotistical sublime." Flynn reads Berryman's Henry as an "unreconstructed child, childish in the way Jarrell's children are not."[37] James Longenbach, meanwhile, presses home the attack on Lowell. He cites Jarrell's insightful early praise of Bishop's first book, which calls her a poet who recognizes that "morality, for the individual, is usually a small, personal, statistical, but heartbreaking or heart-warming affair of omission and commission the greatest of which will seem infinitesimal, ludicrously beneath notice, to those who govern, rationalize and deplore." Longenbach, a sensitive and historically-informed reader, makes the surprising claim that, "I think Jarrell had Lowell in mind here, for if Lowell is anything, he is a poet who governs, rationalizes, and deplores—a poet who does feel that the wickedness and confusion of the age can explain his own."[38]

The tone of moral reprehension found in Longenbach, Flynn, and Bloom is not uncommon in today's readings of Lowell. Longenbach attempts to use *both* Jarrell and Bishop as clubs to beat Lowell, but this interpretation falls apart as soon as one looks at the facts of the case: at what Jarrell actually said and when he said it.

Jarrell alludes to "those who govern, rationalize and deplore" well before Lowell could possibly have been so described. Jarrell's cited review of Bishop appeared in the September–October 1946 issue of the *Nation* when only Lowell's 1944 small-press chapbook *Land of Unlikeness*, published in a run of 200 copies, existed as a public point of reference. When Jarrell wrote that Fall 1946 review of Bishop, Lowell was a promising twenty-nine-year-old poet. Jarrell knew his promise better than most, since he had minutely studied all of his younger friend's forthcoming *Lord Weary's Castle* poems in draft. But Jarrell had every reason to be acutely conscious of the array of established masters—including Eliot, Frost, Pound, Stevens, Williams, Tate, Ransom, and Moore—who stood ahead of Bishop, Lowell, and Jarrell in the literary pecking order of 1946. In the 1942 essay "The End of the Line," Jarrell had written extensively on the problem of following in the wake of the modernist generation. Jarrell was too savvy an observer of the literary scene to have alluded to the all but unknown Lowell, two months before *Lord Weary* appeared in December 1946, as a "governing" force in poetry.

Sergeant Randall Jarrell, only recently discharged from the Army Air Corps, had lived through an extended sojourn as a cog amid the wheels of the world's largest and most quickly assembled military bureaucracy. As an Air Corps instructor and a close observer of contemporary social orders, he had studied at first hand how such a bureaucracy, the forerunner of the Cold War's military-industrial complex, governs and rationalizes the present and future lives of millions of men and women serving under it. Jarrell's war poems are full of pilots and crewmen who "fell into the State / And . . . hunched in its belly" en route to violent, impersonal deaths. These poems repeatedly dramatize the powerlessness of individuals in the grip of governing and rationalizing forces.

Moreover, Jarrell knew quite well that, beyond the scope of his own military bureaucracy, tens of millions of individuals who served and/or were killed in the course of World War II were governed by ferocious rationalizers. Hitler and Stalin deplored racial, ethnic, religious, and political differences in others to the point of employing their soldier-citizens to murder these differing peoples systematically, and by the millions. In the postwar, cold war America of 1946, Jarrell—sounding remarkably like a prophet of the postmodern world then looming into view—had every reason to express anxiety about the leaders of "the practical world of business and science and morality, a vortex that is laboring to suck everything into its transforming revolutions" (*P&A* 99).

It is worth pressing for a historically contextualized reading of Jarrell's remark, in 1946, about "those who govern, rationalize and deplore." This context clarifies Jarrell's position vis á vis the emerging postmodern condition. What's more, clarifying what Jarrell meant speaks to the present image of Lowell as a graceless, dictatorial, and overbearing presence on the poetic scene. Of course, the reputation of any poet as successful as Lowell must provoke an eventual reaction. And Lowell's stock has not been helped by the image projected by recent biographies, which do not sufficiently connect Lowell's life to his creative achievement.

Steven Gould Axelrod has pointed out of Ian Hamilton's biography that "Because Hamilton generally devalues the imagination, and particularly discredits *Lowell's* sort of creativity . . . his book reads less like a literary biography than like a probation report."[39] Even Peter Taylor, who largely admired Hamilton's biography, felt that Hamilton "shows little awareness and no real understanding of his [Lowell's] special brand of humor. . . . and the result is that, with all the book's careful delineation of his madness, there is the danger of his being seen as an unrelieved grotesque. None of his friends saw him as that—not one of them. His teasing was often rough, but he was the most affectionate and loyal of friends."[40] One way to recover an appreciation of "*Lowell's* sort of creativity," and his peculiar humanity, is to read him through the eyes of friends like Jarrell, Bishop, and Berryman, poets who appreciated and frequently shared his personal, cultural, and artistic problems. Current readings of Lowell all too frequently ignore the many ways in which Lowell himself wrote from the perspective of the vulnerable and marginalized, a perspective his friends certainly saw in his work and understood.

As we shall see in some detail in our next chapter, each of these poets, male *or* female, had occasion to view the world through "the eye of the outsider." Could the affinity between these poets be partly explained by a shared experience of outsiderhood? Certainly when Jarrell wrote his review of Bishop in 1946 he identified quite closely with Lowell. Jarrell knew that his friend had refused to rationalize the Allied fire-bombing of Hamburg, in which over 30,000 civilians were killed and 80 percent of the city's buildings were destroyed.[41] Lowell had deplored the act, writing a reproving letter to Franklin Roosevelt, applying for conscientious objector status, and opting for prison when that status was refused. Lowell later recalled with rueful self-deprecation in "Memories of West Street and Lepke," a poem from *Life Studies*, that

> I was a fire-breathing Catholic C. O.,
> and made my manic statement,
> telling off the state and the president.

Jarrell similarly refused to rationalize and deplored in letters to Lowell and Margaret Marshall the dropping of the atomic bombs on Japanese cities in 1945. Jarrell was particularly disturbed by the bombing of Nagasaki, which, he felt "was bombed simply to test out the second type of bomb" (*RJLet* 129, 130–34).

Jarrell sympathized with his friend Lowell's suffering due to manic depression and with his marginality within his own family—dominated by a snobbish, contemptuous mother who bore some resemblance to Jarrell's own. That sympathy, along with his respect for Lowell's political courage, and for his intelligence, talent, wide reading, and devotion to literature, led Jarrell to feel a profound bond with Lowell at just the time (1945–46) when Longenbach was setting up Lowell as a straw man, and using Jarrell's words to apply the torch. As he was embarking on a remarkable series of editorial readings of the poems that would become Lowell's 1946 blockbuster *Lord Weary's Castle*, Jarrell wrote to Lowell from Davis-Monthan Field in Tucson, Arizona, in August 1945. In that letter he expressed both his own profound loneliness and his sense of kinship with Lowell: "I haven't even seen anybody I *know* in three years. You are the only writer I feel much in common with (when I read your poems I not only wish that I had written them but feel that mine in some queer sense are related to them—i.e., if I didn't write the way I do I might or would like to write the way you do; your poems about the war are the only ones I like except my own—both of them have the same core of sorrow and horror and so on) and the only good friend of my own age I have" (*RJLet* 128).

When Jarrell was sending Lowell his last suggested revisions to *Lord Weary* in January 1946, he asked, "But send the manuscript back to me later, will you? Then I can make notes to review it by when it comes out" (*RJLet* 144). For Jarrell was already preparing to write "From the Kingdom of Necessity," a review of *Lord Weary's Castle* that Lowell himself would term (along with Berryman's) "definitive" (*RLProse* 113). Jarrell reads the early Lowell, in a review published just three months after the review of Bishop cited by Longenbach, not as a "governing" force in poetry but as an intrepid explorer of the "realm of necessity." Hence, Jarrell presents the book as a powerful attack on precisely those forces that govern and rationalize, and that deplore and threaten the kind of independent, creative intellects that Lowell and Jarrell were struggling to become.

Jarrell sees the realm of necessity as approximating "that cake of custom in which all of us lie embedded like lungfish," a realm which Lowell's poems fill with "everything that is closed, turned inward, incestuous, that blinds or binds." But Jarrell recognizes a contrary force in Lowell's poetry: "struggling within this like leaven, falling into it like light, is everything that is free or open, that grows or is willing to change: here is the generosity or openness or willingness that is itself salvation: here is 'accessibility to experience'" (*P&A* 208–9). Jarrell does not see the Lowellian individual as seeking absolution in the face of "necessity," but rather as struggling toward survival within necessity's binding, blinding, incestuous strictures and, with luck, escaping into "the realm of freedom." Jarrell's analysis praises as one of the strengths of Lowell's art his "accessibility to experience" of even the most painful kind, his commitment to save what Lowell later termed the "unsavable" by "giving it form."

Rich was speaking of Berryman's *Dream Songs* when she noted, "a certain kind of technical daring and inventiveness combine with historical certainty and total awareness of our language and our tradition. . . . Terrible risks have gone into the making of this poetry."[42] At their considerable best, Lowell and Jarrell, like Bishop and Berryman, connect technical and personal risk to a knowledge of history and tradition in poems that face and explore—in the "realm of necessity"—many of the starkest forms of human constraint, isolation, and loss.

The critics have wrangled, straining at times implausibly to quote these poets against one another. But when one turns back to the poets, whom different critics have condemned explicitly on the grounds of "madness," "inconsistency," "flaunting," or "pathological excesses," one finds them overcoming the potentially divisive effects of rivalry and competition to share a lifetime of friendship, loyalty, collegiality, and mutual admiration. The danger of using one poet as a club to beat that poet's close colleague is that, by exaggerating genuine or imagined differences into full-fledged antagonisms, the critic trivializes literary relations that have great and ongoing cultural importance.

Bishop's declared the grounds of her own affinity with Lowell in a blurb on the very dust-jacket of *Life Studies.* She found Lowell's poems "as big as life, . . . alive, and rainbow-edged," and she read the poems perceptively for their underlying strokes of Jamesian art: "In these poems, heartbreaking, shocking, grotesque and gentle, the unhesitant attack, the imagery and construction, are as brilliant as ever, but the mood is nostalgic and the meter is refined. A poem like 'My Last Afternoon with Uncle Devereux Winslow,' or 'Skunk Hour,' can tell us as much about the state of society as a volume of Henry James at his best."[43]

Lowell observed that "In *Life Studies*, I caught real memories in a fairly gentle style. It's not meant to be extremity" (*RLProse* 286). And he was sufficiently pleased with Bishop's remarks that one finds them reprinted—in full—ten years later, on the dust jacket of his *Notebook 1967–68* (the earliest edition of that work). Bishop's comments are crowded onto the back flap and flyleaf, in small type, along with a verbatim reprint of the lengthy remarks on Lowell with which Jarrell concluded his famous lecture "Fifty Years of American Poetry."

Jarrell's remarks, delivered at the 1962 National Poetry Festival in Washington, D.C., differ from Bishop's in emphasis. He begins with the acknowledgment that, "More than any other poet Robert Lowell is the poet of shock: his effects vary from crudity to magnificence but they are always surprising and always his own." But Jarrell offers a reading of Lowell's most famous book that complements Bishop's: "In *Life Studies* the pathos of the local color of the past—of the lives and deaths of his father and mother and grandfather and uncle, crammed full of their own varied and placid absurdity—is the background that sets off the desperate knife-edged absurdity of the jailed conscientious objector among gangsters and Jehovah's Witnesses, the private citizen returning to his baby, older now, from the mental hospital" (*TBC* 333). And when Jarrell asserts that Lowell "sees things as being part of history," he is in full accord with Bishop, who observes that Lowell's poems give a sense of "exact contemporaneity" while making her more "aware of the 'ironies of American History.'"

Again, Harold Bloom does not think Lowell is "making" poems at all. Bloom, committed to a romantic style that values the imagination's power to transform the past and present world, has a hard time finding value in what Jarrell terms Lowell's portrayal of "his own actual existence in the prosperous, developed, disastrous world he and we inhabit." But Jarrell, like Bishop, knew Lowell's writing process intimately, having assisted in the drafting and redrafting of many Lowell poems. Thus Jarrell had first-hand knowledge of the process by which Lowell's poems had been skill-fully and imaginatively "made." Jarrell praises these poems for "the vivid incongruity [Lowell] gives the things or facts he uses," a trait that Jarrell finds "so decided that it amounts to a kind of wit; in his poetry fact is a live stumbling block that we fall over and feel to the bone" (*TBC* 332).

Bishop, too, praises the way Lowell combines intractable fact and transforming vision. For Bishop, Lowell's poem are like the "powerful reading-glass" she once used to study "my grandfather's Bible" as a child: "The letters assembled beneath the lens were suddenly like a Lowell poem. . . . It seemed to illuminate what it magnified; it could also be used as a burning glass."[44] Bishop and Jarrell recognized in their friend Lowell's work a force of imagination, and a transforming vision, that could by turns refract, sear, enlarge or illuminate the painful facts encountered in the realm of necessity. Detractors of Lowell determined to quote Bishop or Jarrell against him, or to read Lowell as deficient in the practice of his art, must first come to terms with these powerful and authoritative readings by two of Lowell's closest, and most artistically exacting, colleagues.

## Second Problem: The Paradigm Slights Moral and Epistemological Complexities

Not only does the confessional paradigm have a way of skewing critical judgment in directions the poets being battled over would have found surprising, but advocates of the paradigm, caught up in the mantra of "self-revelation," also tend to assume in the poems a "naked" clarity of exposition, completeness of disclosure, and fidelity to fact. Further, the term "confession" implies an acknowledgment on the part of the author that he or she has committed one or more transgressions that must be revealed and expiated. However, the best work of Lowell or Berryman, like the best work of Bishop and Jarrell, contradicts these assumptions.

The writing of these four poets is remarkable for its dramatic realization of the problematic character of human experience and human knowledge. Their poems repeatedly explore problems of memory, consciousness and the unconscious. And many poems, such as Berryman's "Dream Song 29" or Jarrell's "The Truth," turn on the poet's exploitation of the dramatic possibilities created by repression and denial. One encounters constantly in each of these authors poems that dramatize the partial recovery of a half-forgotten memory traced in a context in which, as Bishop phrases it, "emotion too far exceeds its cause" (*EBPoems* 3). In short, these poets make frequent, skillful, and dramatic use of factual or emotional material that is *withheld.* Their poems offer very incomplete disclosure while dramatizing situations involving varying degrees of psychological blockage, of the partial or complete repression of traumatic material. These barriers are in general only partially unraveled in the course of the poem. These poets combine richness of human and cultural detail with a focus on irreversible loss to create a climate of epistemological, moral, and emotional *uncertainty.* This aspect of their work is thoroughly and carelessly elided by the confessional paradigm.

Critical expectations of straightforward self-revelation seem peculiarly at odds with the poet's primordial and unalienable right to alter, invent, or reconfigure facts, often in ways that even the most astute and painstaking critic or biographer would be fortunate to detect. Bishop's poems, despite her famed obsession with accuracy, contain many subtle and not-so-subtle alterations of autobiographical detail. For example, she insisted to one interviewer that the only alteration she had made in "The Fish" was to increase the three actual fish lines to five. But as James Merrill recalls it "*her* fish wasn't let go at all, not in real life; she told in an interview about bringing it proudly back to the dock—intact."[45] And the same kind of pervasive and hard-to-verify alterations occur in Lowell's poems and in Berryman's.

Lowell, for example, stressed that "My 'autobiographical' poems are not always factually true. I've tinkered a lot with fact. You leave out a lot, and emphasize this and not that. Your actual experience is a complete flux. I've invented facts and changed things, and the whole balance of the poem was something invented."[46] One need only study the prose precursors to Lowell's *Life Studies* poems to get a sense of how many facts he alters—yet, for that matter, there is no guarantee of the factual accuracy of the prose versions either. As Merrill observes, the poet's "problem" is "to make it *sound* true. . . . Now and then it's been *true* what I wrote. Often, though, it's been quite made up or taken from somebody else's life and put in as if it were mine."[47]

Merrill concludes that "to all but the very naive reader or writer" it should be clear that one is not dealing with self-photography, with a literal translation of life into art, nor even with a unified, autobiographical self. Rather, the poet goes through an uncertain, intuitive process of reinvention or re-creation by which a poem, even one that appears to closely parallel the author's actual experience, is imaginatively reassembled. This process requires the poet to select, concentrate, organize, invent, and alter while skillfully adjusting the tonal balance of the whole. Thus, if Jarrell's best poems almost always explore his own strongest feelings while inventing *fictionalized* dramatic contexts, neither Lowell nor Berryman felt that this created any sort of divide between themselves and their literary peer and friend. Knowledge of Lowell's or Berryman's biography may elucidate a given poem, but this is just as true for Bishop or Jarrell as for the so-called confessionals, and such biographical backgrounds provide just one of many possible avenues into the poem. Such information might sometimes provide a necessary—but hardly ever a sufficient—condition to support a cogent reading.

Certainly, knowledge of the poet's biography will take one only so far into a poem like Berryman's "Dream Song 31," which concludes:

> Henry Hankovitch, con guítar,
> did a praying mantis pray
> who even more obviously than the increasingly fanatical Americans
> cannot govern themselves. Swedes don't exist,
> Scandinavians in general do not exist,
> take it from there.
>
> (*DS* 31)

Berryman's biography may parallel Henry's in certain respects, but he did not play the guitar, and he was certainly not named Henry Hankovitch. After experiencing this poem's dizzying sequence of puns, non sequiturs, solecisms, anacoulutha, and contrary-to-fact-statements, one emerges rather dazed from the other end of a fictive process in which the poet has in fact "invented facts and changed things, and the whole balance of the poem [is] something invented." Here a surreal irony, an unsettling indeterminacy, reigns—amidst a most emphatic rhetoric. In such a context, as Berryman shrewdly put it regarding his "Ball Poem," "The poet himself is both left out and put in."

If one looks further at the issue of "self-disclosure" or "self-revelation" it becomes obvious that Berryman's *Dream Songs* "confess" only to incidental and symptomatic experiences of suffering and humiliation. A core of crucial psychic material is quite deliberately withheld. Berryman's relationship with his father, who took his own life when Berryman was a boy of eleven, is merely hinted at in a few Songs. Or was his father murdered, and if so, was he murdered by the poet's mother? Or was it by her lover, who soon became the poet's stepfather and changed his surname from Smith to Berryman? Or was it by the two acting together? Neither Berryman nor his biographers have been able to rule out these suppositions in the face of unsettling evidence that leaves murder a distinct possibility. Articulated under the weight of these fearful uncertainties, Berryman's *Dream Songs* are more remarkable for their elisions, emotional blockage, and ambiguity of reference than for specific disclosures.

Berryman, who alludes only fleetingly to his father, has still less to disclose about his dream-haunted, guilt-ridden, and painfully intimate relationship with his mother, a still-living woman whom he hated, feared, and loved. Thus, the most compelling emotional issues of the *Dream Songs* are never *confessed* but exist only as subtext. The poem is much more effectively read for the ways it explores and represents the disturbing, symptomatic consequences of suppressed rage and repressed emotion. It is a dramatization of the desperate search for vital yet unreachable knowledge and a seemingly unattainable solace and maturity, not a catalog of factual disclosures revealing the author's shameful secrets.

The pressures that operate on and beneath the surface of the *Dream Songs* may be seen in microcosm from a mini-sequence of two songs "about" Berryman's terrifying mother. Song 100 is an idealized tribute to "the goodness of this woman / in her great strength, in her hope superhuman." Yet this song, the unvarnished sincerity of which must be considered doubtful, is immediately followed, in Song 101, by a sestet featuring a sequence of disjunctive images and phrases apparently floating up from the unconscious:

> A shallow lake, with many waterbirds,
> especially egrets: I was showing Mother around,
> An extraordinary vivid dream
> of Betty & Douglas, and Don—his mother's estate
> was on the grounds of a lunatic asylum.
> He showed me around.
>
> (*DS* 101)

In the middle sestet of this Song, we learn that the speaker asked friend Don "if he ever saw / the inmates—'No, they never leave their cells.'" This surreal passage set, apparently (if one notes the egrets) in a Florida landscape recalling the locale where Berryman's father met his death, is certainly quite suggestive. A biographically informed reader may be particularly sensitive to Berryman's conflicted feelings about his mother, her possible guilt for the crime of murder, and his father's "imprisonment" in death—condemned, retroactively, as a kind of lunatic by the coroner's jury that ruled his death a suicide. Also relevant are Berryman's own fears of madness, enclosure, or suicide. Yet the Song's disclosures, whatever they are, are certainly far from explicit.[48]

The concluding sestet of Song 101 suggests that there is much Berryman could say by way of interpretation that must remain unsaid. He can disclose his feelings but not their explicit sources, which must remain suppressed or repressed even if the poet were capable of naming them. Nor can he explicate how the images in the dream relate to his feelings:

> I can't go into the meaning of the dream
> except to say a sense of total LOSS
> afflicted me thereof:
> an absolute disappearance of continuity & love
> and children away at school, the weight of the cross,
> and everything is what it seems.
>
> (*DS* 101)

Does this Song render an actual dream the author experienced? Or one he invented or recast? Is it a veiled indictment of the mother he has just roundly (and insincerely?) praised? Is it a "disclosure" of someone's transgression? And if so, whose? Or is it an evasively hermetic treatment of feelings too painful and dangerous to represent directly?

The answers to the preceding questions are far from transparent. The teasing opacity of Song 101 leads the reader to consider the problematic nature of dreaming, owning, knowing, madness, imprisonment, isolation, and such feelings as "an absolute disappearance of continuity and love." Clear enough in the poem, cutting directly through all this opacity, is a cry of pain which I would suggest is not "disclosed" but dramatized, so that it emerges from its indeterminate surroundings with unusual force. Hence the uncanny accuracy of Rich's observation that Berryman "is a bruised, raging and fiendishly intelligent man, and he has found a way to be all three simultaneously." The final line of the Song is the spookiest, for it suggests that life, with all its uncertainties and ambiguities, may really be most difficult to endure when everything *is* "what it seems." What if mother really were the kind of person she appears to be? What if father really is gone beyond recovery, leaving so many questions unanswered and unanswerable? What if I am the dream-haunted, cross-bearing, lonely and raging son, husband, and father that I appear to have become? What if "everything is what it seems"?

This poem veils its emotional issues behind a cryptic sequence of dreamlike non sequiturs, and behind a previous song that imparts a halo of filial praise. Thus, when direct, apparently unambiguous statements do emerge, it seems impossible to attach them to their antecedents with any certainty. Only one Dream Song contains a mildly disparaging reference to Berryman's mother that could be considered in any sense explicit. Song 14 begins: "Life, friends, is boring." The intimately phrased, yet sweeping, generalization in this first brief sentence is immediately qualified by a second brief sentence: "We must not say so." Why must we not say so? Is this because unboring things in fact happen? So it would seem, judging by the qualifiers that immediately follow: "After all, the sky flashes, the great sea yearns, / we ourselves flash and yearn." These observations tie our human inspirations and longings to the largest and most powerful of natural forces.

Yet there is another reason, it appears, why "we must not say so," a reason that grows out of prohibitions learned at the maternal knee:

> and moreover my mother told me as a boy
> (repeatingly) 'Ever to confess you're bored
> means you have no
>
> Inner Resources.' I conclude now I have no
> inner resources, because I am heavy bored.
>
> (*DS* 14)

The poem so far might seem to suggest little more than the mild, ritualized sparring of parent and child. The key phrase, of course, is the one we might notice least: "We must not say so." If we must not ever confess that we are bored, what other more significant feelings must we also not confess? Perhaps this is a poem not merely about boredom but about depression, since what Henry claims to find boring are just those things that Berryman himself found most fascinating. Typically, depression involves ennui in the face of that which would normally delight or fascinate:

> Peoples bore me,
> literature bores me, especially great literature,
> Henry bores me, with his plights & gripes
> as bad as achilles
>
> (*DS* 14)

John Haffenden points out that, "In a conspectus dating from October 1958, Berryman pursued the parallels between Henry and Achilles, describing Henry as 'a man (hero) *deprived*, and *insulted*, sulks (poor will) with enemies *inside* as well as *on* his side.' Specifically, he identified the enemy 'on' Henry's side as his mother, a type of Thetis." Haffenden adds, "It is relevant here to know that, at a poetry reading in Spoleto, Italy, Berryman informed his audience that the name 'achilles' was deliberately 'spelt with rage with a small letter at the beginning.' In conversation, Berryman's mother told me that she had felt outraged at being mocked in that Song, and bitterly pained to have heard it once at a public reading."[49]

Implicit, then, in this song, and arguably in the *Dream Songs* at large, is the notion of Berryman's mother as a central enemy, a figure "on his side" who has "deprived" and "insulted" him and who assumes mythic proportions for Henry/Achilles. But while "the rage of Peleus' son Achilles, / murderous, doomed"[50] is announced as the central issue of *The Iliad* in its opening lines, nowhere is the rage of John Allyn Smith's son (aka John Berryman) toward his own mother explicitly disclosed in the *Dream Songs* as the poems' central conflict. One can well understand why. Martha Berryman, who preferred the bizarre alternative cognomen "Jill Angel" and who still had tremendous emotional power over her son, objected strongly to the relatively mild treatment she received in Song 14. How could Berryman, as a modern, literary "achilles," write a truly "confessional" poem about his relations with this "enemy . . . *on* his side" while the mother with whom he shared a relationship of such "(horrible) *richness*"[51] was still alive?

Hence, most of the "rage" in *The Dream Songs,* as in his life, has to be worked off onto Berryman's long dead father, onto fictionalized self-images such as Henry, or onto the world at large. Rage toward his mother is represented indirectly and cryptically, through implicit correlatives, symbols, allegorical suggestions, or subtle and opaque orthographic devices like spelling "achilles" with "a small letter at the beginning." Read thus, the *Dream Songs,* far from seeming poems of self-revelation, suggest themselves as heavily *encoded* explorations of a powerless son in an impossibly intimate relationship with his mother.

Similarly, Jarrell could hardly write poems exploring his feelings about his own militantly conventional, frequently contemptuous, and perhaps physically abusive mother while she still lived. He chose, instead, to resort to the more indirect methods made possible by dramatic monologues and implicit narratives, in which he could more freely represent feelings without disclosing them. Both Berryman and Jarrell were, in fact, survived by their terrifying, all-powerful mothers. Lowell's apparently more direct mode of writing was, in part, made possible by the death of his two parents, including *his* terrifying mother Charlotte, in the years preceding *Life Studies.* Bishop's parents and grandparents had long departed by the time she came into her own artistically, but her more reserved treatment of her own traumatic childhood was dictated by the habits of emotional restraint she inherited from her family and from her rather tight-lipped Worcester and Great Village communities.

## Third Problem: The Paradigm Slights the Poems' Mobility and Moral Complexity

If one looks to the poems themselves with curiosity about their technique, one encounters still further anomalies between the poems and the confessional paradigm. The confessional model carries strong connotations of hierarchy and stasis. In the Roman Catholic ritual of confession, the supplicant for absolution, his or her identity shielded, kneels in an enclosed space in fixed, hierarchical relation to a father confessor who provides a conduit to God's mercy and grace. But the work of Lowell or Berryman most commonly defined as "confessional" is marked by its roving eye. Looking outside, inside, and around its subjects with an adroitly realized complexity of perspective, their work conveys a constant sense of inquiry, of uncertainty, of temporal and psychological motion. This mobility, moreover, is coupled with an impatience in the face of moral hierarchies.

Lowell's breakthrough poem, "Skunk Hour," provides a clear example. Heavily influenced by the perceptual style of Elizabeth Bishop, the poem is in motion from its first stanza to its last, weaving into, out of, and around the nooks and crannies of a Maine coastal village. Poems such as "My Last Afternoon with Uncle Devereux Winslow," "Memories of West Street and Lepke," "During Fever," and "Sailing Home from Rapallo" are in a similar state of perceptual motion from start to finish. Lowell's *Notebook*, first published a decade after *Life Studies*, itself projects a still more continual state of flux. Both within individual poems, and from poem to poem, one moves rapidly back and forth between the present and the past. The poems briefly touch down on vividly realized moments from the lives of men and women long dead, while bringing to compelling fictive life the passing thoughts, perceptions, and daily experiences of a contemporary individual.

The frame of all four poets is domestic. Berryman's *Dream Songs* is perhaps the most house-bound epic ever written. Its basic setting is the poet, sitting in his study or lying in his bed, musing and dreaming. Yet the Songs are far from static. Each embodies, in a mere eighteen lines, a process of often giddy psychological movement that carries the reader abruptly across multiple planes of experience. Each poet moves around and through and beyond his or her domestic environments, using these as windows onto wide-ranging movements across times, cultures, and versions of the self. In this sense, Lowell's and Berryman's work resembles the temporal, perceptual, and psychological movement of Bishop's "Over 2,000 Illustrations" and her "Crusoe in England," or Jarrell's "A Girl in a Library" and "Siegfried."

This emphasis on movement and change often rises to an explicitly thematic level in the poems, relating movement to risk, discovery, or moral inquiry. Hence, at the end of 77 *Dream Songs* one encounters Henry, learning that with "his head full / & his heart full, he's making ready to move on" (*DS* 77). Where Henry is moving on *to* is unknown, but then, motion may be the only constant in a poem too peripatetic for consistent disclosures. Through Henry, Berryman creates at once a moving perceptual lens and a moving target. The oeuvre produced by Lowell, Jarrell,

Bishop, and Berryman explores the complex layerings of public and private human relations in a spirit of radical inquiry, without fixed notions of right or wrong—and thus it projects an atmosphere as remote as possible from the static hierarchical structure of the Catholic confessional.

## Fourth Problem: The Paradigm Promotes Moral Arrogance in Readers

Another implication of the quasi-religious overtones inherent in the term "confessional" ought to make one still more uneasy. Berryman protested "I understand the confessional to be a place where you go and talk with a priest. I personally haven't been to confession since I was twelve years old."[52] At different stages in their lives Berryman and Lowell each, in fact, knelt at the confessional as Roman Catholic believers, seeking judgment and absolution from sins mortal and venial that otherwise would bar them from God's grace. At least by implication, the confessional paradigm perceives the poet as speaking from a similar—though far more exposed—position of supplication and self-disclosure. Therefore, the paradigm implicitly encourages the poem's every reader, as hearer of the confession, to assume a priest-like—perhaps even god-like—position of judgment and authority over the poet. Was it perhaps the distasteful and anomalous situation implicit here, with its correlative assumptions about his artistic passivity, that most strongly prompted Berryman's raging and contemptuous rejection of the confessional label?

In the process of inventing the term "confessional poetry" in his 1960 review of *Life Studies*, Rosenthal was among the first to sound the note of moral reprehension, describing Lowell's work as resembling "a series of personal confidences, rather shameful, that one is honor-bound not to reveal." Rosenthal characterizes Lowell's as an "impure art, magnificently stated but unpleasantly egocentric—somehow resembling the triumph of the skunks over the garbage cans."[53] Bishop, on the other hand, felt none of Rosenthal's distaste, praising the poems, when she saw them in manuscript in December of 1957, in the highest terms:

> I think all the family group . . . are really superb, Cal. I don't know what order they'll come in, but they make a wonderful and impressive drama, and I think you've found the new rhythm you wanted, without any hitches . . . They all have that sure feeling, as if you'd been in a stretch . . . when everything and anything suddenly seemed material for poetry—or not material, seemed to *be* poetry, and all the past was illuminated in long shafts, here and

> there, like a long waited-for sunrise. If only one could see everything that way all the time! It seems to me it's the whole purpose of art, to the artist (not to the audience)—that rare feeling of control, illumination—life *is* all right, for the time being. Anyway, when I read such an extended display of imagination as this, I feel it *for* you. (*EBLet* 350)

For Bishop, then, the poems that would take shape as *Life Studies* are triumphs of imagination, acts reaching into the past "in long shafts" of light.

In sharp contrast with Bishop's exultant early reading of Lowell's work are such more recent studies as Bruce Bawer's *The Middle Generation: The Lives and Poetry of Delmore Schwartz, Randall Jarrell, John Berryman, and Robert Lowell*, as well as Jeffrey Meyers's "The Death of Randall Jarrell" and his book-length *Manic Power: Robert Lowell and his Circle* (which groups Lowell with Jarrell, Berryman, and Roethke). These critics, apparently encouraged by the implicit logic of the confessional paradigm, assume an all-too-common stance of moral superiority toward the overlapping aggregation of poets featured in their respective studies.

Speaking of the analyst's approach to the patient undergoing therapy, psychotherapist Alice Miller notes, "Certainly, we do not use words like bad, dirty, naughty, egoistic, rotten—but among ourselves we speak of 'narcissistic,' 'exhibitionistic,' 'destructive,' and 'regressive' patients, without noticing that we (unconsciously) give these words a pejorative meaning."[54] Meyers, who consistently disparages both the personal character and the artistry of each of the poets featured in his study, does not bother to veil his own contempt when he asserts that, "The poets competed with each other in madness as in art, and flaunted their illness as a leper shows his sores."[55] The readings of Bawer and Meyers argue for a more or less one-to-one equivalence between a life "driven," in Bawer's phrase, "to pathological excesses" and an art the principal aim of which seems, as these critics understand it, to be to put the authors' human failings on display.

The operation of these pejorative assumptions is obvious in the way Bawer and Meyers represent the life of Randall Jarrell. While Bawer and Meyers make only passing reference to Bishop, each features Jarrell among all-male groupings that include Lowell, Berryman, and (respectively) Delmore Schwartz (in Bawer) and Theodore Roethke (in Meyers). As Richard Flynn suggests, such readings are "inherently Procrustean and break down when they encounter Jarrell."[56] For Jarrell's work, though deeply self-exploratory, refuses even more stubbornly than does Bishop's to conform to the confessional paradigm, as defined by Middlebrook.

Jarrell's poems often confront experiences that are emotionally staggering, yet his work is marked by personal discretion rather than by "flaunting." Characteristically Jarrell speaks through dramatized personae rather than in his own voice—yet his best poems probe incisively into just those issues of loss, unresolved grief, moral, emotional, and perceptual uncertainty and insecurity, and divided selfhood so persistently explored by Lowell and Berryman (and by Bishop).

Lowell's curiosity about, and sympathy for, his friend's method are evident in his characterization of *The Lost World*, Jarrell's last and (his friends agreed) best book:

> Most of the poems are dramatic monologues. Their speakers, though mostly women, are intentionally, and unlike Browning's, very close to the author. Their themes, repeated with endless variations, are solitude, the solitude of the unmarried, the solitude of the married, the love, strife, dependency, and indifference of man and woman—how mortals age, and brood over their lost and raw childhood, only recapturable in memory and imagination. Above all childhood! . . . For Jarrell this was the divine glimpse, lifelong to be lived with, painfully and tenderly relived, transformed, matured—man with and against woman, child with and against adult (*RLProse* 96).

Lowell recognized and understood the complex intersection of the personal and the impersonal in Jarrell's art, appreciating the frequent depth and drama of the psychic subtext in such poems from throughout Jarrell's career as "Losses," "Protocols," "The Truth," "Seele im Raum," "The Night before the Night before Christmas," "A Girl in a Library," "The Black Swan," "A Quilt Pattern," "90 North," "Jerome," "Next Day," "The House in the Woods," and "Thinking of the Lost World."

Lowell recognized that when Jarrell approaches his two great subjects, war and the family drama, he explores, in each arena, the individual's lonely struggle to survive: to emerge emotionally and physically intact, to define a mature self in a threatening environment that demands self-denial, self-forgetfulness, or even self-annihilation. Adrienne Rich noted in her review of Berryman's complete *Dream Songs*, "The dream world that conforms the pain of others to comfortable theory; that will perform the most delicate, insane intellectual contortions to avoid personal risk or vulnerability—this is the world of mind most threatened by the realities of poetry."[57] Arguably, the notion of "confessional poetry" can work as just such a protective device, providing a way of conforming the pain the poet represents to a "comfortable theory" that shields the critic from the "personal risk or vulnerability" that might result from entering into the poem as a creative partner.

In any case, it is from just such an insulated dream world as Rich deplores that Jarrell's ball turret gunner forcibly awakens into the threatening realities of modern, technological war: "I woke to black flak and the nightmare fighters." From a similar dream world, Jarrell's housewife in "Next Day" wakens into realities of loneliness, aging and death that, until now, she has managed to "overlook." The housewife in "Seele im Raum," though returned "cured" from the sanitarium, refuses to wake into reality. Still clinging to the central delusion that provides her life with meaning, she declares: "To own an eland! That's what I call life!" (*RJPoems* 39).

Dreams act ambiguously throughout the work of each of these poets. In many poems dreams serve in Rich's sense, as a haven into which the threatened psyche can desperately (or smugly) retreat. But dreams can also be nightmares, and they may serve as fertile if unreliable resources to be mined by the poet for that precious, painful, and uncertain knowledge —locked away in the unconscious—that constitutes one of the threatening or illuminating "realities of poetry." In this sense dreams represent an important imaginative means of penetrating the unconscious and exploring lost worlds, a means that each of these poets would persistently exploit.

The reader of a "confessional poem," another mere mortal, is in a questionable position when using the poem as a basis for judgment on the author as a person (though as we have seen, this has happened repeatedly). In any case, a critic who assumes the god-like power to judge nonetheless lacks, and in any case rarely seems inclined to exercise, the priest-like power to absolve. Indeed, the critic's or biographer's implicit stance of moral authority over the author has from the beginning served as the uneasy, never-quite-acknowledged moral assumption on which the confessional model rests. This, combined with the corollary assumption that the critic is in full command of the facts and empowered to draw conclusions from the poem about the moral standing of the author, seems antithetical to the open-ended, inquisitive, risk-taking spirit of the poetry itself. Fred Chappell is scarcely exaggerating when he asserts, with reference to Jarrell, that, "The propensity of contemporary biography . . . is to reduce the lives of poets and writers to case histories. Writers are but ambulatory diseases in this view, and criticism is prognosis. Yet such a view is only temporary, the product of smugness that is markedly defensive in nature."[58]

Berryman, in retrospect, appears to have had every reason to be wary of the implication that in his *Dream Songs* he might be read as confessing his transgressions to some semi-official reader who felt authorized by a popular critical paradigm to assume a priest-like authority over both text and author. If one considers where these assumptions lead, it is no longer difficult to understand why Berryman was not just consistent but professional and prudent in rejecting the confessional label. And it should be clear why so many other poets have been decidedly reluctant to have this label govern the reading of their work.

## Fifth Problem: The Paradigm Assumes the Author's Creative Passivity

By contrast with widespread perceptions of Jarrell's brilliance and mastery in three demanding professions—poetry, criticism, and teaching—Bawer insists (in a remark meant to include Jarrell), "All were disabled by emotions upon which they could muse eternally and with great eloquence, but which they were powerless to control. Here lies the ultimate irony of their lives: the very conditions which so tragically crippled them as men also provided their poetry with its greatest beauty and strength."[59] Jarrell himself may have been "disabled by emotions" during the months of his final depression, but his entire poetic *oeuvre* was written before that disabling breakdown. Emotional disorders certainly served these poets as source material that could be shaped artistically, and these problems added urgency to their sense of artistic mission. However, these "emotional problems" did not—and really could not—have "*provided* their poetry with its greatest beauty and strength." Bawer's assertion embodies a peculiarly passive and limited conception of the artistic process, and the creation of what Bawer calls "beauty and strength" in poetry is not a passive but an active achievement.

As the Homeric Greeks knew, poetry requires an act of "making." The biographical and manuscript evidence left behind by these four poets suggests that for them this making was no casual event. It was an act that required, as Emerson put it regarding Whitman's *Leaves of Grass,* "a long foreground somewhere" both in life and in patient, persistent, craftsmanlike effort. For each of these four poets that long foreground included a decades-long process of ongoing self-education, self-exploration, and cultural observation. And despite Rosenthal's claim that in *Life Studies* the "self-therapeutic motive is so obvious and persistent,"[60] it is reductive to read the work of any of these poets as therapy per se. Therapeutic writing is necessarily self-centered while theirs is reader-centered: it consistently assumes and is addressed to that "Indulgent, or candid, or uncommon reader" (*RJPoems* 29) whom Jarrell, for one, sought all his life.

As Jarrell noted early on of Lowell, the work of these poets is consistently "dramatic," presenting "people, their actions, their speeches, as they feel and look and sound to people."[61] Their poems sometimes unfold over years in a multitude of slowly mutating drafts. The poets achieve effects of drama and mimesis by selecting, inventing, combining, and reconfiguring from unconscious, conscious, and discursive mental processes in the crucible of craft. The last step for these poets—which again could be quite prolonged—involved applying the artistic finish, in which diverse and even contradictory materials were phrased and rephrased as they were painstakingly, imaginatively, and lovingly hammered into their places in the poem. This last step often involved a significantly collegial process—it nearly always did for Lowell—of critical reading, editing, and suggestion-making by trusted friends and peers. The resulting end product, if all went well, might give the illusion of being fully alive and bursting with surprise, but this illusion is something made. Anyone who has read a bit of adolescent poetry knows that there's nothing more banal or flatfooted than an amateurish poem about the self. The illusion of casual speech, or even of "naked confession"—as in some of Lowell's latest poems in *Day by Day*—must be recognized as an illusion, even when the poem conforms, to some degree, to known biographical facts.

These poems certainly place extraordinary intellectual and emotional demands on their uncommon readers. And the powerful psychic subtexts that linger in the work of the poets, sometimes close to the surface and sometimes far beneath, were made through skill, imagination, and painstakingly learned technique. This is why only a tiny fraction of individuals who suffer from neurotic symptoms manage to achieve "eloquence, . . . beauty and strength" in poems, stories, or other works of art. Moreover beauty, strength, and artistic eloquence have been realized as well by many individuals who, though driven to create, do not suffer from clinically defined conditions. The question of the relations between art, the artist, the artist's audience, and clinical disorders remains unresolved and requires further careful study. But even at this initial stage, it seems clear that the making of poetry is by no means a passive or merely therapeutic process. Poets may be born, but poems are made.

Artistic achievement must draw on other and more robust resources than neurosis or suffering alone. Speaking of the poets of his own and a previous generation, Lowell observed, "We are more conscious of our wounds . . . than the poets before us, but we are not necessarily more wounded. . . . The difference may be that modern art tries more deliberately to save the unsavable by giving it form. . . . The truth is that no sort of life seems to preclude poetry. Poetry can come out of utterly miserable or disorderly lives, as in the case of a Rimbaud or a Hart Crane. But to make the poems possible a huge amount of health has to go into the misery."[62]

Lowell, a chronic manic-depressive whose family tree contained a long history of bipolar disorder, displayed remarkable recuperative powers throughout his life. He came back time and again from alarming episodes of mania and soul-flattening episodes of depression that might have killed or permanently disabled a less determined man. He returned to his family and to his teaching responsibilities. And he resumed, as well, not just a strenuous life of social, political, pedagogical, and cultural engagement, but also an arduous, prolific, and successful career as a literary craftsman.

Lowell once noted sadly that "Mania is extremity for one's friends, depression for one's self. Both are chemical." And Lowell spoke from experience when he observed that "Depression's no gift from the muse. At worst I do nothing" (*RLProse* 287). Elizabeth Hardwick said he had two engines, one running toward salvation and the other toward destruction. Lowell drew frequently on experiences of emotional breakdown as material for his poetry, but the writing itself was achieved when, released from the hospital, he was struggling toward recovery and self-understanding, rather than during the times when he was actually "disabled by emotions." Lowell acknowledged that he "wrote one whole book [*For the Union Dead*] about witheredness." But, he pointed out, "It wasn't acute depression, and I felt quite able to work for hours, write and rewrite. Most of the best poems, the most personal, are gathered crumbs" (*RLProse* 286).

In order to gather those crumbs and turn them into convincing poems, Lowell had to intervene as an artist. He had to interweave the purposefully expressive strategies of art amidst what he often referred to as the chaotic processes of life. It may be worthwhile to spell out the healthy elements that went into Lowell's own poetry. These include not merely a large measure of artistic talent but other components that friends like Bishop, Jarrell and Berryman deeply respected, such as keen general intelligence (poet Philip Booth said one was "continually knocked over by the intensity of his intelligence"),[63] a profound knowledge and appreciation both of recent developments in poetry and of the literary tradition, a detailed knowledge of Western history along with an intuitive understanding of its application to the present, compassion for his own suffering and the suffering of others, a yearning for beauty and order, a sharp eye for emblematic detail, exceptional long-term memory, a yearning to "save the unsavable by giving it form," and a determination to "get something new into old forms, even at the risk of breaking them." All these qualities combined with an unusual drive, persistence, and artistic commitment that frequently astonished Lowells' friends.[64]

## Advantages of an Exploratory Paradigm

We have seen that the confessional model posits a gulf between intimate friends like Lowell and Bishop, and that it has no place, conceptually, for their close mutual friend Jarrell, whose profoundest psychological explorations appear in the form of dramatic monologues unfolding the inner lives of invented personae. We have seen that the paradigm confronts a mounting body of factual anomalies. We have examined the amorphous quality of the term, its lack of historical integrity or assignable denotative meaning, which forces proponents of the model to defensively accuse *Berryman* of not knowing his business when he disavows the label with "rage and contempt" or insists that "The word doesn't mean anything." We have seen that the term creates lingering discomfort among many of the critics who reluctantly employ it because it skews literary evaluation, reads technical, epistemological, and moral complexities reductively, promotes moral arrogance in readers, and assumes the author's creative passivity. In light of this daunting tangle of negatives, it would be well to consider the advantages of a simple yet potentially profound change in critical perspective that could resolve the decades-long problems the confessional paradigm has imposed on readers. This new perspective would read Lowell, Jarrell, Bishop and Berryman not as evincing a conflict between the reticent and the self-revelatory but as sharing a drive toward the self-exploratory. I suggest that we consider reading Berryman and Lowell not primarily in terms of a "thematic concern with disclosure or shock" but as initiators with Bishop and Jarrell of an aesthetic of psychical and cultural self-exploration. Theirs is a risky, painful, and uncertain poetry of process that explores critical moments in the lives of self-divided individuals struggling to survive and recover in the face of traumatic loss. Such a reading opens the way to understanding what poems such as Lowell's "My Last Afternoon with Uncle Devereux Winslow," Bishop's "First Death in Nova Scotia," Berryman's "Dream Song 1," and Jarrell's "The

Lost World" have always had in common. These poets were drawn so magnetically to one another because each had embarked on a career-long exploration of the problem of selfhood in the postmodern world. Their work shares a preoccupation with feelings of loss, abandonment, and personal or cultural dislocation. Thus, their poems and stories are not primarily engaged in the process of either revealing or reticently shielding the self. Rather they are engaged in a process of *exploring* the self, of reaching back through the uncertainties of the traumatic past to search among its surviving artifacts. Their poems dig through the lingering memory-traces and dreamlike recurrences of the past, as well as among the symptomatic behaviors of the present, for insight into the sources of present dismay.

Most or all of the critical problems outlined above disappear if one reads the work of our midcentury quartet as primarily engaged, not in acts of self-revelation, but in an ongoing exploration of the problems of selfhood in a postmodern world. The individual self at the center of a given poem by a member of this quartet might variously be represented as an invented character, as a version of the author, or as a historical figure. Indeed, each poet employed each of these modes frequently—though with differing emphases at different moments in their respective oeuvres. Their poem's protagonists may at times appear marginal, defeated, aberrant, or otherwise unsavable: even the kings, queens, warriors, and master poets who populate Lowell's *History* seem often to have a desperate air about them. But readers of these four poets are invited neither to exculpate nor to judge the individuals whose lives they are invited to explore. Rather, they are asked to witness and to understand.

We enter into these lives—however strange or foreign they might seem—and explore their personal and cultural situations from the inside out. Hence, in poems such as Jarrell's "Next Day" or "Thinking of the Lost World," Lowell's "Near the Ocean" or "Peter the Great in France," Bishop's "The Riverman" or "Crusoe in England," Berryman's *Homage to Mistress* or *Dream Songs*, the reader enters a lost or somehow foreign world. Often it is a familiar world made freshly unfamiliar, and the reader must confront that world's unsettling physical, cultural, and emotional contours from the viewpoint of a decentered individual.

As one enters into the individual experiences brought to life in these poem, one shares a dramatized individual's pain, doubts, confusion and anxieties. When Jarrell praised, in 1947, Lowell's unusual "accessibility to experience" he saw this quality as related to generosity, and to the yearning for freedom from emotional bondage. Thus Lowell's poems whether wholly or only partly invented reach—like Jarrell's or Bishop's or Berryman's —toward insight into the lonely struggle of individuals who must come to terms with loss, with grief, with loneliness and misunderstanding. These individuals struggle with unsought mental disturbance, with physical and emotional anguish, and with yearnings for survival. They search for self-assertion, for comprehension of the past, and for mature independence.

Robert Pinsky suggests that "knowledge is the geography of survival"[65] in Bishop's work. For each of these poets, the nature and limits of knowledge form an urgent problem, which has its roots in early childhood displacements and losses. Hence survival—both physical and emotional —was a far more pressing consideration than self-revelation. Each of these poets sought knowledge that might reestablish what Jarrell termed (regarding Lowell) "the shaky garden of the heart" as a last, ambiguous refuge in a dangerously decentered world. Beginning with the fragmentary sense of self that emerged from early childhood traumas, and growing up amidst the fragmenting postmodern culture that emerged after World War II and took shape under the looming shadows of the Cold War, the atomic bomb, the emergence of global intercommunications, and the growth of a military-industrial complex, these poets hung on to the embattled individual self as long as they could. They investigated the interpenetrations of complex and challenging inner and outer worlds with sensitivity, artistic tact, technical acumen and quiet experimentality. Their poems represent individual attempts to negotiate survival, self-realization, and even tentative forms of recovery and renewal by means of a range of tactics including camouflage, intransigent resistance, the skillful (or desperate) parrying of overwhelming external forces, and the power that comes from voicing what is silenced.

Reading these poets in terms of an exploratory model avoids many of the specific difficulties that attach to the confessional paradigm. An exploratory model does not prejudice artistic evaluation one way or the other. It avoids the assumption that the poem is a reliable source of factual disclosure. It leaves a reader latitude to respond to the epistemological and moral complexities and uncertainties of the poem. It encourages a reader to consider the poem's perceptual mobility. And it clears the way for readers to recognize and come to terms with the poet's imaginative role as maker.

Moreover, an exploratory model solves many problems that have perplexed recent literary history. For example, an exploratory model makes better sense of the parallel human, cultural, and artistic situations of these four poets, suggesting how a gay woman poet like Bishop could find her most significant connection with three heterosexual males who experienced parallel, though not identical, feelings of outsiderhood. The exploratory model makes better sense of how the earlier, apparently more impersonal work of Lowell and Berryman anticipates and prepares for the later, more overtly self-exploratory work. And of course, this model shows how to account for otherwise anomalous evidence of the extensive and lifelong four-way conversation of Lowell and Berryman with Bishop and Jarrell, allowing a more cogent understanding of the artistic relations of these poets with one another and with the other main currents of postmodern poetry and culture.

Most importantly, perhaps, this exploratory model returns readers to the peculiar richness and surprise of the poems themselves, encouraging readers to open themselves to the suggestive ambiguities of the poetry's dramatic situations. The model provides a means by which readers can appreciate the poems' uncanny, risk-taking investigations of the relations of self, psyche and culture. It allows readers to measure for themselves the extraordinary formal flexibility, inventiveness, and technical resourcefulness of these poets.

It was by means of this resourcefulness that this quartet achieved so many diversely empathetic yet unsentimental renderings of the dilemmas of lonely, vulnerable, emotionally marginalized human beings. These intricate, vividly dramatized poems lead readers into confrontations with emotionally disturbing (and often repressed) psychic material. They deploy the resources of art, exploiting devious adjustments in perspective and scale, and engaging in the "administration" (to use Berryman's droll wording) of oppositional cross-patterns of imagery, grammatical play, diction, wit, narrative, rhyme, repetition, punning, and so forth. Our understanding of these vital dimensions of their work's technique have suffered damage in readings guided by the confessional paradigm.

If one recognizes Bishop's demonstrable importance to a circle once perceived as the sole domain of male poets like Lowell, Jarrell, and Berryman, and if one applies to this expanded circle many of the approaches successfully deployed in the reading of Bishop, one finds the entire dynamic of their relations startlingly changed. Nor is this just because of the addition of a woman, although the expansion of gender is significant. Bishop's example suggests the need to think again about the way we approach the relation between autobiography and fictive art in midcentury American poetry. It further suggests the need to rethink how these poets use childhood as an artistic material, how they construct a grammar of dreams, how they implicate pictures and other visual objects in a verbal space, how they incorporate prose rhythms and speech patterns into their verse, and how they deal with problems of knowledge, history, culture, grief, and loss in an environment of epistemological uncertainty. Such a study will show how each of these artists escaped the limitations of photographic realism and the excesses of confessionalism. For as we shall see, each of these poets, male *or* female, had occasion to view the world through the "eye of the outsider." The affinity between Bishop and Lowell, who spent significant portions of his life under confinement in prison or in mental institutions, and who suffered from a major neurological disorder that remained undiagnosed until well into adulthood, can be partly explained by a shared experience of outsiderhood.

# Part 2

# CHILDHOOD, YOUTH, AND APPRENTICESHIP

# 3 Expulsion from Paradise

## *The Child as Exile and Explorer*

It is surprising what it takes to make an adult human being.

John Berryman

### Expulsion from Paradise

Bishop, Jarrell, Berryman, and Lowell were born under the gathering clouds of humanity's first global conflict and in the midst of modernity's opening phase. Much of their best work would explore the world of the threatened child or the traumatic emotional aftermath for those expelled too quickly from the protected realm of childhood innocence by the conflict, divorce, illness, or death of parents, by one's own diseases and disorders, by war, or by the heedlessness, unconscious manipulation, or conscious cruelty of caretakers.

When Elizabeth Bishop was born in Worcester, Massachusetts, on 8 February 1911, Europe and the Americas were at peace, and the world moved chiefly by steam. Aviation, eight years past Kitty Hawk, remained in its infancy, and radio broadcasts, successful experimentally, were by no means ready to challenge the preeminence of newsprint. Three years later, when Randall Jarrell was born in Nashville, Tennessee, on 16 May 1914, Europe still clung to an uneasy peace. In the five months separating Jarrell's birth from the birth of John Allyn Smith, Jr. (later John Berryman) on 25 October 1914 in McAlester, Oklahoma, the Austrian Archduke Ferdinand had been shot dead at Sarajevo, the "Guns of August" had spoken, and Europe—and Europe's colonies worldwide—had gone to war. When Robert Trail Spence Lowell IV was born on 1 March 1917 at his grandfather Winslow's Chestnut Street townhouse on Boston's genteel Beacon Hill, his father, a naval officer, was away on sea duty, and the United States, its Atlantic shipping the target of unrestricted attack by German U-boats, hovered on the brink of war. In April, Congress affirmed Woodrow Wilson's pledge that "the world must be made safe for democracy" and declared war on Germany and Germany's allies. The United States entered the Great War and made it global.

Bishop recognized and called attention to her own emergence as a child into a world of private and global conflict in the final stanza of "In the Waiting Room," a poem exploring a vertiginous turning point in her own early development. The poem ends with a sequence of factual statements that place her—a six-year-old child—in a specific time and a particular and strangely threatening locality, where she is surrounded (yet somehow conceptually anchored) by a yet more threatening world order.

> The waiting room was bright
> and too hot. It was sliding
> beneath a big black wave,
> another, and another.
>
> Then I was back in it. The War was on. Outside,
> in Worcester, Massachusetts,
> were night and slush and cold,
> and it was still the fifth of February, 1918.
>
> (*EBPoems* 161)

A threatened, intensely reimagined childhood was a pivotal feature in the work of each member of this midcentury quartet. Jarrell, in a 1957 letter noting possible echoes of his own work in Bishop's recently published "Sestina," modestly acknowledged that "I felt as if, so to speak, some of my wash-cloths were part of a Modigliani collage, or as if my cat had got into a Vuillard." Jarrell then adds, "I think too, that all people who really remember childhood and do it at all right sound alike in some ways" (*RJLet* 422). Together, the poets of this quartet, and others of their generation, were engaged in the lonely process—long before it became the focus of White-House-level concern and had gained national attention—of converting the child from the status of a marginalized cultural object into a cultural subject.

Since their brilliant, pioneering efforts that spanned the midcentury era, childhood has become a common, even commonplace, poetic theme. So it is easy to overlook that, for nearly a century, few serious poets writing in English were willing to touch it. Encouraged, in part, by the pervasive influence of poets like Lowell, Jarrell, Bishop, and Berryman, childhood has reemerged over the past several decades as one of the most active fields of investigation for poetry, a position it had not held since the first generations of English and American romantics.

This powerful reemergence of childhood goes unremarked in such conventional accounts of the poetry that followed modernism as M. L.

Rosenthal's *The New Modern Poetry*, James E. B. Breslin's *From Modern to Contemporary*, and David Perkins's *A History of Modern Poetry: Modernism and After*, though the same concentration on recovering the intricacies of early childhood has sometimes been observed in monographs on individual poets.[1] Yet our leading poetry reviews remain full of poems that return memorably to scenes of childhood, often recreated as the site of formative and traumatic early experience.

This recurrent preoccupation with childhood in the several generations that have followed modernism can be profitably examined through the lens of childhood studies, a newly emerging, multidisciplinary field of study of potentially enormous scope and importance that concerns itself with the ways cultures construct childhood. This field explores the many ways that writers and artists represent childhood. A diverse range of postmodern poets, including such first generation postmodernists as Lowell, Jarrell, Bishop, and Berryman, lend themselves to readings from the perspective of childhood studies because of their persistent exploration of the sometimes painful and uncertain processes and anomalies of individual childhood development. The difference between modernist poets, who tend to elide childhood, and postmodernist poets, who richly and variously represent it, is quite marked. This chapter looks at the cultural and personal backgrounds out of which these representations emerge in their work, as well as at the artistic process necessary to create their new aesthetic, and at the work's emotional and intellectual impact and its subsequent implications and influence.

It is no coincidence that the work of poets like Lowell, Jarrell, Bishop, and Berryman combines the representation of childhood with the exploration of loss. For them the problem of recovering childhood experience was intimately intertwined with the problem of confronting and exploring lost worlds. Loss has been a subject of poetry since time immemorial. In most earlier aesthetic frameworks; however, loss involves an alteration of an original, and reasonably sustained, condition of possession or wholeness. On the other hand, poets like Lowell, Jarrell, Bishop, and Berryman created an extensive body of poems that begin in a state of profound and perhaps irremediable loss, loss that accompanies, or even precedes, the protagonist's first moment of conscious awareness or considered selfhood. In poem after poem by this midcentury quartet, the first moment of rational consciousness, the earliest glimmer of mature knowledge, dawns simultaneously with an experience of traumatic loss.

This chapter concentrates biographically on the year 1927 in order to explore a sequence of traumatic "expulsions from paradise" in the lives of these four poets. These premature expulsions from the realm of childhood innocence recur repeatedly in their work in obvious and subtle mutations throughout hundreds of poems. And such experiences in their lives profoundly conditioned their response to the public and private worlds around them.

In Bishop's case, expulsion was quite literal. It took place in 1917, when her paternal grandparents (virtual strangers to her) removed her, an unwilling six-year-old child, from the home she had shared with her maternal grandparents in Nova Scotia after the loss of father and mother. (Her mother had been permanently placed in a mental institution.) These virtually unknown grandparents then transported her to the Bishop homestead in Worcester, Massachusetts. In a recently rediscovered juvenile poem published in a school magazine in 1927, when she was sixteen years old, Bishop voiced a mordantly ironic, if indirect, protest against her own expulsion from paradise.

In the course of that same year, 1927, each of the other poets featured in this study—still in their early youth or adolescence—experienced painful domestic transformations whose effects would continue to appear throughout their mature work. These early childhood losses and displacements would take on an almost mythic intensity of recurrence in their later writing, reappearing in various direct or oblique guises as a series of "expulsions from paradise."

Studying these early experiences of powerlessness and deprivation, and the poets' emotional, intellectual, and artistic response to them, provides insight into that portion of their work written from the perspective of the child. This insight also adds to our understanding of the evolution of their exploratory aesthetic, an aesthetic which drew them persistently back into the lost world of childhood, while encouraging them to explore many other lost worlds—and worlds of loss—in their poetry.

In 1927, each of the other poets was then grappling with recent and traumatic life changes. Berryman, thirteen, had just moved north from Tampa, Florida, to New York City, having recently experienced the sudden, violent death of his birth father—and having acquired a new stepfather, and a new surname—under traumatic and darkly ambiguous circumstances. That same year, Jarrell, also thirteen, was brought back, against his will, to his mother's house in Nashville from the emotionally nurturing family environment created by his father, paternal grandparents, and doting aunt in Hollywood, California. Lowell, ten years old in 1927, witnessed his father bow to pressure from his wife and resign his commission in the navy. Thereafter, in his son's eyes, the senior Lowell had forever lost his last vestige of prestige, personal identity, and moral authority. In Lowell's case, although there was no geographical shift, this was a traumatic event for it proved the absolute power of his terrifying mother and the inefficacy of his morally and emotionally absent father.

These experiences, read against the grounding this generation received in the romantic conception of the child and in the still-emerging and radically revisionary Freudian conception, created powerful and conflicting pressures on their emotional outlook on childhood. These pressures surface in their poetry and function as a series of dialectical oppositions, providing their oeuvre with much of its emotional resonance. One finds them envisioning childhood from a perspective that W. E. B. Du Bois, in a different but not altogether dissimilar context, termed a double-consciousness. In this case the doubleness is dramatized as a gap between the consciousness of the dominant adult culture and the subordinated child culture. Their work juxtaposes not just contrasting layers of adult and childlike perception but also sets the by then conventional—but still cherished—romantic conception of childhood as a paradisal abode of innocence and luminous, intuitive insight against the newly emerging Freudian conception of infancy as itself a locus of suffering and dispossession, as the source of one's first faintly recalled and dimly understood encounters with trauma and loss.

For each of these four poets, the motif of expulsion from paradise reappears in many forms throughout their poetry, marking moments of profound loss that are also points of conscious entry into selfhood, into the pleasures and dangers of the social and material world, and the parallel pleasures and dangers of artistic creation. Childhood is dramatized in their work as the site of one's own first taste of that bittersweet, ambiguous fruit that grows on the tree of knowledge. In this, these poets drew sustenance from that darker, and less popular, view of childhood—seldom mentioned in the histories—found in such romantic verse as Blake's *Songs of Experience* and the more haunted passages in the first book of Wordsworth's *Prelude.* Similar intimations can be found in the early modern poetry of Rilke, who profoundly influenced several of these poets, as well as in many powerful moments in Dickens, Joyce, and Proust.

Sigmund Freud's radical and influential redefinition of childhood in the early decades of the twentieth century laid the groundwork for a new poetics with a radically altered vision of early childhood. Recalling, in his

1914 retrospective *The History of the Psychoanalytic Movement*, the elements that transformed psychology into psychoanalysis, Freud singled out "The doctrine of repression and resistance, the recognition of infantile sexuality, and the interpreting and making use of dreams as a source of knowledge of the unconscious."[2] Each of these elements reappears transmuted in the aesthetic of Bishop, Lowell, Jarrell, and Berryman. Theirs was the first generation of poets for whom Freud was a historical figure rather than a contemporary. His theories had begun to be absorbed into the fabric of Anglo-American culture, and thus they grew up as aspiring writers with the idea that one returns in memory to early childhood experience not in order to recapture a Wordsworthian "visionary gleam" but to recover from neurosis by removing the roadblocks to healthy human development caused by the repression of early traumatic experience. Freud had argued that "It is only experiences in childhood that explain susceptibility to later traumas and it is only by uncovering these almost invariably forgotten memory-traces and by making them conscious that we acquire the power to get rid of the symptoms. And here we reach the same conclusion as in our investigation of dreams: the imperishable, repressed wishful impulses of childhood have alone provided the power for the construction of symptoms, and without them the reaction to later traumas would have taken a normal course."[3] By the time these poets were beginning to come of age in the mid-to-late 1930s, Freud's thesis had come to rival the cultural impact that Jean-Jacques Rousseau's views of the child had on the English romantic poets. Freud's theories of repression, infant sexuality, and the interpretation of dreams "as a source of knowledge of the unconscious" helped to reopen childhood—a subject largely dismissed from the impersonal ideology of modernist poetry for its associations with romantic sentimentality and with late-romantic formalist competitors like Edna St. Vincent Millay—as a field ripe for serious poetic reexploration.

Bishop, Lowell, Jarrell, and Berryman joined with such contemporaries as Theodore Roethke, Muriel Rukeyser, Robert Hayden, Gwendolyn Brooks, Delmore Schwartz, and Dylan Thomas to construct a new poetry and poetics of childhood. Their explorations of childhood would soon be developed in new directions by younger poets as varied as Donald Justice, Allen Ginsberg, James Merrill, W. D. Snodgrass, W. S. Merwin, Philip Levine, Adrienne Rich, Anne Sexton, Sylvia Plath, Sharon Olds, Frank Bidart, Gjertrud Schnackenberg, and Birgit Pegeen Kelly. The particular concern of Lowell, Jarrell, Bishop, and Berryman was on creating an exploratory aesthetic dramatizing moments when an individual's traumatic past, remembered partially and with difficulty in the face of resistance and repression, emerges as the recognized but imperfectly known source of adult emotional disorder. These four poets would sustain their influential preoccupation with childhood experience throughout their careers, developing a probing exploration of the drama of individual human development that was in several respects far from orthodox Freudian thought.

These poets had good reason to share an ongoing concern with the child's traumatic past. For such deeply schooled and imaginative readers who had cut their teeth on romantic poetry in the process of surviving their own traumatic childhoods, the romantic image of childhood as a time of luminous, intuitive rightness retained a strong, lingering appeal. Yet each had suffered tangible and traumatic early abuses and losses that pushed them to question romanticism's construction of childhood as a phase of luminous intuitive certainty as well as Freud's problematic insistence that childhood's partially remembered traumas were wholly or largely fantasies emerging from the realm of infant sexuality which "alone provided the power for the construction of symptoms." The emotional power of their poems of early childhood grows, in part, from the way they dramatize the triangulating pressures of three forces: first, a yearning to recognize and preserve in childhood a paradisal haven of innocence; second, an effort to recover, against repression, unconscious memories of childhood's wishful struggles and fantasies; and, third, an effort to delineate the raw or subtle actualities of a particular child's vulnerability and powerlessness and dawning understanding in the face of deliberate or unconscious adult abuse, seduction, or manipulation.

The series of early poems to be examined in this chapter, some familiar, some comparatively little known, cover a span of nearly two decades, beginning with Bishop's "Ballad of the Subway Train" (1927), moving through Jarrell's "And did she dwell in innocence and joy" (1935) and Berryman's "The Ball Poem" (1942), and concluding with Lowell's "Christmas Eve under Hooker's Statue" (1946). Each of these early poem explores the plight of a child or childlike figure who suffers a profound loss, leading to a traumatic and premature expulsion from a luminous "paradise" of childlike innocence. These early poems begin with children —or their emblematic surrogates—who appear in Jarrell's deliberately Wordsworthian phrase to "dwell in innocence and joy." But these poems center on a moment when these protagonists are forcibly and prematurely expelled from paradise while still children. These poems, and those that follow imply that the recovery of childhood presents an epistemological problem and an emotional challenge that must be faced if one is to achieve anything like maturity, self-protection, self-understanding, or poetic creativity. These poems stand as early tokens of the eventual and decisive emergence of a postmodern aesthetic of childhood. This new aesthetic has long since displaced for most working poets both the romantic myth of childhood as a lost paradise of innocence and luminous perceptual rightness and the modernist myth of impersonality, with its tendency to suppress or elide childhood. The poetics of psychic origins pioneered by Lowell, Jarrell, Bishop, and Berryman continues as a source for original poetry more than half a century after its first tentative appearance in poems such as the ones in this chapter.

## Berryman's "Development of Anne Frank"

Before returning to those early poems, a neglected yet revealing essay on Anne Frank is worth considering. This essay was completed by Berryman in 1967, just as he was finishing *The Dream Songs.* Berryman relates that, upon reading galleys of the soon-to-be-famous *Diary* in the offices of *Commentary* in 1952, "Like millions of people later, I was bowled over with pity and horror and admiration for the astounding doomed little girl. But what I *thought* was: a sane person. A sane person, in the twentieth century" (*JBProse* 91). For Berryman, the genuinely remarkable feature of the *Diary* was simply this: that it recorded a successful process of growing up. Berryman's title is "The Development of Anne Frank,"[4] stressing this overlooked dimension of the *Diary:* "I decided that it was the most remarkable account of normal human adolescent maturation I had ever read, and that it was universally valued for reasons comparatively insignificant" (*JBProse* 91). Anne Frank was the articulate victim of one of "the grand crimes of our age," and while this does much to explain the book's popularity and emotional power, it evades, for Berryman, "the *critical* question. . . . *One finds her formidable:* why, and how, ought to engage us" (his emphasis). Berryman consequently reads the *Diary* as a unique conversion narrative, pointing out that though there are many narratives of religious conversion, "I would call the subject of Anne Frank's *Diary* even more mysterious and fundamental than St. Augustine's, and describe it as: the conversion of a child into a person. . . . Anne Frank has made the process itself available. . . . The reason this matters is that the process we are to follow displays itself in a more complicated fashion than one might have expected: in the will, in emotion, in the intellect, in libido. It is surprising what it takes to make an adult human being" (*JBProse* 93, 96). For Berryman, the making of an adult human being is a rare phenomenon, something to be prized, when it happens, as a genuine accomplishment.

The process of maturation requires that one achieve independence, and one finds Anne Frank formidable because, "Independence comes hard-won and is not friendly" (*JBProse* 98). Berryman's chief tool of inquiry is Freudian analysis. Looking at one of Anne's memories, Berryman remarks, "It is clear that the *meaning* of this experience is not known to the girl, and cannot become known to us, since we do not have her associations; but it is *being reported,* and here is extremely interesting. . . . But there is no need to interpret. The traumatic incident has served its purpose, for her and for our understanding of her development, *in being recollected:* This is the sort of experience that in persons who become mentally ill is blocked, whereas the fullness here both of the recollection (with very slight blockage) and of the affect testifies to her freedom" (*JBProse* 100). For Berryman, the key to maturation, to the achievement of emotional security and independence, lies in the act of working through emotional blockage to recover repressed traumatic experience. When an interviewer asked Tate in 1974, two years after his former protégé's death, "Did you anticipate Berryman's greatness," the seventy-five-year-old Tate replied, "I don't think he was great. He was an original poet and a very interesting one, but he wasn't a great poet. . . . He never grew up. That was his whole trouble. And *Dream Songs* is simply paranoid projections of childhood manias and obsessions."[5] Tate's dismissive treatment of Berryman's *Dream Songs* suggests how little this aged master understood his former apprentice. For it is the very difficulty of growing up, of making oneself into the "adult human being" whom Berryman recognized, envied, and admired in Anne Frank, that emerges as the central drama of Berryman's work, a drama he labored hard to find means to express in verse.

It may seem stunning that so close a mentor and surrogate father as Allen Tate had been to Berryman could coolly flatten the complex dynamics of the *Dream Songs* into a mere projection of childhood "manias and obsessions." But in doing so, Tate was echoing the psychoanalytic convention of his time, which dismissed as mere fantasy the emotional core of his surrogate "son's" work—those traumatic memories and emotions based in childhood which as we shall soon see in Berryman's case had considerable basis in fact. Alice Miller critiques the Freudian reading of childhood trauma because of its assumption of fantasy as a basis for neurosis—and its implied or explicit rejection of actual abuse as an equally powerful or still more powerful source. As Miller sees it "Metapsychology has no model" to deal with the outright abuse that a person like Berryman undoubtedly suffered. For Miller, Freudian analysis can not deal "with facts that at most are taken into account as the patient's fantasies. . . . It is as if we did not dare to take a single step in order to acknowledge the child's reality, since Freud recognized the conjecture of sexual seduction as the patient's fantasy. Since the patient also has an interest in keeping this reality hidden from us, and still more from himself, it can happen that we share his ignorance for a long time. Nevertheless, the patient never stops telling us about part of his reality in the language of his symptoms."[6] In a 1983 lecture on "Violence in the Family," British psychoanalyst John Bowlby agrees. Noting that "Ever since Freud made his famous, and in my view, disastrous, volte-face in 1897, when he decided that the childhood seductions he had believed to be etiologically important were nothing more than the products of his patients' imaginations, it has been extremely unfashionable to attribute psychopathology to real-life experiences." Bowlby, insisting that "no one with eyes to see can any longer doubt that all too many children are battered by their parents, either verbally or physically or both," concludes that "the concentration in analytic circles on fantasy and the reluctance to examine real-life events has much to answer for."[7] Tate's dismissive summing up of his protégé's career suggests just how difficult Berryman's artistic struggle was going to be, since he was learning to write a poetry that tells us about a part of his reality by speaking in the language of symptoms, a language that his close mentor was primed to reject. And that summing up suggests, as well, a significant gulf between the psychological assumptions of "impersonal" modernists like Tate and the emerging perspectives (and needs) of their fractious literary progeny.

Berryman's *Dream Songs* enact the drama of a determined and prolonged —but tragically failed—effort to achieve such maturation and independence as Berryman recognizes in Anne Frank. Berryman presents Henry as a person who may externally look like a grownup, but who displays the symptomatic behaviors of immaturity. In Berryman's *Dream Song* 1, he laments:

> All the world like a woolen lover
> once did seem on Henry's side.
> Then came a departure.
> Thereafter nothing fell out as it might or ought.
>
> (*DS* 1)

Henry should be a grownup by now, but, as the traces of baby talk indicate, he is not fully mature; indeed, the *Dream Songs* persistently characterize Henry as a tragicomic individual whose "conversion from a child into a person" has been dangerously arrested. And in the first Dream Song one learns that Henry has experienced premature expulsion from the lost paradise of childhood. Though, perhaps "Once in a sycamore I was glad / all at the top, and I sang," soon one must descend from this solitary haven of childhood innocence and safety into an intransigent domain where "Hard on the land wears the strong sea / and empty grows every bed." Henry's woolen lover, the source of an earlier sense of security, might itself seem far from perfect, a confused and inadequate substitute for either a living mother or a more warm-blooded lover and companion. Thus, even Henry's paradisal memories are confused and based partly on illusion. Indeed, his original fall may be from the womb itself. Berryman mused in a late conversation recorded by William Heyen, "Isn't it true that the three of us sitting here, began with a great loss, from the controlled environment of the womb? After my son was born, I wrote him a little poem that started: 'Feel for your bad fall how could I fail, / poor Paul, who had it so good.' I have many objections to Freud's findings, but he was right about the importance of the womb."[8] Thus, in the *Dream Songs*, Berryman constructs Henry as a frustrated figure caught tragically between his yearning for two contradictory and apparently unreachable states: the state of preconscious, womblike security and the state of responsible, independent maturity.

Berryman's opening Dream Song posits a dynamic tension between the child that Henry often appears to be and the adult whom he ought to be but cannot fully become. And in this, Berryman bypasses the impersonal ideology of his modernist mentors, particularly Tate and T. S. Eliot, to return to an interest in early childhood development.

## Bishop's "Ballad of the Subway Train"

Berryman's preoccupation with the rigorous drama of individual human development was by no means unique. It is a persistent preoccupation in the work of Bishop, Jarrell, and Lowell as well, a preoccupation one can retrace to the very earliest stages of their writing. In fact, one discovers strong evidence of this preoccupation in the earliest surviving poem that any of them wrote, Elizabeth Bishop's "The Ballad of the Subway Train." In the spring of 1927, when Bishop was a sixteen-year-old high school freshman attending North Shore Country Day School in Beverly, Massachusetts, she published four astute prose pieces—and one remarkable poem—in her school magazine, the *Owl.* Still in her mid-teens, she had already lived through a staggering, and by now oft recited, sequence of losses, losses that shaped what Lloyd Schwartz has recently called "Bishop's now virtually mythic" childhood story.[9] Bishop would respond to these experiences artistically by taking part in the shaping of a subtly controlled, and artistically influential, postmodern poetics of childhood: a poetics of psychic origins. Indeed, close examination of the historical record suggests that, at critical moments in their parallel development as poets, it was Bishop and Jarrell who were encouraging Lowell and Berryman to embark on a deep but artistically controlled exploration of the traumatic psychic origins of the developing, emotionally self-divided individual. It is worth exploring Bishop's childhood experiences at some length because many of the emotional issues she faced are reproduced in slightly different forms for the other poets in her quartet.

In the first six years of her life, Bishop suffered a sequence of early traumas that left a permanent imprint on her art. These include the death of her father from Bright's disease in 1911, when she was eight months old, and the mental breakdowns suffered by her mother, Gertrude Bulmer Bishop, partly, it seems, as a consequence of her father's early death. These led to her mother's temporary hospitalization in 1914 and to her permanent confinement in a Dartmouth, Nova Scotia mental hospital in the summer of 1916 when Bishop was five. After 1916, Bishop would never see her mother again. Thereafter, Bishop experienced a series of wrenching and traumatic dislocations as she passed from one relation to another in the years that followed. But at first the five-year-old Elizabeth, now a virtual orphan, continued living, as she would for more than a year, with her modestly placed but gently affectionate maternal grandparents, the Bulmers, in Great Village, Nova Scotia, a traditional rural community that Bishop vividly recalled in prose and verse from high school on.

In the fall of 1917, when Bishop was six years old, her wealthy and dutiful but emotionally distant paternal grandparents arrived in Great Village to claim Elizabeth and bring her back to Massachusetts. As Bishop recalled the event in a 1964 letter to her first biographer, Anne Stevenson, "The B[ishop]s were horrified to see the only child of their eldest son running about the village in bare feet, eating at the table with the grown-ups and drinking *tea,* so I was carried off (by train) to Worcester for the one awful winter that was almost the end of me. 1917–18."[10] Within months of her removal to Worcester, Bishop began to suffer a succession of illnesses. "I had already had bad bronchitis and probably attacks of asthma —in Worcester I got much worse and developed eczema that almost killed me. One awful day I was sent home from 'first grade' because of my sores—and I imagine my hopeless shyness has dated from then.—In May, 1919, I was taken to live with Aunt Maud; I couldn't walk and Ronald [the Bishop chauffeur] carried me up the stairs—my aunt burst into tears when she saw me." Bishop's traumatic series of losses and displacements is thus explicitly linked to a series of debilitating physical illnesses. She later felt "that stretch is still too grim to think of, almost. My grandfather had gone to see my aunt M[aud] privately and made the arrangements—he said my grandmother didn't 'know how take care of her own children,' most of them had died."[11] Thereafter, under the care of her maternal aunt Maud, Bishop suffered recurrent bouts of asthma that limited her ability to attend school regularly. Bishop had spent much of her isolated youth "lying in bed wheezing and reading."[12]

A contemporary analyst might conclude that in the years following her removal to Worcester, Bishop was suffering from post-traumatic stress disorder. Enumerating the symptoms of this disorder, Dr. Richard Famularo notes in a recent issue of the *Harvard Mental Health Letter* that, "The traumatic experience is followed by recurrent or intrusive recollections, including repetitive play, frightening dreams, reenactment of the trauma, and intense reactions to symbolic reminders of the trauma." Evidence of many of these symptoms reappears in Bishop's extensive writings about the sequence of losses that cut her off from her main sources of nurture and reassurance. In particular, the response to symbolic reminders of the world she had lost in Nova Scotia was visceral and intense. Harking back to the mysterious columns of numbers on the blackboard that she observed as a five-year-old member of a "Primer Class in Nova Scotia" just months after her mother's climactic breakdown, Bishop would write that "Every time I see long columns of numbers, handwritten in a certain way, a strange sensation or shudder, partly aesthetic, partly painful, goes through my diaphragm. . . . The real name of this sensation is memory. It is a memory I do not even have to try to remember or reconstruct; it is always right there, clear and complete" (*EBProse* 3, 4). Bishop's work makes pervasive use of such memory traces. And it frequently attributes long-lasting and profound emotional effects to quite specific and sometimes trivial-seeming incidents from childhood that appear to function as symbolic reminders of trauma. These provoke intense reactions so that, as she suggests in her first mature poem, "The Map" (1935), "the emotion too far exceeds its cause" (*EBPoems* 3). Painfully shy in adulthood, Bishop recalled the intimidating dinner conversation in the home of her Worcester grandparents. "They talked about high prices at the table; I heard that eggs were five cents apiece. And the price of clothes! I rarely spoke, but this time I felt I had something to contribute. I said, 'The last time my aunt in Nova Scotia bought a pair of shoes, they cost three dollars.' Everyone laughed. I lost my courage about making conversation at the dinner table and I have never regained it" (*EBProse* 28). Bishop's genius for investing precisely observed but seemingly trivial detail with great emblematic significance grew in part out of her carefully schooled talent for selecting and placing those details in context so that these symbolic reminders serve as triggers for powerful feeling in the reader as well as the writer—a crucial technique for a writer exploring the secret realms of trauma and repression.

Bishop's resentment of her removal from Great Village, from a landscape she knew and loved and an extended family and village society that she knew and found comforting, remains palpable in the posthumously published autobiographical memoir "The Country Mouse," written in 1960, more than forty years after the event, according to editor Robert Giroux's estimate. "I had been brought back unconsulted and against my wishes to the house my father had been born in, to be saved from a life of poverty and provincialism, bare feet, suet puddings, unsanitary school slates, perhaps even from the inverted *r*'s of my mother's family. With this surprising extra set of grandparents, until a few weeks ago no more than names, a new life was about to begin" (*EBProse* 17). Biographer Brett C. Millier concludes that her abrupt removal from Great Village "sealed little Elizabeth's sense of loss to a permanent condition."[13] Bishop's own later comment was, "I felt as if I were being kidnapped, even if I wasn't" (*EBProse* 14). Of post-traumatic stress disorder, Dr. Famularo adds that "The traumatic experiences of childhood often involve maltreatment by parents or other caregivers. The resulting loss of protection, sense of betrayal, daily fear, and overwhelming sense of helplessness may color all the child's later personal relations."[14] Bishop had simply been appropriated by her paternal grandparents at a time when she was particularly vulnerable, and she never completely recovered, either physically or emotionally, from the sense of helplessness and loss that this heedless act of exile inflicted upon her. Not until she reached sixteen was Bishop finally well enough to enroll full time as a freshman at North Shore Country Day.

She had slipped a year or two behind her age-mates on the academic calendar, but she was already well ahead of them in one important respect: she had molded herself into an accomplished writer of both prose and verse.

The single poem of Bishop's that appeared in that spring 1927 issue of *The Owl,* the brilliant and darkly funny "Ballad of the Subway Train," makes incisive if indirect use of her childhood losses. Only recently republished, the "Ballad" lingered undiscovered for years in the back issue of a high school literary magazine, a quiet, unrecognized literary landmark: a poem that marks the tentative reopening, for Bishop and many other American poets of her generation, of a field of investigation that had long remained closed to serious exploration for poets writing in English: the field of early childhood experience.[15]

Bishop's "Ballad," written when she was sixteen, develops the motif of expulsion from "the lost paradise of the childish past" in a manner at once allegorical and strikingly direct. She evokes a vivid and comically magical scene, in fresh, simple diction.

> Long, long ago when God was young,
> Earth hadn't found its place.
> Great dragons lived among the moons
> And crawled and crept through space.
>
> They bunted meteors with their heads.
> While unseen worlds dropped by;
> And scratched their bronzy backs upon
> The ridges of the sky.[16]

Despite their tremendous size, the demeanor of these "great dragons" seems curiously childlike, even infantile. The primordial world they inhabit, at a time when even "God was young," is expansive and apparently free of law or restraint. Many of Bishop's later poems feature prosaic animals such as a fish, roosters or an armadillo or such fantastic creatures as her Man-Moth, seen partly on their own terms as independent beings and partly in terms that are human and cultural. Here the dragons emerge partly as free inventions but partly as emblematic surrogates of the child. These dragons start their existence in a blissful, premoral state, and like happily occupied children, are so absorbed in play that they remain oblivious to momentous events occurring in the background. Free of shame, innocent of time, and governed by only the most primitive layers of consciousness, these dragons luxuriate for "ten thousand thousand years" in a state of independent pleasure, fulfilling their own narcissistic needs without effort or guidance, enjoying a quasi-mythic scope and power. Yet this state of paradise is suddenly lost, when they are abruptly caught out in a calamitous, if inadvertent, crime.

The aeons came and went and came,
    And still the dragons stayed;
Until one night they chanced to eat
    A swarm of stars new made.

And when God saw them all full gorged,
    Their scaly bellies fed,
His anger made the planets shake
    And this is what he said:

"You have been feeding, greedy beasts,
    Upon the bright young stars.
For gluttony as deep as yours,
    *Be changed to subway cars!*"

The climactic turn in Bishop's ballad offers nothing less than a precocious remaking of an ancient myth that she perhaps first encountered in the old family Bible she features in "Over 2,000 Illustrations and a Complete Concordance" and that finds its most beautiful and sustained expression in Milton's *Paradise Lost.* Certainly Bishop's ability to deploy comedy at this critical moment is a sign of great residual strength, but if God's punishment here is comic, it is also far more terrible and arbitrary than His judgment in Milton's version. According to Milton, Eve and Adam deservedly suffer "loss of Eden." The dragons' "crime," on the other hand, seems little more than an infantile impulse. Nonetheless, God's anger is far swifter and more final in Bishop's version.

The God of Bishop's "Ballad" strikes without warning and departs without a word of hope or consolation. Indeed, God's parting words rub salt into the dragons' wounds:

"No more for you infinite space,
    But in a narrow hole
You shall forever grope your way,
    Blind-burrowing like the mole!"

The word "forever" turns the key on a sentence to life imprisonment and servitude: no whisper here of hope for "paradise regained." The poem's texture is lucid, its imagery precise and vivid, its language comic. But teleologically speaking, this world remains bleak and opaque. God's purposes seem arbitrary and unreadable beyond the motive of mere vengeance, and loss is given only veiled expression, behind the shield of high spirited humor. But Bishop's ongoing preoccupation with traumatic and mysterious loss and her disquiet regarding the nature and sources of human knowledge are vividly prefigured.

These dragons function as poignant, if covert, emblems of Bishop's child-self, their fate paralleling uncannily Bishop's recollections of her own early experiences of displacement and loss. Bishop's early life in Nova Scotia may never have been truly paradisal. She had already lost her father before she first visited Great Village, and her mother suffered an earlier "nervous breakdown" before her permanent exile to a mental institution. "In the Village" takes as its central image a scream Bishop's mother uttered at the moment of that final breakdown. This scream's echo "hangs over that Nova Scotian village. . . . unheard, in memory—in the past, in the present, and in those years between. It was not even loud to begin with perhaps. It just came there to live, forever—not loud, just alive forever" (*EBProse* 251). Bishop's exile from Great Village was not final, though she had no way of knowing. She continued to return for long visits until 1930. But in Bishop's personal mythology, Great Village, though itself the site of painful losses and silences, represented the closest thing to home she had ever known, and it retains its force throughout her work as a kind of irrecoverable Eden: vibrant with loss, perhaps, but also radiant with moments of childlike wonder and natural freshness that make one feel that Bishop was, as usual, far too self-deprecating when she described herself, in a letter to Lowell, as a "minor female Wordsworth."[17]

One symbolic reminder of her traumatic exile from Nova Scotia that forms the decisive image of her 1927 "Ballad," the quasi-comic descent of an angry God upon an unwitting offender, reappears with tragicomic force in the opening scene from the 1960 "The Country Mouse." As the memoir begins, the six-year-old Elizabeth is aboard a sleeper car on "the old Boston and Maine" railroad, being transported from Great Village to the house of her Bishop grandparents in Worcester. In the dead of night the child awakens to observe a startling event. Abruptly, her very tall grandfather, J. W. Bishop, a wealthy and successful building contractor who in the child's mind resembles the "grandfather's clock" of the old song because he, like the clock, was "too large for its shelf . . . snapped on the overheard light again. . . . He had been trying to sleep in the upper berth of our 'drawing room.' Now he descended, god-like and swearing, swept Grandma out of the way, and wedged himself into the lower berth. His thick silver hair and short silver beard glittered, and so did the whites of his eyes, rolled up as if in agony" (*EBProse* 13). Summarily displaced from her berth, "this grandma, jiggling too, stood by helplessly, watching him writhe and grunt." Finally, her husband commands "'Sarah, get in the other way around!' She turned off the overhead light once more and obeyed." Bishop recalls, "I can look back on them now, many years and train trips later, and clearly see them looking like a Bernini fountain, or a Cellini saltcellar: a powerful but aging Poseidon with a small, elderly, curly Nereid" (*EBProse* 14). In this scene, Bishop's own expulsion from the "paradise" of Nova Scotia is comically mirrored in the bizarre and awkward choreography of her grandmother's displacement by a "godlike and swearing" patriarch. J. W. Bishop's startling emergence as a "powerful but aging Poseidon" who descends from on high, commands the moral high ground, and has what it takes to displace others rudely underlines in eerily mythic terms aspects of Bishop's own displacement that she had first dealt with in the 1927 "Ballad."

In her early "Ballad," the experience of arbitrary expulsion from the "lost paradise of the childish past" may have been too close and painful to treat as directly as Bishop would in later poems. Even then, she would leave her most pointed and direct treatment, "The Country Mouse," unpublished. In the 1927 "Ballad" Bishop's experience of expulsion and exile was displaced, through parable, onto the dragons. In her still-early but stylistically mature poems of the mid-to-late 1930s, Bishop would create a series of enigmatic fables such as "The Man-Moth," "The Weed," and "The Imaginary Iceberg" that continue to explore this painful inner world by indirect means. These poems are reluctant to disclose their painful burdens, which often appear to resemble that "one tear, his only possession, like the bee's sting" (*EBPoems* 15) that her Man-Moth guards so carefully. Indeed, Lowell would say of these poems, in the course of a 1947 review, "One is reminded of Kafka and certain abstract paintings, and is left rather at sea about the actual subjects of the poems" (*RLProse* 76). But evidently Bishop's early disposition toward the protective and enabling veil of parable was already in place in the 1927 "Ballad."

Bishop's grandmother, despite her rude treatment at his hands, remains an ally of "this grandfather" in the process of domesticating and Americanizing a granddaughter lifted from another world. "This grandma," Sarah Bishop, appears throughout the memoir as an emotionally distant, formidably proper matriarch who thinks nothing, for example, of dispossessing her small grandchild—who had recently lost her mother and was now losing her home—of all her dolls ("I was quite fond of one or two") because she "found them all in no condition to go traveling in Pullmans." She buys instead a new, more proper (and "totally uninteresting") doll that she insists on naming Drusilla ("I couldn't say that name"). And she "would speak of 'grandma' and 'little girls' and 'fathers' and 'being good'—things I had never before considered in the abstract, or rarely in the third person. In particular, there seemed to be much, much more to being a 'little girl' than I had realized. The prospect was beginning to depress me" (*EBProse* 16). Jarrell, speaking of Christina Stead's *The Man Who Loved Children*, would later remark, "God is, I suppose, what our parents were; certainly the giant or ogre of the stories is so huge, so powerful, and so stupid because that is the way a grownup looks to a child" (*TBC* 32). Here Bishop portrays a child being treated by her grandmother, a new and unwanted caregiver-in-chief, with unconscious contempt. In *Drama of the Gifted Child*, Alice Miller argues relevantly that "In many societies, little girls suffer additional discrimination because they are girls. . . . [Later], these erstwhile little girls can pass on to their children at the most tender age the contempt from which they once had suffered." Here one witnesses a contempt being passed down from "this grandfather" to "this grandma" to a six- year-old child. Miller argues further that "Contempt is the weapon of the weak and a defense against one's own despised and unwanted feelings. And the fountainhead of all contempt, all discrimination, is the more or less conscious, uncontrolled, and secret exercise of power over the child by the adult, which is tolerated by society (except in the case of murder or serious bodily harm.)"[18] Bishop seems to have suffered not merely at the hands of an impersonal fate which caused her father's death and her mother's insanity. She also suffered through the "more or less conscious, uncontrolled, and secret exercise of power" over her life by adults who professed concern for her, and no doubt received society's praise for what they did, but who, if what Bishop records is true, also showed an indifference to the child's feelings bordering on violence.

As Bishop later remembered it, the rangy old Worcester farm house that she was brought to by these new grandparents, set on the fringe of a growing city, was "gloomy," and its several inhabitants—the grandparents, an aunt and an uncle (her late father's sister and brother), and their servants—were "nervous and unsettled." Moreover, this house contained "a whole unknown past I was made to feel I should have known about, and a strange, unpredictable future" (*EBProse* 17). This strange, unpredictable future became Elizabeth Bishop's own painful early life. Bishop never felt at home in this new house. Once, sent to fetch her grandfather's eyeglasses from his empty bedroom, she caught a glimpse "in the long mirror" of the disquieting self she had become: "my ugly serge dress, my too long hair, my gloomy and frightened expression" (*EBProse* 29).

As the young Elizabeth settled into the Worcester house, the creature with whom she most identified was a dog, "a Boston bull terrier nominally belonging to Aunt Jenny, and oddly named Beppo. At first I was afraid of him, but he immediately adopted me, perhaps as being on the same terms in the house as himself, and we became very attached" (*EBProse* 21). Unlike the dog in her late "Five Flights Up," Beppo has a strong "sense of shame," mirroring the exiled late-Puritan child that Bishop had become. "When he was 'bad,' he was punished by being put in a large closet off the sewing room and left there, out of things, for half an hour. Once when I was playing with him, he disappeared and would not answer my calls. Finally he was found, seated gloomily by himself in the closet, facing the wall. He was punishing himself. We later found a smallish puddle of vomit in the conservatory. No one had ever before punished him for his attacks of gastritis, naturally; it was all his own idea, his peculiar Bostonian sense of guilt (*EBProse* 21)." Shortly after Beppo's act of self-punishment, Bishop herself would develop that range of autoimmune reactions including bronchitis, eczema, asthma, and aspects of St. Vitus's dance whose symptoms would follow her dangerously into adulthood. As a child, Bishop felt that there was something both inconvenient and shameful about her own presence in her grandparents' house. She may have been brought there "unconsulted and against my wishes," but she remained, like Beppo, only "nominally" belonging to anyone.

Indirect treatment of grief connected with loss was apparently ingrained in Bishop from the beginning. A taboo on the discussion of her most grievous losses seems to have been maintained by her father's family. The evidence strongly suggests that the breakdowns and institutionalization of her mother were rarely, if ever, mentioned—let alone explained to her—in Worcester. When her Bishop grandfather died, Bishop came under the supervision of his son, John Warren Bishop, Jr., whom she knew as Uncle Jack. Like his father, Uncle Jack was dutifully concerned for his ward but nonetheless aloof from her emotionally. When Uncle Jack enrolled Elizabeth at Walnut Hill, he spoke to administrator Ruby Willis about Bishop's mother's illness. In Willis's notes, he is on record as stating, "These facts are either unknown to Elizabeth or, at most, only surmised by her, since no one has ever spoken to her about her mother and she has never mentioned her." Willis's notes provide remarkable and important external confirmation of the hints in Bishop's writings that, even up to the age of sixteen, she had never been explicitly informed regarding what happened to her mother. An embargo on the topic of her mother was, apparently, quite consistently enforced by her paternal relations, either for the child's "protection" or because the topic was simply too embarrassing or distressing for the family to discuss openly. After a summary of Gertrude Bishop's case, Willis's Walnut Hill notes continue, "Elizabeth's guardian is most anxious that no mention of these facts shall be made to Elizabeth. She had been a 'lonely little girl' and he anticipates much happiness for her at Walnut Hill."[19]

By implication, Bishop's Uncle Jack expected that her new school, in the role of surrogate family, should provide a degree of nurture and concern that might compensate Bishop for the lack of emotional care her losses had received at home. At the same time, Uncle Jack insisted on maintaining the veil of silence about Bishop's mother's condition. It should not surprise one that, as a friend at Walnut Hill recalled, "There was this big gap in Elizabeth's life. Elizabeth didn't talk much about her childhood. It was too difficult." This friend, Joan Collingwood Disney, acknowledged that, "She felt affection for her aunts and they for her," but she continues, "She really had to grow up all by herself. A terrible sadness would cause her to be despondent." Disney concludes, "I remember exactly how she looked one time when she was leaving our house in Plymouth, Massachusetts, after a visit. It was a very sad look and stayed with me. Maybe the right word would have kept her there."[20]

Biographer Gary Fountain, who uncovered this important Walnut Hill material, asks pointedly, "How much did Elizabeth know at this time about her mother?" In response Fountain cites Frani Blough Muser, Bishop's closest friend at both Walnut Hill and, later, Vassar College, "Elizabeth told me that her mother was in an institution. Then she never mentioned it again. Elizabeth felt that fear of inheriting her mother's illness was a horrible thing, but she consciously did not allow it to be a part of her life."[21] In "The Country Mouse" Bishop recalls telling her Worcester friend Emma "in a sentimental voice" that her mother "'went away and left me. . . . She died, too.' Emma was impressed and sympathetic, and I loathed myself." Bishop observes that she loathed herself because she knew she was lying, and "I was aware of falsity and the great power of sentimentality. . . . My mother was not dead. She was in a sanatorium, in another prolonged 'nervous breakdown'" (*EBProse* 31–32). Bishop's self-loathing, quite unmerited, of course, but characteristic of a child's tendency to assume responsibility for what goes wrong, followed her throughout her life, as did a characteristic self-deprecation and an understandable yearning for sympathy and acceptance.

Apparently no one in her childhood attempted, directly at least, to help her to mourn the loss of her father, her mother, or her familiar home in Great Village. Nor did they help her to comprehend and come to terms with the feelings of guilt and abandonment that haunted her as a result of these losses. Instead, she received repeated messages to deny her losses and repress her feelings. Alice Miller argues that, "It is precisely because a child's feelings are so strong that they cannot be repressed without serious consequences. The stronger a prisoner is, the thicker the prison walls have to be, which impede or completely prevent later emotional growth."[22] Bishop would appear to agree, because in this passage, as so often elsewhere in her published and unpublished writings, she claims a direct causal link between quite specific present behavior and the influence of traumatic origins, in this case growing out of unrelieved grief, repressed guilt, and confusion about the propriety of asking for sympathy (via the socially acceptable story that her mother is dead), or speaking the truth (via the forbidden, but factual, story that her mother is "in a sanatorium"). Dr. Famularo suggests that "the child's age and developmental level when the trauma occurs, the kind, duration, and severity of the trauma, the level of parental support, and the psychiatric condition of the parents or other caregivers"[23] may all affect the extent and severity of post-traumatic stress disorder. Given Bishop's very early age, the lack of emotional support or acknowledgment she received from caregivers, particularly after her removal from Great Village, and the psychiatric condition of her one surviving parent, these criteria would suggest that Bishop faced an uphill struggle against the traumatic losses that defined her childhood.

After a series of incidents involving Bishop caused concern for her at the school, Walnut Hill administrator Harriet Farwell wrote to Uncle Jack about a consultation that Farwell had initiated, on her own responsibility, with a certain Dr. Taylor, a woman psychiatrist with offices in Boston. "[Dr. Taylor] did not seem to be worried at all about Elizabeth's heredity. The fact, however, that Elizabeth probably has repressed within her a certain amount of information about her mother, she did consider very serious."

Farwell continued, "I feel very sure myself, in fact, I may say positively that Elizabeth knows some if not all of the truth about her mother. It does not make much difference whether it is some or all—either would be enough to make her very unhappy and keep her in an abnormal state of mind. Dr. Taylor feels very decidedly that submerged facts of this kind are dangerous and should be brought out into the open."[24] Bishop's Uncle Jack finally agreed, at Dr. Taylor's insistence, that the truth should be shared with Bishop. But when Dr. Taylor finally met with her, Bishop refused to speak.

Bishop would later acknowledge in a letter to her first biographer, Anne Stevenson, that these sessions were an "excellent idea," but they had to be discontinued because "Unfortunately, I clammed up and wouldn't talk at all." Brett Millier adds, regarding this unsuccessful attempt at therapy, that "Her teachers at Vassar later made the same suggestion, which she refused."[25]

John Bowlby, the British pioneer of attachment theory, commented in 1988 that, "The belief that children are unable to mourn can . . . be seen to derive from generalizations that had been made from the analyses of children whose mourning had followed an atypical course. In many cases this had been due either to the child never having been given adequate information about what had happened, or else to there having been no one to sympathize with him and help him gradually to come to terms with his loss, his yearning for his lost parent, his anger, and his sorrow."[26] In the above statement, Bowlby seems almost to be reciting the documentary evidence defining Bishop's specific circumstances in relation to the loss of her mother. By her Uncle Jack's own testimony, she was never given adequate information about her mother's breakdown nor did she have anyone to sympathize with her or help her come gradually to terms with her grief. Her refusal to speak to psychologists about her losses suggests that an imperative to maintain silence about central emotional issues had been most firmly ingrained from an early age, and that she had learned to direct her grief and anger and sorrow over her losses inward, upon herself. Yet there was always an element in Bishop of humorous resilience. Richard Howard would remember that, later in Bishop's life, "Adrienne Rich had been to see Elizabeth in Boston and had attempted to persuade her to be more forthcoming about her sexual orientation. Elizabeth did not regard the enterprise with favor. After Adrienne's visit, I remember her describing her new domesticities at Lewis Wharf, 'You know what I want, Richard? I want closets, closets and more closets!' And she laughed."[27]

Bishop would only gradually be able to disclose and explore these painfully repressed experiences in her work, and never without some indirection except in unpublished work, such as the most aggressively critical of her prose pieces, "The Country Mouse." This never appeared in her lifetime, even though the paternal grandparents whose behavior it questions were long dead by the time she completed it in 1960. She would similarly suppress or leave uncompleted much of the most personal of her poetry, such as a number of explicitly erotic poems and that harrowing reminiscence of early childhood "A Drunkard."

Bishop's private feelings of enforced self-constraint and emotional displacement remain alive in an unsettling unpublished poem that exists in a single draft in the Vassar College archive, a typescript that has written above it, in Bishop's hand, "(Poem from 1935)," the year after her mother's death in the Dartmouth, N. S. sanitarium into which she had disappeared so quickly and permanently and from which she never emerged alive.

> The past
> at least
> is polite
> it keeps out of sight.
>
> The present
> is more recent.
> It makes a fuss
> but is unselfconscious.

These quatrains bounce along, quite cheerfully, it seems, with their short, mostly one-foot lines, and oddly slant rhymes, until the line "but is unselfconscious"—a near tongue-twister of a line that sounds anything but unselfconscious, slowing the reader down and preparing one for the fall, which arrives in the third and last quatrain.

> The future
> sinks through water
> fast as stone,
> alone alone.[28]

Written the year after Bishop left Vassar and never published, this well-mannered yet penetrating and ineffably sad little lyric articulates the constrained and isolated psychological position of Bishop's early life. Despite her terrible early losses, Bishop felt that her past must be expected to "keep out of sight," and her present, even when it made a fuss, as it sometimes did, should never be self-conscious, at least in public, about its feelings or behavior. In the face of these implicit demands for silence and good manners, undermined by the unhealed losses she had already experienced, the future must often have seemed to be sinking "through water / fast as a stone." In this it resembled her own mother Gertrude's life, for Gertrude disappeared almost without a trace. In effect she became an unperson in Bishop's world, leaving her daughter Elizabeth both haunted by her own lack of power to shape that future and sensible of being truly "alone alone."

It is hardly surprising in light of her upbringing that as an artist Bishop would be known for her reticence. In her life, the past might be induced to politely keep "out of sight," but in Bishop's poetry and self-exploratory prose its effects would be felt, and perhaps even be intensified, by her skillful management, in poem after poem, of the conflict between emotional constraint and the emergence of symptomatic reminders of traumatic loss and of uncomfortable, repressed truths. In a 1935 notebook, Bishop would write of herself in her tiny, pinched, steeply slanted, and nearly illegible hand that "My friendly circumstances, my 'good fortune,' surround me so well & safely, & only *I* am wrong, inadequate. It is a situation like one of those solid crystal balls with little silvery objects inside: thick, clear, appropriate glass—only the little object, me, is sadly flawed and shown off as inferior to the setting."[29] In one of her Brazilian interviews, which were always franker about her emotional life than her American interviews, Bishop acknowledges that "teaching as I am now doing, I have to keep up a happy front. See, the Americans from New England are great hypocrites. It's part of tradition not to show one's feelings. But sometimes I show mine."[30] Bishop's "reticence" has what Octavio Paz called its "enormous power"[31] because she is able to suggest—perhaps without consciously intending to—the painful depths that lurk beneath her brilliantly polished, "polite" surfaces. She suggests these depths of emotion through the deployment of carefully selected, emblematic details set out against a culturally telling background. As Bishop's oeuvre developed, the past might try to keep politely out of sight, but it never completely succeeds. Bishop once told an interviewer, "Poetry should be as unconscious as possible."[32] The force of the past, lodged deep in the unconscious, keeps reemerging just enough to electrify Bishop's poetry with an enormous sense of latent emotional, moral, and metaphysical power.

## Jarrell and the Family Drama

By 1927, when Bishop as a sixteen-year-old boarding school student published her tragicomically allegorical "Ballad of the Subway Train," Jarrell, just thirteen, was experiencing his own traumatic expulsion from a place he would later remember as a "lost paradise of the childish past." This "Lost World," as he later termed it, was an actual place: a home, complete with toys, a favorite rabbit, and affectionate grandparents on a "Street off Sunset" in Hollywood, California. In 1925, when Jarrell was eleven, his young parents' always-shaky marriage had come apart. The couple separated, and Jarrell's mother left southern California, taking Jarrell and his younger brother back to her home town, Nashville. Soon, however, Jarrell returned alone to California at the request of his father. There, as his widow Mary Jarrell recalled, he "stayed on in Hollywood with his grandparents and great-grandmother on his father's side, who are the Mama and Pop and Dandeen of 'The Lost World.' He was with these old-fashioned people for about a year and the poem says they delighted in *this last child* of theirs *in pride or bewilderment.*" Here was a haven of the imagination, where the young Jarrell might spend the day with his grandfather as he worked in the property department of a film studio or could visit Tawny, the MGM lion. Here his inner life was indulged. He never wanted to leave Hollywood or return to his mother in drab Nashville.

Then, in June of 1927—the same month that Berryman's father met his violent, ambiguous death—Jarrell's mother finally came to California to insist on his return and his grandparents agreed to give him up. This came as a traumatic blow to the young Randall, an experience that emphasized his powerlessness in a way that strikingly parallels Bishop's removal from the enchanting world of Great Village. Jarrell's moment of recognition, in which he faced his own powerlessness and loss so starkly, would be relived frequently in his mature poetry, through the eyes of various dramatis personae: particularly soldiers, women, and children confronting and at least partially recognizing their own crises of dispossession.

Jarrell's "And did she dwell in innocence and joy," published in 1935 in the initial issue of the *Southern Review* when Jarrell was just twenty-one, is an apprentice piece, a poem he never chose to republish. But it remains a revealing artifact of Jarrell's intellectual and emotional development, for, like Bishop's "Ballad," it prefigures the main conflicts that would shape Jarrell's career. Jarrell described Wordsworth "as one of the three or four greatest of English poets" (*KA&Co* 220), yet Jarrell was also drawn to Freud and drank deeply of the Viennese master's prose. "And did she dwell" vividly enacts a then-still-unresolved conflict between Wordsworthian and Freudian myths of the child.

The history books, while largely ignoring the reemergence of childhood in the poetry that followed modernism, have been much more ready to take note of the importance of childhood to such first generation English romantics, already mentioned, as Wordsworth, Coleridge, and Blake. The romantic vision of paradise, embodied in the remembered state of childhood, personalized the paradisal myth romantic poets found in the Bible and Milton by relocating it in one's own remembered past. A second English generation dominated by Keats, Shelley, and Byron largely ignored childhood experience, and childhood was also overlooked by English Victorians poets of high endeavor, though a valorization of the child pervaded Victorian culture more generally. Lowell noted this phenomenon, stating that, by contrast with Wordsworth, "There's no childhood or adolescence in Arnold."[33]

According to this now-familiar myth of romanticism, the childhood state is recollected and yearned for as a lost paradise. Wordsworth works out the dynamics of this process most explicitly in his "Ode: Intimations of Immortality from Recollections of Early Childhood," the locus classicus for a romantic view of childhood. Here Wordsworth posits childhood as a transient but near-Edenic state, remembered and celebrated as a time when

> The earth, and every common sight,
> To me did seem
> Appareled in celestial light."[34]

For a romantic poet like Wordsworth, the child's "visionary gleam" fades inevitably "into the light of common day." It is lost, not through sin, but as a consequence of growing older. To age is to fall—into adulthood. Nearly five decades after the publication of Wordsworth's "Ode," Thoreau paid homage to this well-established conception of the child as standing outside of time, intuitively wise, uncorrupted by society, still in touch with "eternity": "Time is but the stream I go a-fishing in. I drink at it; but while I drink I see the sandy bottom and detect how shallow it is. Its thin current slides away, but eternity remains. I would drink deeper; fish in the sky, whose bottom is pebbly with stars. I cannot count one. I know not the first letter of the alphabet. I have always been regretting that I was not as wise as the day I was born."[35]

According to Alfred Kazin, "To Randall, 'Wordsworth' was not a name, a career—all he is to most cultivated people; he was not a writer whose style and central vision of life one might 'like' or 'disagree' with or 'enjoy'. . . . Wordsworth was a fundamental stage through which the human imagination had to pass; he incarnated fundamental virtù; he was a metaphor of human progress; he was the sacred wood through which Randall's childhood had passed."[36] The Wordsworthian adult of the "Intimations Ode," trapped in a state of imaginative poverty, finds loss where he would dearly love to find childhood rematerialized. The adult *can* rematerialize childhood, it seems, but only evanescently, through a process of imaginative remembering. To recover these "shadowy recollections" is to forge the first link in a chain leading back toward the recovery of imaginative and poetic power. The same might be said for the conception of childhood worked out by Bishop, Lowell, Jarrell, and their contemporaries.

M. H. Abrams suggests that the conception guiding Wordsworth, Coleridge, and Blake toward their vision of the child was the work of a Continental thinker: Jean-Jacques Rousseau. "Modern preoccupation with the experience of childhood has usually, and with some justification, been traced primarily to Rousseau, who wrote, for example, in *Èmile*, 'Nature wants children to be children before they are men. . . . Childhood has ways of seeing, thinking and feeling peculiar to itself; nothing can be more foolish than to substitute our ways for them.'"[37]

In *Centuries of the Child*, Philippe Ariès argues that Rousseau's writings on the theme of childhood and education were aspects of a larger cultural shift, indeed, a revolution in the way childhood was perceived. According to Ariès, in earlier centuries children had been viewed as miniature men or as savage pre-adults, without a distinct existence or consciousness separate from adult consciousness. By the end of the eighteenth century, however, childhood had come to be viewed as a unique phase of human development. Crucial to this conception was the then-new concept of the innocence of the child. The early years of childhood had previously been conceived as an immodest or even savage state predating the age of reason, when moral scruples might be learned. Now, these early years could be reconceived as a presexual and presocial stage whose innocence must be cherished and preserved. Hence Rousseau's assertion that "God makes all things good; man meddles with them and they become evil."[38]

One by-product of this cultural shift was the emergence, for the first time, of a poetics of childhood. Wordsworth's poetry takes Rousseau's conception of the innocence of the child a crucial step further, seeing in childhood not just a distinct and more innocent mode of consciousness, but a privileged state of awareness. For Wordsworth, the child's vision is not merely distinct from the adult's. The child offers a model of imaginative and intuitive perception whose freshness and rightness the mature poet must seek to recapture.

But in the mid-1930s Jarrell was equally devoted to Freud. He majored in psychology for most of his undergraduate career at Vanderbilt University, and he planned a future as a psychoanalyst. Berryman's first wife, Eileen, herself studying for a career as a psychologist, recalled a 1946 conversation with Jarrell: "With Randall that evening, as later, psychology was our subject. His knowledge of the father of psychoanalysis—'a man / sick of too much sweetness'—was broader and deeper than that of many analysts. He knew pages of Freud the way he knew Yeats, Proust, and Tolstoy—by heart."[39]

The opening line in Jarrell's untitled 1935 poem "And did she dwell in innocence and joy" unmistakably echoes Wordsworth's Lucy poems, especially "She dwelt among the untrodden ways," while posing pointed questions about the reality of that Wordsworthian innocence, that joy, where she *seems* "loved, cared-for, a happy child." As in many of his later poems, Jarrell explores his own emotional issues through a feminine persona. Jarrell suggests that had this child ever "lived in splendor and in light" it was only transiently and unknowingly. She must inevitably confront, before she is cognitively prepared, a necessary expulsion from the bliss of precognition:

> But she must strangle in some hooded doom,
> Sheet in vain rhetoric their reader names,
> And, falling, lament the kingdom of the clouds
> (*RJPoems* 423)

Jarrell's innocent girl-child becomes, like Bishop's dragons, a premature exile from paradise. Yet here there seems an explicitly psychoanalytic interposition, given the sense that she will repress this fall, and "afterwards struggle blindly to regain / the most ignorant and most savage moment of her life," which appears to be a Freudian-oedipal lapse from innocence. Here the child's wishful fantasies begin to confront intransigent realities without adjusting to them, and here, apparently, adult neurosis begins to grow. Attempting to articulate what Freud poetically termed the "imperishable repressed wishful impulses of childhood" by reaching back for those "almost invariably forgotten memory-traces" and making "them conscious" through verse, the writer is responding to a

Freudian imperative that in some measure parallels but also contradicts the Wordsworthian imperative to search the "embers" of the past for "something that does live." Rich in Wordsworthian echoes, Jarrell's apprentice poem struggles to articulate an anguished post-Freudian critique of Wordsworth. Yet this early and opaque study of the exiled child is just the earliest in a long series of Jarrellian studies that would focus with increasing clarity and power on a child's specific individual and cultural circumstances. And in this Jarrell was moving from somewhat opaque beginnings toward a penetrating exploration of the power-position or powerlessness of the child.

According to Mary Jarrell, "The household in 'A Street off Sunset' did reassure and guarantee so much in the interim before Randall's mother sent for him. . . . Randall told me he hated to leave. 'How I cried!' he said. And he'd begged them so hard to keep him that when they wouldn't—or couldn't—he blamed them for being cruel and resolved never to think about them again or write them a word. Later on he wrote them a poem instead (though they may not have lived to read it), 'A Story.'"[40]

In this early sestina, published in 1939, Jarrell explores the feelings of abandonment of a small boy sent away to boarding school. Referring to this poem, Jarrell wrote to his former sweetheart Amy Breyer, "I've lived all over, and always been separated from at least half of a very small family, and been as alone as children ever are. . . . I guess nobody else but you would know *A Story* is autobiography. I wrote it with 'I' meaning 'we' for a couple of stanzas before I thought out the story, and then the emotion was certainly mine."[41] Jarrell could not forgive his grandparents for giving him up, and he refused ever to write to them. In "The Lost World," after identifying his great-grandmother with the frightened "little girl" she once remembered being, he regrets the way he neglected her old age:

> real remorse
> Hurts me, here, now: the little girl is crying
> Because I didn't write. Because—
>
> of course,
> I *was* a child, I missed them so.
>
> (*RJPoems* 291)

He can feel his great-grandmother's pain now if he thinks of her, too, as a powerless child. In any case, Jarrell identifies here and elsewhere with powerless individuals who had suffered grievous loss His exploration of their condition was artistically empowering in the same way that Wordsworth regained artistic empowerment by imaginatively recovering his own childhood.

Until very late in his life, Jarrell maintained near-total silence about his childhood in Hollywood—much more so, in fact, than the purportedly reticent Bishop did about her losses in Great Village and Worcester. Jarrell's teacher and close friend John Crowe Ransom, who had known him by then for over thirty years, admitted after Jarrell's death that he was not alone in doubting the veracity of the Hollywood locale of Jarrell's "The Lost World" when it was first published in *Poetry* in 1963.

> It was my impression, and that of my friends, that Randall had spent all of his childhood at Nashville, yet the recitals of the little boy in the poem assumed that the place was Hollywood. Was it a responsible autobiographer who had transferred the scene to Hollywood, because there was more enticing excitement there? But by great luck I was informed, unimpeachably, that Randall had lived as a child for a year or so with his grandparents and great-grandmother, in Hollywood itself. I was chastened of my ugly suspicions. (*RJ1914* 178)

Jarrell's forced removal from a home where he was nurtured and happy was a loss was so great that he would not—or, perhaps, could not—speak of it even to a father-figure like the man he always called "Mr. Ransom." In Nashville the boy found a world entirely different from the "lost paradise" of Hollywood. According to Mary Jarrell, "Randall said, he was 'covered with relatives.' The Campbells (pronounced Cam'll) were an intimate, dominating family of strong wills, the whole of which was not as formidable as its parts. None of them was a listener or a relaxed person, but each on his own level was effective and, as Randall's mother said, 'left tracks'" (*RJ1914* 285). Chief among these relations was his uncle Howell Campbell, his mother's brother, the wealthy founder of the Bell-Camp Candy Company, maker of Goo-Goo Bars, a chocolate-peanut-caramel confection, and a long-time sponsor of "The Grand Ole Opry."

Randall was painfully conscious of his inferior position as the offspring of a poor relation, a child dependent on his uncle's charity. As Mary Jarrell recalls, "In Campbell minds, Randall was expected to Be a Little Man and to aim toward supporting his mother, which, unhappily for Randall, Uncle Howell had done at a very early age" (*RJ1914* 285). Jarrell's father was still alive, but he too was absent, in the "lost world" of California. Jarrell felt that he lost his mother, Anna, too, when she remarried some years later and became Anna Regan. Mary Jarrell recalled that when she told Randall's mother, who was extremely pretty and considered herself a southern belle, that she looked a lot like Randall, her reply was, "I don't look like Randall. Randall looks like me." According to Mary Jarrell, his mother "never ceased criticizing him, belittling him," even in adulthood. Mary Jarrell recalled, for instance, that his mother told Jarrell that she "hated" his beard, which "gave her nightmares."[42] According to Randall's widow, Mary Jarrell, the Campbell family's life revolved around the country club. They placed scant value on young Randall's remarkable literary precocity, his imagination and curiosity, and his acute social conscience. In response, according Mary Jarrell, Randall locked his bedroom door whenever he sat down to write.[43]

Richard Flynn suggests that the rejection was still more disturbing and went deeper. Flynn, author of *Randall Jarrell and the Lost World of Childhood*, has studied Jarrell's early years more closely than any previous scholar. He offers the following account of Jarrell's relationship with his mother.

> Jarrell's mother, Anna, was married at age sixteen, and apparently was quite unstable. Abandoned by her husband . . . and left to raise two young boys, she was subject to fainting spells, often boarding her children with better-off relatives. She seemed to swing between smothering her children with affection or ignoring them (Mary Jarrell, interview with the author, 12 June 1984). In his adolescence, according to Mary Jarrell, Randall often went to the movies on Saturday night with his mother, and was pleased when his friends thought she was his date. There is no direct testimony or evidence that child abuse, repeatedly alluded to in the poetry, ever took place, but "A Little Poem," "Variations," and "The Bad Music" (the latter addressed to "You, Anna") depict abusive mothers as metaphors of a horrifying and abusive world.[44]

We may never know all the salient details of Jarrell's childhood about which Jarrell, though obsessed with childhood experience, had so little to say for so many years. Jarrell was just beginning to write more directly about some of the less painful aspects of that childhood when he died, suddenly, and at the peak of his powers, in 1965. Thus students of Jarrell lack the detailed account provided, for example, by Bishop and Lowell's extensive published and unpublished prose memoirs or by Berryman's hundreds of long and at times unconsciously revealing letters to his mother. Mary Jarrell recalled that she and Randall were shocked to learn when they returned from a trip to Europe that Jarrell's mother, who was caring for Mary's fourteen- and sixteen-year-old daughters, had insisted on personally bathing them.[45] Several of Jarrell's poems depicting abuse involve scenes of a mother bathing a child. Whether this is mere coincidence or evidence of a largely suppressed abusive pattern, it remains clear that Jarrell's conflicted feelings toward his family, and particularly toward his mother Anna, haunted him in later life and shaped his work.

## Jarrell's "The House in the Woods"

Bishop had employed what Berryman termed "parable form" as early as her 1927 "Ballad" for the purposes of dramatizing self-exploration, and she would continue to work within parable structures throughout the 1930s, during the course of a series of fables of enclosure including "The Man-Moth," "The Unbeliever," "The Gentleman of Shallot," "The Imaginary Iceberg," and such stories as "In Prison" and "The Sea and its Shore." But Jarrell was perhaps still more given, in later years, to exploit the psychological possibilities latent in parables. In these, unlike in "allegory forms," as Berryman points out, "There is no point-to-point correspondence, the details are free" (*JBProse* 320). Parable forms continue to function for Jarrell in such mature reconfigurations of the Brothers Grimm as "The House in the Wood" (1964), a late parable that journeys back toward the most distant memory traces to explore the ache latent in a core relationship with the witch-mother. Here is a poem that achieves a complex affect with remarkably simple diction. Moreover, it pursues physical and psychological motion along

> paths I can walk, when I wake, to good
>
> Or evil: to the cage, to the oven, to the House
> In the Wood.
>
> (*RJPoems* 322)

These paths lead one back toward a "part of life, or of the story / We make of life" (*RJPoems* 322). Jarrell here suggests that we can, and often do, make a story of life, turning life into a narrative with a shape and purpose: with a beginning, middle, and end, and with interpretable meaning or meanings. Here Jarrell finds a way of connecting the story he wants to tell with an old tale with familiar furniture: "the cage, . . . the oven, . . . , the House / In the Wood." And this leads the reader into established myth and symbol systems, while opening up the possibility of serious pastiche or creative retelling.

> But after the last leaf,
> The last light—for each year is leafless,
>
> Each day lightless, at the last—the wood begins
> Its serious existence: it has no path,
>
> No house, no story; it resists comparison . . .
>
> (*RJPoems* 322)

Thus the poem quietly embarks on what will prove a harrowing journey into the interior of the self. Yet it creates, very much, its own atmosphere.

> If I walk into the wood
>
> As far as I can walk, I come to my own door,
> The door of the House in the Wood. It opens silently:
>
> On the bed is something covered, something humped
> Asleep there, awake there—but what? I do not know.
>
> I look, I lie there, and yet I do not know.
>
> (*RJPoems* 322)

Jarrell opens the door to the unconscious and confronts what has been "repressed out of existence,"[46] his own early, helpless consciousness, which is so familiar, so close to the bone, that it remains difficult, if not impossible, to recognize. This poem, with its quieter, more uncanny language, places us in a more clearly visualized version of the primal scene Jarrell had long ago treated in "And did she dwell in innocence and joy." At the same time it draws on elements from "A Quilt Pattern" (1953), including the allusions to Hansel and Gretel; the presence of a boy hunched in bed, pretending to sleep; and an adult version of that boy, looking back and attempting to recover the past's obscure and elusive image. The poem contains, as well, a mother figure identified as the witch. This is a "reality" that Eliot said humankind could not bear very much of, where space and time lose their relevance.

> How far out my great echoing clumsy limbs
>
> Stretch, surrounded only by space! For time has struck,
> All the clocks are stuck now, for how many lives,
>
> On the same second.
>
> (*RJPoems* 322–23)

This reality runs very deep and very still, for here, "Numbed, wooden, motionless, / We are far under the surface of the night," and only faint reminders filter in from the external world of time and motion.

Nothing comes down so deep but sound: a car, freight cars,
  A high soft droning, drawn out like a wire

Forever and ever—is this the sound that Bunyan heard
  So that he thought his bowels would burst within him?—

Drift on, on, into nothing.

(*RJPoems* 323)

When Bunyan heard that sound he was on the verge of an overwhelming moment of conversion, and here, too, in a sense, a psychological, rather than religious, conversion seems on the verge of happening.

Then someone screams
A scream like an old knife sharpened into nothing.

It is only a nightmare. No one wakes up, nothing happens,
  Except there is gooseflesh over my whole body—

And that too, after a little while, is gone.
  I lie here like a cut-off limb, the stump the limb has left . . .

(*RJPoems* 323)

In this poem, where the identity of the humped form has now definitively settled down into the first-person singular, and the self is like "a cut-off limb," the image of the sharpened blade recalls the earlier one in Bishop's "Fishhouses" (1951), a blade on an old fisherman's "black old knife" that "is almost worn away." We know Jarrell read Bishop carefully—he commented on this poem in a letter to Lowell, when it first appeared in *Partisan Review* as well as in his review of *Poems.* And curiously both poems associate the image of this "old knife sharpened into nothing" with an impulsive yearning for comfort and nurture from the mother—in Bishop's case through an image of knowledge that is "derived from the rocky breasts forever," those breasts existing at the bottom of a North Atlantic inshore sea that is "cold, dark, deep, and absolutely clear." The problem of finding out what knowledge is, getting down to some source, is indeed the driving force in both poems, which involve imagery of descent from a natural world that is specifically characterized into a deeper world that is more uncanny and symbolic. Jarrell continues,

Here at the bottom of the world, what was before the world
And will be after, holds me to its black

Breasts and rocks me: the oven is cold, the cage is empty,
In the House in the Wood, the witch and her child sleep.

(*RJPoems* 323)

The murderous witch who is burned to death by Hansel and Gretel, becomes the good mother, gently rocking herself and the child to sleep, in the final stanzas of "The House in the Woods." In these stanzas, Jarrell combines terror and comfort into a paradox that defies rational explication. Berryman, who also had reason to fear his mother, would suggest of his own *Dream Songs* that, "These Songs are not meant to be understood, you understand. / They are only meant to terrify & comfort" (*DS* 366). Karl Shapiro has aptly remarked, "Our poets when they deal in the myths do as Jarrell did, following Rilke and other modern artists, analyze and psychologize Orestes or Orpheus. We understand without belief. This is the opposite of using comparative mythology in order to revive and enforce belief, as Eliot did. Our poetry studies behavior and leads us back to the child. With Jarrell, too, the child becomes the critic and the center of value."[47] Jarrell's poem is an exploration of the problems of selfhood in the postmodern world, and his child is an exile, and explorer, and critic, because the child embodies neither a luminous, transcendental vision nor a reasserted myth. Instead, it dramatizes a tentative *process* of experience, leading back through uncertainty toward the ambiguously knowable sources of loss, trauma, and torment. And the child is a center of value because the child's naiveté and vulnerability reflect and amplify the adult's.

In a 1956 letter, Lowell would paint for Bishop—then living in Brazil—an amused and affectionate portrait of the environment their friend Jarrell had created for himself while he served as Poetry Consultant to the Library of Congress, a job that Lowell and Bishop had each held previously.

> Well, Randall! Like the earth he carries his atmosphere with him and is no different in Washington than he is in Greensboro. In the office he has his big Degas, Munch, Klee and Vuillard (?) reproductions and a spectacled photograph, like a picture of one's wife and baby, in a leather frame on his desk: Chekov [*sic*]. At his home in Chevy Chase he has big reproductions of Klee, Degas, Munch, etc. Photographs in the shadowy hall of Wallace Stevens and Marianne Moore and on his desk another photograph—this time without spectacles—of Checkov [*sic*]. . . . Randall is in grand shape and is enjoying the library. . . . He sounds like Bernard Shaw when quoted in the papers. He also has a little white patch in his beard and is ageless—almost. Lonely and wonderful.[48]

Jarrell, who felt ignored, slighted, and, perhaps, threatened as a child, learned to "carry his atmosphere with him," arranging around himself the sacred images of the high art he knew so well, and loved, as an apparent shield against early feelings of insignificance, vulnerability, and powerlessness—

feelings he would never entirely get over despite the many marks of public success and esteem he earned in later life. Jarrell's "transitional objects," as D. W. Winnicott terms them, allowed Jarrell to recreate his identity, surrounded by his "chosen family," no matter where he happened to be.

Yet such a vicariously and imaginatively constructed family could leave Jarrell embattled and "lonely," as Lowell recognized, as well as "wonderful." Jarrell would never cease his search for elective families. Shortly after his return to Nashville in 1927, Jarrell posed for the sculptors of the frieze over the Nashville Parthenon as the figure of Ganymede. According to Mary Jarrell, "Long afterwards his mother said the sculptors had asked to adopt him, but knowing how attached to them he was she hadn't dared tell him. 'She was right,' Randall said bitterly, 'I'd have gone with them like *that*.'"[49]

Elizabeth Bishop said that "I was very isolated as a child and perhaps poetry was my way of making familiar what I saw around me."[50] Like Bishop, Jarrell grew up as a person of great emotional reticence who sought a reflection of and release for his feelings in art. Also, like Bishop, Jarrell was engaged in a lifelong struggle with the emotional legacy left from growing up in the shadow of an absent father and a terrifying mother.

Robert Lowell said without exaggeration that, as a critic, Jarrell had "a deadly hand for killing what he despised" (*RLProse* 91). Jarrell became famous for his incisive skewerings of bad poets, and he was as precise and as fearless as he was witty. Jarrell said that the work of one poet "gave the impression of having been written on a typewriter by a typewriter." He said of Joyce Kilmer, "Some of Kilmer's poems are better than 'Trees,' but not enough for it to matter. He calls the Milky Way 'Main Street, Heaventown,' and ends a Thanksgiving poem, 'And Oh, thank God for God!' But I do not want to give the impression that his poems are unusually absurd—unusually anything; if they had not existed, it would only have been necessary to copy them" (*KA&Co* 38). Jarrell's laceration of the bad—which, as Lowell put it, always had "a patient, intuitive, unworldly certainty"—was, of course, the least significant part of his activity as a critic. Lowell was right to insist that "eulogy was the glory of Randall's criticism. Eulogies that not only impressed readers with his own enthusiasms, but which also, time and again, changed and improved opinions and values. He left many reputations permanently altered and exalted" (*RLProse* 92). Yet there is something uncanny about the way Jarrell uttered those devastating condemnations—with a clairvoyant aptness and memorable finality that some claimed went as far as symbolic murder. Jarrell, who felt so powerless and slighted as a child, later felt compelled to exercise, with a remarkable mixture of canny professionalism, impeccable taste, and childlike candor, his own brand of stern but exact justice in literature, a realm in which he could achieve real authority and power.

Jarrell argued early in his career that modernism was "an extension of romanticism, an end product in which most of the tendencies of romanticism have been carried to their limits" (*KA&Co* 77). But an important difference was that modernist poets continued the general avoidance of childhood found among such eminent Victorians as Arnold, Browning, and Tennyson. The only modernist poet to write more than fleetingly from the perspective of the child was E. E. Cummings, who relied on modernist techniques to give new life to a vision of childhood as a joyful state where

> eddieandbill come
> running from marbles and
> piracies and it's
> spring.[51]

Jarrell found this joyful vision unconvincing—even repellent. For him, "there is a great big moral vacuum at the heart of E. E. Cummings's poetry. As Louise Bogan has written, with summary truth: 'It is this deletion of the tragic that makes Cummings's joy childish and his anger petulant.' What delights and amuses and disgusts us he has represented; but all that is heartbreaking in the world, the pity and helplessness and love that were called, once, the tears of things, the heart of heartlessness—these hardly exist for him" (*KA&Co* 168).

For Jarrell, whom Lowell called "the most heartbreaking English poet of his generation,"[52] a modern poetics of childhood that failed to represent "all that is heartbreaking" was inadmissible. Late in Lowell's life, Helen Vendler recalled crossing Harvard Yard with him, bandying epithets such as "violent" and "comic" that reviewers had recently applied to his work. Lowell confessed dissatisfaction with these terms. "'Why don't they ever say what I'd like them to say?' he protested. 'What's that?' I asked. 'That I'm heartbreaking,' he said, meaning it."[53] When Lowell called Jarrell, his fellow explorer of lost worlds, "heartbreaking," he meant it as high praise.

## Knowledge and Art in Berryman's "Ball Poem"

In 1927, when Bishop's "Ballad" was published and when the thirteen-year-old Jarrell was forced by his mother to return to Nashville, another thirteen-year-old boy had recently experienced a traumatic "departure" of his own. Baptized under the name of John Allyn Smith, this boy was the son and namesake of a failed small-time Florida entrepreneur, John Allyn Smith, Sr. But in 1927 the boy had just moved from Florida to New York with his mother and a new stepfather, John Angus Berryman. Adopting his stepfather's surname, the young John Allyn Smith became John Berryman.

Berryman's natural father had been killed the previous year, on 26 June 1926, by a .32 caliber pistol bullet fired through the heart. According to the coroner's investigation, his father's case was routine, an obvious suicide. The coroner did not attempt to account for the absence of powder burns on John Smith's chest, although biographer Paul Mariani suggests that this absence was "impossible in the case of a self-inflicted wound," a problem also raised by Berryman's previous biographer, John Haffenden.[54] Berryman's first wife, Eileen Simpson, remarked of this event in her unusually sensitive and insightful memoir *Poets in Their Youth*, "The circumstance of his death I heard recounted so often, and so variously, that to this day they remain a puzzle."[55]

Berryman remained haunted by doubts about the role his mother and step-father played in his father's death. As an adult, Berryman found—unlike Bishop or Lowell, whose memories were remarkably visceral and detailed—that virtually his whole childhood had been expunged beyond recall. "'*So few memories!!*' [Berryman would] lament . . . in 1970, while conceding that he retained 'enough feelings to dominate' the *Dream Songs*."[56]

When Berryman told his first wife Eileen of his father's death, "Throughout the narration he behaved, as I told him, as if he were confessing a crime *he* had committed, as if he were responsible for his father's death." Berryman felt intense guilt over allowing himself to be adopted by his mother's lover. "Should he not," Eileen recalls him wondering, "have protested out of loyalty to his dead father? He did not, and his name became John Berryman. 'A good name for a poet, isn't it? Well it's a damn lie. My real name is ludicrously unpoetic. It is Smith. John Smith.'"[57]

Berryman, soon to become a promising Shakespearean scholar, was faced with a situation strangely like Hamlet's: a mother remarrying too soon; a stepfather whom, perhaps with reason, he did not trust; a father certainly dead and perhaps murdered. But Berryman was younger, had less certainty about the nature of his father's death, and had fewer apparent options than the Prince of Denmark.

He acknowledged, in any case, in later life, that he had repressed most of his own past, including intense anger toward his father, his mother, his stepfather, and himself. Key details of this past were apparently irrecoverable, and his main source of information about that past, his "unspeakably powerful possessive adoring"[58] mother, was conspicuously unreliable. Eileen Simpson, always an acute witness, reports that "In the years to come, I realized that the circumstance of her first husband's death were part of an ever-changing myth she periodically reworked, usually in response to her older son's longing to be convinced that she was not responsible for driving his father to suicide."[59] According to the Freudian framework that informed Berryman's thinking, he was trapped in an emotional, psychological, and epistemological impasse: unable to process and get beyond traumatic experiences, mourn his losses, or know the essential facts of his own life, he was doomed to repeat these losses endlessly.

In this context, Berryman's complex love-hate relationship with Freud becomes understandable. In Freud he found a validation for the importance of repressed childhood experience and an analytical approach to dream life and fantasy that he could deploy to telling effect in his most ambitious poem. But he also encountered in Freud a tendency to dismiss the subject's perhaps genuine experiences of loss and abuse as mere by-products of an unformed, childish imagination.

Alice Miller's analysis, written from much the same perspective toward traditional psychoanalysis, provides a remarkably apt description of the operation of Berryman's best poetry. In this work the reality of the author's unmourned grief, confusion, self-hatred, and futile rage are both disguised and constantly revealed in a "language of symptoms" which is, in fact, the prevailing language of the *Dream Songs*. And Berryman created this language of symptoms in the *Dream Songs*, and assigned that language and these symptoms to Henry, by design. As Berryman put it, Henry "only does what I make him do."[60] To a degree, Henry's symptoms may parallel Berryman's, but here they serve the independent purposes of art. These symptoms are evoked through an invented language: drafts of the *Dream Songs* frequently reveal him changing the conventional phrasing of an earlier version into the childlike or bizarre final text. For example, in a draft of "Dream Song 26," Berryman corrects his opening line from the conventional "The glories of the world struck me, made my mind sing, once" to "made me aria, once." And the second sestet, which had begun "All the knobs & softnesses of, my God, / the ducking & trouble it was to Henry" becomes, corrected, "the ducking & trouble it swarm on Henry."

Berryman's work, like that of Bishop, Jarrell, and Lowell, persistently brings alive moments of semiopaque psychological intersection, moments when repressed intimations of past traumatic loss emerge in the context of conscious recognition of actual (or threatened) losses in the present. In poems dramatizing moments of blinding or staggering self-recognition, the figure of the poet—a specific historical personage with a name, a curriculum vitae, and a public and private history—may be variously and complexly implicated. Or this identity may, for personal or artistic reasons, be held in reserve. In a 1965 survey of key developments in his own career titled "One Answer to a Question: Changes," Berryman recounts how in "The Ball Poem" (1942), more than two decades earlier, he first found means to exploit the unsettling drama of psychological intersection.

Berryman first printed "The Ball Poem" privately in December 1942, when he was twenty-eight, as the first in a pamphlet titled *Two Poems*. The newly wed Berrymans sent this pamphlet to friends, as Eileen Simpson later recalled, "in lieu of Christmas gifts which, this year, we couldn't afford."[61] "The Ball Poem" observes a boy who has dropped his rubber ball and who watches, along with the poem's adult speaker, as the ball goes "Merrily bouncing, down the street, and then / Merrily over—there it is in the water!" Here is a clear example, as Bishop put it in an earlier poem admired by Berryman, of a moment of intersection in which "emotion too far exceeds its cause" (*EBPoems* 3). This irretrievable loss of a stock and apparently trivial childhood object triggers a passionate response—in the form of "an ultimate shaking grief"—which so "fixes the boy" that, for the first time, he faces, "well behind his desperate eyes," the problem of "first responsibility / In a world of possessions," and with it, a recognition of the primacy of human loss. The intensity of the child-protagonist's response to his trifling loss is by no means dismissed by the poet-as-empathetic-observer, for it clearly grows out of the frightening, indeed overwhelming, emergence of repressed emotion.

By presenting the ball as an object of symbolic transference, a memory-trace bobbing to the surface, Berryman was finding artistic means to explore repressed emotion, just as Bishop had done much earlier in the "Ballad of the Subway Train." In a famous passage of which Berryman was no doubt aware, Freud speaks of a boy who repeatedly threw a ball away to reenact the experience of his mother's recurring but temporary absences. He concludes that: "Throwing away the object so that it was 'gone' might satisfy an impulse of the child's, which was suppressed in his actual life, to revenge himself on his mother for going away from him."[62] For the child in Berryman's poem, the "accidental" loss of the ball may be read similarly, as both an act of revenge for his father's departure or his mother's betrayal and as an act of self-punishment. As he watches the ball bounce forever out of reach, the child reenacts earlier and no doubt more grievous losses, whose memory he has repressed. In the process, the boy

> is learning, well behind his desperate eyes,
> The epistemology of loss, how to stand up
> Knowing what every man must one day know
> (*JBPoems* 11)

One would perhaps not normally think of a boy facing up to loss for the first time as an epistemologist, but Berryman implies that as one works through denial and repression and faces one's losses, one begins to question the limits and validity of one's knowledge. Without passing through this process of questioning one may never learn "how to stand up." To be fully human is to experience the "ultimate, shaking grief" attendant upon loss, and it is also to be, in effect, an epistemologist, weighing the relative validity of different potent but uncertain, and perhaps contradictory, knowledge sources. The poem ends with an ambiguous moment that moves through both identification and separation:

> A whistle blows, the ball is out of sight,
> Soon part of me will explore the deep and dark
> Floor of the harbour . . . I am everywhere,
> I suffer and move, my mind and my heart move
> With all that move me, under the water
> Or whistling, I am not a little boy.
> (*JBPoems* 11)

In his 1965 commentary, Berryman pointed to his "discovery here . . . that a commitment of identity can be 'reserved,' so to speak, with an ambiguous pronoun. The poet himself is both left out and put in; the boy does and does not become him and we are confronted with a process which is at once a process of life and a process of art. A pronoun may seem a small matter, but she matters, he matters, it matters, they matter. Without this invention (if it is one . . .) I could not have written the bulk of my work so far" (*JBProse* 326–27). Berryman appears to be promising, in one of his earliest successful poems, to create a mobile, flexible, exploratory aesthetic, a poetry of "mind and heart," that will "suffer and move . . . / With all that move me."

Berryman's lyric posits a troubled epistemology anticipating Alice Miller's, where repressed traumatic realities are not truly effaced but reemerge as symptoms. For Berryman this painful, elusive way of knowing may be brought to life with some immediacy by means of a serious playing with words. Berryman's "Ball Poem" implies that the most meaningful knowledge is—like one's ideas of self-hood or identity—by its nature elusive. It suggests that much of the reality about ourselves that we might hope to know lies buried in the unconscious, lost, forgotten, or hidden under layers of repression, and thus at least partly inaccessible to rational processes. One searches the factual markers—photographs from childhood, for instance,—and one's feeling about objects—like, say, a ten-cent rubber ball—to begin to recover even partial knowledge of one's own intimate history. Such rediscovery is posited as vital for emotional recovery or self-understanding, but this painful knowledge remains accessible only through the most unreliable processes. Berryman's poems enact the drama inherent in these processes.

The companion to this penetrating study of loss was "For His Marriage," which was the second of the privately printed *Two Poems* of 1942. The title suggests that this poem concerns the anxieties any young man might face at the approach of the climactic moment of the wedding ceremony, with all his actions witnessed by a large and eager audience. This anticipation is supported, it would seem, by the opening lines:

> Lilies of the valley
> And the face of the priest.
> The pushing eyes
> Upon my back of guest and guest
> Music, and crush of fear
> I never felt before.

But the poem concludes with a rush of discomfitures that emerge cloaked in gothic horror out of Edgar Allan Poe:

> Resist, resist prest Heart,
> In the breast be still.
> If you can still and stay
> Perhaps I will
> Until comes lover to my side
> The terrifying bride.[63]

It is hard not to read "the terrifying bride" in symbolic terms, as she comes to the bridegroom's side rather like the spirit of Poe's deceased Ligeia rising, in another woman's body, to reclaim her errant consort. Berryman here embodies feelings that have less to do with any fear of the flesh and blood bride whom he was about to marry, and more to do with the feared reentry into his life, at the moment of her apparent dispossession, of that most "terrifying," most oedipal of brides—his own mother. Six years after the publication of *Two Poems,* Berryman would dedicate his first book, *The Dispossessed* (1948), to his mother. And he would also dedicate *Delusions Etc.* (1972), his last, to her: "with passion and awe." This poem's oedipal bride, in all her Ligeian power of infinite reconstitution and transfiguration, merges with that still more terrifying bride—death itself. Indeed, the furniture of the opening lines of the poem, the "lilies of the valley," the "face of the priest," the "music," even "the crush of fear / I never felt before" seem as consistent with a disembodied witnessing of one's own burial rites as with a celebration of one's wedding. In his life, as in his poetry, Berryman found it difficult to experience feelings directly or simply, to separate passion from awe, joy from grief, triumph from failure, love from hate, comfort from terror. And in his poetry, he is not so much confessing his own past as exploring the challenges of mature and independent selfhood through the prism of his own traumatic early experience. In this sense "On His Marriage" powerfully confronts the reader "with a process which is at once a process of life and a process of art." This study, too, will continue to explore the parallels and singular intersections of "a process of life and a process of art" as they operate, in "deep and dark" crosscurrents, throughout the work of these four powerful and original poets. Along the way, it will inquire into the various means by which the figure of the poet has been left out or put in to the poem—the artist's identity committed or "reserved"—in works that creatively, wittily, and painfully explore the most intimate and seemingly inaccessible psychological depths, beneath a surface of vividly realized tangible—or intangible—facts.

## Lowell's "Christmas Eve under Hooker's Statue"

In 1927 Bishop was attending North Shore Country Day School and composing her "Ballad," Jarrell was struggling with the anger and frustration that haunted him after his forced return to Nashville, and John Smith, having recently and violently lost his father, was adjusting to his new name—John Berryman. In that same year, Robert Lowell, a ten-year-old boy growing up in a three-story brick rowhouse on Boston's Beacon Hill, was facing many similar issues: loss, abandonment, emotional abuse, and feelings of powerlessness and moral confusion.

On the face of it, Lowell's situation might seem safer and more stable. His parents remained together and would never divorce. He descended, on both sides, from prominent Boston families and his future education was already marked out for him at such exclusive schools as St. Mark's and Harvard University, each of which could claim an ancestor or living relation as president. Still, his first ten years had been haunted by feelings of marginalization and dispossession that would only intensify. In "91 Revere St.," Lowell recalled his feelings about attending "the boarding school for which I had been enrolled at birth, and was due to enter in 1930. I distrusted change, knew each school since kindergarten had been more constraining and punitive than its predecessor, and believed the suburban country day schools were flimsily disguised fronts for reformatories" (*LS* 28).

As Lowell recalled his life on 91 Revere Street, "I felt drenched in my parents' passions." These passions took the form of ongoing, nightly verbal warfare overheard by the young poet-in-the-making during "the two years my mother spent in trying to argue my father into resigning from the Navy" (*LS* 19). Lowell recalled the "arthritic spiritual pains" of this period, during which "Mother had violently set her heart on the resignation. She was hysterical even in her calm." The wrenching effect of this battle of wills went deep into Lowell's psyche. His father's ultimate defenselessness, which led him to mumble "Yes, yes, yes," in nighttime conversations with his wife overhead by their eavesdropping son, made it clear that his father would not be able to defend his son in case of aggression from his mother, whose presence in various subtle forms was a daily experience for Lowell: "I grew less willing to open my mouth. I bored my parents, they bored me" (*LS* 19). In 1927, Lowell's father finally did resign from the Navy, the one institution in which he seemed to have a place, an identity, and a recognized history. Lowell saw this act as marking his father's voluntary renunciation of the last threads of his masculinity and personal identity. Of his father's attempts to explain his resignation to his naval friends, Lowell recalled "Those dinners, those apologies! Perhaps I exaggerate their embarrassment because they hover so grayly in recollection and seem to anticipate ominously my father's downhill progress as a civilian and Bostonian" (*LS* 43). Lowell's ill-matched parents never divorced, but because of their emotional rejection of him—Lowell would learn from his first psychiatrist, the poet Merrill Moore, that, though an only child, he had been "unwanted"[64]—he experienced an early "expulsion from paradise" without ever leaving the Lowell hearthside.

Lowell's conflicted feeling about the military, about his native Boston and about his father's lack of authority—his moral and emotional absence

—in the face of Lowell's threatening, all-powerful mother, are indirectly represented in "Christmas Eve under Hooker's Statue," published in 1946, when the poet was twenty-nine. "Christmas Eve under Hooker's Statue" begins with a modern scene darkened by the Second World War: "Tonight a blackout," then moves immediately to an explicitly biblical framing of the theme of expulsion from paradise, juxtaposed against the celebratory rituals of Christmas.

Twenty years ago
I hung my stocking on the tree, and hell's
Serpent entwined the apple in the toe
To sting the child with knowledge.

(*LWC* 23)

Here a hidden serpent lurks inside a childish token of reward and abundance, the Christmas stocking. But unlike the serpent in Genesis or Milton, Lowell's version of "hell's serpent" is under no obligation to argue a reasoning *adult* into sin. This lurking serpent can strike from a hidden point of vantage, and without warning, at a child innocently going about his business and thereby "sting the child with knowledge." As with Berryman's lost ball or Bishop's heavenly dragons changed to subway cars, Lowell transforms a familiar figure associated with a child's playful and reassuring ceremonies of innocence—a Christmas stocking—and literally "loads" it with original sin, as emblematized by "hell's / serpent" which entwines "the apple in the toe." In this revisionary parable, the Christmas tree, conventionally associated with the birth and enduring life of the redeemer-child, is perverted into a bitterer tree: the Tree of the Knowledge of Good and Evil whose fruit condemned men and women to labor, sin, and death.

The gigantic and imposing figure of General Joseph Hooker enters the poem with emphatic, ironic finality. Hooker's bronze statue stands on a tall and massive marble platform outside the Boston Statehouse. His figure is draped in Civil War officer's tunic, sword, and broad brimmed cavalry hat, and he is mounted on an impressive stallion.

Hooker's heels
Kicking at nothing in the shifting snow,
A cannon and a cairn of cannon balls,
Rusting before the blackened Statehouse, know
How long the horn of plenty broke like glass
In Hooker's gauntlets.

(*LWC* 23)

Despite the massive statue erected in his honor, Hooker was a disaster in his most important Civil War role. Though an effective divisional and corps commander, shortly after Hooker was appointed commander of the Grand Army of the Potomac, he was grievously mauled by Robert E. Lee's Army of Northern Virginia at the Battle of Chancellorsville on 1–3 May 1863 and forced to retreat, at the loss of 17,000 Union casualties despite commanding more than twice as many men. Thus, under Hooker's leadership, the Union suffered perhaps its most humiliating defeat of the Civil War—and Lee won his most glorious victory. When, a month later, Hooker offered his resignation on the eve of the Battle of Gettysburg, it was promptly accepted by President Lincoln, to Hooker's surprise and chagrin. General George Meade, awakened in the field in the dead of night to receive his command, went on to win a decisive Union victory.

When the Union ultimately won the war, Hooker, despite his very public failure at the highest command, was given the monumental treatment by his native state—an irony by no means lost on Lowell, who positions Hooker as a hapless figure uncomfortably yet fixedly representing established cultural and parental authority. Held in apparent honor by society, he is really feckless, "kicking at nothing in the shifting snow." Lowell's Hooker, by analogy to Lowell's father, is a "blundering butcher," his butchery not the consequence of deliberate malice but of hapless incompetence in the face of a more brilliant and determined tactician. In Lowell's view, his father was overwhelmed and defeated by Lowell's mother as clearly as Hooker was outgeneraled by Lee and Stonewall Jackson, leaving Lowell to be "mowed down" like the Union volunteers at Chancellorsville. Lowell's father, firmly identified in Lowell's mind with "the crowd of ruling class Boston" is inadequate to match the insistence, will, and verbal adroitness of Lowell's mother Charlotte.

In Lowell's world, as in Melville's, "all wars are boyish" and thus in Lowell's ironic critique of romantic myths of war, children are by no means exempt either as targets of violence or as its perpetrators. And figures of social or martial authority can themselves be shown to act from a truculent innocence or naiveté that results in human suffering on a massive scale. In this cold, dark world "I ask for bread, my father gives me mould." On the cold, dark Boston Common, alongside the "blackened Statehouse"—blackened to prevent Allied shipping from being silhouetted against a lighted skyline and thereby sunk, as many were, by prowling German U-boats—the threat of premature knowledge lurks much as the threat of a sinful fall had lurked for Lowell's Puritan forebears.

In evoking the motif of expulsion from paradise in "Christmas Eve under Hooker's Statue" in 1946, Lowell was deliberately placing himself at the end of a long tradition of Western literature and thought. In retrospect, one can also see that Lowell was placing himself amidst the still-emerging and intellectually radical mode of understanding childhood that had already engaged poets like Bishop, Jarrell, and Berryman. This approach would, in the next several decades, emphatically and decisively reconfigure the postmodern poet's mythic and personal encounters with childhood.

Lowell would remark in an eloquent posthumous tribute that his friend Jarrell's key subject was his "lost, raw childhood, only recapturable in memory and imagination. Above all, childhood! This subject for many a careless and tarnished cliché was for him what it was for his two favorite poets, Rilke and Wordsworth, a governing and transcendent vision. For shallower creatures, recollections of childhood and youth are drenched in a mist of plaintive pathos, or even bathos, but for Jarrell this was the divine glimpse, lifelong to be lived with, painfully and tenderly relived, transformed, matured—man with and against woman, child with and against adult" (*RLProse* 96).

As should by now be clear, this preoccupation with the "child with and against adult" was by no means the exclusive province of any one of these poets, but would emerge as one of their most pervasive and ongoing mutual concerns. Berryman's *Dream Songs* explore the emotionally tenuous world of "Henry, a white American in early middle age sometimes in blackface, who has suffered an irreversible loss," dramatizing the embattled mental environment of a man for whom the romantic myth of childhood reappears as "only a small dream of the Golden World." Still, as the poet acknowledges sadly, "If the dream was small / it was my dream also, Henry's" (*DS* 132). Bishop, too, would explore childhood persistently in published and unpublished prose writings and in eloquent poems of early discovery and loss like "First Death in Nova Scotia," "Sestina," and "In the Waiting Room." And Lowell, in his poignant, early, neglected "Buttercups" from *Lord Weary's Castle*, or in the vivid childhood passages in "Mills of the Kavanaughs," would presage his own lifelong need to painfully and tenderly relive childhood experience, a need that led Lowell to write many published and unpublished autobiographical sketches in prose, to craft an autobiographical sequence in *Life Studies* that roots itself deeply in childhood, to write the many child-centered poems in *History* and *Day by Day*, and to weave frequent allusions to childhood through dozens of other poems throughout his oeuvre. These include the emotionally ambiguous opening of "Waking Early Sunday Morning," where the poet yearns "to feel the unpolluted joy / and criminal leisure of a boy / —no rainbow smashing a dry fly / in the white run is as free as I" (*NTO* 14) and the equally complex opening of "For the Union Dead," where Lowell recalls the moment when, as a boy, "my nose crawled like a snail on the glass" of the "old South Boston Aquarium," while "my hands tingled / to burst the bubbles / drifting from the noses of the cowed, compliant fish" (*FUD* 70). The yearning to return to the innocence and freedom of a remembered childhood is ironically—and characteristically—undercut in these famous poems by undertones of betrayal, violence, and imprisonment.

In the early and later poems and prose pieces discussed here, each of these poets was struggling to explore and express feelings that would continue to haunt them. For each, the child emerges both as an exile from the lost paradise of the childish past and as an explorer, an active mind and observant spirit driven by the constant impulse to create or invent connections to a lost place or a lost mode of being. The preoccupation of these poets with the child as both exile and explorer would foster a loss-centered yet exploratory aesthetic that avoids the constraints of aesthetic ideologies while stressing surprise, deft and elusive formal innovation, and poignant, ambiguously immediate perception. Each poet's obsessive, life-long preoccupation with the rediscovery and recreation of scenes of irredeemable primal loss suggests that, for each, absence was a source both of pain and of creative discovery. Individually, each poet began his or her career by struggling separately to project a new way of looking at childhood. Together they would combine to fashion this new way of looking into a powerful mode of self-exploration that would allow them to return to and dramatically reimagine painful psychic origins in quest of an elusive understanding of present pain and disorder and a still more elusive state of mature independence.

# 4 Points of the Compass

## *Christmas 1936*

What is in the East? In the West? In the South? In the North?

Elizabeth Bishop, *Geography III*

### Bishop, Lowell, Jarrell, Berryman: Christmas 1936

In 1976, Elizabeth Bishop, looking back over her long career, fashioned extracts from an 1884 elementary school text, *First Lessons in Geography* into the epigraph of her retrospective last book, *Geography III.* She created in the process a peculiar sort of found-poem posing subliminal questions about methods of Western education and about the relation of the individual to a "simpler," seemingly more lucid past. Bishop's epigraph alludes to never-quite-answered questions about her own ambiguous travels—toward those travels' curious gaps and elisions, their arresting silences. Her textbook extract inquires of its unseen map "*What is in the East? In the West? In the South? In the North?*" (*EBPoems* 157) and so on, through all the points of the compass.

As Christmas approached in 1936, four decades before Bishop graced her last book with this intriguing opening, she and the three poets of her generation with whom she would come to feel the keenest affinity—Lowell, Jarrell, and Berryman—were themselves positioned like the points of a compass "in the East, in the West, in the South, in the North." In the east was John Berryman, aged twenty-two. Berryman had just begun a pilgrimage from Clare College in England's Cambridge University, where he was currently a graduate fellow, to Paris, where he was visiting a friend. In the west was Randall Jarrell, also aged twenty-two. Jarrell, living in Nashville, Tennessee, still in his mother's house, was doing graduate work at Vanderbilt University. There, ensconced among the Agrarian school of poets led by John Crowe Ransom and Allen Tate, he was completing an M.A. in English under fellow Agrarian Donald Davidson. Thousands of miles apart, on the eastern and western poles of this notional map, Berryman and Jarrell were in December 1936 already competing for the approval of several of the same elders—the stake being a poetry prize offered by Robert Penn Warren's *Southern Review*—to be judged by Tate and by Berryman's mentor Mark Van Doren.

In the south was Elizabeth Bishop, aged twenty-five. Bishop was visiting Key West, having just made her first foray there from the Florida peninsula while recovering from recent losses and continuing her intensive, artistically self-defining correspondence with Marianne Moore. In the north was Robert Lowell, just nineteen years old. Lowell was a sophomore attending Harvard University, just across the Charles River from his parents home at 170 Marlborough Street in Boston. Like Jarrell he was contemplating some means of breaking free from his confining family environment and expectations.

Three days after Christmas in 1936, Lowell struck his father to the floor in an impulsive act of rebellion. In doing so, he brought his vexed home life to a violent close and set in motion a sequence of events that lead him, an anxious but willing exile from Harvard and Boston, to intersect a few months later with Jarrell at a remote middlewestern college—a place as yet unknown to either—occupying a meeting point between their present poles. It was during that autumn and winter of 1937, in a chilly upstairs room in a central Ohio farmhouse of an elder poet-critic, that Jarrell and Lowell drew upon the experiences of the previous December to spin the first enduring strands in the web of friendship and artistic fellowship that would one day grow to include Bishop and Berryman. Their fellowship would slowly take shape as an unofficial, loosely defined, ever-shifting, but unusually productive and durable artistic circle.

Lowell, Jarrell, Bishop, and Berryman were born under the gathering clouds of humanity's first global conflict in the midst of modernity's opening phase. They came of age as human beings and as writers in the 1930s, that epoch of uncertain peace that T. S. Eliot described in *Four Quartets* as "the world 'entre deux guerres.'" At the same time, each was passing through a rigorous apprenticeship under the eyes of a shifting and overlapping matrix of elder poet-critics that included Marianne Moore, Allen Tate, John Crowe Ransom, Ford Madox Ford, R. P. Blackmur, Richard Eberhardt, Yvor Winters, and Mark Van Doren—an array of elders whom Lowell would later term, in his verse elegy for Berryman, "our galaxy of grands maîtres" (*DBD* 27). They had to manage these complex and often challenging relationships while attempting to discover and project their individual voices. This decade "of waiting for the war," which Lowell believed W. H. Auden had "made immortal,"[1] is the formative period in their development as writers and people examined in the present chapter. The Christmas season of 1936 captures these four poets at a moment, just before their first meetings, when, through their publications and their overlapping array of mentors, their lives and careers had begun their independent directions on paths that would one day intersect. Each of these poets' life texts and literary texts would come to be linked in an enduring web of connections. Examining their complex emotional, intellectual and cultural positions in the mid-1930s in the context of personal, cultural, and global change, offers insight into their later intricate four-way conversation.

By 1936 each member of this emerging quartet had passed through a childhood marked by traumatic losses, by indelible feelings of abandonment. One effect of this experience was to make them readers. Each had, in Berryman's phrase, "read omnivorously when quite young."[2] Berryman's first wife, Eileen, recalled that "when I banished books (which I suspected would always preempt any living space we shared) from the kitchen" of 49 Grove, Berryman's former bachelor apartment on Boston's then "rundown, even seedy-looking" Beacon Hill, "he protested, 'All that *beautiful* space will go to waste.'"[3] Bishop recalled having spent much of her isolated, asthmatic youth "lying in bed wheezing and reading."[4] Jarrell, meanwhile, was devouring whole libraries while still a child, and as a precocious high school student he read vast quantities of Shaw, Ibsen, Chekhov, Flaubert, Dostoyevsky, Faulkner, Eliot, and Proust.[5] Jarrell also boasted, plausibly, at fifteen in a review of a performance of the play for his high school literary magazine, the *Hume-Fogg Echo*, that he knew by heart "the soliloquies a number of the scenes in 'Hamlet.'"[6] Still, Jarrell always felt on the ragged edge of having nothing to read. In an address to a group of librarians Jarrell later admitted that, "If people were like me, libraries and not religion would be the opium of the people," and he added that, "Will Rogers said that he never met the man he didn't like. If it hadn't been for *Main Street* I could have said this, once, about books. When I was eight, we lived in my aunt's apartment until *Main Street* was the only book left. I read it the way people in a famine eat bark: it seemed to me that Sinclair Lewis had left out of *Main Street* everything you read a book for—to me the only thing worse than reading *Main Street* was not reading anything."[7] At the moment of this famished reading experience, the marriage of Jarrell's parents was coming apart, and he was living in his aunt's apartment as a consequence of the split. Later, in "Children Selecting Books in a Library," Jarrell would suggest that "if we find Swann's / Way better than our own, . . . / . . . it is because we live / By trading another's sorrow for our own" (*RJPoems* 107). Each member of this emerging quartet would face—and each was learning to represent in his or her work—the problem of the individual attempting to cope with a traumatic past while living in, and somehow confronting, a bewildering, dangerous present. Their work was already contemplating and would later persistently return to the torment of powerlessness and emotional abuse, of unhealed loss and repressed grief, sometimes brought to life in the form of "another's sorrow," sometimes acknowledged as one's own.

This chapter will examine in turn the personal and artistic situation of each of these poets, when, spread out across the globe as Christmas approached in 1936—and as yet unacquainted personally—each faced a pivotal moment in his or her development as a person and a poet. Spread out across the old and new worlds over thousands of miles, each was brooding separately and eloquently on the problems to be overcome in defining a workable human and literary identity.

By late December 1936, Bishop, Jarrell, and Berryman, the three eldest of these four fledgling poets, had already begun submitting poems to national magazines and had impressed influential elders. The distinctive artistic profile of each was already beginning to emerge. Moreover, while they had yet to meet, their unpublished papers reveal that even then these widely scattered poets were beginning to read and comment privately on one another's work.

As that ominous year 1936 approached its close, each was struggling to mediate the gap between word and world, each was preparing to celebrate a somewhat isolated Christmas, and each was feeling, perhaps, some of the loneliness of genius. Eventually, as they broke out of their isolation into more public identities, this breakout would be supported, in great measure, by the private network of collegial relations they succeeded in forging as friends, as fellow artists, and as literary peers.

Concentrating on these separate but parallel moments in late December 1936, this chapter will study the difficult and painful sequence of steps by which each was passing through apprenticeship and beginning to discover a voice and style, and an array of thematic materials, that would become their own. In this period these poets came gradually to replace their "galaxy of grands maîtres" with a new array of touchstones selected from among their contemporaries. Individually and collectively these four poets would come to forge a powerfully exploratory aesthetic that could move dramatically from the private sphere to the public, from the local to the global, or from the individual into the realms of memory, dream, myth, and history. Through these labors, they came increasingly to recognize, appreciate, and acknowledge in one another the parallelism of their respective artistic situations and responses. Thus they gradually emerged as points on one another's compass.

But throughout the 1930s, as these poets were struggling to articulate and explore both a global and an individual perspective, each was also to struggling toward self-definition as a person. In this early phase of their parallel development, each of these poets was grappling with troublesome, unresolved family issues that would continue to shape, define, and energize their work well into maturity. Thus, for each of these poets Christmas 1936 marked a point of intersection between their already long-established life-texts and their emerging literary texts, at a moment of great uncertainty for Western civilization at large.

## In the East: John Berryman, Christmas 1936

In the east as Christmas approached in 1936 was John Berryman. Cold, hungry, and dispirited, he shivered alone in a cheap hotel room off the Faubourg Montmartre in Paris, holding loneliness at bay by writing long letters home to his mother. As the year 1936 drew to a close, Berryman, then aged twenty-two, had done everything his elders might expect of a young poet—everything, that is, except produce a completely successful poem. Still, he had an impressive resumé. Berryman had studied with Mark Van Doren at Columbia University and become Van Doren's protégé and friend. One Columbia classmate, Robert Giroux, already Berryman's close companion, would in time become the friend and publisher of each member of this midcentury quartet.

In 1935, Berryman had won the prestigious Kellett Fellowship from Columbia, which was currently funding the first of two years of graduate study at Clare College, Cambridge. In the spring of 1936, Berryman had graduated Phi Beta Kappa from Columbia, and Van Doren had written that in his absence, "Columbia is going to be barren bricks this winter."[8] The following fall, Berryman would carry away Cambridge's prestigious Oldham Shakespeare prize, his triumph in this unsigned British competitive examination marking him, a mere colonial (or in Berryman's words "a completely unknown 'American with a beard,'")[9] as one of the most promising young scholars in England. His Cambridge tutor, George Rylands, remembered Berryman as being "strange and wayward and original and much loved and admired by his friends who believed in his future." Rylands also recalled that Berryman was "exceedingly interested in all the problems and potentialities of verse composition."[10]

By the age of twenty-two, Berryman had met and corresponded with R. P. Blackmur and Allen Tate (each of whom would later offer Berryman a teaching post that would rescue him from desperate personal and professional straits). He had worked as Tate's assistant at the Columbia Summer School. (Tate wrote: "You helped me greatly with my lectures. I regret that I couldn't make them more interesting for you; but you know what the audience was like."[11]) He had engaged in lively colloquy with Auden and received a cordial note of reply from the great William Butler Yeats himself, promising an audience when mutually convenient. Soon, Berryman would remark in a letter to his Columbia friend Milt Halliday that he was "drinking and reading poems by the hundreds with . . . Dylan Thomas, a young Welsh poet who is highly touted and actually has some merit."[12] Before long, Berryman would be taking tea with the revered Yeats at the Athenaeum, Yeats's decorous London club. Dylan Thomas found the solemnity of Berryman's veneration for Yeats—as Berryman would later recall—"the funniest thing in that part of London."[13] So Thomas endeavored to get Berryman roaring drunk just before his scheduled meeting with Yeats. (Thanks to a cold bath at his flat, Berryman sobered up just in time.)

While pursuing his successful studies at the alma mater of Milton and Wordsworth, Berryman would give a well-attended lecture on Yeats at Cambridge and write a series of self-absorbed but often brilliant letters home to his mother on his feelings, his evolving ideas about aesthetics, and his artistic intentions, letters now available in a selection superbly edited by Richard J. Kelly. He remarks in one of these early epistles that "letters can form a style."[14] Berryman was working hard, by every means available, to form that style. But he had not yet succeeded, as he well knew. Despite his brilliance and skill, the invention and crafting of a consistently effective poetic voice would elude Berryman for nearly twenty years. For real fame he would have to wait even longer.

In July of 1936, Berryman had submitted the poem "Ritual at Arlington" to a contest sponsored by the newly founded *Southern Review*, which offered a prize for the best long poem. The judges happened to be Berryman's own mentors, Van Doren and Tate, each of whom, reading four hundred-seventy-eight anonymously submitted manuscripts, had placed their protégé's poem high on their respective shortlists. Van Doren wrote, by way of consolation, "You may or may not enjoy hearing that Ritual averaged on our two lists the fifth place among forty-five poems; and it may do you good to know that in our present bleariness it could well be higher still. The point is that both of us must have liked it greatly. Believe me I did." Van Doren went on to add, perhaps presciently: "It is a noble poem; much your maturest thing to date; and concerned with something vastly more important than Arlington itself. Something, I should say, called Death; and the best set of parallels (your word) along which to sight at the thing called Life."[15]

Tate was also moved to write to Berryman in Cambridge, balancing consolation with specific technical advice: "I should like to hear about the progress of your studies. . . . If your poem had been cut down to proper length considering the form I should have placed it first. There are very fine passages in it, the best I thought in the whole contest. But the sort of thesis-antithesis development of the theme seemed to me mechanical, not dramatic—though I felt a kind of affection for it since I used it in my Ode. The prize went to Jarrell. He didn't have your line by line excellence, but what he had was better subdued to form."[16] Tate's insinuation of imitativeness to his own "Ode to the Confederate Dead" tactfully implies a censure that Berryman would frequently hear from the editors and reviewers who perused his early verse. The extraordinarily individual voice that first emerged in "Homage to Mistress Bradstreet" and would later shape the unique verbal environment of *The Dream Songs* required almost twenty further years of unremitting labor.

Van Doren, too, had a tactful suggestion, dropped in the midst of praise for the poem's "magnificent indirection" and its "symbols of permanent bronze," regarding what Van Doren called "your latinity": "I like it; am familiar with it; know you by it; but do not care to imagine its ever becoming a manner with you. Don't believe me at once or ever, perhaps. Simply consider; and perhaps try now and then the bonier music of monosyllables."[17] The bony, and predominately monosyllabic, music of many lines from the *Dream Songs*, like these opening ones from a song in his initial book—"I am the little man who smokes & smokes. / I am the girl who does know better but. / I am the king of the pool. / I am so wise I had my mouth sewn shut. / I am a government official & a goddamned fool" (*DS* 22)—show Berryman crafting a virtuoso response to this early admonition of Van Doren's, for here the hilarious explosion into self-mocking polysyllables in the last quoted line is comically prepared by that hammering, monosyllabic prelude. At their best, Berryman's individual Dream

Songs compress a complex and dramatic psychological journey, complete with telling, surprising rhymes and sharp turns of feeling and thought, into three six-line stanzas. Their terse punch represents Berryman's achieved response to Tate's suggestion about subduing "length" to "form." No doubt the achievement actually exceeds what Tate envisioned.

But for now Berryman was writing to Tate from Cambridge: "Thanks very much for your letter and the criticism therein—your use of 'form' still puzzles me a bit." He then adds, immediately, "I'm glad Jarrell won—he writes damn good poems."[18] Jarrell, whom Berryman had not yet met, was already a rival (and potential colleague?) as early as 1936. Jarrell, Tate's former student at Vanderbilt University and his current protégé and friend, had won the prize for his long poem "Orestes at Tauris." That Berryman already knew this exact contemporary's "damn good poems" suggests that though he was now immersing himself in Shakespearean scholarship, he was far from ignoring the writing of his immediate contemporaries. Berryman keenly followed the contemporary poetic scene. The Jarrell poems Berryman had spotted may have included the group of five poems Jarrell published in the May 1934 issue of the short-lived *American Review* (edited by Tate), or the single poems published in the December 1934 *New Republic* and the winter 1935 *Westminster Magazine*. They certainly included the two poems Jarrell had published most recently, in the inaugural issue of the *Southern Review*,[19] which appeared in July 1935, since that was a journal Berryman followed closely from its inception. One of these "damn good poems," heavily revised, became Jarrell's frequently anthologized "The Elementary Scene." The other, "And did she dwell in innocence and joy," though never republished by Jarrell, was discussed in the previous chapter in relation to the motif of "expulsion from paradise." Lowell would later comment, regarding his two friends' relative stature at the moment of their first meeting, at a party given by the *Nation* in Jarrell's honor in 1946, "Compared with other poets, John was a prodigy; compared to Randall, a slow starter" (*RLProse* 112).[20] By 1946, Jarrell's powerful war poems of the mid-1940s, collected in the 1945 volume *Little Friend, Little Friend*, had already distinguished him at a time when Berryman was struggling to find a voice. Lowell had no way of realizing that his comparison of the two in 1946—Jarrell as admired "prodigy," Berryman as comparative "slow starter"—had been felt already by Berryman a decade earlier.

For Berryman, a mere five months Jarrell's junior, would publish no poem in a national magazine until 1938, when the *Southern Review* brought out a group of four. By that time, Jarrell would have more than two dozen poems in print, as well a series of well-placed reviews. Though few of these early poems of Jarrell's are now well remembered, Berryman must have felt, even in 1936, a certain belatedness in relation to his precocious contemporary. Berryman, however, could not complain, at present, of being ignored. Both of the contest's judges had written offering personal consolation and technical advice. And the *Southern Review*'s editor, Robert Penn Warren, also wrote to Berryman, on 7 October 1936, suggesting that, "Although your poem did not receive THE SOUTHERN REVIEW prize, the judges were enormously interested in it; and so are we." Echoing Tate's hint that "certain sections resemble too closely, even to the point of imitation, Tate's 'Ode to the Confederate Dead,'" and indicating that "At times the composition appears chopped and crabbed," Warren continued, "Please take these remarks in the spirit in which they are meant. We simply feel that because your work is so good we owe you an explanation for not publishing it as it stands. We are positive that in the near future we shall be able to arrange a large display for you in THE SOUTHERN REVIEW, if your present poem can be a fair sample of your general performance."[21] When, a year later, after some negotiation, the *Southern Review* did in fact accept a group of his poems, Berryman, worn out by his night-and-day cramming for the Oldham Shakespeare prize, noted in his Cambridge journal for 11 November 1937, "Letter from Warren accepting five poems and asking to see more: I am a little too dead for elation, but glad; 'Last Days of the City' is taken. I wonder if I shall live long enough to write the great poetry I know I can."[22]

Despite these marks of promise, when Christmas arrived in 1936, Berryman was in awkward circumstances that emphasized his isolation. He had arranged to spend Christmas in Paris with the amusing Basque caricaturist Pedro Donga, whom he had met on the SS *Britannic* en route to England that September. (Six months later, in June of 1937, Bishop would arrive in Cork, Ireland aboard this same ship, the *Britannic*, and would retain memories from nearby Dingle harbor that she would weave into her 1948 chef d'oeuvre "Over 2,000 Illustrations and a Complete Concordance.") But for the moment Berryman found himself more or less stranded in the City of Light when it turned out that Donga, the only person he knew in Paris, had recently begun a passionate love affair and had little time for his friend. Moreover, funds on which Berryman had been counting did not arrive at the American Express office for several days, leaving him nearly broke, without money even for food. Trapped in these faintly ridiculous circumstances, Berryman was reduced to taking long walking tours during which he "systematically followed" and noted the names of Paris streets—and to writing lonely letters home to his mother. After an attempt to put up a brave front, his Christmas letter concludes, "It's late and my pencils are all dulled and I feel like hell and after all Christmas is a poor day to pass without seeing a single person you know or speaking to anyone but the Concierge and not even Beetle or writing cheers me and I've got a poem going in my head that I can't get on paper and in fact DAMN and damn again. Good night, Mum—I suppose all this is excellent for me, but it's difficult to see how—I'm going to bed before I dissolve in tears of self-pity. Christ & hell. I've not even a decent pain, merely boredom and nothing. *Nothing*."[23] Berryman's "I suppose all this is excellent for me" should be recognized as more than a conventional remark. Its roots (as Kelly indicates) lie in Mrs. Berryman's repeated warnings to her son "of the dangers that personal happiness might hold for his work."[24] Internalizing this dangerous message from his mother, Berryman would later state in an interview, "The artist is extremely lucky who is presented with the worst possible ordeal which will not actually kill him. At that point he's in business."[25]

Berryman, deep in the reading of Shakespeare, went on next day to plan a classical tragedy, "The Architect," whose one memorable feature is the name of its title character, Alan Severance, a revealing appellation that Berryman would use again for the protagonist of his posthumously published semiautobiographical novel on the rigors of alcoholism, *Recovery*. Kelly suggests that "A persistent thread throughout his letters is a desire to please Mrs. Berryman with his accomplishments. It is as if love manifests itself in achievement and, despite what she says, he cannot be truly loved for what he is, only for what he does. Very early on he evidently came to believe that he was responsible for her health and happiness and well-being."[26] Lowell, who spent much of his early life defiantly at odds with his parents, once remarked to Helen Vendler "for children selfishness *is* character."[27] By contrast, three days before his twenty-third birthday, Berryman would write in his notebooks on 22 October 1937: "Found two letters from Mother: one of them birthday, speaking of her own life, caused me the greatest and purest grief I can remember—unable to weep, but long dry sobs tore me to pieces; I vow to achieve her happiness in all ways open to me. Pray these prizes give me a start."[28]

A month later, on 24 November 1937, in response to financial and emotional worries that his mother confided in a letter, Berryman would write, "Think of me as a cushion who loves you devotedly, will always be there for you to sit on, and will endeavor constantly to be as comfortable for you as possible. This is not self-abnegation, despite my unhappily persistent capacity for self-pity; I am perfectly aware of my value; but I know yours."[29] In this remarkable offer—disturbingly submissive and transparently oedipal, despite Berryman's disclaimer—Alice Miller might have recognized the sort of gifted child whose drama she wrote of with such subtle attention, for certainly Berryman seems here to meet her criteria: "intelligent, alert, attentive, extremely sensitive, and (because . . . completely attuned to her well-being) entirely at the mother's disposal and ready for her use."[30] But Berryman's submissive attitude should be understood in the context of Berryman's ongoing, silent, and as-yet-unacknowledged rage toward his mother both for her frequently overbearing way of treating him and for her ambiguous contribution to his father's suicide (or murder). Berryman would later note that he once accused his mother when "drunk & raging, of having actually murdered him & staged a suicide," a view by no means implausible, as we have seen, in light of the coroner's report on his father's death, a document Berryman never consulted.[31] Miller goes on to say that her "gifted child" will be "transparent, clear, reliable, and easy to manipulate—as long as their true self (their emotional world) remains in the cellar of the transparent house in which they have to live."[32] Considering what Berryman would later term "the (horrible) *richness*"[33] of his relationship with his mother, it is clear that key issues of the *Dream Songs* lurk in the subtexts of these highly charged, emotionally convoluted letters, and that Berryman's lengthy struggle toward artistic expression would remain a struggle to find a form with sufficient drama to obliquely express—and with enough opacity to allow him to conceal—thoughts and feelings that he could not express more directly. For, despite his anger, Berryman's sense, not just of his mother's power, but of her emotional dependence on him, even late in life, was far from misplaced. Kelly notes that Mrs. Berryman wrote to her son on 3 January 1971 that when a doctor expressed surprise at her quick recovery from a serious illness, she replied, "'my son's letters were all I needed.'"[34]

Despite the miles of ocean separating Berryman from his mother and his artistic mentors, he remained entrapped by the extensive reach of their expectations. He had partly internalized these expectations, and did not yet consciously understand how directly they obstructed his not yet fully understood or articulated yearnings for self-exploration and self-expression. Van Doren's sheer moderation, good will, good taste, and common sense would always stand as an unattainable standard of human and literary deportment for Berryman. Tate, on the other hand, while chiding Berryman for imitating him too closely in "Ritual," also objected when Berryman later swerved too far from his own practice.

Given how the cards were stacked, it should come as no surprise that in the mid-1930s, Berryman was still pursuing the austere, impersonal artistic norms he had absorbed from Van Doren and Tate, and those more remote high modernists, Eliot and Yeats. For the impersonal norms of these modernists "fathers" seemed to echo and reinforce his mother's desire that he serve her needs and keep his own painfully repressed and raging emotional world locked in the cellar of the "transparent house" they symbolically shared. Berryman would write to his mother, always a seductively responsive audience, on 14 February 1937: "My enemies are extravagance of speech, irrelevant interests and sympathies I find within myself, and the current time, the world, the Body of Fate."[35] Speaking of the early verse Berryman produced according to these principles, Lowell later remarked, "His proper bent seemed toward an intense and unworldly symbolic poetry" (*RLProse* 105).

To achieve his mature style Berryman would have to learn to employ the high modernist's austere inflections as merely one range of colors in that dazzling kaleidoscope of hues that would inform his singularly elaborate stylistic palette. The artistic remaking of his own version of a postmodern aesthetic would be an arduous process for a poet faced with daunting and confining expectations from his mother and from his literary "fathers," those "high judges" who guided his early promise. Yet by the late 1950s, when he began producing Dream Song after Dream Song in a steady stream, Berryman had learned to project a vividly nuanced voice definable by the very qualities he had termed his "enemies" in that 1937 letter to his mother—a voice raising "extravagance of speech" to new levels, a voice yoking heterogeneous "interests and sympathies" by violence together, a voice that could investigate "the current time, the world, the Body of Fate" against a backdrop of just such faintly ridiculous situations as the one that had trapped him in Paris in December of 1936. These elements offered few of the building materials of classical tragedy. But combined and in dynamic interaction, they could bring to giddy life the "plights and gripes" of Henry, the tragicomic alter ego of Berryman's *Dream Songs*. By then, Berryman, exploiting "all the possibilities of verse composition" that he had explored since 1936, had at last created a language that could oppose and balance, in a single Song, sentences like:

"Rilke was a *jerk*," or "My psychiatrist can lick your psychiatrist," against such a curious, lyrical opening as "Acacia, burnt myrrh, velvet, pricky stings" (*DS* 3).

In that high-toned, high modernist February 1937 letter to his mother Berryman wrote, "What we require is armor."[36] By the mid-1950s, as Berryman was seeking means to dramatize the vicissitudes of "Henry's fate" (*DS* 6), he came to share Lowell's determination, voiced in a 1957 letter to Bishop, to get rid of "my medieval armor's undermining."[37] Berryman, too, would learn to project the physical and psychic struggles of an apparently defenseless Henry whose "pelt was put on sundry walls / where it did much resemble Henry and / them persons was delighted" (*DS* 16). Lowell termed Berryman's harrowing ordeal of artistic remaking "a long, often backbreaking search for an inclusive style, a style that could use his erudition and catch the high, even frenetic, intensity of his experience, disgusts, and enthusiasm" (*RLProse* 105). Chapter 5 will further explore Berryman's painful and protracted development as an artist.

## In the West: Randall Jarrell, Christmas 1936

Five thousand miles to the west of Berryman, Randall Jarrell was still living in his mother's modest brick house at 2524 Westwood in Nashville, Tennessee, as he worked to complete a master's thesis in English (on A. E. Houseman, since his original choice of Auden was refused) at Vanderbilt University, under the direction of Fugitive poet and scholar Donald Davidson. Jarrell, like Berryman, had an impressive résumé for a twenty-two-year-old. Among his early achievements he had, as we have seen, beaten out Berryman himself in September for that *Southern Review* poetry prize,[38] eliciting thereby Berryman's praise to Tate of his "damn good poems."

Like Berryman, Jarrell was still fighting free of family entanglements—and at much closer quarters. Several years earlier, Jarrell's wealthy uncle Howell Campbell, the brother of his divorced mother, had agreed to fund Jarrell's undergraduate degree from Vanderbilt on condition that he continue to live at home. Berryman's relationship with his mother might seem dangerously intimate, given the burden of resentment he also carried, but Martha Berryman, though she lacked her son's brilliant opportunities in education, was herself an extremely intelligent, well-read, and ambitious woman who had achieved business success while nursing frustrated aspirations of her own as a writer. Berryman obviously relished sharing his evolving literary ideas in singular detail with this seductively receptive audience. Berryman's future friend Jarrell would have to look outside his home to find that "Indulgent, or candid, or uncommon" reader whom he invokes at the beginning of "A Conversation with the Devil" (*RJPoems* 29), and whom he had never found, to his lasting regret, among his own Nashville family.

Jarrell began his famous 1962 lecture "Fifty Years of American Poetry" with the declaration, "In 1910 American poetry was a bare sight" (*TBC* 295). When Jarrell was delivering this lecture as the featured speaker at the National Poetry Festival in Washington, he could look out on an audience filled with famous poets of several generations and observe with confidence that with "the generation of American poets that included Frost, Stevens, Eliot, Pound, Williams, Marianne Moore, Ransom . . . and . . . the Irishman Yeats, we realize that the whole center of gravity of poetry in English had shifted west of England" (*TBC* 296).

In 1935, Berryman had sojourned eastward, where his Cambridge tutor Rylands temporarily shook his faith in American letters by insisting on the inadequacies of recent American criticism and verse. Lowell would later recall that as a young writer Berryman had "clung so keenly to Hopkins, Yeats and Auden that their shadows paled him" (*RLProse* 112). Berryman brought back with him a habit of British orthography ("we dream of honour") that he would never relinquish and an English accent that annoyed old college friends like Milt Halliday. The latter acquisition proved a serious hindrance, for Berryman would have to relearn a native inflection for his verse. Berryman's first wife, Eileen Simpson, recalled that, "John, whose speech had been as formal as his poetry and his style of dressing when I first met him, had been dismayed by my slangy way of talking. . . . Later, . . . he took over the phrases."[39] Jarrell, on the other hand, was experiencing an important phase of that shift of poetry "west of England" commonly known as the Southern Renaissance, and he did so while continuing to occupy the room in his mother's house whose door he had been locking, when he sat down to write, ever since junior high.

For Vanderbilt University was anything but "a bare sight," poetically, in 1936. At Vanderbilt, such Fugitive poet-critics as Ransom, Tate, and Davidson—who had come to prefer the term Agrarians, expressive of their wish to return to a simpler, more rural, less technology-centered culture—had long since taken their stand. The left-leaning Jarrell, whom Lowell later called "no agrarian, but a radical liberal" (*RLProse* 98), read Marx and Engels and Freud along with Rilke and Kafka and Proust.

Though far from sharing the political views of his Agrarian mentors, Jarrell loved the South and relished the fact that at Vanderbilt literature mattered. There he developed friendships with Tate and Robert Penn Warren, and he haunted the office of that courtly and incisive poet-critic he would always call Mr. Ransom. Ransom felt, "even then, when you came to read what he had written, you knew that he had to become one of the important people in the literature of our time."[40] Tate vividly recalled meeting Jarrell as a Vanderbilt freshman in 1931 when Tate himself was a thirty-two-year-old rising star. He would later recall that Jarrell "seemed as an undergraduate to have read all English poetry—John Ransom once said to me that Randall knew more than he did."[41] Tate was impressed by Jarrell's "formal mastery" in such early poems as "A Description of Some Confederate Soldiers," a mastery which, according to Tate, "I, nearly fifteen years older, could not have equaled."[42] But from the beginning Jarrell projected an air of independence toward his elders that both impressed and unsettled them. According to Tate, "Our rather highfalutin talk about the Southern tradition . . . left Randall cold."[43]

Jarrell, an avowed Marxist in the 1930s, began his own career much further from the Agrarians politically than did Lowell. Still, Jarrell shared with mentors like Ransom and Tate not just their talent for observation and their respect for the dynamics of poetic form but for their tragic view of history, a view that placed Jarrell at a considerable remove from mid-1930s Marxist orthodoxy. In a remarkable recording made at Greensboro the 1960s, Jarrell and Ransom discourse—companionably and without an audience—about several of the elder master's poems. Jarrell remarks of one of Ransom's infrequently requested religious poems, "I think "The Puncture" is a wonderful title and it's so unpleasant and truthful. It's . . . as if you saw the whole New Testament as a tire that was once full of air and now is punctured and it all goes out. [Ransom replies: "Could *be*!"] And yet in the end here it has all its human force." [Ransom, quietly: "Yes."]"[44] Speaking of another neglected Ransom poem requested by Jarrell, "Vision by Sweetwater," the former explains that he chose the Far West as its setting because it was "a place of great innocence," while the South has "a grim sense of history." But for Ransom, the effects of history are regional or national, and Ransom's vividly drawn characters—his Captain Carpenters, his gentlemen in dustcoats, his Judiths of Bethulia, his lovely ladies of high degree—remain what Jarrell terms in their recorded discussion "archetypes" rather than individuals.

Lowell, speaking in a 1965 interview of his own complex response to

Agrarian mentorship, observed that "in the Thirties . . . [the] 'Southern Renaissance' . . . was, perhaps, the strongest single element in American culture. . . . Somehow this whole Southern view didn't make sense morally; but it was observant of life and talked a great deal about the 'tragedy of life.' The Southerners no longer seem to have that strength."[45]

Lowell, Jarrell, Bishop, and Berryman would each come to see the problem of making sense of the world morally not in terms of an ideological struggle between cultural poles (agrarianism vs. technology, poetry vs. science, good vs. evil) but as an *individual* struggle. A detailed background of cultural markers functions importantly from poem to poem in the work of this midcentury quartet but each rejected the idea that moral authority must (or can!) be recovered through a reassertion of the fading values of the past—a stand taken by the Agrarians and voiced strenuously, too, by Eliot and Pound. Jarrell's praise of Bishop in 1946 suggests his own shift in moral concern toward the problems of the individual. "She is morally so attractive, in poems like 'The Fish' or 'Roosters,' because she understands so well that the wickedness and confusion of the age can explain and extenuate other people's wickedness and confusion, but not, for you, your own; that morality, for the individual, is usually a small, personal, statistical, but heartbreaking or heartwarming affair of omissions and commissions the greatest of which will seem infinitesimal, ludicrously beneath notice, to those who govern, rationalize and deplore" (*P&A* 235).

Writing about Jarrell after his younger friend's death, Ransom put his finger on a key difference between them: "What Rilke and Jarrell had in common was their obsession with their remembered childhoods, beset with terrors as they were; a thing I confess is not at all the picture of my own childhood, so safe and commonplace."[46] For Jarrell and his contemporaries, as for Rilke, a childhood "beset with terrors" helped to focus their sense of history on the specific and personal. Even when their poems focus on invented or historical protagonists, they tend to explore a uniquely remembered (or repressed) individual past.

The impact of Jarrell's unsettling childhood was obvious to Ransom, who understood that the young Jarrell, even as he enjoyed the clash of intellects growing out of their obvious political and literary differences, very much depended on the support and praise of his mentors. In his memoir "The Rugged Way of Genius," Ransom recalls the early Jarrell as "an insistent and overbearing talker" when he was "a sophomore and '*enfant terrible*' in my writing class at Vanderbilt." As Ransom gracefully phrased it, "I guessed that he had had an unhappy childhood and was bent on identifying himself as a man."[47] Ransom noted that as Jarrell matured "he learned to use his power properly, like a good magistrate; becoming always gentler and less aggressive. . . . Settled at last in Greensboro, it is my understanding that he was loved or admired by everybody in the place."[48] Ransom's view is confirmed by the reports of many Greensboro students and colleagues. One of the former recalled, after Jarrell's death, that "while he was capable of devastating wit as a literary critic, toward his students he was understanding and kind,"[49] while another student stressed "his warmth, his flashing wit, his brilliant mind, his unerring and intuitive critical ability, his exuberant enthusiasm, his sudden flights into a gay and spontaneous joy. . . . His zest for enjoying the sudden delightful moments in life was contagious."[50]

But while Jarrell was still in his twenties, Ransom saw many occasions when "the naked pride of his incisive mind" could intimidate even well known literary elders. Robert Penn Warren recalled serving as Jarrell's instructor in the "top section" of the "standard Sophomore survey—Beowulf to Thomas Hardy." Jarrell, just a freshman, had been placed in at this advanced level because, as Warren recalled, he "had read everything, and remembered everything." Warren, himself twenty-six and a beginning instructor, noted that soon the students were looking not to him but to Jarrell "to see how they were doing. So did the instructor, and on days when the hour passed with not once that certain expression of glazed pity on the skinny young man's face, the instructor took a deep breath and hurried out to light a cigarette. The instructor learned a lot in Sophomore Survey. He had to."[51] Warren saw too how Jarrell's manner gradually eased: "The severe passion for high standards of intelligence and reason turned more and more inward into a self-demanding scrupulosity seasoned by humor and untainted by self-importance. The genuine appreciations and joy at achievement with an undertone of pity for human failing and pity for human feeling."[52] Impressed with this "skinny young man," Warren launched Jarrell's career as a critic by assigning him to review a stack of novels in August 1935, when Jarrell was barely twenty-one and Warren was putting together the second number of the *Southern Review.*

Jarrell similarly impressed such fellow students as the fiction writer Peter Taylor, a Vanderbilt freshman in 1936 who would soon become a lifelong friend of both Jarrell and Lowell. Taylor paints a vivid portrait of a literary circle that grew up spontaneously around Jarrell "on a grassy plot outside the student union building" during touch football games. "It was Randall's talk we wanted of course, and his talk on the sidelines and even while the game was in progress was electrifying. It was there that I first heard anyone analyze a Chekhov story. I have never since heard anything to equal it." Taylor adds that, "On the sidelines of one of those games I once suggested to him that probably we couldn't know just how good Chekhov's stories were unless we could read them in Russian. He laughed at me. . . . On that occasion he said, "Even in Constance Garnett's translation, Chekhov's stories are the best in the English language. . . . Even then Randall could talk about a story you had read, and make you feel, make you realize, that you had never really read it before."[53] These observations—from a writer who would come to be termed an American Chekhov—suggests again the impact of Jarrell's mind and personality on a range of talented friends and contemporaries, an impact it had altogether failed to have within the family circle. And they suggest just how intensely Jarrell's creative impulse intertwined with his aggressive, independent, and magnetically attractive critical intelligence.

Jarrell remained at Vanderbilt in December 1936, with Davidson directing Jarrell's master's thesis, "Implicit Generalization in Houseman." Later Jarrell would emerge as a dazzlingly insightful reader of the generalizations implicit in Bishop, Lowell, Berryman, and many other poets. In his review of *Lord Weary's Castle*, Jarrell would praise Lowell as a "dramatic poet: the poet's generalizations are usually implied, and the poem's explicit generalizations are there primarily because they are dramatically necessary" (*P&A* 217).

By Christmas 1936, several poets and critics identified with the Agrarians had departed Vanderbilt. Tate settled with his wife Caroline Gordon near the Kentucky border fifty miles to the northeast of Nashville in an old farmhouse, "Benfolly," a site that would become a magnet for an international array of literary talent, including, that summer, the young Robert Lowell—to the detriment of the house's ancient plumbing. Cleanth Brooks accompanied Warren to Louisiana State University in Baton Rouge, where together they founded the *Southern Review*. And in a move that would prove fateful to the development of this circle, Dr. Merrill Moore, a prolific sonneteer, moved to Boston. There he established a psychiatric practice and began treating Charlotte Lowell, Robert's mother.

The details of Jarrell's Christmas in 1936 have been lost to history. Perhaps he visited quietly with his cultured Nashville friends the Starrs, a surrogate family who recognized and appreciated his talents. But Jarrell left an imaginative and vividly dramatized record of the loneliness and confusion he associated with that season in the mid-1930s in a complex and powerful poem, "The Night Before the Night Before Christmas," published in 1949 in the *Kenyon Review*. This poem presents the complex and painful inner experience of a lonely, precocious fourteen-year-old girl during one night of her life. Mary Jarrell later described it as "Jarrell's longest poem to date, 300 lines; and . . . the first of Jarrell's semi-autobiographical poems that culminated in the three-part *Lost World*" (*RJLet* 191). Reviewing Jarrell's *The Seven-League Crutches* (1951), Lowell called this poem "perhaps, the best, most mannered, the most unforgettable, and the most irritating poem in the book" (*RLProse* 89). This long lyric narrative explores an adolescent's unresolved and largely repressed traumatic experience of emotional isolation, powerlessness, and the impending death of a loved one in the context of a foreground of everyday domestic routine.

The poem anticipates not just Jarrell's later work, but also, for example, Lowell's or Bishop's self-exploratory poetry of the 1950s, though Jarrell renders his own psychic history indirectly rather than in his own person. As Richard Flynn observes, Jarrell "distances himself from the teenage protagonist in three ways. He writes the poem in the third person, alters the gender of the child, and places the poem in 1934, somewhat later than his own early adolescence."[54] Protected by these strategies, Jarrell can explore a mirror-image of his own emotional situation in the mid-1930s through a process of gender reversal. By making the protagonist female, and younger than himself in 1934, Jarrell underscores the child's vulnerability and powerlessness. Jarrell's own lost sister—stillborn a year before Jarrell's birth and idealized and mourned by his mother ever after—reappears in the poem as the adolescent girl's younger brother, still alive but dying of an unnamed chronic disorder. The girl's clubbable and well-meaning but imaginatively limited father ("poor Lion / poor Moose") mirrors Jarrell's mother. The girl's mother—"two years dead" (*RJPoems* 40)—mirrors Jarrell's father, not dead but left behind in California for exactly two years when Jarrell was himself a fourteen-year-old boy after his unwilling removal to Nashville by his mother. Only the girl's scantly characterized aunt is the same gender as the invalid aunt who shared Jarrell's small house.

The girl is never named, suggesting the character's lack of externally recognized identity. Yearning for transcendence in a world of unglamorous commonplace actualities, this "good" daughter labors dutifully to care for her ailing brother—feeding him meals on a tray and reading him stories in their common bedroom, a quiet enclave of childhood or emerging adolescence. Privately, however, the girl engages in small, silent acts of rebellion and wrestles with her rarely verbalized longing for political or religious belief, faiths that might allow transcendence of one's unsatisfactory self. Flynn suggests: "Beginning to read the Marxist and proletarian literature of the 1930s in an effort to understand her feeling of alienation from the frightening world, the girl is caught between childhood and adulthood. . . . In her confusion between the child-self lost too soon, and the adult-self arriving too soon, she is unable to figure out who she really is."[55] "The Night Before the Night Before Christmas" poses with greater clarity, specificity, and emotional power many of the issues explored earlier in "And did she dwell in innocence and joy" (1935). A girl-child faces the dilemmas of a threatening world in which she must grow up too fast and whose threat is represented symbolically by a frigid out-of-doors that also offers the poem's few fleeting glimpses of release into purity and beauty. As the girl of "The Night Before the Night Before Christmas" drifts toward sleep, her unconscious floats free of her bedroom's warm, banal protection into the wintry night, a realm of the imagination that transforms the familiar into something lovely, something pure, something unknown—something dangerous.

> In the fields outside
> There is not one step on the snow,
> And each bough is bent with the burden
> That is greater, almost, than it can bear.
> The breaths of the world are webs
> Of angelhair,
> Of glass spun, life by life,
> Into the trees' earned, magic tinsel.
>
> (*RJPoems* 49)

The beauty of this frigid world is insentient, apparently cut off from those transcendental meanings associated with the birth of Christ.

> In the fields there is not one angel.
> In all these fields
> There is not one thing that knows
> It is almost Christmas.
>
> (*RJPoems* 50)

Lowell recalled how, in the winter of 1938, Jarrell shocked Gordon Chalmers, the president of Kenyon College (in Lowell's words, "a disciple of the somber anti-romantic humanists") when—as they skied together on the low snow-covered hills near Gambier, Ohio—Jarrell exclaimed "'I feel just like an angel.'" Lowell recalled, "Randall *did* somehow give off an angelic impression" (*RLProse* 91).

Jarrell, like Chalmers, was a humanist—and in many respects a disappointed one—but he was neither somber nor anti-romantic. He wished romantic dreams *could* be fulfilled, and his yearning for the transcendent, the angelic, is mirrored here in the yearnings of this fourteen-year-old child, yearnings that are all the more poignant in the context of Jarrell's (and the girl's) equally strong intellectual and emotional belief that such experiences are, in all likelihood, illusory. The child, in an earlier moment of intellectual pride, pities the ignorance of someone who does not even know

> Enough not to believe in God . . .
> She thinks, as she has thought,
> Her worn old thought,
> By now one word:
> "But how could this world be
> If he's all-powerful, all-good?
> *No*—there's no God."
>
> (*RJPoems* 45)

But despite her doubts she too yearns to believe: in God, in humanity, in Marx's vision of a proletarian utopia, in something larger, more important, more permanent than her vulnerable self.

The frozen out-of-doors of "The Night Before the Night Before Christmas" combines in the girl's dreams with a wishful realm of the unconscious where she can meet her dying brother and discourse with him in a new way.

> The boy and girl in the leaves of their grave
> Are the wings of the bird of the snow.
> But her wings are mixed in her head with the Way
> That streams from their shoulders, stars like snow:
> They spread, at last, their great starry wings
> And her brother sings, "I am dying."
>
> (*RJPoems* 50)

In fantasy, the girl takes on angelic attributes she has yearned to find outside her self, and, at the same moment, she faces and silently acknowledges the human mortality she shares with her brother. Brother and sister have never found words with which to address the fact of his approaching death. But in this frigid dream-realm, "a cave opening into the dark," what had remained unsaid becomes spoken, while the protective lie one ordinarily speaks fades back into thought. Hence, as her brother sings "I am dying," he renders sayable—and turns into art—a fact that he and his sister separately apprehend but feel they cannot share. The girl responds first with the false, protective untruth that she would normally say but now only hears in her mind,

> "No: it's not so, not so—
> Not *really*,"
> She thinks
>
> (*RJPoems* 50)

But this is immediately followed and contradicted by her sad-but-true speech, which is so painful that she immediately tries to retract it in the face of his own denial:

> but she says, "You are dying."
> He says, "I didn't know."
>
> And she cries: "I don't know, I don't know, I don't know!"
>
> They are flying.
> They look down over the earth.
> There is not one crumb.
> The rays of the stars of their wings
> Strike the boughs of the wood, and the shadows
> Are caught up into the night,
> The first faint whisper of the wind:
> *Home, home*, whispers the wind;
> There are shadows of stars, a working
> Hand in the . . .
>
> (*RJPoems* 50–51)

The children seem in fantasy at least to lift off the earth's banal surface as they finally confront, even if fleetingly, the unconfronted fact of imminent death that haunts their days. When the girl who (like Jarrell?) shields herself by a screen of intellectual superiority—when the girl who seems to know it all—at last confesses "I don't know, I don't know, I don't know!" she lets go of the weight that is crushing her. She voices her own till-then-unacknowledged confusion and fear and, in her dream, the children begin to soar. But their imagined journey through the frigid darkness of the unconscious is brief: "Home, home whispers the wind." The quotation's last, uncompleted, phrase, "There are shadows of stars, a working / Hand in the . . . ," suggests that the child feels a transitory yet powerful impulse to perceive at work the hand of a God whose existence she believes, intellectually, that she must deny. At last, each child faces his or her own grave, and each reads the inscription thereon.

> There are words on the graves of the snow.
> She whispers, "When I was alive,
> I read them all the time.
> I read them all the time."
> And he whispers, sighing:
> "When I was alive . . ."
>
> (*RJPoems* 51)

This poem suggests the paradox that a fleeting, necessary, sense of liberation and power can be grasped only through a confrontation with and acknowledgment of realities of loss, of powerlessness, of mortality. In a 1948 letter, William Carlos Williams, in the act of praising several of Jarrell's recent war poems, expressed concern about some of their endings. Jarrell replied, in a letter that included a typescript of "The Night Before the Night Before Christmas," which Jarrell describes as "a long poem I've been working on for six months." Jarrell responds, "I'm sure that, sub specie aeternitatis, what you say about the best poems having a 'return' from the losses must be true; but when you write about a war, really write about it, you haven't that much choice, and feel a direct responsibility to the facts i.e., people in it (most of which have no "return" mixed in at all)" (*RJLet* 190–91). But Williams's demand for a "return" from the experience of losses, while certainly present in this poem, is fulfilled quite ambiguously. The poem concludes with the girl returned to her bed and poring, in her dream, over a book with invisible pages.

> And, moving her licked, chapped, parted lips,
> She reads, from the white limbs' vanished leaves:
> *To End Hopefully*
> *Is A Better Thing—*
> *A Far, Far Better Thing—*
> It is a far, far better thing . . .
>
> She feels, in her hand, her brother's hand.
> She is crying.
>
> (*RJPoems* 51)

In her dream, if not in physical fact, brother and sister have journeyed far. Hence, the poem points to a psychic process of departure and return, offering the closeness of affection and the catharsis of tears. But the willed "hopefulness" of the ending combines curiously with the tears, which somehow seem more real than the curious and ironic echoes of the heroic but doomed gallows-words that conclude *A Tale of Two Cities.*

Berryman was certainly thinking of this poem in one of his *Dream Song* elegies for Jarrell, which uncannily echoes language and imagery of "The Night Before the Night Before Christmas."

> In the night-reaches dreamed he of better graces,
> of liberations, and beloved faces,
> such as now ere dawn he sings.
> It would not be easy, accustomed to these things,
> to give up the old world, but he could try;
> let it all rest, have a good cry.
>
> (*DS* 90)

Berryman, perhaps even more than Jarrell, lived "in the night reaches"—Mary Jarrell recalled his "2 A.M. telephone calls long distance" to Randall[56] —and he often, as well, "dreamed . . . of better graces, / of liberations and beloved faces," as the strangely inverted lyrical moments in the *Dream Songs* make clear. The dream in "The Night Before the Night Before Christmas" represents an unfulfilled yearning to imaginatively confront losses, mourn unprocessed griefs, and acknowledge real or imagined powerlessness, a yearning that both of these poets understood in the work of the other. And Berryman understood, better than many of Jarrell's critics, that representing a character who is having "a good cry" does not in itself render Jarrell's work sentimental. Rather, Jarrell is representing an experience of catharsis, one act in the process of coming to terms with loss, a process that in Jarrell's poem, is tinged by a tender, almost ineffable affection and irony.

## In the South: Elizabeth Bishop, Christmas 1936

Far to the south in late December 1936, Elizabeth Bishop was sailing from the (then) rustic Gulf coast community of Naples, Florida, on her first voyage to Key West—the extreme tip of the Florida Keys, the southernmost point in the United States, and Bishop's future home for more than ten years. Bishop's arrival in Key West—which along with other Floridian sites would become the setting for such poems as "Florida" (1939), "Roosters" (1941), "Cootchie" (1941), "Seascape" (1941), "Songs for a Colored Singer (1946), "Anaphora" (1945), "Little Exercise" (1946) and "Faustina, or Rock Roses" (1947)—opened a new phase in her career both as person and as artist. Life in Florida and later Key West encouraged Bishop to develop the incisive and flexible style that became the basis of an approach to poetic structure that will be defined in the next chapter as "narrative postmodernism." Bishop's successful experiments in this new mode caused Lowell to observe in 1962 that "Her rhythms, idiom, images, and stanza structure seemed to belong to a later century." Bishop's early reshaping of narrative along postmodern lines influenced the form of Lowell's *Life Studies*, helping him to "break . . . through the shell of my old manner" (*RLProse* 226), and it still serves, today, as a model in creative writing seminars nationwide.

Engaged by her isolated, frightening, loss-beset, and lonely childhood, Bishop's imagination was intensely, darkly, and wittily hermetic in those earlier poems she had been writing up to December 1936. And her work would continue to develop along these lines over the next two years, inspired, in Bishop's words, by those "awful fable ideas that seem to obsess me." But Bishop's imagination was stimulated in new directions by her travels, luring her to engage more directly with the seemingly endless variety of the world's flora and fauna, as well as with cultures different from her own. The remoteness, exoticism, and cultural diversity of these settings would provide Bishop not just with materials for her art, but with protective coloration that would help her to discover and explore a lifestyle radically different from that pursued by her male contemporaries. In Key West, Bishop began to attend to natural and cultural detail with a fresh and precise attention that would lead her to create poems that could hold inner and outer realities in peculiar and telling balance, and that would eventually lead her back to an artistically fruitful reexamination of her remarkably detailed childhood memories of Nova Scotia and Massachusetts.

In December 1936, Bishop could not point to anything like Berryman's or Jarrell's extra-poetic literary accomplishments. But Bishop had already accomplished something that would elude her slightly younger colleagues-to-be for years to come: she had published many poems of lasting value. When she wrote to Moore in August that she was ready to quit poetry and take up "medicine or biochemistry. . . . I feel I have given myself more than a fair trial, and the accomplishment has been nothing at all," Moore was able to reply, encouragingly and accurately, "To have produced what you have—either verse or prose is enviable."[57] By the time Bishop arrived in Key West in December 1936, she had already published a series of significant poems, many of which still hold their own in anthologies, and none of which have lost their vitality or their capacity to surprise. These include "Some Dreams They Forgot" (1933), "The Imaginary Iceberg" (April/June 1935), "The Man-Moth" (Spring 1936), "Casabianca" (April 1936), "The Colder the Air" (April 1936), "The Gentleman of Shallot" (April 1936). Already in draft as she began her voyage to Key West were several more poems, including "The Weed" (mentioned in an 18 October letter to Moore and published in February 1937,) "Paris, 7 A.M.," "A Miracle for Breakfast," "From the Country to the City" and "Song" (most or all begun by December 1936 and all published within the next three years). Thus, by the time Bishop reached Key West, she either had published or drafted nearly all of the "northern" poems in her first book, *North & South*, a book that would not appear for ten years, in 1946. Florida in general, and Key West in particular, gave Bishop's poetry a new and important arena of experience: a radically different culture and fresh and colorful new topography. And the dynamic opposition of diverse cultural mindsets that would be central to her Brazilian work was already beginning to emerge.

And, by December 1936, though Bishop had as yet no way of knowing it, she had already won John Berryman as a lifelong reader and admirer. When Bishop wrote a 1968 fan letter in praise of *His Toy, His Dream, His Rest*, Berryman replied: "Thank you for your lovely letter. . . . There is no one living whose approval I would rather have. I've admired & loved your work since I read 'The Imaginary Iceberg' in *Trial Balances* when I was an undergraduate at Columbia."[58] Berryman's memory, though understandably a trifle imprecise after nearly thirty-five years, reveals just how intensive and complete was his coverage of the literary scene in the mid-1930s. It was Bishop's "The Map"—not her "Imaginary Iceberg"—that first appeared (along with four earlier and lesser poems she later chose not to collect) in *Trial Balances*, an historic volume of "trial" poems by fledgling poets "balanced" with introductory essays by established masters. Introducing Bishop was Moore herself, who noted presciently: "the rational considering quality in her work is its strength—assisted by unwordiness, uncontorted intentionalness, the flicker of impudence, the natural unforced ending."[59] It was this "flicker of impudence" peeking out from Bishop's style that would trouble Moore in "Roosters" and that would eventually emerge as one of the salient characteristics of Bishop's poetry.

That Berryman transposed "The Imaginary Iceberg" and "The Map" in his memory shows that he also must have read and remembered Bishop's "Imaginary Iceberg" on its first publication, for it, too, appeared in 1935, while Berryman was still at Columbia, not in *Trial Balances* but in the short-lived little magazine *Direction*. Bishop would write in reply, "I was amazed at your remembering 'Trial Balances'—but then, I have a copy of 'Three Young American Poets' right here."[60] Bishop's memory was also misleading her slightly in a way that looks quite like a Freudian slip. This 1940 New Directions volume, edited and published by James Laughlin, is actually titled *Five Young American Poets*. Laughlin had strongly urged Bishop to appear in this very book, even journeying to Key West from his offices in Connecticut to plead his case. Bishop refused because she did not want to supply the self-defining essay and the picture that Laughlin demanded, and because she wanted to wait until she had enough poems for a volume of her own. She was also offended by Laughlin's suggestion that she would provide the "sex appeal" in an otherwise all-male collection. Bishop's slot as the fifth poet and sole woman would be filled by Mary Barnard, the four others being taken by Berryman, Jarrell, and two poets who have been more or less forgotten: George Marion O'Donnell (a former Vanderbilt rival of Jarrell's) and W. R. Moses. By remembering this volume's title as "*Three* Young American Poets," Bishop seems, in 1968, to be unconsciously reshaping the book into the collection it might have been: an extraordinary introduction, at the dawn of their careers, to the work of *three* young American who would one day join with Lowell—then just twenty-three and without the poems, as yet, to even to share a volume with other poets—in the unofficial and enduring midcentury quartet that is the subject of this chapter, and this book.

Berryman's comment about "The Imaginary Iceberg" and, by implication, "The Map" establishes that he "admired & loved," from the moment of their initial publication, the first two poems of real merit that Bishop published anywhere outside school magazines. Unlike the early poems of Berryman or Jarrell, now largely forgotten, these two 1935 poems of Bishop's continue to be anthologized, repaying one's attention along with such intriguing poems of 1936 as "Casabianca," "The Colder the Air," "The Gentleman of Shallot," and, especially, the extraordinary "The Man-Moth." Bishop and Berryman would be the last of these poets to forge a significant personal connection. Even then, separated by great physical distance, they had to rely on letters.[61] But the evidence suggests that even as early as the mid-1930s, Bishop, along with Jarrell, was already beginning to emerge as one of the points on Berryman's compass.

Since graduation from Vassar College, Bishop's life had centered, uncomfortably, in New York City. Bishop had several excellent instructors at Vassar, including Miss Rose Peebles, whose course in "Contemporary Prose Fiction" brought inspiration to her junior year. But only now was she beginning to enjoy the informal but close mentoring of a real poet, Marianne Moore, though, in December 1936, Bishop was still a year-and-a-half away from Miss Moore's invitation to address her by her first name, Marianne (see *EBLet* 76). Bishop described herself as being, in her last year at Vassar, "painfully—no, *excruciatingly* shy" (*EBProse* 122). So this intensely shy, intensely proud, intensely inward, and habitually self-deprecating young poet found the New York literary scene—with its attendant egos and self-promotion, the clatter of its glittering cliques and claques—overwhelming. When Bishop sailed to Key West, "a place," she wrote her friend Frani Blough Muser, "that had never even entered my consciousness,"[62] on a charter boat over Christmas 1936 from her recently established base at the Keywaydin Fishing Camp, she was pursuing, for the moment, not literary reputation, but a simpler, more remote lifestyle, complete with wild flora and fauna, brilliant sunlight, swimming, and good fishing. By the following winter, Key West would become Bishop's artistic refuge and her primary place of residence—though she continued to make fairly frequent trips north, to New York, where she kept a small apartment, and—still further north—to Boston, the Maine coast, and Nova Scotia: the northerly perimeter of her first book, *North & South* (1946). Key West would remain the southern pole of Bishop's personal geography until 1951, when she settled still further south, in Brazil. But in December of 1936, accompanied by her college friend and frequent traveling companion Louise Crane, Bishop was exploring Key West for the first time.

She had recently experienced another unsettling loss, when she learned that a college boyfriend, Bob Seaver, a young man who had more than once begged her to marry him, without success, had died—a death "reported by the medical examiner as suicide," though this finding was disputed by his parents—on 21 November 1936. Seaver's sister, Elizabeth Seaver Helfman, recalled that, before his death, "It was clear to me that Robert and Bishop were very fond of each other. I assumed that they would get married. . . . I think that her relationship with my brother worried her because she did care so much about him. That's my theory. In a way she never really wanted to get involved. She said she was never going to marry anyone, and she never did. He was very much in love with her. I don't doubt that. He had so many girls, but she was the only one he really cared for."[63] Bishop's feeling for Seaver were complicated by Bishop's fierce sense of independence, her urge for privacy, and, of course, by her as yet incompletely acknowledged lesbian sexuality. Before Seaver's death, he sent Bishop a note which she received in the mail only after the event. This note, she told a friend, Barbara Chesney Kennedy, read, "Elizabeth, Go to hell," a fact she would later confirm to Frank Bidart. Kennedy recalled that Bishop, naturally, "sounded very upset." According to Millier, Bishop would later retell this story "in her most abject moments of guilt and self-recrimination."[64] Already, in early adulthood, Bishop had received unnerving confirmation of her early intimations of love's inextricable dangers and sorrows.

Ten years earlier, John Berryman, then just eleven years old, had lost his own father in Florida, "close by a smothering southern sea," and this death, too, had been reported by the coroner as suicide. As we have seen, Berryman's first wife Eileen reported that when he told her the details of his father's death for the first time, he behaved "as if he were confessing a crime *he* had committed, as if he were responsible for his father's death."[65] Though one might feel that Berryman and Bishop should not be held responsible for the deaths of these independent adults, each would remain haunted by guilt and an unrelieved sense of loss as a consequence—feelings that were confirmed and intensified, in Bishop's case, by the suicide of her former lover Lota de Macedo Soares in 1967. Bishop's trip from New York to Florida, retracing Berryman's migration north to New York ten years earlier following his father's death and his mother's prompt remarriage, may have been motivated, in part, by a desire to escape her own anxiety and guilt. Bishop's room at the Keywaydin Fishing Camp in December 1936 little resembled, in externals, Berryman's elegant student chambers at Clare College, Cambridge. Still, both Cambridge and coastal Florida offered radical changes of external setting that must have been comforting and stimulating for poets wounded inwardly: a place remote from home and one's own grievous history—a place with a history of its own, offering much to learn, and space to be apart. For Bishop, the further sojourn to Key West promised a setting still richer in repose and full of exotic and unlikely natural beauty. It also offered a place to define and come to terms with the lesbian sexuality, already implicit in high school poems like the "Dead" and stories like "The Thumb," a still not completely acknowledged sexual orientation that must have lent a troubling undercurrent to her relationship with Bob Seaver.

Bishop had arrived in Florida for the first time on 18 December 1936. She was then twenty-five, the eldest of the four poets under discussion here, and the only one no longer connected to a college or university. Bishop had graduated from Vassar College in 1934—and, with inheritances from her father and her paternal grandfather that would provide financial independence for the next two decades, and with no living parents or grandparents to offer guidance, affection, encouragement or restraint—Bishop was on her own far more completely than slightly younger contemporaries like Berryman, Jarrell, or Lowell.

Not only did Bishop have no family either to check or support her, but, in 1936, and for a decade to come, she had no close friends her own age who were poets, no contemporaries with whom to share the triumphs, frustrations and confusions of her art. On the other hand, Marianne Moore, twenty-four years older than Bishop, played the role of mentor, and perhaps, within the bounds of both poets' elaborate sense of propriety, surrogate parent. Moore read every piece of Bishop's writing, editorially, before the latter submitted it for publication, and several pieces benefited from Moore's scrupulous care with diction. When Bishop, with apologies to her mentor, admitted sending a story that had not yet passed under Moore's eyes to the *Partisan Review* to meet a contest deadline, Moore chided her protégée with the remark, "It was very independent of you to submit your prize story without letting me see it. If it is returned with a printed slip, that will be why."[66] Bishop's independence was rewarded, however, when the story won *Partisan*'s $100 prize, cementing an editorial relationship that would lead them to publish most of Bishop's best work until the early 1950s, when the *New Yorker* took over as her main periodical outlet. Even when Bishop refused one of Moore's suggestions, she did so politely and apologetically. Yet at this early stage in their relationship, both the elder and the younger poet had already begun to take note of tacit—but marked—differences in sensibility and aesthetic principle, differences that would later come to a head with Bishop's rejection of Moore's attempt to expurgate and recast the versification of one her greatest early poems, "Roosters" (1941).

Bishop had many friends with artistic leanings: painters Margaret Miller and Loren McIver, the critic Lloyd Frankenberg (McIver's husband), Frani Blough Muser, her old Walnut Hill School and Vassar College classmate, who would become for many years the editor of *Modern Music*, and Louise Crane, another Vassar classmate and the wealthy heiress-to-be of the Crane Paper fortune, who would soon emerge as an impresario of jazz and avant garde art. Bishop had attended Vassar with writers who would one day become famous, including Mary McCarthy, Eleanor Clark, and Muriel Rukeyser, but each was temperamentally quite different from Bishop, and none turned out to be a colleague with whom she could freely share ideas.[67] Millier notes that when Bishop shared a "literary lunch" in New York in January 1938 "with Mary McCarthy, F. W. Dupee, and Philip Rahv, a group then associated with the *Partisan Review*," and thus a group who already looked favorably on her work, this meeting "sufficiently fueled" the shy and insecure Bishop's "anxiety about writing to give her nightmares." Millier adds that: "In her notebook she recorded a series of transparent dreams that link the tools of her trade, particularly typewriters, with images suggesting war. In one dream, the typewriter keys are a code she must solve."[68] In 1936, Bishop had, in effect, no real poetic colleagues, and, abetted by her shyness and uneasiness about literary conversation, and her frequent sojourns to remote locales, this condition of comparative artistic isolation would persist for another decade, until a dinner party in New York that took place in 1947, when she met and formed lifelong friendships with Robert Lowell and their host, Randall Jarrell, the latter of whom had already produced, and the former of whom would soon produce, glowing reviews of her first book.

While Lowell would soon respond to his suffocating family situation with outright rebellion and even violence, by 1936 Bishop had no family to rebel against, and she had already internalized a quieter, more indirect, and possibly more traditionally "feminine" way of responding to painful emotion, by submerging it rather than by letting it burst violently forth. Florida would open the possibility of a more overtly observational kind of poetry, but even before she discovered the exoticism of the subtropics, she was already creating poems of great originality and subtlety that explore her lonely and painful inner world with a combination of wit, mystery, narrative surprise, metrical invention, and dazzling imagistic virtuosity. For even in such early, pre-Florida fables as "The Man-Moth," set in a surreal, nightmare version of Manhattan, Bishop was already creating poems of great complexity, wit, and emotional power. These poems offer an intensely hermetic but remarkably rich, subtle, and comprehensive treatment of her own emotional situation, represented in such a way that the emotional intensity lurks just beneath the enigmatic surface. About this most stunning of the poems she published in 1936, Lowell would later say, "In Elizabeth Bishop's 'Man-Moth' a whole new world is gotten out and you don't know what will come after any one line. It's exploring. And it's as original as Kafka. She's gotten a world, not just a way of writing. She seldom writes a poem that doesn't have this exploratory quality; yet it's very firm, it's not like beat poetry, it's all controlled."[69] Already Bishop was finding her way toward an aesthetic that could be "firm," yet exploratory, in which "a whole new world" could be "gotten out" while maintaining a mysterious emotional reserve. In several respects, "The Man-Moth" reads like a revisiting of "The Ballad of the Subway Train." Both poems begin above ground, then descend into a subway and explore its subterranean depths. And both involve curious, invented creatures. But the Ballad's "great dragons" who come into being "when God was young" and "earth hadn't found its place," are here supplanted by a still stranger and more surprising creature, the Man-Moth. The dragons are childlike and are punished like naughty children, but the Man-Moth is an adult and his human-like qualities are made more explicit. He is already wounded when we meet him. He mostly lives underground, making only "rare, although occasional" visits above ground. Unlike the dragons, he cannot fly, as a moth, of course, normally could. His human weight forces him to try to get aloft by scaling the buildings, dragging his wings behind him like a photographer's cloth, as he tries to crawl through the moon, "a small hole at the top of the sky, / proving the sky quite useless for protection." The journeys of Bishop's Man-Moth are strange, obsessive, thwarted quests that circle back to the original point of departure. When one corners the Man-Moth, one may attempt to extract his secret token of sorrow: "one tear, his only possession, like the bee's sting" (*EBPoems* 15). The weight of unmourned losses and griefs seems concentrated in this single tear, whose loss might prove fatal to its owner.

In her later work, the exploratory quality Lowell shrewdly noted in "The Man-Moth" would project both inward and outward in an uncanny and elusive way. Lowell was thinking in part of this poem when he articulated a theme of Bishop's poetry, the opposition of "motion, weary but persisting . . . stoically maintained" and terminus "rest, sleep, fulfillment or death" (*RLProse* 76–77). Bishop's 1927 dragons had combed the sky freely and joyously in a world before sin, but the Man-Moth inhabits a fallen urban world from the poem's outset, and, despite his wings, and his constant state of motion, he cannot fly. In "The Man-Moth" Bishop created one of the earliest of her many "complex self-portraits," a form widely employed by each of these poets in which not just the protagonist (here the imaginary Man-Moth) but every figure in the poem—the moth's useless wings, the coolly observing "Man," who does not share the Man-Moth's illusion, the tall, imprisoning buildings, the subway, with its "artificial tunnels" where one "dreams recurrent dreams," the "third rail, the unbroken draft of poison," and that elusive tear, serve as elements of a complex psychic portrait that the poem invites one to explore with immediate surprise and lingering wonderment.

## In the North: Robert Lowell, Christmas 1936

Lowell's Christmas 1936 has by no means been lost to history. It marked a sharp turning point in his life, and contributed quite directly to the beginnings of the midcentury quartet. In December 1936 the nineteen-year-old Lowell was halfway through his second year at Harvard, living in college rooms not far from his parents' townhouse in Boston's fashionable Back Bay. Lowell had been engaged in a running battle with his parents for years and lately these relations had undergone steadily increasing strain. One bone of contention was Lowell's determination to become a poet. His parents intended that he graduate from Harvard, settle into a profitable business career, and marry a woman of the Boston social elite.

His mother Charlotte was by all accounts focused almost entirely on externals and in the process persistently denied the emotional life of her son. Charlotte claimed that "Neither Daddy nor I wish in any way to force you into our way of life or behavior." Still, they would withhold any future financial support unless he complied.[70] In a late poem Lowell recalled his mother complaining of "Your profession of making what can't be done / the one thing you can do . . ." (*DBD* 36). Lowell resented that Harvard had been chosen for him by his parents, chiefly his mother, just as she had chosen his boarding school, St. Mark's, and before that, the Brimmer School—which was primarily for older girls. Lowell recalled that, while there, "I wished I were an older girl. I wrote Santa Claus for a field hockey stick. To be a boy at Brimmer was to be small, denied, and weak" (*LS* 27).

Lowell would remark of his five months in prison as a conscientious objector in 1943, "I was thankful to find jail gentler than boarding school or college—an adult fraternity." Lowell noted that he "grew congenial with other idealist felons, who had homemade faiths" and added slyly that after reading Samuel Butler "and God knows what . . . a thousand pages of Proust. I left jail more educated—not as they wished *re*-educated" (*RLProse* 279). Seven years before his imprisonment, Lowell, who had yet to publish a poem, had already developed his own homemade faith—in poetry. And he had already dedicated himself with an almost religious fervor to becoming a poet: a plan that, of necessity, and perhaps by intention, set him at odds with his family. Lowell read and wrote poetry tirelessly. Ransom would later comment, "His way of reading literature was to devour it, to get it quickly into his blood stream."[71] Already displaying what would emerge as a kind a genius for discipleship (paralleling what Stanley Kunitz called his "great gift for friendship"[72]), Lowell by 1936 had worked closely with the poet Richard Eberhardt, a teacher at St. Mark's, then shifted his attention to James Laughlin, recently returned from a visit to Pound at Rapallo and completing a degree at Harvard en route to the founding of the publishing house New Directions and such books as the 1940 *Five Young American Poets*.

Lowell's parents stood in the way of more than his plans to become a poet. They moved to break up his "unsuitable" engagement to Anne Dick, a woman of middle-class origins six years Lowell's senior. (The engagement would burn itself out of its own accord in a few months.) On 22 December 1936, urged on by Charlotte Lowell, Lowell's father wrote a stiffly formal and disapproving letter to Anne Dick's father, objecting to her visits to his son's college rooms. "Such behavior is contrary to all college rules, and most improper for a girl of good repute." Paul Mariani observes that "If the letter was meant to wound, it certainly succeeded."[73]

Lowell, who had long displayed signs of the manic-depressive disorder that would remain undiagnosed into the 1950s, responded with bewilderment and rage when Anne Dick handed him the letter on 27 December. As a small child, Lowell had worried that "to judge from my father, men between the ages of six and sixty did nothing but meet new challenges, take on heavier responsibilities, and lose all freedom to explode" (*LS* 28). On that day, Lowell himself exploded. He asked Anne Dick to drive him to his parents' house and there he knocked his father down, after presenting him with the note he had sent to the parents of Anne Dick. In a poem from *Lord Weary's Castle* explicitly titled "Rebellion," Lowell would make the first of a series of attempts to come to terms with this event, whose symbolic and practical import would take him a lifetime to unravel.

> There was rebellion, father, when the mock
> French windows slammed and you hove backward, rammed
> Into your heirlooms, screens, a glass-cased clock,
> The highboy quaking to its toes. You damned
> My arm that cast your house upon your head
> And broke the chimney flintlock on your skull.
>
> (*LWC* 35)

The passive voice ("There was rebellion") seems less than forthright: does it reflect an implicit attempt on Lowell's part to relieve himself of responsibility for his own actions? The fact that the "mock / French windows," providing entrance to 170 Marlborough Street, "slammed" before his father hoves backward, suggests that in this version Lowell enters the house violently. The poem, while still addressing "my father," then shifts to a dreamlike and wishful present.

> Last night the moon was full:
> I dreamed the dead
> Caught at my knees and fell:
> And it was well
> With me, my father.
>
> (*LWC* 35)

On this moonlit night, the speaker's dream seems to take him to the Vergilian underworld, where the dead reach out in supplication, "And it was well / With me, my father." Is there a certain feeling almost of triumph here? Has the rebellion succeeded? And will the apocalyptic process continue?

> Then
> Behemoth and Leviathan
> Devoured our mighty merchants. None could arm
> Or put to sea. O father, on my farm
> I added field to field
> And I have sealed
> An everlasting pact
> With Dives to contract
> The world that spreads in pain
>
> (*LWC* 35)

Yet this wishful dream of personal beneficence, in which one tries to sign a pact with the great merchant (Dives) to shrink the world's spreading miseries, falls apart when the son contemplates his past action: "But the world spread / When the clubbed flintlock broke my father's brain." The poem now no longer addresses the father, and it moves ever farther afield from biographical fact. Lowell didn't hit his father with a clubbed "flintlock" and he did not break his father's brain. And the sense of contrivance here is palpable, in a way that is completely eliminated in his later treatments of his relations with his father. This poem suggests an impulse to explore his own experience in verse, but he has not yet mastered a way of presenting such experience with an effective sense of scale. By sheer persistence and skill, Lowell would one day master this difficult art. This poem remains a remarkable document of a son's ambivalent feelings toward a father who can rebuke but not protect him.

It is worth comparing Lowell's treatment of this incident in 1946 with his more artistically mature treatment in *Notebook*. In the first version of that volume, *Notebook 1967–68*, Lowell addresses his memories in an unrhymed sonnet spoken to his former fiancée, Anne Dick, exploring the crisis that would soon lead to his departure to Kenyon College and Ransom's tutelage. Lowell's poem opens with Proustian detail, quieter memory-traces that gather toward a traumatic center.

> My father's letter to your father, saying
> tersely and much too stiffly that he knew
> you'd been coming to my college rooms alone—
> I can still almost crackle that slight note in my hand.
> I see your outraged father; you, his outraged daughter;
>
> (*Notebook 1967–68* 37)

Then the scene shifts to Lowell's own deeply troubled isolation, to his memory of reciting "Lycidas," a poem he was already turning to in times of trouble. And, then, suddenly, a shift to irrevocable action:

> myself brooding in fire and a dark quiet
> on the abandoned steps of the Harvard Fieldhouse,
> calming my hot nerves and enflaming my mind's
> nomad quicksilver by saying *Lycidas*—
> then punctiliously handing the letter to my father.
> I knocked him down.
>
> (*Notebook 1967–68* 37)

Lowell's great physical strength here frightens even him. As Jahan Ramazani notes, "Because of its highly wrought form, the elegy ["Lycidas"] calms and cools the young rebel. But it is not merely a break on his oedipal episode: it also plays the opposite role, 'enflaming' the poet's restless imagination. . . . Far from pacifying him, the recitation of the elegy is an act of symbolic rebellion that prepares for and parallels the physical act."[74] Yet the style of this passage is far from the floridly wrought diction of "Lycidas." Each image is like a little snapshot and together they form a disconnected sequence. The reader has to infer the transitions and the connecting motivations. As Ramazani suggests, "whereas Milton displaces the struggle for power from the domestic realm to the literary, Lowell redomesticates and literalizes it." But the action is not merely literal, and here the implied connections between the form and fire of poetry and domestic rebellion are surprising and cogent. For Lowell's family viewed his devotion to poetry as an act of rebellion. And in Lowell's poem, the act of knocking down his father follows almost immediately upon the recitation of "Lycidas," interrupted only by the formal gesture of "punctiliously" handing over his father's offending letter. Lowell's phrasing suggests that in his own former mind he was acting as if presenting a gentlemanly challenge in a duel. Except, of course, one doesn't challenge one's own father and in fact this particular fight took place without the formal controls and courtesies of a duel. Here, the awkward and awful just happens, and there is no way to return it to the consoling cycles of nature.

Then Lowell has to deal with the immediate consequences of his impulsive violence: consequences for his father, his family, his planned marriage, and himself.

> He half-reclined on the carpet;
> Mother called from the top of the carpeted stairs—
> our glass door locking behind me, no cover; you
> idling in your station wagon, no retreat.
>
> (*Notebook 1967–68* 37)

The carpet on which his father half-reclines links to the carpeted stairs his mother calls from. Then the objects seem to take over: "our glass door locking behind me, no cover." His parents, now protected, can see out at him, exposed. Will he ever see his way back into their house? And "you / idling in your station wagon, no retreat"—his fiancée is also behind a glass shield—only he is exposed. Although she drives a rather domestic-sounding getaway car, her claims on him, and her own function as a witness to this humiliating domestic violence, actually cut off his immediate escape from humiliation. One encounters no claim to authorial privilege here; the author renounces both the grand style of "Quaker Graveyard," which had once been native soil, and the privileges of implied moral superiority over the parents against whom he rebels. Whatever their own abuses, he knows this is an act that he cannot justify. This young poet may know "Lycidas" by heart, but his emerging command of the poetic tradition does not help him to deal with the stresses and conundrums of ordinary life. This poem may be read as a kind of elegy for the concept of the privileged author. Yet it is by no means a "naked confession," either. For all its elements of literalness, it may best be read as an exploration of memory and self, exploring without sentimentality, rationalization, or posturing an event that might relate to a reader's own awkward and impulsive actions, actions that he or she might wish to be able to retract, actions one reviews among the private stations of one's own secret humiliation and grief. As Lowell puts it in a subsequent poem:

> I struck my father; later my apology
> hardly scratched the surface of his invisible
> coronary . . . never to be effaced.
> (*Notebook 1967–68* 37)

Lowell's impulsive explosion, his act of striking his father to the floor, would precipitate the first in the series of connections that linked these poets in an unofficial network. Lowell's conflict with his parents over his fiancée was only the most recent in a long line of mysterious and disturbing actions by a son who would not be diagnosed manic-depressive and treated for nearly two decades. Dr. Merrill Moore, a thirty-three-year-old psychiatrist and a member of the Nashville Agrarians who was already treating Charlotte Lowell, was called in to consult on the case of Robert. Moore's diagnosis might be summed up as: too much family, too much Harvard, too much Boston. And his prescription, to send Lowell to visit Allen Tate and John Crowe Ransom at Vanderbilt University, would have lasting implications for literary history. Dr. Moore provided good personal and literary advice, but not much psychiatry; he didn't get at the root causes of Lowell's problems. But he set Lowell on a course that would shape his career.

Lowell attended classes at Vanderbilt in the spring of 1937, spending the summer with Allen Tate, his wife Caroline Gordon, and the visiting Ford Madox Ford and his young wife. When Caroline Gordon said she had no room for him in the house, and added jokingly that he'd have to sleep in a tent in the yard, Lowell went out and bought the tent. Here was a young man desperately in need of a sympathetic familial and literary environment. And when, that fall, Ransom moved from Vanderbilt to a new position at Kenyon College, Lowell followed as his newest protégé.

## Convergence of the Twain: Jarrell and Lowell at Kenyon

Jarrell expected to spend the 1937–38 academic year completing his masters degree at Vanderbilt. But in the spring of 1937, Gordon Chalmers, president of then-little-known Kenyon College, and Jarrell's future skiing companion, offered Ransom a Carnegie Professorship. Mary Jarrell recounts what happened next:

> "Ransom submitted the proposal to his English department, supposing that (after some twenty years of teaching, several published books, and many editorships, prizes, and distinctions) Vanderbilt would match little Kenyon's offer and all would continue as before. To the astonishment of many and the outrage of Jarrell, mighty Vanderbilt decided to pass. In a fury, Jarrell circulated a petition to keep Ransom, and got hundreds of signatures from faculty members and students. But the English department were unmoved, and Ransom went" (RJLet 49).

Where Ransom went, Jarrell followed. The gentlemanly, acerbic southerner of forty-nine and the skinny, athletic enfant terrible of twenty-three arrived in Gambier, Ohio, in the fall of 1937, Jarrell in the role of tennis coach and part-time English instructor. At Kenyon, Jarrell would live away from home for the first time, sharing an upstairs room rent-free in Ransom's house with a newer protégé of Tate's, and yet another young man in need of a surrogate father—a brawny, handsome, learned, high-spirited, unkempt twenty-year-old refugee from the constraints of Harvard, upper-crust Boston, and his parents home "on Boston's / 'hardly passionate Marlborough Street'" (*LS* 85).

As Ransom later remembered it: "Jarrell and Lowell, and I and my family, descended upon Kenyon at the same time, and for the first year they lived in the cold upstairs of our farmhouse on the campus. They took to each other at once, and made everlasting compact of friendship. No fear that they might be competitors, though we all knew they were destined to be writers; these were God's own originals."[75] Elsewhere, Ransom recalled of Lowell, "His animal spirits were high, his personality was spontaneous, so that he was a little bit overpowering. But a natural goodness shone from his face. We had Randall Jarrell in our house too, an M.A. graduate; and if a few others came in sometimes, our tone became that of a hilarious party, and Lowell was the life of it."

According to Lowell, the Jarrell of that period was "unsettlingly brilliant, precocious, knowing, naive and vexing" (*RLProse* 90). Their complex friendship involved, perhaps, a dash more rivalry than Ransom was inclined to acknowledge in 1965, but it also involved an unusual measure of mutual support, understanding—and tolerance of one another's eccentricities. Lowell would later write, in his prose elegy of Jarrell, of the young man he had known at Kenyon in 1937, "He had the harsh luminosity of Shelley—like Shelley, every inch a poet, and like Shelley, imperiled perhaps by an arid, abstracting precocity. Not really! Somewhere inside him, a breezy, untouchable spirit had even then made its youthful and sightless promise to accept—to accept and never to accept the bulk, confusion, and defeat of mortal flesh . . . all that blithe and blood-torn dolor!" (*RLProse* 91).

What did these poets share, aside from their literary precocity, that allowed Jarrell to appreciate the "vivid incongruity" (*TBC* 333) he found in Lowell's writing, or that allowed Lowell to savor the "blithe and blood-torn dolor" he found in Jarrell's? Not only was each drawn to the unusual level of talent, learning, imagination, and intelligence he saw in the other. In addition, each recognized that he shared with the other a common set of difficulties. Each had had an unhappy, traumatic childhood, marked by the physical or emotional absence of the father and dominated by a terrifying, prestige-driven and frequently contemptuous mother who had consistently slighted her son's intentions and wishes in the past. Each had met the other on their first excursion from the troubled family circle. Each was struggling toward personal maturity, and toward a viable artistic persona, in the context of a family environment explicitly opposed to a career in writing and unable to bestow unconditional love. And they shared the same chief mentors, especially John Crowe Ransom and Allen Tate.

## Beginnings of a Four-Way Conversation

In "From the Kingdom of Necessity" Jarrell reads his friend intuitively, seeing a conflict of opposites that resembles the conflict between motion and terminus Lowell saw in Bishop's *North & South*. He suggested that "perhaps people will understand the poetry more easily, and find it more congenial, if they see what the poems have developed out of, how they are related to each other, and why they say what they say" (*P&A* 208). Jarrell, without explicitly revealing the contours of Lowell's own early family life speaks very closely about them, arguing that the conflict in Lowell's *Lord Weary* is between a "realm of necessity" dominated by "custom" and "everything that is free or open, that grows or is willing to change." Without untoward disclosures, Jarrell's exposition neatly summarizes Lowell's family conflict. Parents driven by custom and social prestige have erected a looming framework of necessity from which the nearly-adult son struggles to escape.

Jarrell notes that "the poems can have two possible movements or organizations: they can move from what is closed to what is open, or from what is open to what is closed." Citing an example of the latter, "'unhappy ending'" type of poem, Jarrell mentions "Between the Porch and the Altar," with "its four parts each ending in constriction and frustration and its hero who cannot get free of his mother, her punishments, and her world even by dying, but who sees both life and death in terms of her." Jarrell notes, however, that "normally the poems move into liberation," adding that "In 'Rebellion' the son seals 'an everlasting pact / With Dives to contract / The world that spreads in pain'; but at last he rebels against his father and his father's New England commercial theocracy, and 'the world *spread* / When the clubbed flintlock broke my father's brain.' The italicized words ought to demonstrate how explicitly, at times, these poems formulate the world in the terms that I have used" (*P&A* 210).

Jarrell was no doubt speaking from his own intimate knowledge of Lowell when he said of him a quarter-century later, in 1962, "Perhaps because his own existence seems to him in some sense as terrible as the public world—his private world hangs over him as the public world hangs over others—he does not forsake the headlined world for the refuge of one's private joys and decencies, the shaky garden of the heart" (*TBC* 333). To undertake their arduous parallel journey in search of the "shaky garden of the heart," Lowell and Jarrell, like Bishop and Berryman, would need companionship, as well as the kind of learning that comes from an interchange marked by alternating discipleship and confrontation. And it was just such patterns of responsiveness that would develop between this midcentury quartet of poets.

Bishop, in one of her many long letters to Lowell from Brazil, cites a practitioner of another art on this very point: "Vergil Thomson says, 'One of the strange things about poets is the way they keep warm by writing to one another all over the world'" (*EBLet* 416). She interrupted another long, newsy letter to Lowell from Brazil in 1961 with a still more telling remark, aimed, apparently, at supporting her friend through a recent depression: "Dear Cal—if you only knew how many imaginary conversations I have with you all the time and how little any of this [her own letter] represents what I am really thinking, doing, etc.—Lota [de Macedo Soares] and I talk about you a lot and we both hope and pray you are better, that things are going well, and that your life is matching the splendour and success of your work."[76] She went on a few months later to insist, "You have no idea, Cal, how really grateful to you I am and how fortunate I feel myself in knowing you, having you for a friend—when I think how the world and my life would look to me if you weren't in either of them at all—they'd look very empty I think. . . . I don't seem to need or enjoy a lot of intellectual society—but I certainly need you."[77]

Jarrell had sent a remarkably similar letter to Lowell in August 1945, just after Japan's surrender brought World War II to a close. Written from the Air Corps post at Davis-Monthan field in Tucson, Arizona, where Sgt. Randall Jarrell was serving as a Celestial Navigation Trainer, he declared —the year before his important meetings with Bishop and Berryman— "I'll certainly be glad to see you. I haven't even seen anybody I *know* in three years. You are the only writer I feel much in common with (when I read your poems I not only wish that I had written them but feel that mine in some queer sense are related to them—i.e., if I didn't write the way I do I might or would like to write the way you do; your poems about the war are the only ones I like except my own—both of them have the same core of sorrow and horror and so on) and the only good friend of my own age I have" (*RJLet* 128). The friendships with Bishop and Berryman that Jarrell would soon develop thus helped this brilliant and singular individual to fill a real void in his intellectual and emotional life. Mary Jarrell, the poet's widow, would later recall that on the rare occasions when Jarrell and Berryman could get together, the intellectual sparks flew, and she further recalled that Jarrell was on the receiving end of several of Berryman's anxious, inebriated 2 A.M. telephone calls.[78]

The years just after World War II marked the beginning of a decisive convergence among this quartet of poets. One of them, Elizabeth Bishop, found a place in the circle after a single memorable evening early in 1947. Jarrell, discharged from the Army Air Corps and standing in for Margaret Marshall for his year as literary editor of the *Nation*, had recently and fleetingly met Bishop, and, as a longtime admirer, he promptly invited Bishop to dinner with Lowell. For all three poets, this would prove a fortunate meeting. James Merrill, noting how Bishop's example helped him solve the problem of "day-to-day living" as a poet, commented: "Like her I had no graduate degree, didn't feel called upon to teach, preferred to New York's literary circus the camouflage of another culture."[79] Bishop felt deeply uncomfortable in New York, surrounded by the "literary circus," but immediately felt at home with Jarrell and Lowell, despite qualities in each of them that other writers found formidable or even threatening. It is likely that Bishop was drawn by the intelligence, imagination, deep reading, and artistic seriousness she found in both. She was drawn to Jarrell's lack of pretension, his boyish frankness, his uncanny critical acumen, and his spontaneous good spirits when excited by the presence of writers he admired—including, especially, Bishop and Lowell. She later wrote, in response to Jarrell's glowing and prescient review of *Poems*

(1955), "Sometimes I have the odd sensation that I am writing solely for you—which, after this piece, I don't mind a bit but shall try to relax and enjoy" (*EBLet* 312).[80]

She was drawn to Lowell's deference, collegiality, good looks, bearish sense of humor, and thinly masked vulnerability, as well as by his profound admiration of her poems, which rivaled Jarrell's. Almost immediately, Lowell took over Marianne Moore's role, vacated since the dispute over "Roosters" in 1941, as Bishop's professional mentor. For the rest of Bishop's life, she would depend on Lowell, though he was six years her junior, for help in finding financial support through grant opportunities and, later, teaching jobs. Lowell and Bishop became one another's correspondents-in-chief, and they would exchange hundreds of long letters over the next thirty years, letters—constituting one of the extraordinary literary correspondences of the twentieth century—whose bounty can only be suggested in these pages. Also, despite Bishop's predominantly lesbian sexual orientation, and the fact that she was six years Lowell's senior, there was a barely latent erotic dimension to their mutual attraction that led Lowell to yearn to propose marriage on more than one occasion.

After this single meeting in January 1947, Bishop, previously almost alone amidst the contemporary literary circus, entered the intimate circle formed by Lowell and Jarrell ten years before. Each of these poets, Berryman and Bishop as well as Jarrell and Lowell, would slowly put behind them the impersonal poetics of high modernism and learn how to explore "the shaky garden of the heart" in poetry that convincingly represents the inextricable intermingling of the private and the public.

# PART 3

# MAKING A POSTMODERN AESTHETIC

# 5 The Problem of Selfhood in the Postmodern World

No ideas but in things.

William Carlos Williams

There are no things in a poem, only processes.

Randall Jarrell

## Randall Jarrell and the Poetry of Process

Commenting on the massive cultural shifts that had created romanticism and modernism—and anticipating further shifts that might soon lead to "the sort of poetry that replaces modernism"—Randall Jarrell, a twenty-six-year-old poet and part-time university instructor composing his first extensive critical essay, observed in 1940 that "the great changes in literature are non-literary in origin; and the same causes that produce the new work produce, in time, its audience. Wordsworth's poems did not produce the Wordsworthians—the things that made Wordsworth write a certain type of poetry at the beginning of the nineteenth century, by the middle of the century had prepared its readers" (*KA&Co* 48). At this point in his career, Jarrell—who had not yet achieved his personal voice as a poet though he was finding it as a critic—felt himself hovering on the cusp of the postmodern world.

Five years later, in the prose poem "1914," Sgt. Jarrell would look back on the Great War that had confirmed the presence of the modernist era: "Now it is no longer the war, but a war: The World War is only the First World War; and, truly, these are photographs not of the world, but of the first world. But for twenty years, while the wire and trenches in the mud were everybody's future, how could any of it seem old-fashioned to us? —it was our death. But when we died differently we saw that it was old" (*RJPoems* 201).

In James Laughlin's New Directions volume *Five Young American Poets*, which also included Berryman and would have included Bishop had Laughlin gotten the young woman poet he most wanted, Jarrell announced combatively at the start of the essay (part of the preface that Laughlin had demanded): "I may as well say what the reader will soon enough see, that I don't want to write a preface. . . . I don't want the poems mixed up with my life or opinions or picture or any other regrettable concomitants" (*KA&Co* 47). Jarrell devoted most of his essay to developing the thesis that modernism was "essentially, an extension of romanticism," which by 1940 had reached a "culminating point" (*KA&Co* 48). His last sentence makes his first and only reference to his own artistic intentions, acknowledging that "the reader may have thought curiously, 'Does he really suppose he writes the sort of poetry that replaces modernism?' Let me answer, like the man in the story, 'I must decline the soft impeachment.' But I am sorry I need to" (*KA&Co* 51). John Crowe Ransom, reviewing *Five Young American Poets* in a 1941 issue of *Kenyon Review*, called Jarrell "the most brilliant of the five." And drawing on his own intimate familiarity with the twenty-seven-year-old author under review, he observed, not without a trace of irritation, that "In the prose conclusion, as in the poetic sequel, Jarrell forbids us to say yet that he is a post-modernist. But probably he will be. It is self-consciousness which stops the young poets from their own graces; too much thinking about all the technical possibilities at once, as well as too much attention to changes in fashion."[1] Ransom's is the earliest documented use of the much debated term "post-modernist" in a literary context, predating—by at least six years—other references cited as "the earliest."

Even as the New Criticism, which picked up its own name from the title of a 1941 anthology of *Kenyon Review* criticism edited by Ransom, was taking on a public identity and beginning its rapid progress toward academic hegemony, Jarrell was pointing toward a "post-modern" position that would, in the long run, undercut several of the New Criticism's soberest aesthetic assumptions. It was precisely by "thinking about all the technical possibilities at once" *without* excessive concern for "changes in fashion," but with an intuitive awareness of the cultural context and the requirements of the particular poem being written, that poets such as Bishop, Berryman, and Lowell would mark this line of postmodern development.

Artists such as Jarrell, Bishop, Lowell, and, Berryman were among the first to sense a major shift in the cultural climate, a shift that would one day come to be named "the postmodern condition." Certain of these poets, especially Jarrell and Berryman, began to find a need for the term postmodern. And they began to use it and to speak in ways that provoked others to so describe them, in the early to mid-1940s, as they went through the process of working out their own early aesthetic formulations. More importantly, they wrote poems (at first tentatively, but soon with more confidence and power) that bring to dramatic life their growing intuition of cultural change. Significantly, by the late 1940s these poets had identified in one another's work trends that seemed postmodern and that seemed to suffice. For after Berryman's 1948 essay "Waiting for the End Boys," which praised Bishop energetically and agreed with Jarrell's 1947 attribution of postmodern qualities to Lowell, these poets simply abandoned discursive use of the term "post-modern," and addressed themselves to the primary business of writing poems. In the process they continued to develop postmodern techniques reflecting their perception of a new constellation of cultural conditions and their implications for the individual human self.

By the 1970s these changes in the condition of western culture became both so profound and so pervasive that they began to appear on scholarly radar screens. By the time the discourse of postmodernism grew to a position of real scope and influence, and as it aspired toward ever more comprehensive claims, several of postmodernism's most important originators and artistic pioneers had long since dropped off the radar screens and their contributions came to be elided. This sort of elision has of course often been the fate of artistic or intellectual pioneers, whose contributions then have to be recovered, in part by a careful sifting for evidence of the documentary record.

On 30 April 1942, a twenty-seven-year-old poet-critic named Randall Jarrell gave the Mesures Lecture at Princeton University. Jarrell was quite young to be invited to take part in such a prestigious series, which had previously featured R. P. Blackmur and Kenneth Burke. But Jarrell had already made a name for himself as a critic, having recently produced such important white papers on current letters as "Contemporary Poetry Criticism" and "The End of the Line," as well as penetrating evaluations of individual authors such as "The Morality of Mr. Winters," "Tate Versus History," and "The Development of Yeats's Sense of Reality." At the same time, Jarrell was acquiring a reputation as the most fearsome, witty, and insightful poetry reviewer since Edgar Allan Poe. In an April 1942 letter to fellow Marxist critic Edmund Wilson, recently his editor at the *New Republic*, Jarrell described his forthcoming lecture: "it's about *Structure in Poetry*. . . . to the effect that the 'logical' structure of poetry is, very often, roughly dialectical, this with many examples; but don't tell this to my friends, for they would disown me, or to my superiors, for they would discharge me—or would if they knew or cared what *dialectical* meant" (*RJLet* 59–60). Jarrell's "friends" were socially conservative mentors such as Ransom, Cleanth Brooks and Allen Tate, members of the Fugitive Movement in poetry with whom Jarrell had studied at Vanderbilt University in the mid-1930s. Jarrell's "superiors"—senior professors in the English Department at the University of Texas at Austin, where he was then serving as a part-time instructor—already disapproved pointedly, as he noted with amusement to Tate, "of having my things in 'that radical magazine, *The Nation*'" (*RJLet* 51).

Previous scholars have concluded with William H. Pritchard in his 1990 *Randall Jarrell: A Literary Life* that "the lecture has not survived."[2] Yet it appeared complete, with my introduction, in the winter 1996 issue of the *Georgia Review*, including a clinching citation mentioned in his letter to Wilson: "a charming quotation from Blake: 'In poetry Unity and Morality are secondary considerations.' I'm kidding—halfway" (*RJLet* 60). The document, a relatively clean twenty-two-page typescript with a few handwritten corrections, caught my eye as I was browsing among Jarrell's papers housed in the Berg Collection of the New York Public Library, where it is catalogued under the intriguing heading "Criticism is Impossible." Jarrell in fact jotted "Crit. is impossible" at the top of his typescript, which has no title page, perhaps as a reminder to make a conversational introduction to a text that begins rather abruptly. It may also have been an afterthought, since his argument, radical for 1942, received a frosty reception from its initial Princeton audience, according to a letter from Allen Tate to Cleanth Brooks indicating that Jarrell's lecture ranked a poor eighth in popularity among the Mesures lectures. The lecture appeared in the *Georgia Review* as "Levels and Opposites"—the title Jarrell employed at Princeton—with the descriptive subtitle of "Structure in Poetry" borrowed from his letter to Wilson.[3]

To understand the intellectual sources that stimulated Jarrell, one must return to the fall of 1937, when Jarrell and Lowell shared rooms in the chilly upper story of John Crowe Ransom's house at Kenyon College. Lowell recalled in a 1965 memoir of his recently departed comrade-in-the-arts that "Ransom and Jarrell had each separately spent the preceding summer studying Shakespeare's Sonnets, and had emerged with unorthodox and widely differing theories. Roughly, Ransom thought that Shakespeare was continually going off the rails into illogical incoherence. Jarrell believed that no one, not even William Empson, had done justice to the rich, significant ambiguity of Shakespeare's intelligence and images. I can see and hear Ransom and Jarrell now, seated on one sofa, as though on one love seat, the sacred texts open on their laps, one fifty, the other just out of college, and each expounding to the other's deaf ears his own inspired and irreconcilable interpretation." In a letter written two decades after this memorable argument about Shakespeare's sonnets, Lowell recalled in a letter to Elizabeth Bishop: "You know Randall has his own flippant natural language. . . . Randall and Ransom sat talking one evening and every minute Randall got more enthusiastic about Shakespeare and more and more breezy about Ransom's critical points. At the end Ransom said, 'That boy just doesn't have a critical vocabulary.'"[4]

Ransom's views appeared promptly in the essay "Shakespeare At Sonnets," collected in *The World's Body* (1938). Ransom argues that the *Sonnets:* "are generally ill-constructed. They use the common English metrical pattern, and the metrical work is admirable, but the logical pattern more often than not fails to fit it." Jarrell names neither Ransom nor the *Sonnets* in his 1942 "Structure in Poetry," but the lecture grows very clearly out of Jarrell's "own inspired and irreconcilable interpretation." Jarrell insists that, "Poetry loves contradictions, real ones; logic denies that they exist. . . . The structure of logic is the wrong *sort* of structure for poetry; to say that the structure of a poem is logical is not only not a guarantee that the structure is effective, it is a guarantee that this structure, unless assisted by another variety of structure, will be thoroughly ineffective."

Jarrell is outlining the basis for an alternative critical paradigm of poetic structure that strikes at the conceptual roots of Ransom's neoclassical formalism. Jarrell rejects the New Critical conception of the poem as a static unity, a "verbal icon," and he rejects as well the corollary assumption that the tension in poetry tends always toward a state of equilibrium—or "balanced poise," as I. A. Richards put it. For Jarrell "the poem is completely temporal, about as static as an explosion; there are no things in a poem, only processes." Jarrell points out that, "In our time there has been a tremendous emphasis on the irony and ambiguity of poetry; critics like Richards, Cleanth Brooks, and Empson have pushed these partial, and extremely valuable, views to the limit. But ironic or ambiguous structures are merely special varieties of dialectical structures." And Jarrell soon makes clear that dialectic is just one example chosen from a dizzying multiplicity of structural possibilities. For Jarrell, "There are *many* different sorts of structure in poetry, *many* possible ways of organizing a poem; and *many* of these are combined in the organization of a single poem."

Displaying a wide-ranging "critical vocabulary" that incorporates and then goes well beyond Ransom's own, Jarrell's conception of poetry in 1942 displays many of the characteristics now commonly associated with a postmodern poetics. Jarrell argues that "Poetry is interested in communicating extremely complicated systems of thoughts, perceptions, and emotions, which have extremely complicated non-logical structures; for this, logical structure is pathetically inadequate. In poetry we are trying, often, to do things which logic cannot do, which can be done only in defiance of logic: to reconcile the individual to both sides of an inconsistent world order, to console him for the inconsolable, to unify things which cannot be unified and which any submission to reality should make us differentiate." In Jarrell's subsequent work, and the work of contemporaries like Lowell, Bishop, and Berryman, the attempt to "unify things which cannot be unified" is often in fact abandoned, and the poems end without ever achieving, or attempting, closure.

Jarrell's second major target in his lecture, after the emerging doctrine of logic, balance, and symmetrical order fundamental to New Criticism, was the then "famous" discussion of structure in Yvor Winters's 1937 *Primitivism and Decadence*, which Jarrell questions a good deal more explicitly, and far less politely, than he questions Ransom. Despite the fact that Winters's discussion "has . . . been praised as the critical feat of the time," Jarrell finds it woefully inadequate and incomplete, an atavistic projection of "all the abstract, static, rationalistic, metaphysical side of Western thought."

Jarrell argues that the tendency of elders like Winters, Ransom and Tate to cling to these abstract modes of thought is "as great a hindrance in criticism as it is in anything else." And he wonders why, "if two thousand years of these proper and traditional views have left the criticism of poetry in the profoundly, the traditionally unsatisfactory state in which we find it, why should anyone on earth believe that the preservation or restoration of these views will *save* our criticism? I should think that critics would welcome some improper views, for a change." Jarrell suggests that a more satisfactory state of criticism will only be achieved when readers begin to develop "a dislike of all the systems or generalizations that actual observation does not justify."

Describing his progress on the Mesures lecture to Edmund Wilson, Jarrell remarks, "I have about a pound of notes." And his analysis of the "*many* different sorts of structure in poetry" is in fact extremely perceptive and uniquely extensive. Citing these as "a few from many," Jarrell fills a typescript page with thirty-one distinct "structural methods" observable in existing poems, including the following characteristically suggestive foursome: "dream-structure, Freudian ambivalence, and so on; symbols, considered as matrices of incipient judgments; consistent levels of imagery, formality, vocabulary; logical fallacies, pseudo-logic." By arguing for the presence of several (perhaps contradictory) organizing principles operating at once in a good poem, Jarrell is emphasizing the importance of process, of dramatizing the mind in action, of simultaneity, of polyvocality and multiple points of view, and he is thus anticipating the translation of Mikhail Bakhtin's *The Dialogic Imagination* (1981) into English by nearly forty years.

Jarrell's studies in the dialogics of poetic structure helped equip him to become a nearly unerring judge of excellence in poetry. In particular, Jarrell's studies in poetic structure made him the outstanding early reader of contemporaries such as Lowell and Elizabeth Bishop, and to foresee the most profitable future direction for the work of the young Berryman.

Jarrell was certainly paraphrasing his own unpublished lecture when he said of Lowell's *Lord Weary's Castle* in 1947, "The poems understand the world as a sort of *conflict of opposites*," and he paraphrases further as he observes that "the shifts of movement, the varied pauses, the alternation in the length of sentences, and the counterpoint between lines and sentences are the outer form of a subject matter that has been given a *dramatic, dialectical internal organization;* and it is hard to exaggerate the strength and life, the constant richness and surprise of metaphor and sound and motion, of the language itself" (*P&A* 208, 215–16; emphases added). Jarrell was prepared to understand the aesthetic, cultural, and emotional oppositions and to enjoy the "constant richness and surprise" animating Lowell's poems (and to help Lowell realize their potential more fully in the extraordinary series of critical readings Jarrell gave the book in manuscript) because Jarrell had already worked through the functions of such oppositions in his own mind.

Why the lecture was not published shortly after its delivery cannot be determined with certainty, but we should not disregard Jarrell's references to his "friends" and "superiors" in the letter to Wilson. That is, Jarrell may have refrained from rushing into print trenchant disputes with two of the leading and most powerful critical theorists of his day, John Crowe Ransom and Yvor Winters. Jarrell had recently experienced more than his share of controversy when he took a public buffeting for his pointed 1941 critique of Conrad Aiken in the *New Republic.* He knew that Winters would be a formidable opponent. In his lecture, Jarrell acknowledges that

"No matter how sure I may be that one of [Mr. Winters's] decrees is nonsense, I always . . . feel the greatest trepidation about questioning it."

But Jarrell was not a critic to be guided by his fears. It seems more likely that he chose out of loyalty to defer the publication a piece that would certainly have been judged as a direct attack (despite his never being named) on Jarrell's respected and beloved "Mr. Ransom." Of course, Jarrell may simply have been enlisted for service in the Army Air Corps too soon after giving his lecture to give the text his customary stylistic finish. He describes his prose in the letter to Wilson as not "anything very elegant." But it is characteristically funny, lucid, and engaging, and the final polish couldn't have cost much effort.

Jarrell's analysis of poetic structure remained in typescript during 1946–1947, when he was literary editor of the *Nation.* In 1950, when editor John Ciardi aimed a battery of questions at the youngish authors anthologized in his *Mid-Century American Poets*, he asked, among other things, what guides "YOUR attitude" toward "the structure of the total poem; what makes its unity?" Jarrell's replies to Ciardi's questionnaire were as a rule terse and reluctant, but here he bordered on the enigmatic and evasive: "An answer would take too many pages."[5] The present rediscovery makes clear that the "too many pages" Jarrell referred to are the twenty-two pages of his 1942 Mesures lecture, since it explores, quite specifically, "the structure of the total poem." This, then, was a typescript Jarrell would neither release, summarize, nor destroy. Even years later, it remained in Jarrell's mind, yet also firmly in his desk drawer—only now to emerge at long last as the century draws toward its close.

Whatever his motives for not publishing his theory of poetic structure, Jarrell's reluctance has contributed to the unfortunate current impression that this poet's keen critical judgment lacked a theoretical center and that his insights were solely the product of intuition. Years ago, I remember praising Jarrell's criticism to a fellow graduate student and being met with the scornful rejoinder that Jarrell's writings contained "not a single theoretical formulation!" Bruce Michelson similarly laments in a recent study that "because reviewing was the craft he commonly practiced, his writing shaped itself to that craft, and a price of sorts had to be paid. Short was the space he could give to any one subject, and so he became famous for the quick, venomous strike, rather than for cooler, more patient, more precisely constructive criticism."[6]

These assessments overlook a great deal of published Jarrell, including his extensive, precise and influential discussions of poets and fiction writers such as Frost, Whitman, Kipling, Marianne Moore, and Christina Stead. Jarrell's patient, constructive criticism often left their subjects' reputations, as Robert Lowell phrased it, "permanently altered and exalted." The previously unpublished Measures lecture ought to put to rest lingering stereotypes of Jarrell as a primarily negative—and wholly instinctive—critic by revealing the dynamic understanding of poetic structure that informed his critical and artistic practice.

In 1947, the same year he reviewed *Lord Weary's Castle* so incisively, Jarrell produced an influential critical study of "The Other Frost" that forever redefined Robert Frost for serious readers. Acknowledging Frost's public success as a cracker-barrel philosopher, Jarrell drew attention cogently—and for the first time—to Frost's darker side: his complex and at times unnerving character portraits, his dramatic poems that uncannily blend wit, craft and a dazzling bleakness. Behind Jarrell the critic stands an elusive yet powerful poet who is himself dark, witty, crafty and at times uncannily bleak, a poet one might term "The Other Jarrell." Jarrell remarked in his last interview, "in most works of art, you're concerned with showing things that are often repressed out of existence; you want to show what the world's really like." [7]

Jarrell's poems, at their best, probe beneath the shell of the outer self, in search of that core of loss, abandonment, anxiety, or alienation that was at the center of his own experience. Jarrell will receive the fuller understanding and appreciation he deserves when readers return to his poems in search of the "disrupting tension," the "dramatic struggle of opposites," the uncanny, sometimes shattering, intimacy that are beautifully, painfully and sensitively realized in such poems as "Protocols," "Losses," "Eighth Air Force," "A Quilt Pattern," "The Black Swan," "Seele im Raum," "Jerome," "Cinderella," "The House in the Wood," "Next Day," "The Lost Children," and "The Old and New Masters."

## Jarrell's "Siegfried"

Jarrell completed his Mesures lecture in the spring of 1942. By October he had enlisted in the Army Air Corps, and, unable to qualify as a pilot, found himself, along with 50,000 other soldiers, at Sheppard Field, an Army Replacement Center in Wichita Falls, Texas. Writing to his first wife, Mackie, Jarrell confided that "Being in the army is like being involved in the digestive processes of an immense worm" (*RJLet*, 70).[8] It was while serving as a Celestial Navigation Trainer in the years that followed that

Jarrell wrote his extraordinary sequence of poems exploring the lives of children, pilots, and bomber crews in World War II. For Jarrell, the Second World War would provide a dynamic arena in which to test and bring to life a conception of poetic structure as involving multilayered strata of competing dialectics. Here were the elements of a postmodern aesthetic, in the hands of a poet avowedly searching for a way to get beyond modernism. And that poet found himself placed in the middle of the immense military-industrial complex that emerged during the course of the war and that social critics frequently cite as an originating agent of postmodern culture. Not surprisingly, these conditions induced Jarrell to produce the postmodern poems he had been yearning to write at least since 1940.

If one looks solely for visibly experimental formal operations—the clash, say, of razor-sharp edges—Jarrell's poetry may seem too traditional to read as postmodern in any useful sense. But if one looks for a convincingly realized critique of modernist systematizing and depersonalization, of what Jarrell called in his Mesures lecture "all the abstract, static, rationalistic, metaphysical side of Western thought," one finds these in many of his poems of the World War II, including "Siegfried" (1945).

"Siegfried" is a poem composed in hypnotic iambics that builds a web of subtle and penetrating cultural critiques out of a layered series of opposing dialectics. The poem takes one by gradual, indivisible stages into the life of a flesh and blood individual who seems in no obvious way to resemble Wagner's mythic hero. Wagner's Siegfried, a young man equipped with magic sword and disappearing helmet, heads off to do battle with the murderous man-dragon Fafner for a Ring that allows its owner to control the world, if the curse it carries does not kill him first. Jarrell's tone, however, is cool, distant, sober, and dreamlike—apparently impersonal and hardly Wagnerian. And the poem unfolds in an unhurried, slow-motion fashion. The fast-breaking, violent action—the attack of a cannon-firing Japanese Zero on a B-29 and the return of fire with the machine guns of the protagonist, a turret gunner—appears as in a trance:

> In the turret's great glass dome, the apparition, death,
> Framed in the glass of the gunsight, a fighter's blinking wing,
> Flares softly, a vacant fire. If the flak's inked blurs—
> Distributed, statistical—the bombs' lost patterning
> Are death, they are death under glass, a chance
> For someone yesterday, someone tomorrow; and the fire
> That streams from the fighter which is there, not there,
> Does not warm you, has not burned them, though they die.
>
> (*RJPoems* 149)

Here is a world in which every reality seems unreal. The actual fighter seems an apparition, and death—real for many on this day, if not for the gunner himself—also seems far off and insubstantial. The attacking fighter really is on fire, and if that fire does not warm the gunner, it does burn "them" in the enemy plane, whoever they might be. Here, then, is a world that only *seems* impersonal, in which the "distributed, statistical" antiaircraft fire certainly kills real individuals, in which the "bomb's lost patterning" is no mere idea of order but is actually killing people on the ground miles behind and below the bomber, though to the crew the smoke rising from bomb's explosions might seem merely to be dissipating, aestheticized patterns. And all of these actual, individual deaths will, of course, return again—as statistics. The B-29's defensive machine guns, unlike those of a B-17 or B-24, were now for the first time in history remotely controlled by an early computer. And since the gunner operated them from a distance, within the comparative comfort of a pressurized cabin, he, too, could not be quite convinced of the reality of his actions, nor of whether it is he who performs them:

> Under the leather and fur and wire, in the gunner's skull,
> It is a dream: and he, the watcher, guiltily
> Watches the him, the actor, who is innocent.
> *It happens as it does because it does.*
> It is unnecessary to understand
>
> (*RJPoems* 149)

This poem has a curious way with pronouns. The reader begins by seeing the action from the gunner's point of view, from within the framework of the turret's "great glass dome," yet sees no clear individual within that dome, at least at first, and has no hint that the dome is even occupied until the enigmatic address to "you" (the gunner) and "them" (the burning fighter's crew) in line eight. One has to puzzle out the antecedents of these pronouns. Soon, though, the crewman is addressed in third rather than second person. And he seems to see himself, too, in a strangely bifurcated third person, presenting the gunner as a voyeuristic and thus guilty "watcher" of his own "innocent," if fatal, actions: "and he, the watcher, guiltily / Watches the him, the actor."

But *who* is saying that it is "unnecessary to understand"? Wagner's powerful, magically armed, but guileless Siegfried is sent off on his mission to kill Fafner by Mime, who wants the Ring for himself. Mime hopes Siegfried will not understand what is afoot and will hand the Ring over to his weaker but craftier elder, who pretends to be Siegfried's father. Does the voice of the dominant culture, in Jarrell's poem, standing in for Mime, make the claim: "It is unnecessary to understand"? Slyly, in mid-sentence, the pronoun reference, which had been third person ("he, the watcher"), again shifts to second person ("if you are still / In this year of our warfare") and the poem begins to narrow in on the guilt, the losses, and the uncomfortable knowledge experienced by an individual:

> if you are still
> In this year of our warfare, indispensable
> In general, and in particular dispensable
> As a cartridge, a life—it is only to enter
> So many knots in a window, so many feet;
> To switch on for an instant the steel that understands.
>
> (*RJPoems* 149)

The tone has a cool finality, despite its riddling diction, that, I would argue, represents an impersonation of modernist infallibility—if one understands modernism in its ordering, system-building sense—that might extend to political myth-makers and the constructors of massive military machines as well as to poetic systematizers. The lines on the page look like iambic pentameter, but the somewhat unusual, trancelike feel arises because these lines are really hexameters, six-foot iambic lines, generally lightened by a three-beat foot or two somewhere, and hence contain thirteen or more syllables. And, combined with this concealed prosodic art, the enigmatic play with pronouns suggests the difficulty of establishing and maintaining an identity in a postmodern world where, it often seems, it is not the individual but "the steel that understands." As the gunner enters "So many knots in a window, so many feet," he is supplying information about speed and altitude that will allow his aircraft's bombs to find their targets accurately:

> So the bombs fell: through clouds to the island,
> The dragon of maps; and the island's fighters
> Rose from its ruins, through blind smoke, to the flights—
> And fluttered smashed from the machinery of death.
> Yet inside the infallible invulnerable
> Machines, the skin of steel, glass, cartridges,
> Duties, responsibilities, and—surely—deaths,
> There was only you
>
> (*RJPoems* 149–50)

This time the formerly elusive "you" of the poem lands with startling weight. There is no one else on the scene to blame or hold responsible for the killing described. For in this setting merely to survive and fulfill one's assigned responsibilities is to become both a killer and a victim.

In classical drama, the recognition of the hero's true identity takes place in a public arena, as when Oedipus learns most publicly that it is he who has brought the plague on his own city, he who has killed his own father, and he who has married his own mother. But this gunner, apparently no classical or Nordic hero, experiences a different sort of recognition, one that is entirely private and internalized. This person wishes not for recognition but release. He longs to return to his former life without loss, without guilt, without change:

> the ignorant life
> That grew its weariness and loneliness and wishes
> Into your whole wish: "Let it be the way it was.
> Let me not matter, let nothing I do matter
> To anybody, anybody. Let me be what I was."
>
> (*RJPoems* 150)

But a "shell with your name / In the bursting turret"—the only thing so far in this poem with the gunner's (unspecified) name on it—causes, in fact, an irremediable loss.

> the terrible flesh
> Sloughed off at last—and waking, your leg gone,
> To the dream, the old, old dream
>
> (*RJPoems* 150)

With this loss, and this waking, comes real loss and the now "old, old dream" of a return to "the way it was," along with the hint of possible understanding but,

> if you wake and understand,
> There is always the nurse, the leg, the drug—
> If you understand, there is sleep, there is sleep . . .
>
> (*RJPoems* 150)

Soon the recuperating gunner finds himself "Stumbling to the toilet on one clever leg," and not long after that he finds himself in his home town,

> staring
> Past the lawn and the trees to nothing, to the eyes
> You looked away from as they looked away.
>
> (*RJPoems* 150)

Here, back in the vernal if not altogether welcoming bosom of small town America, the gunner "understands"—and what he understands is his own, and his world's, difference.

If, standing irresolute
By the whitewashed courthouse, in the leafy street,
You look at the people who look back at you, at home,
And it is different, different—you have understood
Your world at last: you have tasted your own blood.
(*RJPoems* 150–51)

The poem ends with a sudden and wrenching recognition. Despite the gunner's prayer to "Let me be what I was," that perhaps simpler or more innocent "what I was" is the one thing he can never be. For what he did, and what he does, and what has been done to and through him actually does matter. His own lost leg cannot be "whitewashed" from the scene, nor can the deaths he helped to cause be washed away, despite their apparent remoteness both then and now.

When Wagner's Siegfried slays the dragon Fafner with his magic sword, he dips his finger into the dragon's blood, and by tasting it, gains understanding. He can hear new forms of speech and learns to see through his pretended father Mime's hypocrisy and understands, too, other murderous designs and dangers that surround him on all sides. He comprehends how others have imposed duties on him and worked to manipulate his youth and strength. The queries raised by the Jarrellian dialectic in "Siegfried" pile up in intersecting layers: Is this gunner a knower or a fool? Is he innocent or guilty? Victim or conqueror? Hero or dragon? By tasting his *own* blood, he learns that he is both Siegfried and Fafner, both the hero and the beast.

At last, then, the gunner at the end of "Siegfried" finds that his world "is different, different" not merely because he has lost a leg, but because he has "understood" his own willing or unwilling complicity in "both sides of an inconsistent world order." The poem's voice does not seek "to console him for the inconsolable, to unify things which cannot be unified and which any submission to reality should make us differentiate." Rather, it confronts both the poem's protagonist and the reader with this polyvocal message and in the process suggests the need for a new mode of understanding.

One complex fact that Jarrell presciently understood as early as 1945, more than a decade before Dwight Eisenhower named it in his farewell speech as president, was the arrival of the military-industrial complex, with its intersecting vectors of technology, profit, and death. And Jarrell anticipated too the conflicted intimations of power, powerlessness, knowledge, ignorance, abundance, and anxious mortality that would haunt the postmodern world he saw emerging out of the shadow of the twentieth century's second global war.

## Bishop and the Origins of Narrative Postmodernism

One of the last poems Elizabeth Bishop published during her lifetime, "Santarém" (1978), begins with an idiomatically convincing, but syntactically curious, sentence: "Of course I may be remembering it all wrong / after, after—how many years?" (*EBPoems* 185). Bishop's sentence starts out as a quite tentative declarative, only to trail off into still greater uncertainty as a question. Such self-interruptions and self-questionings, common enough in Bishop, have generally been read as disarmingly candid, off-the-cuff disclaimers, dropped into descriptive lyrics by a modest poet obsessed with factual precision. But an alternative reading might perceive this opening as a slyly sophisticated postmodern gambit, embodying a tactic whose appealing modesty is disingenuous, quietly subversive, deflecting modernist conceptions of the poet as an ordering self. According to this alternative reading, Bishop deliberately breaks through the just-emerging narrative frame of "Santarém" in order to slightly but effectively de-center the authority of each detail in the vivid stream of (apparently uncalculated) recollection that follows. Bishop's subtle, unobtrusive opening calls into doubt not just the modernist poet's aspirations to an ordering vision but even those more modest claims to exactitude of recollection and observation that critics both friendly and unfriendly had long since granted to be Bishop's forte.[9]

The argument put forward here is for the validity of *both* these lines of interpretation. Bishop's opening gesture melds a seductive casualness with a quite uncanny level of self-consciousness and sophistication, creating an artistic resource of great subtlety and surprising power. And the tactics represented here have been employed, not just by Bishop, but by a diverse range of poets who came of age in the midcentury period and after, many of whom are still actively producing poetry. Langdon Hammer has recently asserted that, "No poet has more widely or powerfully influenced current poetic practice than Bishop"[10]—yet the basis for Bishop's pervasive current influence seems to leave most commentators puzzled.

If one examines Bishop's originating role in the important and still influential line of poetic development that has been sketched here, the reasons underlying the depth and breadth of her current influence become clear. This line of development will be named "narrative postmodernism" in this study. Jay Clayton has recently argued in *The Pleasures of Babel* for the operations of narrative in postmodern fiction, but he does not carry his analysis into poetry, where the resurgence of narrative in postmodern forms has been similarly striking. The aesthetic of "narrative postmodernism" operates thematically as a layered, interactive web of dialectics, and operates formally by combining conventional narrative elements with the subtle but pervasive evocation of the mind in action, of surreal or dream textures, of temporal multiplicity or simultaneity, of poly-vocality, and of a deliberate acknowledgment of process.

Exploiting these techniques, this quartet of poets focuses acute attention on the problem of selfhood in the postmodern world, raising questions about the unitary or divided self, about centrality and marginalization, about psychic health or disorder, and about authorial privilege and the elusive nature of knowledge. But the complex and subtle techniques and thematic implications characteristic of narrative postmodernism—though widely exploited by successive generations of poets—have not been explicitly theorized and thus have been more or less elided from literary history.

This elision grew in part out of the way Bishop and her colleagues answered questions such as that battery of inquiries into poetic technique and structure that John Ciardi also posed to Randall Jarrell in 1950. Bishop's reply, unlike Jarrell's, has been rediscovered and is now famous: "To all but two of the questions raised here my answer is *it all depends*. It all depends on the particular poem one happens to be trying to write, and the range of possibilities is, one trusts, infinite. After all, the poet's concern is not consistency. I do not understand the question about the function of overtone, and to the question on subject matter (any predilections? any restrictions?) I shall reply that there are no restrictions. There *are*, of course, but they are not consciously restrictions."[11]

Bishop resists the process of critical appropriation that, in the years since midcentury, has become an almost inevitable consequence of literary fame. In fact, Bishop rejects the assumption of the poet's *conscious* command of artistic processes implicit in every one of Ciardi's questions, while she politely but firmly insists on the broadest possible latitude for technique and for subject matter ("there are no restrictions"). What matters most, for Bishop, are the requirements, not just of the individual poet, but of "the particular poem one happens to be trying to write."

While Bishop's Vassar classmate Muriel Rukeyser's response to Ciardi's questionnaire was an essay defining a universal psychology of poetic composition (based, of course, on her own practice), Bishop expresses grave doubts about the means by which aesthetic theory might actually shape practice: “No matter what theories one may have, I doubt very much that they are in one’s mind at the moment of writing a poem or that there is even a physical possibility that they could be. Theories can only be based on interpretations of other poet’s poems, or on one’s own in retrospect, or wishful thinking.”[12] But significantly Bishop, like Jarrell, had in fact formulated a rather elaborate theory of poetic form, as well as a partial theory of creative psychology, as far back as the mid-1930s, while she was still at Vassar. (She uses the word “theory” when alluding to her approach in a letter to Moore—without describing the theory.)

Bishop, however, like the other members of what would become her informal artistic circle, remained extremely guarded about revealing in public that her work might be supported by an even partially formulated set of cognitive principles. And if one analyzes Bishop’s privately held ideas about the dynamics of poetic construction, one finds that they bear a striking family resemblance to Jarrell’s own emerging ideas about poetic structure. This, despite the fact that neither could have read the other’s views, and they did not sit down to share ideas about the writing of poetry until January of 1947.

“It all depends” remained a characteristic Bishop phrase, one she would revert to again in 1966 in reply to interviewer Ashley Brown’s question about the need to have “a ‘myth’—Christian or otherwise—to sustain” the work. Bishop responded: “It all depends—some poets do, some don’t. You must have something to sustain you but perhaps you needn’t be conscious of it. Look at Robert Lowell; he’s written just as good poetry since he left the Church. Look at Paul Klee: he had 16 paintings going at once; *he* didn’t have a formulated myth to look to, apparently, and his accomplishment was very considerable.”[13] When Brown rejoined, “But some poets and critics have been terribly concerned about this, haven’t they?” Bishop replied, simply, “Some people crave organization more than others—the desire to get everything in place.”[14]

Bishop was joined in her insistence on freedom in the choice of technical resources and subject matter by her friend Lowell, cited above, as well as by her colleagues Jarrell and Berryman. Even when they were partly conscious of principles that sustained them, they were reluctant to admit these principles in public (a reluctance hardly shared by most of their poetic contemporaries and elders, who as a rule were bristling with principles and would state them at the drop of a hat.) Starved for freedom of action in their youth, these poets went to extraordinary lengths to maintain the freedom of the poem to become itself on its own terms.

Bishop's private experimentation with the dynamics of postmodern voicing can be traced through the documents as far back as the mid-1930s, when she was a senior at Vassar College and her poems were just beginning to appear in national magazines. Working alone, Bishop described features of her new aesthetic in such Vassar essays as "Time's Andromedas" (1933)—an essay which, in many ways, anticipates contemporary chaos theory—and "Gerard Manley Hopkins: Notes on Timing in His Poetry" (1934), as well as in a series of 1933–34 letters to her generally uncomprehending contemporary Donald Stanford. If we look at Bishop's emerging aesthetic during this period, we find her speaking concretely and locally about the same problems of timing and diction in poetry that Jarrell was tackling more generally and abstractly, through the principles of a dialogic poetic structure. Working separately, and almost simultaneously (though Bishop, three years older, began somewhat earlier), these two poets were piecing together the features of the new aesthetic that I am calling narrative postmodernism.

Given the refusal of the original narrative postmodernists to formalize their aesthetic position, given their indifference to founding a publicly recognized school of poetry, given the wide and eclectic reach of their technical apparatus, and given widespread assumptions that narrative and postmodernism are mutually exclusive, it is by no means surprising that this remarkably extensive line of poetic development has been largely overlooked or misplaced by literary historians. Hence, though this line of development has been much read and widely discussed, and has created a most impressive body of poetry across four or five poetic generations, its aesthetic characteristics remain poorly defined and fragmentarily understood, more than sixty years after this aesthetic first began to emerge in the mid-1930s. There are three major reasons for this lingering confusion.

First, Bishop, Lowell, Jarrell, and Berryman, all of them working under socially conservative modernist mentors, were reluctant to open to public discourse the complex, powerful, and carefully worked out aesthetic positions (now recoverable in archival manuscripts), that served as the cognitive wellsprings of their poetry. Second, those easy, conflicting, and misleading labels—"confessional" and "impersonal"—that literary journalists pasted on the careers of these four close friends and colleagues while they lived continue to obscure intriguing parallelisms in their literary and personal development. And finally, uncertainties persist about the denotative and connotative import of that damned elusive term *postmodernism*. Yet the power of the line of development these four poets inaugurated derives precisely from its ability to merge elements of postmodern skepticism, indeterminacy, or heterogeneity with techniques and attitudes pioneered by their modernist mentors in their earlier and more experimental phases, as well as with more commonplace narrative elements drawn from the rich world of social markers and cultural conventions, creating what Bishop called, in a now famous phrase, "the always-more-successful surrealism of everyday life."

But the devices of postmodern narrative, even at their most radical and effective, have most often been examined in isolation—and, because they frequently disguise themselves under a disarmingly casual surface, they are not infrequently condemned as insufficiently new or experimental, as in the dismissive portrait of "the apparent defeat—the absence" of Bishop and other "middle generation" poets in James E. B. Breslin's 1984 survey *From Modern to Contemporary*.[15] Bishop's tactics for de-privileging the poet, for example, were noted by earlier critics often enough, but until recently, at least, these de-privileging tactics have generally been cited as evidence of Bishop's lack of importance.

Thus in 1973, five years before the publication of "Santarém," Jan B. Gordon complains that Bishop gains "a certain surface tension" by "the loss of poetic *privilege* in every sense of the word: the narrator's sense of an advantage to perspective; an access to secrets, unknown to the protagonists of her poems; or even the subtlety of an untrustworthy vision which might confer aesthetic advantage by granting the reader the right to acknowledge a false subjectivity."[16] By assuming a "*loss*" of privilege (how was it lost?), rather than a renunciation, Gordon makes Bishop's technique sound passive, even weak. Yet from the start of her career, this renunciation of privilege functioned as a key feature of Bishop's elusive style, allowing her to explore perspectives of outsiderhood or marginalization. These perspectives include the outsiderhood of lesbian identity identified by Rich, along with the outsiderhood of the denied child, the provincial, the colonial subject, the observer, the dreamer, the endangered animal, the neglected art object, the disparaged cultural position—in poems that do their subjects the honor of close attention while refusing to claim the privileges of prescriptive ethical authority.

While the poets of high modernism struggled, in the 1920s, to reassert a vanishing cultural, spiritual, or metaphysical order, proclaiming with Eliot at the end of *The Waste Land* that "These fragments I have shored against my ruin," the poets of the later generation to which Bishop belonged found themselves, by the early 1930s, already living among those ruins. Yeats, Eliot, Pound, Stevens, and even Williams, in *Paterson*, when he posits "that a man is himself a city, beginning, seeking, achieving and concluding his life in ways which the various aspects of a city may embody,"[17] represent a last brilliant reconception of the notion, romantic in origin, of the poet as imaginative center, as unacknowledged lawmaker, as imperial self. Even when the modernist poet acknowledges with Stevens that, "I cannot bring the world quite round, / Although I patch it as I can,"[18] or acknowledges with Pound, in his final Canto volume, *Drafts & Fragments*, that "I cannot make it cohere,"[19] the expectation remains that the poet must labor to impose some kind of order.

Even in her earliest poems, Bishop never tried to present herself as such a privileged observer, and she rejected the stance of an observer with claims to privilege. By the mid-1930s, Bishop was already writing from her lonely, painful, and fragmentary inner world with a combination of wit, mystery, narrative surprise, metrical invention, and dazzling imagistic virtuosity. Hence, in the poem "Cirque d'Hiver," an observer studies a "mechanical toy," a "little circus horse with real white hair" who "bears a little dancer on his back." Is this toy an object or an emblem? When we learn that the horse's "mane and tail are straight from Chirico" or that "He has a formal, melancholy soul" or that "He feels her pink toes dangle toward his back / along the little pole / that pierces both her body and her soul / and goes through his, and reappears below, / under his belly, as a big tin key," it is hard to avoid the emblematic reading. Yet the direction in which this reading leads remains curiously inconclusive, even in the poem's final five-line stanza (in which "He" is her circus horse):

> The dancer, by this time, has turned her back.
> He is the more intelligent by far.
> Facing each other rather desperately—
> his eye is like a star—
> we stare and say, "Well, we have come this far"
> (*EBPoems* 31)

Rather than claiming the privilege of normative interpretation, this poem ends on a note of dogged persistence: all the elegance and charm of the toy, all the probing of its soul, all the emblematizing skill of the poet, have produced a startlingly inconclusive, yet effectively desperate conclusion: an ending that one couldn't have predicted when the poem began, and that still surprises after many readings.

When Bishop was a senior at Vassar in the fall of 1933, Yvor Winters, acting as a regional editor of *Hound and Horn*, noticed Bishop's work (submitted for a contest) and suggested that she correspond with another protégé of his, Donald Stanford, then a budding poet and scholar doing graduate work at Harvard. Bishop revealed some of the most important features of her early aesthetic in letters written to Stanford from Vassar.

After the startling early achievement of "The Ballad of the Subway Train" in 1927 for North Shore Country Day School's *The Owl*, Bishop's high school poems for *The Blue Pencil*, written under the influence of the sentimental Miss Eleanor Prentice, are notable for their smoothness, their conventional lyric polish, their adherence to what Cheryl Walker has recently termed "the nightingale tradition." Four years of poetic silence followed Walnut Hill, during which time Bishop seemed to be quietly distancing herself from this premodernist aesthetic. She began to publish poems again in 1933, and these poems, "A Word with You," "Hymn to the Virgin," and "Three Sonnets for the Eyes," which appeared unsigned in the April and November issues of the renegade Vassar school magazine *Con Spirito*, read like a series of deliberate experiments with the extremities of poetic voice. Bishop acknowledged in a November 1933 letter to Stanford:

> If I try to write smoothly I find myself perverting the meaning for the sake of the smoothness. (And don't you do that sometimes yourself?) However, I think that an equally great "cumulative effect" might be built up by a series of irregularities. Instead of beginning with an "Uninterrupted mood" what I want to do is to get the moods themselves into the rhythm. This is a very hard thing to explain, but for me there are two kinds of poetry, that (I think yours is of this sort) *at rest*, and that which is in action, within itself. At present it is too hard for me to get this feeling of action within the poem unless I just go ahead with it and let the meters find their way through. (*EBLet* 11)

Two years later, in 1935, Bishop would achieve an active poetic voice that would get "the moods themselves into the rhythm" in two poems that Berryman admired on their first publication, "The Map" and "The Imaginary Iceberg." Her remarks to Stanford cited above suggest that this achievement was the result of conscious, deliberate, and lonely effort—effort that had already begun before she met her mentor Marianne Moore in 1934.

In a letter to Stanford, Bishop relates her notion of a poetry that is "in action" to Gerard Manley Hopkins, a poet whose influence she would soon find means to successfully internalize, and thus disguise. Bishop also cites the writings on baroque prose of scholar M. W. Croll: "But the best part, which perfectly describes the sort of poetic convention I should like to make for myself (and which explains, I think, something of Hopkins), is this: 'Their purpose (the writers of Baroque prose) was to portray, not a thought, but a mind thinking. . . . They knew that an idea separated from the act of experiencing it is not the idea that was experienced. The ardor of its conception in the mind is a necessary part of its truth'" (*EBLet* 12).

Displaying one of his many points of affinity with Bishop, Berryman—another poet who invented his own poetic conventions and learned quite well how to dramatize the mind thinking—chided Tate in an 11 October 1936 letter, "How can you dismiss Donne's prose in so offhand a manner, incidentally—I love the stuff."[20] Berryman's proclivity for the intricate syntax of baroque prose and verse, syntax that captured the "ardor of conception in the mind" and maintained a sense of action, helps to explain his promptness to "admire and love" Bishop's early work.

Bishop would write to Stanford, "Have you ever noticed that you can often learn more about other people—more about how they feel, how it would feel to be them—by hearing them cough or making one of those innumerable inner noises, than by watching them for hours? . . . Do you know what I'm driving at? Well . . . —that's what I'm trying to get into poetry" (*EBLet* 18). Berryman, who would later write the words "Starts again always in Henry's ears / the little cough somewhere, an odour, a chime" (*DS* 29) certainly would have known what Bishop was driving at. But Stanford, the recipient of these early aesthetic confidences, was not prepared to sustain a true give-and-take with a poet as groundbreaking as Bishop. Moreover, her letters make clear that she hardly expected him to comprehend much of what she said and that she distrusted many of his more or less conventional assumptions about art—and about her. Hence, she would write, "And one more thing—what on earth do you mean when you say my perceptions are 'almost impossible for a woman's' 'Now what the hell,' as you said to me, 'you know that's meaningless.' And if you really do mean anything by it, I imagine it would make me very angry. Is there some glandular reason which prevents a woman from having good perceptions, or what?"(*EBLet* 12).

Bishop, though painfully shy, did not suffer fools gladly, and she knew how to nail interlocutors firmly to the wall. She needed to find her true artistic peers, and her correspondence with Stanford would soon end. Significantly, Bishop did not directly explore these same ideas with Marianne

Moore, in the correspondence that began with her in 1934, in part because she may have wanted to preserve her autonomy in the face of this established elder while developing her own aesthetic.

As the years passed, working first in parallel and later in conversation with such emerging friends and contemporaries as Robert Lowell, Randall Jarrell, and John Berryman, Bishop would create the poems that quietly established narrative postmodernism as one of the most engaging, powerful, and influential contemporary modes of poetic discourse—as she was all the while refusing, along with her friends, to explicitly state a poetic doctrine. Ransom, in the process of labeling Jarrell as an incipient postmodernist in 1941, had regretted his protégé's inclination to think "about all the technical possibilities at once." But this very tendency to consider "all the technical possibilities at once" may be taken as the defining characteristic of this quietly experimental mode of writing. With it, these poets consistently found the means to create fresh and surprising poems that synthesize imagist, surrealist, modernist, objectivist and/or formalist elements. These poems employ a flexible and inclusive aesthetic to compress extensive cultural, emotional, moral, and epistemological complexities into a surprisingly brief verbal compass.

Narrative postmodernists who have specifically acknowledged Bishop's importance include: James Merrill, John Ashbery, Adrienne Rich, Amy Clampitt, Frank Bidart, Robert Pinsky, Dana Gioia, William Logan, and Gjertrud Schnackenberg. Bishop's particular contribution to postmodern narrative grew out of her extraordinary early focus on the poem as a dramatization of "the mind in action." Her experiments with timing, with the balancing of realism and abstraction, and with the stripping away of authorial privilege, experiments that began as early as 1933, combined with her uncanny ear for the right diction to produce a mastery of the intricacies and uncertainties of a convincing postmodern voice.

Returning then to "Santarém," the extraordinary descriptive paragraph that follows Bishop's disarmingly ambiguous opening query sets a scene bathed in a stately romantic aura. The speaker seems, despite the opening disclaimer, to be recalling the scene with great and authoritative precision while summoning echoes of earlier literary convergences:

> That golden evening I really wanted to go no farther;
> more than anything else I wanted to stay awhile
> in that conflux of two great rivers, Tapajós, Amazon,
> grandly, silently flowing, flowing east.
>
> (*EBPoems* 185)

Here one can sense the numinous tranquillity echoing many generations of romantic river literature. American readers are bound to think of the great conjunctions of the Missouri and later the Ohio Rivers with the Mississippi. But this sense of tranquillity, and these grand associations, are almost immediately disrupted:

> Suddenly there'd been houses, people, and lots of mongrel
> riverboats skittering back and forth
> under a sky of gorgeous, under-lit clouds,
> with everything, gilded, burnished along one side,
> and everything bright, cheerful, casual—or so it looked.

Now the frame of reference veers away from that romantic literature of the river toward Bishop's own previous writings about disorderly water scenes. This scene, with its "mongrel / riverboats skittering back and forth" is curiously reminiscent, in particular, of "The Bight," with its "frowsy sponge boats" that "keep coming in / with the obliging air of retrievers" (*EBPoems* 60). Each scene is characterized and personalized, but in the context of a recognition that this is just one person's rather external view of the scene, one person's way of recalling a particular moment:

> I liked the place; I liked the idea of the place.
> Two rivers. Hadn't two rivers sprung
> from the Garden of Eden? No, that was four
> and they'd diverged. Here only two
> and coming together. Even if one were tempted
> to literary interpretations
> such as: life/death, right/wrong, male/female
> —such notions would have resolved, dissolved, straight off
> in that watery, dazzling dialectic.

The authority of the poet is undercut by her inability to accurately remember her allusions (imagine T. S. Eliot or Marianne Moore misremembering their carefully documented sources?). While Eliot, Pound and Moore each make a point of the fact that they are citing from a printed source, Bishop, although she no doubt did check the reference at some point in the writing process, makes it seem as though she is thinking, imperfectly, aloud. And by her undercutting of traditionally dyadic structures, those weary old dualism rehearsed in the poem, Bishop shows these held in a "watery, dazzling dialectic" that poses all the components against each other dazzlingly and inextricably: one can still tell the Amazon from the Tapajós. Such a stress on the dynamism of a multiplanar dialectic shows

Bishop's sympathy, once again, for the conception of poetic structure held in reserve by her friend Jarrell.

Prismatic imagery, which, due to its multiplanar, de-centered character, seems deftly if quietly postmodern, runs throughout Bishop's poetic oeuvre, from "Florida," in which "After dark, the fireflies map the heavens in the marsh / until the moon rises" (*EBPoems* 33), through the "rainbow, rainbow, rainbow" that glows in the oily pool of bilge in the bottom of the boat in "The Fish" (*EBPoems* 44), through the fighting cocks of "Roosters," who, as they do battle, display "all the vulgar beauty of iridescence" (*EBPoems* 37). Consider also "Over 2000 Illustrations and a Complete Concordance," in which:

> The eye drops, weighted, through the lines
> the burin made, the lines that move apart
> like ripples above sand,
> dispersing storms, God's spreading fingerprint,
> and painfully, finally, that ignite
> in watery prismatic white-and-blue.
>
> (*EBPoems* 57)

Bishop's prismatic images, as one can already see, evoke many differing tones and feelings, many differing emotional weights, but they seem to be a product of her multifaceted way of looking, her intuition both that the ordinary can suddenly blaze out with surprising beauty and complexity, and that nothing is reducible to plain black and white. Even the engravings in an old family Bible finally and painfully ignite "in watery prismatic white-and-blue." For this prismatic imagery is associated with movement, with the unpredictable. Hence, in "Quai d'Orléans,"

> We stand as still as stones to watch
>     the leaves and ripples
> while light and nervous water hold
>     their interview.
> "If what we see could forget us half as easily,"
>     I want to tell you,
> "as it does itself—but for life we'll not be rid
>     of the leaves' fossils."
>
> (*EBPoems* 28)

Bishop's absorption in the complexities of perception, exemplified by her fascination with shifting effects of light of movement, works always in nervous conjunction with her prismatic aesthetic of "the mind in action."

## Berryman's Artistic Struggle

The previous chapter argued that Berryman, among all of this quartet's members, had most thoroughly internalized modernist principles of impersonality and the effacement of self. Piety and rage, both linked to feelings about his mother, provide the pattern for Berryman's interaction with the world, and of all these poets his early relationships with modernist mentors were the most worshipful. He thus faced the longest and most painful struggle to make his own version of a postmodern aesthetic. Berryman's artistic struggle, which I propose to further trace here in the context of an evolving postmodern voice, was in large part a struggle to extract himself from an exaggerated piety toward his artistic predecessors that was bound up with his exaggerated respect for, and need to serve and please, his terrifying, all powerful mother. Perhaps for that very reason his voice emerged, at last, as the most radical.

From many likely examples of Berryman's early struggles with voice, we will begin with a poem that occasioned a stinging critique by Jarrell, an eventual friend and admirer who was also the critic of his own generation that Berryman most respected. This poem is worth looking at, as well, because it marks a farewell to the keenly cherished illusions of many intellectuals of Berryman's generation. Titled simply "Communist," the poem —based on "Lord Randall"—is dated October 1939 and responds directly to recent and cataclysmic events. For as Stalin signed the infamous Non-Aggression Pact with Hitler, conspired in the partition of Poland, and gobbled up the Baltic States, he was also crushing the idealistic hopes of many Marxist intellectuals in America and helping to usher in World War II. The poem begins:

> 'O tell me of the Russians, Communist, my son!
>  Tell me of the Russians, my honest young man!'
> 'They are moving for the people, mother; let me alone,
>  For I'm worn out with reading and want to lie down.'
>
> 'But what of the Pact, the Pact, Communist, my son?
>  What of the Pact, the Pact, my honest young man?'
> 'It was necessary, mother; let me alone,
>  For I'm worn out with reading and want to lie down.'
>
> (*JBPoems* 280–81)

Commenting on a group of Berryman's poems, including this one, that appeared in James Laughlin's *New Directions in Prose and Poetry* for 1941, Jarrell wrote, "John Berryman's 'Five Political Poems' have lots of Yeats, lots of general politics, a 1939 reissue of *1938*, and a parody of 'Lord Randall' that—but nothing can make me believe that Mr. Berryman wrote this himself, and is not just shielding someone" (*KA&Co* 86).

Jarrell's barb points toward the peculiar incongruity with which the famous border ballad is grafted onto contemporary events. This incongruity is no doubt at least partly intentional, but Jarrell saw clearly enough that Berryman was not fully in control of its effect. But there is also, rather unusually for Jarrell, an implied compliment in Jarrell's suggestion that Berryman ought to know better. While the poem involves an obvious "dialectic" between mother and son, it is the cookie-cutter clarity of this sequence of oppositions that put Jarrell off.

Despite this tough review, when the two poets met for the first time some five years later, in 1946, they easily made the transition from confrontation to companionship. Berryman's first wife Eileen Simpson recalled that "their exchanges at their first meeting were so easy and good-natured that, though it meant missing the train John had said we must take home, we lingered over dinner."[21] Simpson notes that before this meeting the parallels and attractions were already obvious to both: "He and Randall, who were the same age, had corresponded at the time *Five Young American Poets* was published, and knew each other's work intimately, but had never met. John was so eager to talk to the poet he admired, the poet-critic he thought was the most original of their generation" that he "came up from underground"[22] during a period of intense writing, and attended a party given by *The Nation* in Jarrell's honor.

Berryman observed after Jarrell's death that he "hated bad poetry with such vehemence and so vigorously that it didn't occur to him that in the course of taking apart—where he'd take a book of poems and squeeze, like that, twist—that in the course of doing that, there was a human being also being squeezed." Of course, before he found his voice Berryman himself had been squeezed. But he admired Jarrell's critical perception and respected his critical judgment enough to benefit from the confrontation. In 1951 Jarrell would write to Mary von Schrader, soon to be Mary Jarrell, that during a conversation at Princeton about Housman and Frost, "Berryman astonished me by saying he thought and had thought for many years that I was the best reviewer of poetry alive. Was I dazzled and grateful!" (*RJLet* 309).

When Jarrell's *Poetry and the Age* appeared two years later, Berryman would praise it in the *New Republic* as "the most original and best book on its subject since *The Double Agent* by R. P. Blackmur and *Primitivism and*

*Decadence* by Yvor Winters." There he termed Jarrell "the most powerful reviewer of poetry active in this country for the last decade," appreciating characteristics such as his "rare attention, devotion to and respect for poetry," his "natural taste," his "restless, incessant self-training, [and] strong general intelligence" which "make up an equipment that would seem to be minimal but in fact is unique."[23] Given his respect for Jarrell as a critic, Berryman could be expected to take seriously both his negative and his positive criticism.

Jarrell had privately been casting his sharp critical eye on Berryman's writing even earlier. Jarrell wrote to Allen Tate, a mentor they shared, that Berryman had more of "the negative virtues" than George Marion O'Donnell, Jarrell's rival at Vanderbilt and a poet with whom he and Berryman appeared in Laughlin's 1940 anthology *Five Young American Poets*, though, as Jarrell went on, "as for positive ones, there the difference is smaller. I think Berryman has a pretty inferior feel for language, for one thing; and to talk of your old favorite, the poetic subject, he's obviously not really found his" (*RJLet* 30).

In order to fashion an idiom that would allow him to project his really excellent and highly individual ear, Berryman was beginning in some of the poems that followed his 1940 contribution to *Five Young American Poets* to abandon his clear advantage in the negative virtues. In the process he was risking bad taste in order to find his "subject" and his "language." Berryman's "Communist" provides a curious glimpse into this process of stylistic unmaking or remaking. "Communist" concludes,

> 'O I fear for your future, Communist, my son!
> I fear for your future, my honest young man!'
> 'I cannot speak or think, mother; let me alone,
> For I'm sick at my heart and I want to lie down.'
> (*JBPoems* 281)

One senses with the aid of hindsight that there is a vein valuable ore, a yet-to-be-extracted lode of excruciating feeling and perception, running through this retro-ballad's crude sedimentary rock. Looking back at "Communist" from the perspective of the later work, one is tempted to point out the long list of characteristics this poem shares with the *Dream Songs*. I count at least six, including: 1) traditional poetic form—here, the ballad—stretched to its limits, 2) grave or distasteful contemporary events referenced against the past, 3) the presentation of major public occasions through the prism of an individual's private disaffection, 4) a fantastic dialogue between two intimately antagonistic interlocutors serving to highlight a disturbance in the dominant voice, 5) a queasy juxtaposition of the tragic and the comic, and 6) a mordantly sharp ironic intelligence. Indeed, even if one accepts Jarrell's judgment, the poem's failure is by no means a failure of what John Dryden would have called "Wit" or what a journalist today might call editorial savvy. Berryman has accurately diagnosed the malaise of many thoughtful left-leaning idealists and intellectuals of the 1930s and brought the cause of that malaise home with crushing if perhaps heavy-handed irony. Only by *dis*honestly ignoring or rationalizing the intentions of Stalin can this "honest young man" cling tenuously to his illusions in the face of events that in fact make him 'sick at my heart.' Berryman brings all this out while taking risks with voice that he was perhaps not quite ready to control.

Thematically, then, the poem functions pointedly, as a sharply conceived dialectic, and its problem is primarily one of vocal insecurity. Why is this problem so vexing to the poem's intended effect? Why would an unconvincing or incongruous voice override other substantial and hard-learned virtues? The poet John Haines suggests a possible answer, "It is the voice of the poet, no two alike, that determines the line, rhythm, structure, everything. . . . The voice refined becomes the poet's style. Unfortunately, the voice is one thing that can't be taught in any school or class, nor can it counterfeited. It is discovered in the act of living and working, and nourished until it becomes as much a part of the person as an arm or leg."[24] If Haines is right, then one must look at the "line, rhythm,[and] structure" of "Communist" for symptoms of insecurity. Doing so, one finds lines that are awkwardly stressed, and one sees, as well, that the stanzas unfold in a predictable and "static" succession that leads to a unified conclusion. This conclusion is sufficiently cogent, but certainly falls well short of the charged "conflict of opposites" and aura of live improvisation so dazzling in the best *Dream Songs*, which really are "about as static as an explosion."

Later, if parodying a source like "Lord Randall," Berryman would have played far more freely with the source's diction, structure, and syntax. Indeed, Berryman's *Dream Songs* rely persistently on what Yeats called, in their London interview, "a more passionate syntax."[25] The syntactic predictability of this early poem, therefore, omits what would turn out to be, for Berryman, a necessary artistic resource. Only after a painful decades-long process of discovery "in the act of living and working" would this particular poet find means to make the words on the page conform at last to the jagged contours of his mind.

Berryman's friend Lowell was fascinated by Berryman's early artistic development, in part because Berryman's evolution toward maturity of voice was a slower and more painful version of Lowell's own. It was Lowell who suggested that Berryman collect some of his Dream Songs, which he had projected to run to more than 350, into a preliminary volume. The resulting *77 Dream Songs*, published in 1964, when the poet was fifty, marked Berryman's first real breakthrough from comparative obscurity into fame. In his review of this volume, which won the Pulitzer for 1965, Lowell produced a vivid and perceptive portrait of his friend's development from earnest, driven, unworldly youth to bristling, articulate, worldly maturity. "In his twenties, he was already a keen critic and a distinguished scholar. . . . He vibrated brilliantly to all significant influences and most of all to the new idiom of Auden. His proper bent seemed toward an intense and unworldly symbolic poetry." Lowell adds pointedly that "In the beginning, Berryman might have grown into an austere, removed poet, but instead he somehow remained deep in the mess of things. His writing has been a long, often backbreaking search for an inclusive style, a style that could use his erudition and catch the high, even frenetic intensity of his experience, disgusts and enthusiasms" (*RLProse* 104–5).

The sketch he produces here typifies Lowell's distinctive brand of criticism, which, unlike Berryman's or Jarrell's, relies more on the acute character portrait, placing its object in a specific personal and cultural context, than on structural analysis. When Helen Vendler was "a special student in transit from chemistry to English" at Boston University in 1955–56, she frequented Lowell's lectures. Vendler later recalled how "Lowell began his classes on each successive poet with . . . remarks on the poet's life and writing; the poet appeared as a man with a temperament, a set of difficulties, a way of responding, a vocation, prejudices."[26] If one tries to see Berryman in late 1930s in terms of the temperament, the set of difficulties, the way of responding, the vocation, the prejudices that Lowell stressed when he spoke of poets to his own classes, one can more readily understand how Berryman might have written a poem such as "Communist" and how this poem can offer an entrée into his later work.

One must start with Berryman's vocation, since this vocation was ever in the forefront of his thinking and drove him compellingly. Berryman's vocation, early on, was simply to become a great and famous poet in the grand style. "Yeats's way was the ideal way," he told his first wife, Eileen, a few years later, comparing his own slow start to his friend Delmore Schwartz's swiftness out of the gate. "A long slow development, the work getting better, the character stronger, until the late great poems and world fame."[27] A master poet in the Yeatsian mold, such as Berryman then aspired to be, had to comment for eternity upon the crucial events of his day, to speak powerfully and universally as Yeats had spoken about "mad Ireland." Berryman's adoption of Yeats as a model for his own development may have encouraged him, in his early verse, to overreach and to propound sententiously, just as he preferred bow ties for years because Yeats had worn a bow tie to their single meeting. But it also meant that he was willing to risk early weakness, even failure, in order to achieve later success.

In his prose elegy, Lowell aptly characterized the conflict of opposites in Berryman's temperament as a person and artist. On the one hand "An indignant spirit was born in him; his life was a cruel fight to set it free." On the other, the young Berryman was frequently worshipful. Indignation and worship, usually directed at the same object, are the central, conflicting, emotions in many of Berryman's mature poems, and in some early poems as well.

Berryman's intense, conflicted temperament had its roots in his embattled, embittered, childhood, particularly in his relationship with his mother, which contained strong measures both of worship—the attitude he had been taught to take toward her—and of indignation—a feeling, overwhelming in its power, that he was taught, early on, to suppress. In "Communist" one sees the worshipful, nearly slavish, imitation of a classic border ballad. Hadn't Yeats drawn on Celtic mythology? Hadn't Hopkins and Auden echoed the Anglo-Saxon epics? At the same time, one sees an indignant protest against the contemporary betrayal of an ideal. This uneasy balance of adulation and indignation, here externalized onto literary history and contemporary events, remains unresolved in early Berryman and threatens to tear many poems of his long apprenticeship to pieces. But this same tension—in the form of a keenly dramatized dialectic—would one day provide the fuel for many a Dream Song.

Berryman's chief artistic prejudice as he emerged from the 1930s was a commitment to aesthetic over political values in poetry—though a response to political issues always had a place in his writing. For Berryman, poetry might articulate the present moment, but it must be judged according to the standard of the best poetry of the past. "Communist" suggests, through its appropriation of an archaic form to comment on contemporary events, the standpoint of a writer who wants to see current events through the prism of the eternal. It would take Berryman many years to solve the problem implicit in this aesthetic, but the result would be a voice of significant temporal range and of almost unparalleled originality.

Berryman's "set of difficulties" have been outlined, so far, with emphasis on his concerns as an artist. But his personal difficulties cannot be omitted from the profile. Berryman had lived, as we have seen, through a childhood dominated by unresolved traumatic experiences, stemming partly but by no means exclusively from his father's reported suicide (and possible murder), and he remained in complex relationship with a doting, possessive and sometimes frightening mother who shared and encouraged his intellectual ambitions while often subjecting him to rigorous cross examination or to bouts of non-stop talking. Paul Mariani indicates that as early as 1938 Berryman "had discovered that the only way to stop Jill's monologues was to faint."[28]

Berryman, too, was aware of his own eccentric personality, the way his passionate intellectual self-absorption, his fierce bouts of reading, and, later, his equally fierce bouts of drinking, consumed his life and set him apart from others. This self-absorption was balanced and complicated by a searching and intelligent awareness of current events, and by a deep introspection schooled by a detailed technical knowledge of Freudian psychoanalysis. Berryman's introspection was made all the sharper by his keen, if sometimes helpless, identification with the suffering of others, an identification limned in writings such as his story "The Imaginary Jew." Each of these elements may be noted in "Communist." Meanwhile, the verbal Ping-Pong match between mother and son, with mother smashing hard slams to the backhand and son just barely keeping the ball in play, suggests a dimension of his own interior conflict of opposites that would remain at the core of his work.

To take up the last remaining Lowellian category cited by Vendler above, let me suggest that Berryman's most persistent "way of responding" artistically to the world as he ambivalently saw it, a trait he shared with Lowell, Bishop, and Jarrell, was to dramatize an individual experiencing the shocking recognition of crushing displacement or personal loss. In "Communist" it seems that the "honest young man" may have begun, by the end of the poem, to move from denial of his lost illusions toward recognition that his ideals have been misplaced and his illusions have, indeed, been lost. Implicitly, this young man will have to reconstruct his system of beliefs in response to shattering realities. Berryman's later poems often leave us at just this moment, staring loss straight in the face and wondering unceremoniously, "What next?"

## "Changes and Discovery" in Berryman

The difference idiom can make, which suggests the vigorous manner in which Berryman would finally address his artistic difficulties, may be illustrated by two passages Berryman wrote about his friend Delmore Schwartz. The first is from "At Chinese Checkers," yet another poem written in 1939:

> Deep in the unfriendly city Delmore lies
> And cannot sleep, and cannot bring his mind
> And cannot bring those marvellous faculties
> To bear upon the day sunk down behind.
>
> (*JBPoems* 28)

Jarrell calls this "monumental bathos" in his 1948 review of Berryman's *The Dispossessed*, but he asserts in the same paragraph that "Berryman is a complicated, nervous and intelligent writer whose poetry has steadily improved." The intimate frame of reference that would work in the *Dream Songs* doesn't work here, because of a slight staleness of phrasing and, worse, a lack of specificity.

Most interestingly for our present purpose, at the end of his 1948 review Jarrell praises "The Nervous Songs"—now clearly recognizable as prototypes of *The Dream Songs.* Jarrell had a well-known flair for chucking authors who displeased him definitively into the waste bin, but in this case he prophesied with uncanny accuracy that Berryman "ought in the end to produce poetry better than the best of the poems he has so far written" (*KA&Co* 152–53). Lowell once said that a "true review . . . sinks into the reviewed's mind, causing changes and discovery" (*RLProse* 275) and that almost certainly happened in this case.

The potential latent in Berryman's "Nervous Songs" lingered in Jarrell's mind. Speaking in 1950 of Howard Nemerov's second book, *Guide to the Ruins,* Jarrell said, "many of them might be given the name that John Berryman, a better poet with whom Nemerov has something in common—gave to some of his, 'The Nervous Songs'" (*KA&Co* 164). Jarrell was so closely attuned to the potential of the "Nervous Song" language because this language was perfectly in keeping with his conception of poetic structure as dynamic, as dialectical, as existing in a state of becoming—"about as static as an explosion."

In Berryman's many *Dream Song* elegies to his friend Delmore, the monumentality and grandiloquence Jarrell criticized have been displaced by a dazzling and dazed simplicity, a poem representing "the mind in action":

> I need to hurry this out before I forget
> which I will never He fell on the floor
> outside a cheap hotel-room
> my tearducts are worn out, the ambulance came
> and there on the way he died
> He was 'smart & kind,'
>
> a child's epitaph. He had no children,
> nobody to stand by in the awful years
> of the failure of his administration
> He was tortured, beyond what man might be
> Sick & heartbroken Henry sank to his knees
> Delmore is dead. His good body lay unclaimed
> three days.
>
> (*DS* 151)

Using Berryman's *Dream Song* voice to exemplify the characteristics of poetic diction after modernism, Robert Pinsky has commented, "Perhaps the most important point to be made is that the colloquial words and the gag-words are not the words for which the extravagant style provides a kind of license or passport. Rather, the colloquial words help the syntax, the gags, and the personae in a general effort to admit another kind of phrase—like 'a smothering southern sea'—just as in ordinary talk tough-slangy tag lines such as 'all that jazz' often excuse and qualify a phrase the speaker fears may seem too elevated or pretentious."[29] Pinsky's argument seems all the more cogent when set against the actual record of Berryman's artistic struggle. The elevated and pretentious diction toward which he was originally drawn resulted for him, at least, in what Jarrell called a "posed, planetary melodrama" (*KA&Co* 152). The character of the experience he was trying to bring across into verse resisted being treated in an unrelievedly elevated tone—as readers and critics whom Berryman respected continually reminded him.

Instead, Berryman was to find that the conscious and deliberate (rather than inadvertent) breach of good taste was essential to the development of his voice, and might even be essential to the floating of those oddly turned, mock-pretentious, but nonetheless elevated and moving phrases in which the *Dream Songs* seem uniquely to specialize.[30] Of course, there is a necessary element of brinkmanship in any ambitious aesthetic, but particularly so in this one. The lapses and incongruities must seem purposeful, and the poet must somehow appear to retain a measure of control over the dynamic dialectic of his stanzas, at once comic and tragic, learned and profane, blunt and riddled with paradox. No wonder it took Berryman so many years of living and working to evolve this voice. As Berryman's career progressed he was not attempting to "remake" himself, as Yeats claimed that he was doing, "When ever I remake a song." Rather, he was painfully remaking his line into an echo of his voice, so that its sound would linger even past his own death, so that a friend like Lowell could finally recognize "a voice on the page, identified as my friend's on the telephone, though lost now to mimicry."

## Lowell's "Falling Asleep over the Aeneid"

As he was writing "Falling Asleep over the Aeneid," just following the end of World War II, Lowell was much involved with all three of his friends. While the poem was still in an early draft in May of 1946, Jarrell wrote to Lowell that "Your 'Falling Asleep over the Aeneid' is the best title I ever heard, almost" (*RJLet* 161). When the poem appeared in *The Mills of the Kavanaughs*, a book Jarrell generally found disappointing, Jarrell commented, "I cannot think of any objection at all to 'Mother Marie Therese' and 'Falling Asleep over the Aeneid,' and if I could I would be too overawed to make it. 'Mother Marie Therese' is the best poem Mr. Lowell has ever written, and 'Falling Asleep over the Aeneid" is—is better" (*P&A* 255).[31]

Bishop had met Lowell recently, and in the second of the hundreds of letters she sent to Lowell—and the first that she addressed "Dear Cal"—she begins by stating, "I am terribly impressed with your dream poem and I gather from it that when you dream you dream in colors all right. . . . It is a really *stirring* poem; I don't think I've enjoyed a poem in that particular way since reading Macaulay when I was little." She then provides a very detailed reading of the phrasing of the text she had in hand, which, as Robert Giroux summarizes it, "caused Lowell to change 'mass" to 'morning service,' to spell 'turms' (squadrons of horsemen) correctly, to delete 'Johnny Comes Marching Home Again,' to revise 'Mass is over' to 'church is over,' and to make other minor improvements."

But Lowell's formative interactions with contemporaries who had a shaping influence on "Falling Asleep over the Aeneid" began still earlier. In July 1946, with the war over and travel again unrestricted, a promising scholar and poet in his early thirties named John Berryman came to the door of an early-nineteenth-century frame house in the Maine coastal village of Damariscotta Mills. He arrived with his talented first wife Eileen —later a psychologist, novelist, and brilliant memoirist. The town, as Eileen Simpson later remembered it in *Poets in Their Youth*, "looked as though it had been scrubbed and polished, so bright was the light, so transparent the air."[32]

The Berrymans planned to spend a literary weekend with some newfound friends. Waiting at the door was another promising poet, still in his late twenties, and recently released from prison where he had been confined as a conscientious objector. The poet was Robert Lowell, whom the Berrymans knew slightly and wanted to know better. Lowell was working on an early version of "Falling Asleep over the Aeneid" on that day in July 1946, a few months after Jarrell's "Death of the Ball Turret Gunner" appeared in *Partisan Review*, and a few months before Lowell's own *Lord Weary's Castle* would appear in print. Eileen would later recall that Lowell "greeted us as if he had been impatient for our arrival." He showed this eagerness by carrying their suitcases, "heavy with books rather than clothing," up the stairs two steps at a time. Lowell's own first wife, Jean Stafford, had bought this house, the first home any of the four had owned, with the proceeds of her best-selling first novel, *Boston Adventure*.

For much longer than the weekend originally planned, Stafford's recent investment provided shelter for this unusual concentration of emerging literary talent. Berryman, Lowell, and their gifted wives enjoyed this idyll of writing, walking, drinking, and conversation—punctuated by Stafford's droll and penetratingly ironic observations. Berryman wrote his mother of this foursome's "lazy, agreeable, interesting & alcoholic" two-week sojourn, saying of Lowell, "I haven't found anyone so pleasant since Delmore [Schwartz] in 1939." He went on to say, "Cal (Lowell) & I are working our way, comparing opinions, through the whole of western poetry."[33] When they reached the twentieth century, and it emerged that Yeats was Berryman's favorite modern poet, Lowell insisted that his friend name Yeats's three greatest poems and then "his three greatest lines." Berryman protested, "Greatest lines? Must we select?" As Eileen recalled it, the next comment was Stafford's: "'Cal gets that from Randall,' Jean said, not quite sotto voce and looking as if she'd swallowed her tongue. 'Randall has a passion for the Three Greatest. Cal's caught it.'"[34]

Jarrell, Lowell's old friend from Kenyon College and his recent close collaborator on the final revision of *Lord Weary's Castle*, was many hours drive to the south in New York City. There, newly discharged from the Army Air Corps, he was beginning his year as literary editor of *The Nation*, replacing Margaret Marshall, who was on sabbatical. Even at such a distance, Jarrell's critical habits had a way of making their presence felt. But it was Berryman rather than Jarrell—who was serving as an instructor when Lowell, an undergraduate, knew him at Kenyon—of whom Lowell would later say, "I think he was almost *the* student-friend I've had, the one who was the student in essence" (*RLProse* 111). This visit is the chief source of that memory, suggesting that as late as 1946, Lowell viewed himself and the thirty-one-year-old Berryman as still students of the art of poetry. As Lowell recalled it, "John was ease and light. We gossiped on the rocks of the millpond, baked things in shells on the sand, and drank, as was the appetite of our age, much less than now. John could quote with vibrance to all lengths, even prose, even late Shakespeare, to show me what could be done with disrupted and mended syntax. This was the start of his real style" (*RLProse* 112).

The Berrymans had planned no more than a weekend stopover, but when the time came for them to go, Stafford and Lowell insisted they stay on. As Eileen later recalled it, "We must stay, Cal said. How could John even consider going when they hadn't discussed 'Lycidas.'"[35] Indeed, one of the keys to the artistic relationship of Lowell and Berryman, each among the most heartbreaking and innovative of recent elegists, can be acquired only by examining their relation to "Lycidas."

Samuel Johnson had famously condemned "Lycidas" as a poem in which "the diction is harsh, the rhymes uncertain, and the numbers unpleasing. . . . It is not to be considered as the effusion of real passion; for passion runs not after remote allusions and obscure opinions. . . . Where there is leisure for fiction there is little grief. In this poem there is no nature, for there is no truth; there is no art, for there is nothing new. Its form is that of a pastoral, easy, vulgar, and therefore disgusting . . . ; its inherent improbability always forces dissatisfaction on the mind."[36]

More recently Ezra Pound, reviewing the various styles available to modern poets, condemned "the Miltonic, which is a bombastic and rhetorical Elizabethan coming from an attempt to write English with Latin syntax."[37] T. S. Eliot, echoing Pound, had insisted on what would emerge as the standard high modernist view that Milton was a master of the "*artificial* style" whose poetry "triumph[s] with a dazzling disregard of the soul."[38] And W. H. Auden, aligning himself with this tradition of reading, would soon assert that: "At first reading, *Lycidas* seems to be by Prospero, for it purports to deal with the most serious matters possible—death, grief, sin, resurrection. But I believe this to be an illusion. On closer inspection it seems to me that only the robes are Prospero's and that Ariel has dressed up in them for fun. . . . If *Lycidas* is read in this way, as if it were a poem by Edward Lear, then it seems to me one of the most beautiful poems in the English language: if, however, it is read as the Prospero poem it apparently claims to be, then it must be condemned as Dr. Johnson condemned it, for being unfeeling and frivolous, since one expects wisdom and revelation, and it provides neither."[39]

This ongoing catalogue of high-level reproof from important poet-critics, articulating neoclassical, high modernist, and late modernist paradigms, makes clear that despite its lofty (and apparently unshakable) canonical rank, an imposing succession of authorities had deemed Milton's "Lycidas" "disgusting," "bombastic and rhetorical," "artificial," "frivolous," and "unfeeling." In short, it was an alluring and potentially dangerous literary influence, making it a poem worth attacking.

By contrast, Eileen Simpson recalled that when Lowell and Berryman took up "Lycidas" in the summer of 1946, they "had no trouble agreeing it was one of the greatest poems in the language."[40] Indeed, "Lycidas" had an usual importance for each of these poets, a fact Jarrell recognized regarding Lowell when he observed of the latter's 1944 small-press volume *Land of Unlikeness* that Lowell's "essential source is early Milton." Jarrell further noted that Lowell "is sometimes able to exploit the resources of language and the world for the organization of a poem almost exactly as some of the poets of the seventeenth century were able to" (*KA&Co* 132). Two years later, Jarrell would speak of the longest poem in *Lord Weary's Castle*, "Quaker Graveyard in Nantucket," as an "extraordinary rhetorical machine" and a "baroque work, like *Paradise Lost.*"

Jarrell praised Lowell's as a style in which things have "necessarily, been wrenched into formal shape, organized under terrific pressure, but they keep to an extraordinary degree their stubborn, unmoved toughness, their senseless originality and contingency" (*P&A* 216). There was something liberating for Lowell in those very characteristics of Milton's, in "Lycidas" and elsewhere, that Johnson, Pound, Eliot and Auden had lined up to condemn as improbable, vulgar, arbitrary, or artificial. A remark from Coleridge's *Table Talk* is helpful as one asks what this liberating quality might be: "In the Paradise Lost—indeed in every one of his poems—it is Milton himself whom you see; his Satan, his Adam, his Raphael, almost his Eve—are all John Milton; and it is a sense of this intense egotism that gives me the greatest pleasure in reading Milton's works. The egotism of such a man is a revelation of spirit."[41]

Berryman too, was intensely involved with "Lycidas," as his posthumous story "Wash Far Away" reveals, and his true style, too, would be one of the elements of which are "wrenched into formal shape" and "organized under terrific pressure." For each of these poets, the "egotism" of Milton—combined in "Lycidas" with his extraordinary erudition, his command of a varied array of potentially contradictory literary traditions, and with the buildup of an intense range of partly conscious, partly buried and inarticulate feelings—emerged as "a revelation of spirit." "Lycidas" includes Milton's responses to "the most serious matters possible—death, grief, sin, resurrection," and thus provides both Lowell and Berryman support for the arduous emotional and artistic work that they had undertaken.

Lowell's mentor John Crowe Ransom read "Lycidas" with a wariness understandable in the context of the remarks of Johnson, Pound, and Eliot—critics he respected—but also with a tentative sympathy for the strengths Lowell and Berryman found in it. He remarked in 1938, exactly three hundred years after the poem was first published, and a year after he took on Lowell as a protégé, that "Lycidas" was "done by an apprentice of nearly thirty, who was still purifying his taste upon an astonishingly arduous diet of literary exercises. . . . The poem is young, brilliant, insubordinate. In it is an artist who wrestles with an almost insuperable problem, and is kinsman to some tortured modern artists."[42] Ransom's description of a young poet at work in 1638 perhaps reflects his own still active experience with apprentice-poets such as Lowell and Jarrell. It is certainly prescient of the affinity Lowell and Berryman would come to feel toward the Milton of "Lycidas" when, more than three centuries later in 1946, each was a young, brilliant, insubordinate, and tortured modern artist of about thirty, struggling to emerge from a state of apprenticeship after having purified his taste upon an "astonishingly arduous diet of literary exercises."

Yet, unlike the romantic Coleridge, for whom Milton's "intense egotism" gave "the greatest pleasure," Ransom reads Milton's poem in the context of the prevailing, anti-romantic modernist belief that, "Anonymity, of some real if not literal sort, is a condition of poetry." Ransom is perturbed and not a little fascinated by the "excited Milton, breathless, and breaking through the logic of composition." And Ransom highlights the way the poem operates within—yet constantly threatens to break through—the limits of prosodic and elegiac conventions. For Ransom this suggests that "we may believe that Milton's bold play with the forms of discourse constitutes simply one more item in his general insubordinacy. He does not propose to be buried beneath his own elegy." Hence Ransom concludes that "*Lycidas*, for the most part a work of great art, is sometimes artful and tricky. We are disturbingly conscious of a man behind the artist. But the critic will always find too many and too perfect beauties in it ever to deal with it very harshly."[43]

Is it any wonder that Lowell, coming of age under the watchful eye of Ransom and struggling to find a language for his own early verse, would be drawn magnetically to Milton, and specifically the Milton of "Lycidas"? Here is a poet challenging enough to offend authorities ranging from Johnson to Auden, articulating an egotism that Coleridge found a "revelation of spirit," yet with sufficiently compelling beauties, and sufficient command of traditional forms, so that even though Ransom feels "disturbingly conscious of the man behind the artist," he cannot bring himself to deal with the poem (or the poet) very harshly.

Through his absorption of the range of possibilities latent in the Miltonic model—tentatively approved by his mentor Ransom—Lowell would leverage out the space he needed to create his early work. In *Lord Weary's Castle* and, still more conspicuously, in soon-to-be-written poems such as "Falling Asleep over the Aeneid," he created poems unimpeachably classical in origin, cogently formed and apparently impersonal, but that nonetheless insubordinately disturb one with the presence of the man behind the artist. At the same time, Lowell dramatizes the feeling of wrestling with almost insuperable problems that are at once artistic and personal.

"Falling Asleep over the Aeneid," generally recognized as one of Lowell's best poems, has received surprisingly sparse critical discussion. Possibly this is because of its sheer difficulties of structure, which in fact make it a quintessentially postmodern narrative, particularly in its multiplanar treatment of time, culture, character, and psychological states. Four temporal levels are embodied in the poem: the time of Trojan Aeneas; the time of Roman Vergil; the time of the Civil War, when the protagonist's Uncle Charles is buried; and the present, when the octogenarian protagonist falls asleep while reading the Aeneid and dreams his way back into the previous time frames.

Lowell offers a postmodern take on problems of memory and self-representation. Lowell knew classical languages, having majored in the classics at Kenyon. He was also steeped in American history, and the lore of his own family. Few would question that Robert Lowell's poetry is deeply involved with loss, but he is not so often associated with epistemology. This is a major oversight. The problem of knowledge, what one can know, and how one can know it, is at the center of his work—knowledge as burden and knowledge as opportunity. And many of the most central poems from each phase of Lowell's career seem to beg for discussion in light of the poetic materials he shared with other members of his circle.

Such major poetic statements as "Christmas Eve under Hooker's Statue," "The Mills of the Kavanaughs," "Falling Asleep over the Aeneid," "Beyond the Alps," "Memories of West Street and Lepke," and "Near the Ocean" present individual losses framed by history, and they employ all, or nearly all, of the poetic materials I have been highlighting. Each presents a fragment of the poet's, or an invented character's, autobiography in verse and makes significant use of such materials as childhood, visual objects and dream-like textures. For example, "Falling Asleep over the Aeneid" locates its invented protagonist, "an old man in Concord," in the historical context of abolitionist Massachusetts, a culture that was fast approaching extinction when Lowell published the poem at midcentury. Lowell explores this loss while presenting fragments of the protagonist's life in the form of a self-referential internal monologue. He makes symbolic use of domestic visual objects—a parlor saber, a group of stuffed birds, a "bust / of young Augustus"—that are alive with familial, cultural, and historical associations. As Lowell describes his protagonist in the epigraph, "He falls asleep, while reading Vergil, and dreams that he is Aeneas at the funeral of Pallas, an Italian prince." The poem unfolds by transcribing this dream with surrealistic intensity. At last the protagonist awakens to confused memories of his childhood, memories that serve to emphasize the approach of his own death and the inevitable extinction of his native culture.

Despite the dramatic shifts in style that characterized Lowell's work and that, in the minds of some readers, seem to indicate radical discontinuities in Lowell's career, many of the materials on which he drew, and the stylistic possibilities he exploited, remained self-consistent—and consistent, too, with the work of his closest contemporaries. Even quite early in his career, before he had published any of the poems for which he is now remembered, Lowell saw the issue of memory as problematic. In a remarkable 1941 letter to his friend Peter Taylor, whom he met several years earlier through Jarrell at Kenyon College, Lowell wrote in a way that displayed his early sophistication and insight into the problematic relation between art and memory. The letter, written on *Southern Review* letterhead, begins "The problem of Proust's memory fascinates me. Jean [Stafford] is writing a Proustian novel and you have turned to remembrance. I'll dash off a few definitions and aversions, not to Proust, who is one of the world's few tremendous writers but to his method and its implications." Lowell continues, almost as if he is composing a formal essay, stating that "Memory is not an end but an invaluable means for selecting and accumulating, for holding an experience as in a pair of tongs so that the intellect may intuit it from many angles, distort, refine, invent and develop. Memory is only a power for summoning images and consequently sub-intellectual and à fortiori sub-mystical. As an idol, as 'something terribly important' (precious?), it leads to illusion."[44]

Lowell saw memory, in its full epistemological complexity, as a tool both valuable and potentially dangerous. It is most valuable as a "power for summoning images," but these images should not be considered on the level of the "precious," the "terribly important," or even the true. In that they are, of logical necessity, "sub-intellectual" and "sub-mystical," memories must be processed by the intellect and/or the imagination before their value can be established in the realm of art. For Lowell, the illusions that memory can lead to include the following:

> 1) The nostalgia of recapturing mentally what can never be recaptured in life, i. e. the Past as passed, there mysterious, pathetic; 2) a perilous severance from substantial objects, a subjective state to be distinguished from Plato's realism, viz. the Ideas are external, more in opposition to Aristotle by terminology than intention; 3) a solipsism: what I think, what I reconstruct, what I feel is reality. This results in hideous violence to nature and tendencies to pamper one's faculties of introspection and self-criticism. Proust has five or six marvelous strategies for escaping such pit-falls.

One wishes Lowell had expatiated further on these Proustian strategies. Even so, this letter suggests that long before Lowell began to write a directly self-exploratory poetry, he had anticipated most of the epistemological pitfalls that later entrapped the confessionalist critics. And this letter suggests further what Bishop observed of *Life Studies*, that Lowell's art was deliberately designed to evade just such pitfalls.

Certainly, in his best work, Lowell displayed his own "marvelous strategies" for escaping the pitfalls of memory. In Lowell's work, one is always conscious of the rememberer observed in the act of remembering, and there is no suggestion that the past is fully recaptured. There is by no means a "perilous severance from substantial objects"—rather, the past in Lowell's work is built out of an extraordinarily vivid and tangible matrix of objects made as substantial as words can make them. And solipsism is avoided because of the intent focus on other people who have their own, divergent realities. Thus, in "Falling Asleep over the Aeneid" we have a culturally situated individual engaged in the act of memory. We have several vividly realized scenes and a number of vividly realized characters.

The poem's four parts are woven together with dreamlike transitions. The first part establishes the context of a man in Concord who dreams over the Aeneid instead of going to church. The second is an extended bravura passage about the funeral rites of Pallas, focusing on the bird priest, a passage not in Vergil that Lowell simply invented. The third is a loose translation of a passage on the rites of Pallas that actually is in Vergil. This transitions into a fourth part that returns us to Concord in the present, overlapping with memories from the distant past.

The poem provides the intersection and exploration of literary, historical, psychological, and mythic levels. The historical layers are several: a series of lost worlds recovered and explored. The protagonist of the poem, an inhabitant of Concord born in the nineteenth century and surviving well into the twentieth, explores through his dream the barbarous and ceremonious culture that Vergil evokes as the world of Trojan Aeneas. The poem, which is in many ways an exploration of the world after World War II, after one awakens from a dream of barbarism, juxtaposes pagan values against Puritan, Christian values, without showing a clear preference for either. At the same time, the poem's imagery has an unsettling immediacy, which contrasts with contemporary sobriety.

The first part of the poem introduces the subject through the title, epigraph and opening two-and-one half lines:

> The sun is blue and scarlet on my page,
> And *yuck-a, yuck-a, yuck-a, yuck-a,* rage
> The yellowhammers mating.
>
> (*LWC/MK* 101)

Much is accomplished in these opening lines. They link up, through a simple color association that will run as a leitmotif through the poem, with the second part:

Yellow fire
Blankets the captives dancing on their pyre,
And the scorched lictor screams and drops his rod.
(*LWC/MK* 101)

The association of bird imagery and the color yellow is here established. The second section creates an imaginary mythic sacrifice for which there is no precedent in Vergil. Moreover, Vergil's third person treatment of Aeneas becomes first person. The unnamed Concord gentleman becomes Aeneas, who goes by the epithet "pious" in the Aeneid but who can seem to modern readers both a loyal son and friend and a bloodthirsty imperialist. The bird-priest represents a different and more barbaric but also more exciting kind of religion than the staid Puritanism of latter-day Concord. Dido's sword is one of many objects that cross the temporal barrier, later turning into the Concord gentleman's "parlor saber." It is, in its Vergilian phase, a "bloody implement," since Dido used it to commit suicide because of Aeneas's desertion.

The third section of the poem is the translation from Vergil. Dryden had translated Vergil into heroic couplets, but Dryden's heroic couplets are nothing like Lowell's. Lowell's couplets are sinewy and at the same time rather elusive. The yellow imagery comes from Vergil but is developed far more extensively by Lowell, who uses it as a link between the ancient and modern worlds.

The fourth section, which takes us back into the modern world, is the poem's most startling and impressive section. Bishop praised the transition from past back into present, and from waking back into sleep. Jarrell speaks of the "conclusion in which all the terms of the poem coalesce . . . as the ending of this poem, an ending with every term prepared for, every symbol established, it is as magnificent as it is final" (*P&A* 257).

Church is over, and its bell
Frightens the yellowhammers, as I wake
And watch the whitecaps wrinkle up the lake.
Mother's great aunt, who died when I was eight,
Stands by our parlor sabre. "Boy, it's late.
Vergil must keep the Sabbath." Eighty years!
It all comes back. My Uncle Charles appears.
Blue-capped and bird-like. Phillips Brooks and Grant
Are frowning at his coffin, and my aunt,
Hearing his colored volunteers parade
Through Concord, laughs, and tells her English maid
To clip his yellow nostril hairs, and fold
His colors on him. . . . It is I. I hold

His sword to keep from falling, for the dust
On the stuffed birds is breathless, for the bust
Of young Augustus weighs on Vergil's shelf:
It scowls into my glasses at itself.

(*LWC/MK* 103)

The temporal layers, and the layers of history, myth, and self, converge on the remarkable final lines. As in many of Bishop's best works, most of Lowell's poem is description, yet the description keeps piling up symbolic associations that come powerfully together in the end.

Reading this poem, Bishop asked Lowell in 1948: "How do you feel about Browning and why don't the critics ever mention him in connection with you?—although give me you any time" (*EBLet* 154). Bishop is suggesting here Lowell's mastery of literary personae, his ability to project present-day issues and personal concerns back into the past. Though scholars of Lowell often emphasize the schism in his work, it is helpful to keep the technique of a large-scale early poem like "Falling Asleep over the Aeneid" in mind when reading the unrhymed sonnets of *History*. There one finds the same sudden shifts from the apparently descriptive to the symbolic, the same startling juxtapositions of self, history, and myth.

# 6 Exploring Lost Worlds

## *Developments in Narrative Postmodernism*

In Elizabeth Bishop's 'Man-Moth' a whole new world is gotten out and you don't know what will come after any one line. It's exploring.

Robert Lowell, Interview with Frederick Seidel

### Exploring Lost Worlds

Robert Lowell's unrhymed sonnet "Charles V by Titian"—which appeared in *Notebook 1967–68*, in the revised and expanded 1970 *Notebook* (under the headings "Power" and "The Powerful"), and in a slightly improved version in *History*—addresses the problem of reading history, or recovering it, through artifacts that survive from the past. In this particular case, Lowell explores the way heroic portraiture may project a stage-managed version of individual character or historical fact. Certainly, for Lowell, the past cannot be unproblematically recovered through such artifacts, even as they appear to bring the past alive:

> But we cannot go back to Charles V
> barreled in armor, more gold fleece than king;
> he haws on the gristle of the Flemish world,
> his upper and lower Hapsburg jaws won't meet.
> The sunset he tilts at is big Venetian stuff,
> the true Charles, done by Titian, never lived.
> The battle he rides offstage to is offstage.
>
> (*History* 63)

Here, as so often in Lowell, one is confronted by an unresolved "conflict of opposites" such as Jarrell described in his 1942 Mesures lecture. Is Titian's heroic version of Charles V—resplendently armored, mounted on a plumed charger, backed by a sublime if stagey-looking sunset, and confidently presenting his lance—really the "true Charles"? Or is it more to the point that such a triumphantly "true" figure "never lived"?

Although Charles V (1500–1558), like most of the Hapsburgs, spoke with a stammer, he ruled more countries than any previous European monarch. But he spent most of his life harassed by debt and civil war, struggling to hold his fractious empire together. In 1557, nine years after the triumphant Titian portrait was painted, and the year before his death, Charles V abdicated his imperial crowns in favor of his son and younger brother and retired to the monastery of Yuste.

> No St. Francis, he did what Francis shied at,
> gave up office, one of twenty monarchs
> since Saturn who willing made the grand refusal.
> In his burgherish monastery, he learned he couldn't
> put together a clock with missing parts.
>
> (*History* 63)

In his retirement Charles V has relinquished the theatrics of equestrian portraiture only to become a curious, voluntary iteration of Lowell's Czar Lepke:

> Flabby, bald, lobotomized,
> he drifted in a sheepish calm,
> where no agonizing reappraisal
> jarred his concentration on the electric chair—
> hanging like an oasis in his air
> of lost connections.
>
> (*LS* 86)

Like that latter-day Czar of crime, Charles V's life is built on irreconcilable contradictions: "He had dreamed of a democracy of Europe, / and carried enemies with him in a cage" (*History* 63). Here, as in so many of the unrhymed sonnets of *History*, Lowell is exploring a lost world juxtaposed with an implicit or explicit authorial present that is just as complex.

It is easy enough to find implicit parallels between Charles V and Lowell-as-author. Each was the beneficiary and victim of inherited privilege and inherited disabilities. Each bore for most of his life the mantle of expectation and lived with the rewards and challenges of power. Each projected an heroic yet vulnerable public image that partly expressed, and was partly at odds with, the private self. Each was drawn to high ideals, yet had to struggle with a streak of violence, even vengefulness, in his own character. Each in several different ways was trying to put together "a clock with missing parts."

Lowell, however, is not only exploring—and thereby implicitly linking with—a lost *character*, but also that character's world. Sixteenth-century

Europe, as it appears in the poem, connects by several points of analogy to Lowell's Vietnam-era America. For example, Charles V's unruly, perhaps ungovernable European empire mirrors a contemporary imperial America doomed "until the end of time / to police the earth" (*NTO* 20). And Charles's abdication reflects on President Lyndon Johnson's decision not seek another term after Eugene McCarthy's surprising success against him in the 1968 New Hampshire primary. Lowell's exploration of the lost world of Charles V may be read, in part, as self-exploration and in part as an exploration of the plight of the contemporary wielder of power who finds the world fractious beyond his control. The poem is a portrait of a portrait of a portrait that works simultaneously on multiple planes.

Like Lowell in "Charles V by Titian," Jarrell, Bishop and Berryman, his colleagues in our midcentury quartet, were engaged throughout the mature phase of their careers in the emotionally risky, intellectually uncertain, yet illuminating and intriguing process of exploring lost worlds. In these explorations, which deal intimately with cultural and psychical history in poems that pass with deceptive ease between conscious and unconscious layers, this quartet was developing the art of postmodern narrative, an aesthetic whose origins are outlined above. This chapter will examine a sequence of poems written during the course of the 1950s, under the heavy shadow of the Cold War, and under the lingering shadow, as well, of each of these poets' traumatic early experience. These poems exploit the multilayered narrative time-frames and multilayered frames of cultural and psychological reference that had become standard equipment in each poet's artistic repertoire. The poems include Jarrell's "A Quilt Pattern" (1953), Berryman's "Homage to Mistress Bradstreet" (1953), Bishop's "Sestina" (1956), and Lowell's "Skunk Hour" (1959). Each of these Fifties poems places its individual protagonist in the context of a historical condition that seems at once familiar and radically new, and each involves an unsettling confrontation with loss, emotional disorder, and the problem of identity. Each poem exploits dream states as vehicles of transition between planes of time, planes of consciousness, and cultural difference. Moreover, all four narratives allude, directly or distantly, to the traumatic family experience that each author had survived.

Such poems have no immediate precedent. The dramatic monologues of Tennyson or Browning lack this degree of complex temporal layering: most often there are two levels, the past and, implicitly, the author's present. Modernist poets such as Eliot and Pound pioneered the technique of complex temporal juxtaposition, but to achieve this effect they strove to fragment traditional narrative structures and depersonalize the individual. In Pound or Eliot, or in Williams's *Paterson*, the transitions between temporal layers is *not* intended to appear seamless, but rather to strike the reader as deliberately jagged or jarring. Hence Eliot's "Gerontian," or the fleetingly dramatized figures in *The Waste Land*, or Pound's Odysseus or Malatesta, like Williams's Dr. Paterson, are fragmentary characters. By comparison Lowell's Charles V is placed vividly before us in a few deft strokes, holding Titian's two-dimensional representation against the historical individual so that we may contemplate their differences. Lowell's achievement in this short, coherent, yet multiplanar poem required extraordinary technical invention and skill.

Critics who isolate single features of the dynamic aesthetic examined in this chapter, by which art conceals itself, may be tempted to condemn it on technical grounds. They may particularly object to its characterization as "postmodern," asserting that it is insufficiently new or experimental. Yet when one looks at the eclectic mix of modern and traditional elements that this aesthetic can marshal together in a single poem, in a pastiche that does not look like a pastiche, one begins to appreciate the remarkable intricacy and freshness of this style. Lowell, Jarrell, Bishop, and Berryman, as they evolved the techniques of this aesthetic, found means to combine modernism's complex, disjunctive temporality with a return to elements of traditional narrative continuity. Thus the poems are able to explore the felt losses, confusions, and disordered affective lives of *credible* individuals—individuals who face severe difficulties integrating the conflicting elements of their personalities.

## Jarrell's Versions of History

In his own approach to history, Jarrell aligns himself with a focus on the individual. He attacks the dissimulations of a more official mode of history in one rarely mentioned poem with an ironic attitude toward the soporific and oversimplifying effect of historical monumentalism. This attitude is implied by the poem's title, "A Lullaby." Here an ordinary foot soldier

> Is lied to like a child, cursed like a beast.
> They crop his hair, his dog tags ring like sheep
> As his stiff limbs shift wearily to sleep.
>
> (*RJPoems* 169)

In sleep, alone, the soldier finds respite, and only there, in the unrecorded corridors of the unconscious, does he connect, fleetingly, with the people and the life he left behind:

> Recalled in dreams or letters, else forgot,
> His life is smothered like a grave, with dirt;
> And his dull torment mottles like a fly's
> The lying amber of the histories.
>
> (*RJPoems* 169)

Jarrell would remark in his last interview, "In any . . . in most works of art, you're concerned with showing things that are often repressed out of existence; you want to show what the world's really like."[1] To recover and dramatize the "dull torment" of the individual, whose "family and days" seem to be inevitably lost when encapsulated in the "lying amber" of monumentalist history, would become a key artistic project for each of our four poets. Each would evolve a technique that could bring to life both the quotidian immediacy and the repressed psychic background of their characters' experience. In the process, their poems project a richly detailed imaginative history that, at its most telling, dramatically recreates both a cultural environment and the hidden emotional life of a culturally determined individual.

Jarrell's "A Quilt Pattern" was written in 1953, several years before *Life Studies.* The poem offers its own penetrating exploration of a lost world. The child protagonist, like Lowell's Concord gentleman in "Falling Asleep over the Aeneid," is on the verge of sleep as he lies in bed, but his mind ranges through different layers of consciousness, entering, in particular, the mythic story of Hansel and Gretel:

> The blocked-out Tree
> Of the boy's Life is gray
> On the tangled quilt: the long day
> Dies at last, after many tales.
> Good me, bad me, the Other
> Black out, and the humming stare
> Of the woman—the good mother—
> Drifts away; the boy falls
> Through darkness, the leagues of space
> Into the oldest tale of all.
>
> (*RJPoems* 57)

The central conflict here is between the child and the child's mother. Is this "the good mother" or some other mother, and am I "good me' or "bad me" or "the Other"? This is a poem in which exploration correlates with eating the house, and when

> The boy holds out the bone of the finger.
> It moves, but the house says, "No, you don't know.
> Eat a little longer."
> The taste of the house
> Is the taste of his—
>                  "I don't know,"
> Thinks the boy. "No, I don't *know!*"
>
> (*RJPoems* 58)

Clearly the suppressed word is "the taste of his *mother*," and the child in this case knows, but does not want to know what he tastes.

In poems such as "A Quilt Pattern," these poets were completing the transition away from modernism toward a new style, one that would be anything but impersonal, a style that would return to narrative while retaining the disjunctive elements of modernism. This style would be able to explore lost worlds on many levels, in the realm of personal loss, in the realm of history, in the realm of myth. It would be immersed in domestic detail, yet also full of dream textures, constantly juxtaposing the tangible against the unconscious. It would be ironic, yet full of stubborn facts, full of necessity, yet equally full of life and surprise. Literary historians have tended to valorize later breakthroughs, emphasizing what is new about the "confessional" style of Lowell and Berryman in the late 1950s and through the sixties. But an examination of these earlier post–World War II poems shows just how much groundwork went into the creation of that new style. It also suggests how poets such as Bishop or Jarrell could importantly influence Lowell and Berryman, and why these four would continue to appreciate one another. Together they pursued common interests in the problem of self-exploration and exploration of the domestic, historical, and mythic backgrounds that help to shape one's perceptions of the self. They had an ambivalent attitude toward cultural tradition, but an effective way of making use of it.

## Berryman's "Homage to Mistress Bradstreet"

Anne Bradstreet served as a brilliantly chosen transitional figure for Berryman. As a senior poet she could serve as an object of pious adoration, and his title *Homage to Mistress Bradstreet* implies that intention. As an American, she could represent a return to native models, after his 1930s' infatuation with things British. As his projection of a desirable woman, remote in the past, she could represent the occasion for a safely imaginary seduction. As a Puritan wife, she could offer stiff resistance. But as a comparatively unschooled wordsmith whose "bald / abstract didactic rime I read appalled / harassed for your fame / mistress neither of fiery nor velvet verse" (*JBPoems* 135), she might stand as a figure with whom the superbly trained yet strangely voiceless Berryman could unite. Together they might join in finding a voice that would more fully express each poet's isolated contemporary situation. Casting himself in the conflicting roles of muse, confidant, and seducer, Berryman took up, for the first time, the great dramatic part he would play for the rest of his literary career—his pose as The Other. As Berryman alternately centers and de-centers the voices of his *Homage*, he and his richly historicized and extravagantly imagined Mistress Bradstreet explore fictively the temptations and risks of breaking free from their different—but equally constraining—temporal situations. Through the creation, or re-creation, of Mistress Bradstreet, as later through the invention of Henry, Berryman would find means of summoning to uncanny half-life figures of his own capable imagination: quasi-historical, quasi-fabricated characters, whose represented and representative lives unfold against intricate physical, cultural, and psychic backgrounds.

Here then is another postmodern narrative. Berryman began the poem in 1947, shortly after he and his first wife Eileen visited Lowell and Jean Stafford in Damariscotta Mills, Maine, in the summer of 1946. He completed it in 1953, when it appeared in *Partisan Review*, and he published it in book form in 1956. Berryman had certainly read and been impressed by Lowell's Jonathan Edwards's poems from *Lord Weary's Castle*, which versify extracts from Edwards's own writings and recreate him in modern terms. In this homage Berryman also explores a lost world, in this case the historical world of early Puritan Boston. The recreation of that lost world is often magical, as when Anne, early in the poem, recalls the privations of their first season in the Bay Colony:

> How long with nothing in the ruinous heat,
> clams & acorns stomaching, distinction perishing,
> at which my heart rose,
> with brackish water, we would sing.
> When whispers knew the Governor's last bread
> was browning in his oven, we were discourag'd.
> The Lady Arbella dying—
> dyings—at which my heart rose, but I did submit.
>
> (*JBPoems* 134)

Berryman, an avid reader, had immersed himself in the lore of Puritan Boston with a zeal that rivaled Hawthorne's a century earlier, and like Hawthorne, he used the strengths and contradictions of America's early Puritan culture as a vehicle for exploring the problems of the present. Two years after completing the poem, Berryman sketched a list of its central concerns on the page of a notebook:

> Themes
> poet in anti-poetic society
> demon lover & Belle Dame sans Merci
> The Sense of the Past—(her nostalgia & mine)
> The Great Goddess—ancestress—first poetess—Mother-Mary (St Anne—Mary's mo.)
> Utter Conservatism & Rebellion
> —Amer. origins
> a woman's life (esp. children)
> 30 May 55[2]

I have not found a published critical account that outlines the overlapping emotional and thematic concerns of the poem as comprehensively as does Berryman's brief list. Many readings of this poem have been quite narrow, reducing it to a single one of the elements listed by Berryman. Thus that list makes a useful point of departure, suggesting several levels on which the poem can be read. The "poet in an anti-poetic society" suggests both a level of personal identification by Berryman with Bradstreet and an urge to compare their cultures. An element of romantic mythology emerges in the "demon lover & Belle Dame sans Merci." "The Great Goddess—ancestress—first poetess—Mother-Mary (St Anne—Mary's mo.)" conflates the myths of Mediterranean paganism with the Christian myth of the immaculate conception. "The Sense of the Past" shows each poet as suffering from and motivated by nostalgia. "Utter Conservatism & Rebellion" was both a reading of Bradstreet and a trait of Berryman's own, derived from his mixture of worshipful and raging attitudes toward his mother. In this poem he can explore these elements culturally, on the level of their "—Amer. origins."

Berryman, noting that, "an American historian somewhere observes that all colonial settlements are intensely conservative, except in the initial break-off point," maintained that in *Homage* "Trying to do justice to both parts of this obvious truth. . . . I laid the poem out in a series of rebellions. I had her rebel first against the new environment and above all against her barrenness (which in fact lasted for years), then against her marriage (which in fact seems to have been brilliantly happy), and finally against her continuing life of illness, loss, and age. . . . Each rebellion, of course, is succeeded by a submission, although even in the moment of the poem's supreme triumph—the presentment . . . of the birth of her first child, rebellion survives" (*JBProse* 328–29). Berryman's own character, shaped by his relationship with his mother, also combines the worshipful and the rebellious, and rebellion always survives, even in moments of triumph.

One of the major focuses of the poem, though, is on "a woman's life (esp. children)." Bradstreet is a woman who yearned to be a mother, was infertile for a long time, and finally produced many children. As such, she is not an impossibly unreachable figure but complex, a real woman, with, for Berryman, an attractively maternal side. Berryman said, "I did not choose her—somehow she chose me—one point of connection, at any rate, being the almost insuperable difficulty of writing high verse at all in a land that cared and cares so little for it" (*JBProse* 328).

Berryman felt that the personal connection between himself as poet and Anne had received excessive attention. "Noting and overconsidering such matters, few critics have seen that it *is* a historical poem, and it was with interest that I found Robert Lowell pronouncing it lately, in *The New York Review*, 'the most resourceful historical poem in our literature'" (*JBProse* 329).[3] The poem takes many liberties with historical fact, but it remains rooted in historical detail. Berryman had been well trained as a literary scholar at Columbia and Cambridge Universities, as a biographer of Stephen Crane, and as an editor of King Lear. He describes his research as intensive: "for four-and-a-half years. . . . I accumulated materials and sketched, fleshing out the target or vehicle, still under the impression that seven or eight stanzas would see it done. There are fifty-seven" (*JBProse* 328).

Speaking of the blend of history and imaginative transformation in "The poem in which everything flowers for Berryman" (*RLProse* 105) after his "long, often back-breaking search for an inclusive style," (*RLProse* 107) Lowell said of *Homage to Mistress Bradstreet*, "It is wonderfully wrung and wrought. Nothing could be more high-pitched, studied and enflamed. . . . It . . . reproduces the grammar, theology, and staid decor of the period. The poet, however, heightens the action by imagining his heroine with the intensity of a seizure of hallucination. . . . Here Berryman's experiments with music and sentence structure find themselves harnessed to a subject and trial that strain them to the limit. His lovely discordant rhythms ride through every break, splutter, archaism, and inversion" (*RLProse* 107).

The individuals in the poem, and particularly Anne Bradstreet, emerge out of a psychologically determining cultural and historical context. Recovery of that lost world in the historically informed, imaginatively reconstructed arena of the poem involves both significant fidelity to the texture of early life *and* significant alteration. All of Anne's rebellions, except the act of writing poetry, are private. For the remarkable childbirth scene Berryman drew on experiences of contemporary women friends, whom he interviewed in some detail about their childbirth experiences. He captures the phase of early pregnancy, and what follows: "My world is strange / and merciful, ingrown months, blessing a swelling trance." The language is an uncanny blend of seventeenth century archaisms and modern elements. For Lowell, "The old rustic, seventeenth-century, provincial simplicity survives and is greatly enriched by the jagged intellectual probing and techniques of the modern poet." All of this comes together in the stanzas on childbirth:

> So squeezed, wince you I scream?" I love you & hate
> off with you. Ages! *Useless.* Below my waist
> he has me in Hell's vise.
> Stalling. He let me go. come back: brace
> me somewhere. No. No. Yes! everything down
> hardens I press with horrible joy down
> my back cracks like a wrist
> shame I am voiding oh behind it is too late
>
> hide me forever I work thrust I must free
> now I all muscles & bones concentrate
> what is living from dying?
> Simon I must leave you so untidy
> Monster you are killing me Be sure
> I'll have you later Women do endure
> I can *can* no longer
> and it passes the wretched trap whelming and I am me
>
> drencht & powerful, I did it with my body!
> One proud tug greens Heaven. Marvellous,
> unforbidding Majesty.
> Swell, imperious bells. I fly.
> Mountainous, woman not breaks and will bend:
> sways God nearby: anguish comes to an end.
> Blossomed Sarah, and I
> blossom. Is that thing alive? I hear a famisht howl.
>
> (*JBPoems* 137–38)

A generation of fathers who have been present as birth coaches can testify, along with the many women Berryman interviewed about bearing a child, to the extraordinary vividness and accuracy of this representation of unmedicated childbirth. Rebellion and submission, unfathomable pain and triumphant physicality, biblical lyricism, and the bluntest frankness intertwine and merge in a passage that is a triumph of the empathetic imagination. The poem ends on a similarly high note that expresses both resignation and exaltation in opaquely lyrical language:

> O all your ages at the mercy of my loves
> together lie at once, forever or
> so long as I happen.
> In the rain of pain & departure, still
> Love has no body and presides the sun,
> and elfs from silence melody. I run.
> Hover, utter, still,
> a sourcing        whom my lost candle like the firefly loves.
>
> (*JBPoems* 147)

Berryman said that "In the Bradstreet poem, as I seized inspiration from [Saul Bellow's] *Augie March*, I sort of seized inspiration from Lowell." The parallel is not a matter of voice, as Berryman correctly pointed out: "I can't think, offhand . . . of a single passage which distinctly sounds like Lowell."[4] The parallel arises more out of the very detailed but also dreamlike entry into a lost world of the past, and the connection between this quasi-historic, quasi-mythic lost world and a troubled present individual. In this sense Lowell's Jonathan Edwards poems and "Falling Asleep over the Aeneid," as well as Jarrell's "Girl in a Library" (1951), which explores a sleeping young woman's inner life as "an object among Dreams," were sources of inspiration waiting to be seized. Berryman had written that first, precious stanza of his *Homage* in 1947, a year before the publication of "Falling Asleep," when he conceived of the poem as a brief lyric, but the full development and elaboration of the poem came in 1953, well after Lowell's and Jarrell's explorations had appeared.

## Bishop's "Sestina"

One Bishop poem that explores a world of silent rebellion, which Berryman's Anne Bradstreet might of have understood, is "Sestina" (1956). The familial imperative that Bishop internalized, which enjoined her to remain silent about painful truths, to leave grief unexpressed and losses unmourned, may have begun with her maternal grandparents (the Bulmers) in Great Village, Nova Scotia. Bishop witnessed her mother's climactic breakdown over the fitting of a purple dress, a dress that would have removed her, after five years of mourning, from a widow's black. Bishop certainly overheard fragmentary discussions of these events by her Bulmer relatives, and she was frequently asked to deliver packages to the post office marked with her mother's address at the Dartmouth mental hospital. But, even if her mother's illness was tacitly acknowledged, Bishop's Bulmer grandparents, like, later, her Bishop grandparents and uncle, seem never to have fully explained what happened to her mother. Instead, they allowed her to infer what she could, which was clearly quite a bit. But as a child Bishop lacked the skills to understand her loss, and she was apparently not invited fully to share in the family's process of mourning. Bishop inferred from her experiences in Great Village and especially, I think, Worcester, that her own role within her family was to conspire to maintain the veil of silence, whatever she might surmise in private.

A scene remembered from shortly after the moment her mother left for the institution in Dartmouth is evoked in the 1956 "Sestina." In this scene, Bishop's Bulmer grandmother is vividly represented as struggling to maintain an aura of normalcy while disguising her own grief:

> September rain falls on the house.
> In the failing light, the old grandmother
> sits in the kitchen with the child
> beside the Little Marvel Stove,
> reading the jokes from the almanac,
> laughing and talking to hide her tears.
> (*EBPoems* 123)

Bishop here invents new psychological and narrative uses for the sestina form. The constant repetition of five of the six rhyme words, "child," "tears," "house," "stove," and "almanac," functions rather like a Freudian "repetition" of repressed material the unfolding psychological implications of which remain unacknowledged by the "grandmother," the figure who provides the sestina's sixth rhyme word. This grandmother thinks, apparently, that she has successfully disguised her own tears, but the child not only notes them but surmises much of what they mean. And she surmises as well that this is a house in which grief must remain unspoken. The grandmother:

thinks that her equinoctial tears
and the rain that beats on the roof of the house
were both foretold by the almanac,
but only known to a grandmother.
The iron kettle sings on the stove.
She cuts some bread and says to the child,

*It's time for tea now;* but the child
is watching the teakettle's small hard tears
dance like mad on the hot black stove,
the way the rain must dance on the house.
(*EBPoems* 123)

For this child tears are by no means eliminated because they are not acknowledged. Despite the attempt to disguise them, these tears are everywhere. Dancing off the sides of the hot kettle, beating on the roof of the house, these "equinoctial" tears are like tropical rainstorms: they will keep coming back, intensely, inevitably, at all the solstices of mourning. Indeed, they are everywhere, endowed with a purpose of their own. The teakettle's "small hard tears / dance like mad on the hot black stove," and the grandmother's teacup, too, seems "full of dark brown tears."

All these tears emblematize a grief that is repressed but nonetheless felt—and clamoring to be expressed. And it is the child who must do this expressive work since the grandmother will not. When the child draws a house she "puts in a man with buttons like tears / and shows it proudly to the grandmother." This picture's latent emotional material is received without comment, "But secretly, while the grandmother / busies herself about the stove," the action of the poem shifts to the ignored house the child has drawn. The house mirrors the actual house that the grandmother and child live in, but from which the child's mother, who is also the grandmother's daughter, has been exiled. She is never named in the poem, just as she has been effaced from the house.

Icons of sorrow and loss detach themselves from the static field of the almanac and enter the dynamic field of the child's drawing, taking on a dreamlike life of their own:

the little moons fall down like tears
from between the pages of the almanac
into the flower bed the child
has carefully placed in the front of the house.
(*EBPoems* 124)

These tears, and the child's imagination, become the sole entities of vitality in a world of absence. As in such poems as "The Weed," "Some Dreams

They Forgot," and the fourth "Song for a Colored Singer," here the tears are fruitful and they surreally multiply. The sestina concludes:

> *Time to plant tears*, says the almanac.
> The grandmother sings to the marvellous stove
> and the child draws another inscrutable house.
> (*EBPoems* 124)

Fear, overdelicacy, and a sense of propriety may get in the way of direct expression of emotion, but the child strives to express that emotion nonetheless, even if her expression must remain encoded. With the work of mourning undone, tears will remain a piece of the child's unresolved emotional material. The child repeats her action, drawing "another inscrutable house" because the first has engendered no response. Instead of empathy, reassurance, or the gift of necessary, if painful, knowledge, the child faces a frightening and inscrutable unknown, papered over by convention and the moral law.

## The Making and Reading of "Skunk Hour"

Perhaps the best single focus for a discussion of the elective affinities, mutual influence, and parallel development of this midcentury quartet emerges if one studies their different roles in the making of, and their various readings of, Robert Lowell's "Skunk Hour." This is a key poem in Lowell's development. It is also a poem in which both Bishop, the dedicatee, who helped to inspire it and provided the basis for its structure and technique, and Berryman, whom Lowell (and Bishop) considered the poem's most inspired and penetrating interpreter, each hold a stake.

David Kalstone, speaking of the impact of Bishop's "The Armadillo" on "Skunk Hour," the first poem that Lowell completed in his *Life Studies* style, observes acutely that Lowell's breakthrough was "in part nourished by Lowell's confused feeling for Bishop as admired writer, rival poet, unattainable and renounced love, and fantasy Muse." But Kalstone misses one of the genuinely vital points of connection between these two poets when he insists that Lowell's is a "much more *historical* poem" (his emphasis). Kalstone contends that "in 'Skunk Hour' [Lowell] separated himself poetically from Bishop."[5] But one might argue, to the contrary, that this is precisely the point at which his aesthetic most fully and fruitfully connected with Bishop's. Bishop's own poems are historical in much the same way as Lowell's, placing a vulnerable individual in a context surrounded by objects emblematic of that individual's psyche and cultural history. And "Skunk

Hour" and the poems that followed show Lowell comprehensively absorbing and adapting Bishop's technique of emblematic observation drifting toward a surprisingly decisive conclusion. Lowell himself remarked in a letter to Bishop that in "Skunk Hour," "really I've just broken through to where you've always been and gotten rid of my medieval armor's undermining." In a later letter, which Kalstone does not cite, Lowell went so far as to claim that, "I used your Armadillo in class as a parallel to my Skunks and ended up feeling a petty plagiarist."[6]

Why did Lowell feel his debt to Bishop so strongly—and in the poem in which he broke through to the *Life Studies* style? With all due respect to Kalstone, with whom I disagree reluctantly, the imprint of history and culture on human behavior is perhaps *the* key subtext of "The Armadillo." The poem's "frail, illegal fire balloons," so lovely and so destructive, are seen "rising toward a saint / still honored in these parts" as "the paper chambers flush and fill with light / that comes and goes like hearts" (*EBPoems* 103). Here are echoes of human aspiration and feeling that suggest that these balloons are very much a product and expression of the culture that launches them.

The quiet accretion of significant detail throughout "The Armadillo" writes a subtle cultural "history" of Brazil—a culture in which the observer ambivalently participates—in much the same way that "Skunk Hour" inscribes a cultural history of New England. And the impulses that lead, in Bishop's poem, to the release of the balloons, balloons that carry liquid fire and that destroy rain forests with an effect suggestive of defoliants or napalm, may remind the reader of still more violent personal or cultural impulses. Each poem explores, by implication, the way subtle cultural conditioning shapes overt human behavior, and each poem builds quietly to a disturbing climax.

No doubt Kalstone has a different and more conventional definition of history in mind. But a fascination with the artistic possibilities of history in the sense I am articulating here—that subtly revealing history embedded or encoded in overlooked cultural detail—was one of the most fundamental characteristics linking Bishop to more obviously public poets like Lowell, Jarrell, and Berryman. In 1957, Lowell was seeking a new style, and he felt indebted to Bishop not just for the tone and structure of his breakthrough poem—Lowell told A. Alvarez "I was reading Elizabeth Bishop's poems very carefully at the time and imitating the loose formality of her style. . . . You dawdle in the first part and suddenly get caught in the poem"[7]—but also for the way it modeled a technique by which psychically and culturally revealing detail, detail pregnant with individual human history, could be dropped into a casual background of what Lowell calls "drifting description."

By June 1957, when Bishop sent Lowell a typescript of "The Armadillo," she had already published such explorations of embedded individual and cultural history as "Roosters" (1941), "Songs for a Colored Singer" (1944), "Faustina, or Rock Roses" (1947), "Over 2,000 Illustrations and a Complete Concordance" (1948), "The Prodigal" (1951), "Filling Station" (1955), and "Exchanging Hats" (1956), along with that remarkable poem about childhood losses, "Sestina" (1956). Bishop's series, while generally more indirect in its self-referentiality than Lowell's later self-explorations—even "Sestina" speaks of "*a* child" and "*a* grandmother"—establishes Bishop's own preoccupation with telltale psychical and historical messages. In another poem published before Lowell's "Skunk Hour," "Questions of Travel" (1956), Bishop explicitly suggests the rewards of having "studied *history*" (my emphasis) in "the weak calligraphy of songbirds' cages" (*EBPoems* 94). Similarly, Bishop's earlier "At the Fishhouses" (1951) is built on an exploration of the effects of history, through a study of a declining Nova Scotia fishing village whose weathered and eroding but still lovely artifacts stand for much that remains unstated. These artifacts adjoin and are weathered by the North Atlantic, a vast body of "chill gray icy water" whose emblematic significance slowly emerges as the poem unfolds. This water, "Cold dark deep and absolutely clear, / element bearable to no mortal," begins to seem like the chill waters of the past. The poem concludes, referring to this icy sea:

> If you tasted it, it would first taste bitter,
> then briny, then surely burn your tongue.
> It is like what we imagine knowledge to be:
> dark, salt, clear, moving, utterly free,
> drawn from the cold hard mouth
> of the world, derived from the rocky breasts
> forever, flowing and drawn, and since
> our knowledge is historical, flowing, and flown.
> (*EBPoems* 66)

Bishop not only states that "our knowledge is historical," but this is the premise on which the whole poem depends. The ending derives its surprising power in part from the fact that we have been, throughout, witnessing the pervasive and subtle effects of history without quite realizing it. Bishop's work is about history, loss, knowledge, and one's complex relation to the past as clearly as it is about anything at all. And this helps to explain not just the deep mutual affinity between Bishop and Lowell, despite the obvious differences in their temperaments and style, but also her keen affinity for the world of Berryman's *Dream Songs* and for the work of Jarrell —just as it explains the pronounced affinity of the latter two poets for her. With Lowell, Jarrell, and Berryman, Bishop helped to create a new and influential aesthetic that explores psychic origins (and other lost worlds) through the vehicle of postmodern narrative. And very often she was leading the way.

Bishop not only anticipated, in verse, Lowell's absorption with the intersection of the cultural, the psychological, and the autobiographical. She also anticipated it in prose. "In the Village"—a story that fascinated and obsessed Lowell to the point that he created a verse imitation, "The Scream"—was published in the *New Yorker* in 1953, four years before "Skunk Hour." Lowell would later acknowledge that, "'The Scream' owes everything to Elizabeth Bishop's beautiful, calm story, *In the Village*" (*FUD* 1). Three years after the publication of Bishop's story, Lowell would begin exploring his own past in prose.

Lowell published in the winter 1956 issue of *Partisan Review* that now-famous memoir of his own childhood, "91 Revere Street." Many forget that this story was already in print a year before Lowell began writing of any of the *Life Studies* poems. Bishop congratulated Lowell on "91 Revere Street" in a letter from Brazil, in 1956, immediately after she saw it in *Partisan.* "It is *very* good; I feel as if I'd sat through one of those Sunday dinners. And being thrown out of the Garden, just like Adam, is marvelous. I hadn't realized before how closely connected with the Navy you were. In fact it is all fascinating and I hope I see more soon" (*EBLet* 332–33). Bishop may have forgotten that it was she who first sounded the theme of "being thrown out of the Garden, just like Adam" thirty years earlier, as a sixteen-year-old school girl, in that precocious poem of 1927 "The Ballad of the Subway Train."

When M. L. Rosenthal declared Lowell a "confessional poet" in a 1959 review of *Life Studies*, and went on to develop this premise in a series of widely read and influential books, he proclaimed Lowell's work a breakthrough and in the process drew a line around Lowell and several other poets. This line separated Lowell from Bishop, though Bishop had been for years one of his closest friends in the arts and perhaps the living poet he most admired. Rosenthal's approach, which has generally been followed by subsequent historians, also drew a line implicitly separating Lowell's work after 1959 from all that had gone before. This act, in effect, treated as naught the substantial process of mutual interchange and influence ongoing between Bishop and Lowell since their first meeting in 1947. If Lowell actually separated himself from Bishop in "Skunk Hour," as Kalstone—following the paradigm laid out by Rosenthal—contends, why had she anticipated the poem so thoroughly in her own previous work? And why did she follow it, almost immediately, with her own exploration of psychic and cultural history, the posthumously published memoir "A Country Mouse"?

The real separation between Bishop and Lowell, if it can be called that, came much later, over Lowell's use of, and changes to, his estranged wife Elizabeth Hardwick's private letters in *The Dolphin* (1973). But this was a far more specific and local difference, arising from what Bishop considered the alteration and misuse of another person's private correspondence, and it occurred much later than the general aesthetic separation announced by Rosenthal, Kalstone, and numerous other historians. Moreover, despite the strain this disagreement put on their relationship, Dana Gioia and his classmates would occasionally see Bishop and Lowell in 1975, two years after this dispute, "casually walking together near Harvard Square."[8] In the last year of Lowell's life, 1977, Bishop announces in a letter to her friend Margaret Miller that she is making fudge to celebrate Lowell's birthday.

As a result of the critical construct created by Rosenthal, and echoed by critics and historians ever since, Lowell came to be viewed as the spokesman for his generation. Bishop's image, on the other hand, was miniaturized, and she has only now begun to be seen as Lowell always viewed her: as Lowell's artistic peer, and, perhaps, in some respects at least his superior. Still, if one thinks of Lowell's poetry less as an act of "confession" than as an act of self-exploration, the many parallels that Bishop and Lowell shared throughout their long artistic association become much clearer. Bishop and Lowell emerge as fellow pioneers, partners in the development of an aesthetic of psychic origins. And in matters of narrative style, as in many others, Lowell looked to Bishop—his elder by six years—as a model and as a teacher.

Lowell, commenting on essays by fellow poets at a symposium devoted to his recently published "Skunk Hour," stated that "The dedication is to Elizabeth Bishop, because rereading her suggested a way of breaking through the shell of my old manner. Her rhythms, idiom, images, and stanza structure seemed to belong to a later century. 'Skunk Hour' is modeled on Miss Bishop's 'The Armadillo,' a much better poem and one I had heard her read and later carried around with me. Both 'Skunk Hour' and 'The Armadillo' use short line stanzas, start with drifting description, and end with a single animal" (*RLProse* 226). Dana Gioia says that Bishop claimed she couldn't remember why the poem was dedicated to her, except that she was present during the actual arrival of the skunks. But then, Gioia remembers, Bishop gave the poem an uncharacteristically tight close reading. In an unfinished memoir, however, Bishop acknowledged that her role in the writing of "Skunk Hour" was one of the things in her entire life that made her proudest.

If Lowell makes it clear that he saw Bishop as a key source in the writing of the poem, he likewise makes it clear that Berryman's, among the three critical readings of his "Skunk Hour," comes closest—in fact, uncannily close—to his own modes of thinking and feeling. Lowell praises the acuteness of attention in John Frederick Nims's reading, but, he adds, "I get a feeling of going on a familiar journey, but with another author and another sensibility." And, Lowell adds, "This feeling is still stronger when I read Wilbur's essay." On the other hand, "With Berryman, too, I go on a strange journey! Thank God, we both come out clinging to spars, enough floating matter to save us, though faithless" (*RLProse* 229). Lowell acknowledged that in his astute, and sometimes harrowing reading, Berryman had "hit a bull's-eye."

Berryman's first bull's-eye was his recognition of the poem's most immediate technical inspiration. Unaware at this moment of the factual background, Berryman nonetheless recognized Bishop's influence on the poem's opening stanzas. "The four stanzas are unemphatic, muted. But their quiet, insistent mustering of the facts of an extant world opens toward the danger of its being swept away, into delirium. I have seldom seen stanzas . . . so un-self evident. He's holding fire, let's say. Down-rhyme, casual, unlike earlier Lowell, suggests Miss Bishop's practice; to whom the poem is dedicated; though the heavy, fierce rhyming of 'The Quaker Graveyard' will be admitted in the final stanzas" (*JBProse* 319–20).

Berryman begins his inquiry into the poem with the remark: "A title opaque and violent. Since it throws, at once, little or no light on the poem, we inquire whether the poem throws any light on it, and are underway. Our occasion is the approach of a crisis of mental disorder for the 'I' of the poem—presumably one leading to the hospitalization, or hospitalizations, spoken of elsewhere in the volume, Life Studies, where it stands last. Lowell's recent poems, many of them, are as personal, autobiographical, as his early poems were hieratic; and it is certain that we are not dealing here purely with invention and symbol. One thing critics not themselves writers of poetry occasionally forget is that poetry is composed by actual human beings, and tracts of it are very closely about them. When Shakespeare wrote, 'Two loves I have,' reader, he was not kidding" (*JBProse* 316).

Berryman's own title for his reading of "Skunk Hour" is "Despondency and Madness." For this title he draws on another *Life Studies* poem, "To Delmore Schwartz," which addresses Schwartz with the recollection that, "You said, we poets in our youth being in sadness, / Thereof in the end come despondency and madness." Berryman is alluding to a core of emotion in the poem that connects Lowell with Wordsworth, who had claimed that "poets in our youth begin in gladness," with their mutual friend Delmore, and, implicitly with Berryman himself. Berryman resumes, "Back to the title then. The Hour of the Skunk, I suppose, would be one of the most unprepossessing times of the day. . . . The skunk is a small, attractive, black-and-white creature, affectionate and loyal when tamed, I believe, it suffers (or rather it does not suffer, being an animal) from a bad reputation, owing to its capacity for stinking. (The poet, in the identification, knows: and suffers.)"

The poet's symbol-making and associational powers help to achieve the poem, but they also occasion emotional suffering. The skunk has a peculiar kind of power. "Cornered, it makes the cornerer wish he hadn't. Painful, in symbolization, is the fact that its sting, so to speak, can be drawn, its power of defending itself removed—as the poet can be made helpless by what is part of his strength: his strangeness, mental and emotional; the helplessness of a man afraid of going mad is the analogue. The skunk is an out cast; this is the basis of the metaphor, and how a mental patient feels. . . . . We like, in mature professional life, to know who we are; which may be on the point of becoming out of the question for the 'I' of the poem" (*JBProse* 316–17). If a threatened loss of identity emerges into the foreground of this piece, Berryman recognizes that the yearning for maturity and control provides the background: "His target is the dreadful aura—in epileptic analogy—the coming-on, handled by Hölderlin in 'Hälfte des Lebens,' which may be the deepest European poem on this unusual theme. You feel you're going too fast, spinning out of control; or too slow; there appears a rift, which will widen. You feel too good, or too bad" (*JBProse* 317).

Berryman seems to be speaking from experience here, and out of an empathy not always found among Lowell's critics. Using what appear to be the New Critical tools of asking appropriate questions of the poem and following where they lead, Berryman draws conclusions that are far from the New Critic's emphasis on impersonality, drawing one deep into the psychological position of the poet as "an actual human being." Lowell was forced to acknowledge the uncanny, intuitive rightness of Berryman's analysis, "What I can describe and no one else can describe are the circumstances of the poem's composition. I shan't reveal private secrets. John Berryman's pathological chart comes frighteningly close to the actual event. When I first read his paper, I kept saying to myself, 'Why, he is naming the very things I wanted to keep out of my poem.' In the end, I had to admit that Berryman had hit a bull's-eye, and often illuminated matters more searchingly and boldly than I could have wished" (*RLProse* 226).

Berryman, however, sees the poem not as an act of self-photography, but as something made, an artistically wrought structure with a careful array of balances and controls. Hence, he says, "I must pause, briefly, to admire its administration of time. In general for it time narrows: a vista of decades, 'the season's ill,' one night, and so down to the skunk hour. But I notice two substantial exceptions to the method. The second stanza opens a longer vista still than the first, with 'century.' And the 'Hour' is nightly, expanding again into a dreaded recurrence. Most real poets work in this way, but Lowell decidedly rather more than most" (*JBProse* 321).

The identity of the poet, the problem of the poet's relation to the persona who stands for him, remains a state of affairs requiring careful delineation. As Berryman put it, "For convenience in exposition, with a poem so personal, I have been pretending that 'I' is the poet, but of course the speaker can never be the actual writer, who is a person with an address, a Social Security number, debts, tastes, memories, expectations. Shakespeare says, 'Two loves I have': he does not say only two loves, and indeed he must have loved also his children, various friends, presumably his wife, his parents. The necessity for the artist of selection opens inevitably an abyss between his person and his persona. I only said that much poetry is 'very closely about' the person. The persona looks across at the person and then sets about its own work" (*JBProse* 321).

In support of Berryman's view, it's worth adding that, along with selection, there might also be alteration, or addition. Lowell claims that he invented the voyeuristic "love cars" scene, which most readers find the most perverse and/or disturbing moment in the poem. "Lowell works rather in parable form than in forms of allegory. There is no point-to-point correspondence, the details are free" (*JBProse* 320). Hence, the overtly autobiographic "Skunk Hour" (which Berryman reads as covertly a parable) moves into a position of immense analogy with Bishop's "The Prodigal Son," which is overtly a parable and covertly autobiographic. In Bishop's "Prodigal," too, "there is no point-to-point correspondence," and "the details are free." In his reading of "Skunk Hour," Berryman was outlining a methodology for reading his own poetry, and the poetry of Bishop, Lowell and Jarrell. This methodology has too often been ignored. One must read the work of these four poets for its exploratory character, with a sense that, even when the work is very closely about the poet, there are no absolute correspondences and the details are free. In this way one can begin to take an adequate measure of the many parallels in their development, and of the full dimension of their artistic achievement.

We shall now pass on to a discussion of this midcentury quartet that will carry us into the 1960s and 1970s, when such outstanding books as Lowell's *For the Union Dead, Near the Ocean* and *Day by Day*, Jarrell's *The Lost World*, Berryman's *77 Dream Songs* and *His Toy, His Dream His Rest*, and Bishop's *Questions of Travel, The Complete Poems*, and *Geography III* appeared for the first time. Chapter 7, "Displacing Sorrow," will explore the role these poets played in the development of the postmodern elegy. My eighth and final chapter, "A Cycle of Elegies," will study in cultural and biographical context the series of heartbreaking postmodern elegies in which this quartet of poets took leave of one another and faced the inevitability of their own deaths.

# Part 4

# POSTMODERN ELEGIES

# 7 Displacing Sorrow

## Studies in Postmodern Elegy

When I died they washed me out of the turret with a hose.

Randall Jarrell, "Death of the Ball Turret Gunner"

### Peculiar Monodies: Elements of Postmodern Elegy

In Randall Jarrell's 1942 essay on "The Development of Yeats's Sense of Reality," published the same year as his recently discovered "Levels and Balances: Structure in Poetry," Jarrell argues that Yeats became a great poet only after he faced up to the painful losses in his own life. "The dreams that made up his life were going to pieces and his poetry changed with their ruin. He had loved and worked for several things, and only one of them (mysticism, supernaturalism) remained whole. . . . It is this, and what happened because of it, that began to put reality into Yeats's poetry" (*KA&Co* 96–97).

In one of these poems of loss, "The Irish Airman Foresees His Death" (1918) Yeats elegizes Major Robert Gregory, an officer, a gentleman, and the son of his most generous patron who had died recently in aerial combat. He represents Gregory as soliloquizing fatalistically on his future, "I know that I shall meet my fate / Somewhere in the clouds above." Yeats's Major Gregory, disenchanted with the modern world, acknowledges that "Those that I fight I do not hate, / Those that I guard I do not love." Yet despite his then-ultramodern means of combat, Gregory's expressed values, as they appear in the poem, touch at many points on the chivalric tradition that Yeats reasserted so ardently in those later, loss-dominated years. Of Yeats's use of elegy, Jahan Ramazani observes that "Recuperating myth and ritual for his contests with death, Yeats also shares with such writers as Nietzsche, Hemingway, and Stevens the historical project of reconstructing a literary heroism. In his lyrics of tragic joy, the speakers laugh into the face of death."[1]

Yeats's reconstruction of a chivalric tradition is, of course, significantly problematized in his poem. An almost suicidal wish is implied for Gregory, who upholds this tradition in isolation from his own needs or the specified needs of his countrymen. He meets his chosen fate alone, seized by "a lonely impulse of delight" enjoyed through a canvas-rigged and petrol-powered contrivance of the modern age. Ramazani argues that in this modern context, "Yeats clutches all the more vehemently to exemplary heroes who belong 'to a dead art'; he suppresses the dehumanization of death by keeping before his mind heroes whose last moments 'will, it may be, haunt me on my death bed.' This last phrase suggests that, for Yeats, the literary reconstitution of a disappearing heroism provided above all an *ars moriendi*, a way of training himself aesthetically for his own death."[2]

When he contemplated Yeats's poetry in 1942, Jarrell was soon to write of war in the air, but his commonplace crewmen and pilots and civilians—rarely officers and never gentlemen—struggle to survive the century's second global war not as the objects of a reconstructed "literary heroism," nor as in any sense "exemplary heroes." They confront death not with a sense of tragic joy, but with a bewildered vulnerability in the face of the enormous power of high-tech weaponry and the ravenous demands imposed on its citizens by "the State." In Yeats's modernist elegy of aerial death, it does remain possible to reconstruct a post-chivalric concept of literary heroism. In Jarrell's early postmodernist poems on the same theme, such reconstructed heroisms must be washed "out of the turret with a hose."

In 1943, the year after publishing his Yeats essay, Jarrell stopped teaching "freshmen to punctuate" at the University of Texas at Austin and began teaching air crews to navigate, as a Celestial Navigation Trainer in the Army Air Corps. The crewmen he trained in the arcana of reckoning by the stars would soon be operational cogs in the massive Eighth Air Force, flying through fighter-and-flak-infested skies to bomb "the cities we had learned about in school" (*RJPoems* 145). Jarrell's orders posted him to training bases in the American southwest, far from these scenes of combat. But while he taught, Jarrell contemplated the inevitability of death awaiting a random sampling of the airmen he was educating and a similarly random sampling of the civilians living and working amongst their targets. Jarrell, a talented and prescient systems analyst, was aptly placed to contemplate the beginnings of postmodern military bureaucracy and to study its systematic regulation of human effort to achieve sudden death on a massive, impersonal scale in the name of a just cause.

And Jarrell was aptly placed to experiment with modes of elegy in response to the realities that were already shaping the postmodern world into a new kind of "inconsistent world order."[3] Jarrell was working in parallel with Robert Lowell, Elizabeth Bishop, and John Berryman to develop a postmodern mode of elegy in which many of the elements intrinsic to the elegiac tradition are subtly displaced, allowing him to write perhaps the most powerful poetic response to World War II in the English language. The postmodern elegies of the midcentury quartet achieve a quiet yet decisive break from the traditional elegy that had run through poetry in English for centuries and still survived as recently as the reconstructed literary heroism Ramazani locates in Yeats.

Beginning with the Greek elegies of Theocritus, the Western tradition of the elegy had remained predominantly pastoral, featuring a formal and sustained lament for the death of an individual placed in a natural setting. This pastoral tradition survived with only slight modification through Matthew Arnold's "Thyrsis: A Monody" (1867) in which Arnold's friend and fellow-poet A. H. Clough is mourned as the Arcadian shepherd Thyrsis. The pastoral elegy maintained so strong a hold on the Georgian poets who served as front line soldiers in World War I that one finds Wilfred Owen, Siegfried Sassoon, and others of that brilliant cadre consistently evoking pastoral motifs, if only for ironic contrast, in their threnodies from the trenches. As late as 1946, Lowell would evoke Milton's "Lycidas," the most ambitious of all Britain's pastoral elegies, in his own wartime funeral elegy for his cousin Warren Winslow, "A Quaker Graveyard in Nantucket."

Ellen Zetzel Lambert argues in a classic study of the elegy tradition that: "The basic thrust of the pastoral elegy is to affirm continuity; life, albeit in new forms, goes on. . . . The pastoral elegist . . . considers human death by placing it in nature's world, within her annual cycle of decay and generation."[4] This pattern of placing death within the cycles of nature is central to Whitman's "When Lilacs Last in the Dooryard Bloomed" (1865), despite the absence in Whitman's great elegy of Milton's Arcadian trappings. This pattern of lingering pastoralism continues to serve Yeats amidst the hard-nosed modernities evoked in "Easter 1916" and "Lapis Lazuli." But it would not serve Jarrell as he contemplated deaths occurring with dismaying suddenness and in dismaying numbers in the flak-filled skies over Schweinfurt, or in the sudden, lethal dogfights over carrier groups in the Pacific, or among the blazing urban blocks of Hamburg or Tokyo, or on the barges filled with Jewish children towed by German soldiers into the harbor of Odessa for drowning. Jarrell, responding specifically to each of these and similar subjects, created a radically new elegiac form adequate to the urgent demands of these unprecedented and disturbing events. His elegy placed individuals within the numbing routines of everyday military life, while conveying the wrenching, dislocating horror, the unnaturalness, impersonality, and surprising finality of death in modern war. The form he evolved would be developed promptly in other contexts by fellow members of his midcentury quartet.

One day while on KP duty, Jarrell was hosing out a trash can when an image struck him that would inspire his most famous poem, "The Death of the Ball Turret Gunner." Jarrell scrawled the initial version of the poem —first published in *Partisan Review* in the winter of 1945—at the bottom of a typescript draft of a far less famous poem, "The Wide Prospect." This pervasively anthologized poem of five pentameter lines reached its final form quickly, as did so many of the poems Jarrell composed during World War II, Jarrell's speed of composition reflecting his long background of arduous self-training.

Jarrell's biographer William Pritchard dismisses "The Death of the Ball Turret Gunner" as "a favorite of the undergraduate neophyte poetry reader." For Pritchard the poem "doesn't demand long acquaintance for its impact to be made; nor does it grow in the mind on rereadings."[5] However, with all the respect due to Pritchard as a critic and reader, the poem is of crucial importance to the development of a new and influential poetic mode and has not yet received all the recognition nor quite the understanding that it deserves. For this is not merely an effective anthology piece. It connects with Jarrell's best poems of World War II as one of the originating works in the postmodern mode of elegy, a now widely practiced mode of composition that is among the most original, emotionally powerful, and influential of postmodern poetry's many genres.

Lambert observes of the traditional pastoral elegy, "The pastoral landscape pleases us not, like the vanished groves of Eden, not because it *excludes* pain, but because of the way it includes it. Pastoral offers us a vision of life stripped not of pain but of complexity."[6] "The Death of the Ball Turret Gunner," by contrast, places the reader in anything but a pastoral world. Jarrell notes that "a ball turret is a plexiglass sphere set into the belly of a B-17 or B-24, and inhabited by two .50 caliber machine-guns and one man, a short small man" and that this man's bomber is attacked by fighters "armed with cannon firing explosive shells" (*RJPoems* 8). Nor is this world of harsh, surreal realities at all simple. Despite its brevity—a mere five lines of unrhymed pentameter stretched out, in the final line, to thirteen words, and fourteen agonizing syllables—the poem complexly embodies just the sort of unresolved contradictions Jarrell celebrated in his 1942 essay outlining a dialectical theory of poetic structure.

Jarrell's gunner experiences a web of interrelated losses: not simply death, the ultimate, inevitable loss, but earlier, the fall from the womb and then the loss of connection to earth and its comfortable "dream of life." Yet the gunner, nominally a man, has never grown up. Jarrell's uncanny technical, intellectual, and moral accomplishment is to transform his poem's apparently simple language into a language peculiarly multiple in its frames of reference so that the poem seamlessly operates across multiple temporal, psychological, and cultural planes. Through a series of slight but effective shifts in perspective, this apparently conventional narrative, like many of Jarrell's best poems, lands the reader in an intensely foreign, yet strangely familiar place where the nerve endings are peculiarly raw. Behind its childlike and dreamlike foreground, the whole poem disguises the sharply reasoned, historically informed, yet complexly intuitive poet. Jarrell is a profoundly learned, long-term student of contemporary social, biological, technological, and psychoanalytic systems. His comprehensive intelligence makes possible a poetry that compresses yet dramatizes the vulnerability of the childlike individual in the postmodern world.

In this 1945 poem, Jarrell exemplifies principles laid out in his 1942 "Levels and Opposites," conveying "extremely complicated systems of thoughts, perceptions, and emotions" in a taut yet elusive "non-logical" structure.[7] This structure can be defined through several of the poem's unusual features. First of all, the poem compresses an entire autobiography into three declarative sentences. Moreover, this autobiography is extensive and complete, starting before birth, passing through a series of distinct developmental stages, and ending with the "ceremonial" aftermath following the protagonist's violent death. And this death and its aftermath—"When I died they washed me out of the turret with a hose" —itself resembles an aborted birth. For the protagonist of the poem, despite living to adulthood, mustering into the Air Corps, undergoing specialized training as a ball turret gunner, fighting, and dying suddenly and violently, has never quite been alive. Uncannily, this as-yet-unborn yet already dead individual actually *speaks* his own compressed life story, though he has never quite awakened "from his mother's sleep." Rather he has passed from a condition of sleep in one womb into a similar, though less comfortable, condition of sleep into another. Specifically, "From my mother's sleep I fell into the State / And I hunched in its belly till my wet fur froze." His turret, a high-tech womb provided courtesy of the State, holds him inverted beneath the heavy bomber, but, unlike his mother's warm, nurturing, natural haven, this armed, plexiglass womb is cold, transparent, fragile, and unable to protect.

To summarize the postmodern clash of temporal and psychological planes: this dreaming fetus-like creature "woke" at last from a "sleep" that was not quite his own into another, more chaotic and terrifying sleep-or-dream-state, also not quite his own: "Six miles from earth, loosed from its dream of life, / I woke to black flak and the nightmare fighters." Unfortunately for the ball turret gunner, this particular dream-state is a "nightmare" all too actual, and when he dies his instant, shattering death receives no independent treatment, even as *he* tells the story. Rather, he tucks it into a subordinate clause ("when I died") in a sentence that focuses on the "ceremony" through which his innocence is both "drowned" and washed out of sight and out of mind. One never learns the gunner's name: one knows him only by his stated function as a human cog in the machinery of war. The shock effect of the final line, which for many readers does not wear off, depends on the fact that it is "me" who is being "washed" by an undesignated "they," like so much garbage "out of the turret with a hose," taking us back to the original image that arrested Jarrell's imagination while on KP. This shocking final moment might seem to hint at a bitter awakening for the gunner, but the poem ends too abruptly to disclose whether any such awakening has occurred, and since the gunner is in any case already dead, he might appear beyond the reach of any "awakening."

"The Death of the Ball Turret Gunner" derives much of its power from the fact that the dead ball turret gunner is the speaker of the poem, a fact not fully disclosed until the poem's final line. This disclosure, built into the poem from its beginning, reveals at last that the gunner is speaking his own elegy. Here, as so often in Jarrell's work, art conceals itself. Experienced readers who assume they know this oft-anthologized poem have confessed surprise when they are brought to recognize that the poem's speaker is dead.

Also "concealed," through a kind of stylistic understatement, is the degree to which the poem's language is alive and full of art. Jarrell's phrasing is quietly, fiercely witty, yet the speaker appears unaware of the intricate, developing verbal play on words like "sleep," "fell," "State," "belly," "wet fur," "dream," "woke," "nightmare," and that problematic "me" whom "they washed . . . out of the turret with a hose." How much of "*me*" can actually be left to experience this washing? And is it "me" who is being cleansed? Or aren't "they" rather washing the turret clean of the loathsome offal of "me," since "they" no doubt plan to repair this costly, damaged, powerful bomber and return it to the air over Germany? The gunner, speaking from death as from a trance, seems in no way conscious of the repeating, uncompleted, chimerical cycles which make this poem an example of what Bishop termed the "always-more-successful-surrealism of everyday life." Nor can the apparently uneducated speaker be aware of the poem's fleeting echoes of Marx, Auden, Rilke, Freud, and Grimm.

How different are the conditions of death in Jarrell's poem from the conditions noted by Yeats's "Irish Airman," and how abrupt a departure is Jarrell's poem from the chivalric literature of the past. French cultural historian Phillipe Ariès explores this tradition in *The Hour of Our Death*, a monumental study of the evolution of Western customs of death and dying from the Middle Ages to the present. Ariès observes that "the knights . . . in the *Chanson de Roland*, the stories of the Round Table, and the poems about Tristan. . . . do not die just anyhow: Death is governed by a familiar ritual that is willingly described. The common, ordinary death does not come as a surprise, even when it is the accidental result of a wound." Ariès argues that in a chivalric poem, death's "essential characteristic is that it gives advance warning of its arrival: 'Ah, good my lord, think you then so soon to die?' 'Yes,' replies Gawain, 'I tell you that I shall not live two days.' Neither his doctor nor his friends nor the priests (the latter are absent and forgotten) know as much about it as he. Only the dying man can tell how much time he has left."[8] According to Ariès, this measure of conscious control and acceptance at the moment of death, a characteristic he notes as typical of the premodern way of dying, allows both the one who is dying and those who survive to assimilate the experience: "Thus, regret for life goes hand in hand with a simple acceptance of imminent death. It bespeaks a familiarity with death."[9]

Lambert argues that making death familiar is a key characteristic of the pastoral elegy, and for Ariès, "Familiar simplicity is one of the two essential characteristics" of what he calls "The Tame Death." For Ariès, "The other is its public aspect, which is to last until the end of the nineteenth century. The dying man must be the center of a group of people."[10] Significantly, the death of Yeats's Irish airman, not long after the close of the nineteenth century, lacks this public aspect. By its nature, his death in "this tumult in the clouds" cannot be public. In fact, it is not "public men nor cheering crowds" that bid him fight, but rather, "a lonely impulse of delight." Yet Yeats's poem alludes to past norms in that his Major Gregory has what Ariès terms "advance warning" of death's arrival. As stated in the poem's title, Gregory "foresees his death," and because "I balanced all, brought all to mind," this death as still, in a sense, "tame" and "familiar," a death heroically accepted as a deliberate choice.

By contrast, in Jarrell's poem, ceremony and human control are absent; the protagonist, apparently an ordinary citizen, makes no choices, and death remains sudden, frightening, unpredictable, and unfamiliar, even to the dead speaker himself. With the tools of war available in 1945, a cannon-firing fighter attacking a bomber could shatter a healthy, isolated, glass-enclosed human body in a micro-second. Yet that bomber, only slightly damaged, could continue toward its target, drop a payload of incendiary bombs on an urban district, and return to its base with a trivial gash in its fuselage. In Jarrell's vision of postmodern war, the conscious knowledge and recognition of one's passing at the moment of death, an aspect of "the tame death" described by Ariés, has been rendered void. Jarrell implies that "placing sorrow" in postmodern war or rendering its griefs into the pastoral or chivalric frameworks of the past is now impossible.

Jarrell's war elegies break radically and finally with the traditional pastoral elegies: they increase rather than shed complexity; they *displace* rather than "place" sorrow. Jarrell implies the difficulty of achieving mature recognition of one's condition amidst the accelerating cycles of postmodern life. The ball turret gunner has not had a living instant to achieve the self-recognition celebrated by Ariès or Yeats's Major Gregory. A glimmering of conscious awareness comes to him, if at all, only after the moment of death.

"The Death of the Ball Turret Gunner" is one of the earliest of postmodern elegies of a type that might well be termed "peculiar monodies." Traditionally, a *monody* is an elegy uttered by a single voice, whereas a *threnody* is choral. The poems under discussion in this chapter are *peculiar* monodies partly because of the peculiar placement of the poem's speaker and because of the peculiar relation of that speaker to the figure being mourned. The peculiarity of Jarrell's monody derives in large measure from the fact that the monodist is already dead: he is both the subject of the elegy and his own sole mourner. And "The Death of the Ball Turret Gunner" was published five years before Billy Wilder popularized the technique of narration-after-death in the 1950 film noir *Sunset Boulevard.*

Another peculiarity of this new form of monody involves its uncanny inquiry into the rites of mourning. In Jarrell's "Death of the Ball Turret Gunner," this rite of passage—"When I died they washed me out of the turret with a hose"—is so lacking in dignity, that it functions not to express nor to relieve but to *suppress* grief. G. W. Pigman, in his sensitive study of *Grief and English Renaissance Elegy* asserts, "The essential concept for understanding the process of mourning is denial. Mourning, in the words of Martha Wolfenstein, is a 'painful and protracted struggle to acknowledge the reality of the loss.' The stages of mourning represent the development of this acknowledgment at the expense of the desire to deny the loss. Unresolved mourning represent the triumph of denial; the bereaved clings to the dead to avoid conflicts of guilt and self-reproach or suppresses grief as if no loss had taken place."[11] In Jarrell's poem, mourning seems impossible and grief is suppressed in the face of a death so shocking and so quickly dismissed that it remains impossible to process emotionally. The gunner remains the only sentient being left to witness or acknowledge the reality of a death that the rest of the world has simply washed away. He lingers still, a disembodied survivor whose voice hovers tentatively while his existence and his death have equally been denied.

Jarrell was not alone in his exploration of this denial of loss and grief in the postmodern world. By confronting and exploring the manifestation and suppression of grief in a wide range of contemporary forms, the peculiar monodies of Jarrell, Lowell, Bishop, and Berryman confront the anomalies of loss and death in a postmodern world that, in Ariès' words, finds death "so terrifying that we no longer dare say its name."[12]

## Berryman's "Dream Song 29"

Following Jarrell's extensive pioneering efforts, the other members of the midcentury quartet produced their own varied array of postmodern elegies. The remainder of this chapter explores a sequence of such poems that Berryman, Bishop, and Lowell produced in the early 1960s when they were at the height of their powers. The first poem is one of Berryman's most peculiar monodies and one of his most famous poems, "Dream Song 29" ("There sat down, once, a thing on Henry's heart"). The others to be discussed are Bishop's "First Death in Nova Scotia" and Lowell's "For the Union Dead."

In Berryman's "Dream Song 29," the relation of the protagonist to the death being mourned and to the feelings of grief being experienced is more convoluted and conflicted than in Jarrell's "Ball Turret Gunner." Certainly the occasion for grief is more ambiguous. This Song is clearly centered on a terrible loss, but *whose* loss? And *what* has been lost? And where, and when, and how, and why?

> There sat down, once, a thing on Henry's heart
> só heavy, if he had a hundred years
> & more, & weeping, sleepless, in all them time
> Henry could not make good.
> Starts again always in Henry's ears
> the little cough somewhere, an odour, a chime.
>
> (*DS* 29)

Here is a truly displaced elegy. Loss appears not as a deprivation but as an arrival in the form of an oppressive psychic visitation: "There sat down, once, a thing on Henry's heart." In the first sestet, neither the nature of the thing that "sat down . . . on Henry's heart" nor the time of its encroachment is spelled out. "The little cough somewhere, an odour, a chime" that "Starts again always in Henry's ears" suggest that these are possible memory triggers, recalling in some way the cause of the oppression that "sat down, once . . . on Henry's heart," but how can "an odour" start in "Henry's ears"? And why, exactly, should Henry have to "make good"? One colloquial meaning of "make good" is to "succeed," a demand parents are wont to place on their children; another connotation is to "make good" on a debt or to make up for an omission or transgression. The poem may be an elegy for childhood losses. But here, unlike Jarrell's "Ball Turret Gunner," a child's consciousness is suggested not through the direct evocation of a child's experiences (a womb, birth, "my mother's sleep"), so much as through the preservation or stylized re-creation of childlike forms of speech ("in all them time," "só heavy," "could not make good"). These childish or childlike forms of speech convey Henry's feeling of his own incomplete maturity, the struggles caused by the fact that a part of himself remains locked in childishness, emotionally uncompleted.

*The Dream Songs* emerged out of a period of intensive dream analysis for Berryman. And the poem's sudden shifts and surprising juxtapositions reflect his extensive exploration of and immersion in unconscious experience:

> And there is another thing he has in mind
> like a grave Sienese face a thousand years
> would fail to blur the still profiled reproach of. Ghastly,
> with open eyes, he attends, blind.
> All the bells say: too late. This is not for tears;
> thinking.
>
> (*DS* 29)

Henry feels the reproach of that grave Sienese face, no doubt a Madonna, and the language evokes other religious and ceremonial elements (such as "the bells") that here float in an unsettling sea of indeterminacy that may be drifting toward nondisclosure. Yet is there any reason for reproach? Has any crime been committed? Most important, if this is an elegy, whose death is being mourned?

> But never did Henry, as he thought he did,
> end anyone and hacks her body up
> and hide the pieces, where they may be found.
> He knows: he went over everyone, & nobody's missing.
> Often he reckons, in the dawn, them up.
> Nobody is ever missing.
>
> (*DS* 29)

This monody is peculiar in part because the reader discovers that there has been no death, certainly no murder, since "Nobody is ever missing." Despite feelings of grief and guilt, particularly over a urge to commit violence to women, reenacting, in effect, Edgar Allan Poe's "Black Cat," there seems to be no deceased object nor any specific action to which Henry can attach his disconcerting feelings of guilt and grief. Yet the feelings of guilt and grief remain, and they assume a character of unusual intensity and duration: "só heavy" and so lasting that "weeping, sleepless, in all them time / Henry could not make good."

Much later, in "Dream Song 327," Berryman concludes that "Freud was some wrong about dreams, or almost all," in part because he saw dreams not as "a transcript / of childhood & the day before," which is how Henry, apparently, sees them, but as "a panorama / of the whole mental life." But Berryman also objected to Freud, that "Grand Jewish ruler, custodian of the past / our paedegogue to whip us into truth" because "you wholly failed to take into account youth." It was in Berryman's youth that the violent death of his father and his own abrupt transformation from the Floridian Catholic John Smith to the Manhattan unbeliever John McAlpin Berryman occurred, in the context of abuses whose pervasive reality Freud's system chose not to acknowledge.

Berryman had reason to fear his mother, both as a possessive and judgmental presence in his life and as his father's possible murderer. Moreover, his father was definitely, if ambiguously, "missing." In "Dream Song 29," he dramatizes the problem of radically displaced emotion that "too much exceeds its cause" or that remains free-floating, unattached to any assignable cause. Perhaps this is because, despite deep self-analysis and even self-punishment, the real cause of Berryman's blocked emotion is too painful to name and thus has been most savagely repressed. And in his quest for self-knowledge and maturity, Berryman would conclude of Freud that "I tell you, Sir, you have enlightened but / you have misled us" (*DS* 327). Berryman exploits the postmodern elegy to explore the lost world of repressed emotion, that elusive yet strangely imperial kingdom whose hegemony is chiefly felt, and in *The Dream Songs* expressed, through the language of symptoms. And for insight into this world, Berryman felt sure, Freud's work provides only a partial key.

## Bishop's "First Death in Nova Scotia"

The quiet, gradual unfolding of Bishop's "First Death in Nova Scotia" (1962) might seem worlds apart from the terse forward drive of Jarrell's "Ball Turret Gunner" or the peculiar tragicomedy of "Dream Song 29," but each of these three poems employs a range of common formal and substantive elements, and the thematic overlaps are fascinating. Each poem is spoken in the first person and presents a kind of autobiography: Bishop narrates a single experience that seems to be hers, Berryman explores a moment of psychic crisis, and Jarrell invents a character who summarizes his life as a soldier for the state. In each case, loss is the condition of the poem, a condition to which a childlike understanding attempts to respond. Berryman gives us a sophisticated, troubled adult manifesting specific childlike vestiges, and Jarrell portrays a young man whose awareness is linked by metaphor to that of a child, but Bishop presents an actual child of four. In each poem an individual, isolated even when surrounded by others, faces loss in a historically determined space.

In Bishop's poem the frame is characteristically domestic and the determining historical elements largely familial and cultural. Bishop's poem focuses on a child's confusion in the face of death, showing how the child tries to come to terms with the permanence of this loss in the context of her culture's traditional ceremony. Bishop employs devastating, if quiet, wit—of which the protagonist is unconscious—for the child facing her cousin's death is unaware of the poem's gentle ironies, which are directed at her inability to comprehend the finality of death and at the failure of the adult world to help her.

In "First Death in Nova Scotia," as so frequently in Bishop, common household objects latent with family and cultural significance command the foreground of the poem. The first two stanzas appear to describe little else, though they omit much that might seem more important:

In the cold, cold parlor
my mother laid out Arthur
beneath the chromographs:
Edward, Prince of Wales,
with Princess Alexandra,
and King George with Queen Mary.
Below them on the table
stood a stuffed loon
shot and stuffed by Uncle
Arthur, Arthur's father.

Since Uncle Arthur fired
a bullet into him,
he hadn't said a word.
He kept his own counsel
on his white, frozen lake,
the marble-topped table.
His breast was deep and white,
cold and caressable;
his eyes were red glass,
much to be desired.

(*EBPoems* 125)

The dead cousin and her mother are merely mentioned by the childlike voice who tells this story. Arthur's "laid out" body, not specified as dead (except in the title), is defined almost entirely in terms of its contextual relationship to parlor ornaments: a pair of chromographs and a stuffed loon. These seem from the start to provide the girl with a way to defer confronting death although they just as quickly lead her back to that unavoidable reality. The loon is a family heirloom with a history. The child recognizes that the loon has been silenced by a bullet fired by Uncle Arthur, but in her imagination, this stillness is not final. This loon remains curiously charged with the attributes of life. What would the loon say if he could speak? The deep white breast, "cold and caressable," is associated with beauty and (implicitly) with the allure of death, but the child's yearning for his red eyes seems at once a yearning for their illusory fire of life and a recognition that the loon is merely simulating life, and these jewel-like eyes are a detachable part of that tempting illusion.

Red and white images run throughout the poem with white, the more frequent color, consistently associated with stillness, cold, and death, and red associated with a peculiar simulacrum or representation of life. Bishop actually did lose a cousin, Frank Boomer, when she was a four-year-old child in Great Village, Nova Scotia, but in case one is inclined the read the poem as literal fact, it is worth pointing out that her cousin Frank's tombstone clearly indicates that he died in June 1915. The poem's winter setting, so central to its symbolic effect, was a product of Bishop's imagination: either a sheer invention or a conflation of other memories.

The British royal family, standing framed above the scene as color lithographs on the cold parlor's wall, insure, through their vicarious presence in this provincial outpost of the Empire, the ceremonial nature of the event, underscoring quietly the need to maintain a stiff upper lip. Evidence from the poem underlines a series of parallels with the British prince's own suspended life. This is the same royal Edward who had remained for more than six decades the Prince of Wales under the eye of his own long-lived mother, Queen Victoria. At last, in 1901, at the age of sixty-one, this no longer young prince was finally crowned Edward VII. When he died nine years later, at seventy, in 1910—the year before Bishop's birth—he had lent his own name to an epoch, now seen as transitional: the Edwardian Age. The cultural assumptions on which Edward's era were founded would soon meet an abrupt end in the muddy trenches and cratered no-man's-lands of Paschendale, Verdun, and the Somme, at about the same time that Bishop was peering into her dead cousin's coffin. But in the poem's chromograph he remains "Edward, Prince of Wales." His coronation and death are facts of which the child may not be aware—are deaths never explained to her?—but they serve as subliminal indicators that these images of Edward and his future queen, frozen at a moment before they had at last come into their own, are themselves echoes of the dead cousin, Arthur. Here are still more figures locked in incompletion, maintaining a pale, colored-in, shadow of life.

Some significant aspects of Bishop's family history are implicit in "First Death." Readers familiar with Bishop's own life and with works like the remarkable autobiographical story "In the Village" (1953), which was published along with this poem in *Questions of Travel* (1965), may see connections in the way Bishop's mother treats Arthur's death. Bishop's mother, Gertrude Bulmer Bishop, went mad and was permanently institutionalized when her daughter was five. And as "In the Village" makes clear, Gertrude Bishop was unable to come to terms with the early death of her husband, Bishop's father, when their daughter was eight months old. After several earlier episodes, the decisive incident in Gertrude Bishop's madness, after which her daughter never saw her again, was linked in "In the Village" to the stress of moving out of widow's black. Gertrude Bishop was being fitted for a purple dress, after four years of deep mourning, when she had her final breakdown. Clinging to widow's weeds, Bishop's mother is shown trying frantically to control grief through ceremony, but tragically, this approach failed. In this poem, too, the mother is shown only as she is insisting on ceremony: laying out Arthur and later placing the lily of the valley in her daughter's hands and telling her to "say good-bye." But the child's questions remain unanswered.

In his discussion of the English Renaissance elegy, G. W. Pigman draws on the shaping influence of cultural attitudes toward grief and mourning. Controversy over how much grieving is permissible was common in England circa 1600. Pigman notes that Ben Jonson takes the Puritan-influenced line that would place strict limits on the duration and intensity of grieving. "His elegy contains almost no expression of sorrow that is not at once rejected; some of the poems, in particular 'On My First Sonne,' are especially moving because of a tension between contradictory desires to express and suppress grief." Pigman observes that in the more recent psychoanalytic literature about mourning, unlike almost all other fields of psychoanalysis:

> agreement on matters of substance is profound. Mourning is a process set in motion by the death, or sometimes by the anticipation of the death, of a person to whom the bereaved is attached. In everyday speech "grief" is a synonym for "mourning," and some theorists prefer it as the technical term, but there are advantages to distinguishing between the two. I use "mourning" to refer to a process and "grief" to refer to an emotion, intense sorrow. This makes it possible to realize that the condition first described by Helene Deutsch as "absence of grief" is a form of mourning.[13]

"Absence of grief" is a powerful presence in "Death of the Ball Turret Gunner," and it figures ambiguously in most postmodern elegies, which gain much of their power from a conflict, implicit, rather than explicit as in Ben Jonson, over "contradictory desires to express and suppress grief." This same kind of tension operates in Bishop's poetry, which grows from and remains closely attached to the same Calvinist roots that informed Ben Jonson's approach to grieving.

In "First Death," the child's already active imagination really goes to work when it observes Arthur. He, too, is rendered as an attractive visual object, but he is newly so and the transformation is not quite convincing. Arthur's coffin is "a little frosted cake," while Arthur himself is:

> all white, like a doll,
> that hadn't been painted yet.
> Jack Frost had started to paint him

the way he always painted
the Maple Leaf (Forever).
He had just begun on his hair,
a few red strokes, and then
Jack Frost had dropped the brush
and left him white, forever.
(*EBPoems* 125)

The stanza's final words, "white forever," hint at the child's dawning recognition of the finality of death.

But the child invents another life for Arthur, using all the visual materials the poem has quietly assembled. She combines fantasy and ceremony in her notion of Arthur's invitation "to be / the smallest page at court," but such fancies do not help her to understand her cousin's death nor to resolve her grief. The royal couple are "warm in red and ermine." If one looks back over the poem's symbolic color scheme, in both previous instances the color red—the loon's red glass eyes and the corpse's red hair—had been associated not with the real warmth of life but with eerie imitations of life. And the white of death is subliminally alluded to also in that elegant, regal, white fur—ermine—which seems, like the caressable breast of the loon, alluring and warming, and which appears to offer Arthur (and the child?) an escape from the cold parlor.

The final lines represent a dead end for these fancies. Who will answer the girl's poignant questions? These questions tenderly evoke a young child's groping for accommodation with loss, but they suggest also—despite an apparent "absence of grief"—the child's underlying confusion and desperation. The child's speech is mixed with elevated and adult speech, suggesting that behind the child's viewpoint stands the viewpoint of the mature poet. This added layer of understanding points every seemingly innocent declaration with delicate irony, acknowledging with a hint of nostalgia the charm and beguiling elegance of post-Victorian ceremony while also implying the need to confront death less euphemistically. Less thoroughly institutionalized forms of denial might permit a child to learn to face life's inevitable losses more familiarly, more directly, and with better understanding.

Bishop's poem is uniquely arranged in five stanzas of ten lines each, unrhymed (though there are some near rhymes, such as "counsel," "table," "caressable" in stanza three) with two exceptions: single exact rhymes clinching the third ("cake" and "lake") and the last stanzas ("go" and "snow"). The short, three beat line employs Bishop's trademark version of sprung rhythm, an understated, often prosaic meter employing a fixed number of beats but a freely varied number (and placement) of unaccented syllables. The versification contributes to that air of quiet, wholly unrhetorical speech crucial to the poem's calmly devastating effect. The invention of unique stanza forms and the unconventional handling of standard forms is characteristic. The poem might seem itself a model of decorum, yet Bishop's writing is deftly and subtly exploring and protesting against decorums that deny the reality of death. As in Jarrell's or Berryman's postmodern elegies, Bishop's poems confronting death establish a matrix of intersecting psychological and contextual levels through which to explore and critique cultural and familial norms that block the completion of the grieving process. The peculiar monodies of each of these poets dramatize how blocked grieving intensifies problems of selfhood by displacing rather than placing sorrow.

## Lowell's "For the Union Dead"

Lowell's "For the Union Dead" vastly expands the context of individual experiences of loss presented in more concentrated form in the previous poems. In a succession of subtly linked vignettes, Lowell probes the personal, intellectual, cultural, and political ramifications of an array of locally defined losses. Vanished buildings, displaced monuments, misplaced childhoods, crumbling traditions, frayed dignity, and annihilated cities are represented in successive quatrains through the eyes of a historically aware individual—apparently a dramatized avatar of the poet—reviewing the changes rapidly overtaking his native city and its once dominant Brahmin culture. The texture of the poem fluctuates between graphic, hypercharged super-realism and a curiously distanced, dreamlike reverie. It alludes to Lowell's childhood tellingly in its second stanza, and a "cowed," childlike confusion in the face of unfathomable experience is invoked again later in the poem.

But perhaps most tellingly, Lowell objectifies the process of loss by his persistent attention to visual objects. Often these visual objects are monuments of some public note. After an Latin epigraph that slightly but significantly alters the motto to the Saint-Gaudens statue dedicated to Colonel Shaw's regiment (the altered version translates as "They relinquished everything to serve the Republic" instead of "He relinquished . . ."), the poem proper begins by examining visual evidence of other forms of relinquishment. This examination starts with a public monument whose significance seems largely personal, the "old South Boston Aquarium." Not yet torn down, this structure has relinquished its old function. It "stands / in a Sahara of snow now. Its broken windows are boarded. . . . / The airy tanks are dry" (*FUD* 70). A diminished survivor, the aquarium is just the first of many attenuated monuments that populate the poem. Soon center stage shifts to Saint-Gaudens's "shaking Civil War relief," now "propped by a plank splint against the garage's earthquake," and to the neighboring Statehouse, another monument, that relinquishes its own traditional centrality and dignity. Braced and held upright by girders and gouged out underneath to make room for a parking garage, it appears as a symbolic victim of the modern, mechanical dynamism that persistently displaces the traditional past.

Such local cultural attrition provides the context for losses of a different order. These begin, of course, with reflections on the death of Colonel Shaw and his black regiment during the Civil War, losses that, despite their tragic nature, had a lofty social purpose. But this is balanced by modern destruction of a still more devastating order, represented by a advertising poster of "Hiroshima boiling." This visual object points with casual indifference toward two dominant postmodern fears that disturbed all four of these poets: the threat of nuclear holocaust and the onset of a devouring commercialism. For example, the nuclear destruction of Hiroshima and Nagasaki in 1945 dismayed Randall Jarrell as profoundly as the firebombing and massive destruction of Hamburg did Lowell (see also Jarrell's own quietly heartbreaking "The Angels at Hamburg" for his response to the destruction by firestorm of this German city, where the death toll, by some estimates, exceeded that of Nagasaki.) The age of nuclear anxiety that followed Hiroshima and Nagasaki (so vividly crystallized in Lowell's "Fall 1961") provides a backdrop for Lowell's mature poetry as well as for the poetry of Berryman and Jarrell. And there is evidence in the polemical essays of Jarrell's prose collection *A Sad Heart at the Supermarket* and in poems like "Next Day," as well as throughout Berryman's *Dream Songs*, of the degree to which the burgeoning of a callous and triumphant commercialism in the fifties and sixties disturbed them. During these same years, Bishop moved to Brazil in part to evade the mass-production culture that was increasingly dominating her native land.

Just as Lowell's "For the Union Dead" presents its catalog of losses, so, too, does it present a peculiar, and parallel, catalog of survivors: almost nothing mentioned in the poem quite disappears. The aquarium stands in ruins, but it stands. Its "cowed, compliant fish" may be no more, but a "bronze weathervane cod" still sits atop the roof, even though it "has lost half its scales" (*FUD* 70). Later the fish reappear, in the angry final lines of the poem, having suffered metamorphosis into dynamic, mechanical monsters:

> Everywhere,
> giant finned cars nose forward like fish;
> a savage servility
> slides by on grease.
>
> (*FUD* 72)

These two versions of the fish-as-survivor characterize the two opposing types of survivor in the poem. Survivors appear either as static and attenuated simulacrums of their former selves, or brutal mechanical transformations. Some of the poem's many figures have lost all but a vicarious existence, and live on in the form of monuments, statues, pictures, and other visual objects. These icons are static except in the sense that they suffer physical erosion and a parallel erosion of their dignity, through desecration, displacement, or neglect. But there is a different order of survivor, like the extinct dinosaurs, who reappear as devouring steam shovels, or the Mosler safe, whose commercial viability overshadows in the minds of its promoters the human losses at Hiroshima, or the new mechanical fish that end the poem. Each of these survivors embodies a new, aggressively commercial, mindless, and mechanistic order.

By contrast, the displaced Saint-Gaudens statue is the central image linking the first group of survivors. It preserves in vicarious stasis its "bronze Negroes," who maintain a curious simulation of life (William James could "almost hear [them] breathe"), a life mirrored by the "stone statues of the abstract Union Soldier[s]," who "doze over muskets / and muse through their sideburns." But the Saint-Gaudens statue differs from all the other static monuments in one sense: it "sticks like a fishbone / in the city's throat" because it is an uncomfortable survivor, reminiscent of such values as heroism, sacrifice, and racial equality, that no longer seem relevant in downtown Boston. This is true in part because racism and racial tension also survive, as does a replica of the ditch in which Colonel Shaw and his black Massachusetts volunteers were buried without the customary military honors by the Confederate soldiers who mowed them down at Fort Wagner. The form of that ditch is further replicated in the very "underworld garage" being gouged beneath the Statehouse. The continuing reality of racism reappears in "the drained faces of Negro school-children" whom the narrator observes on television attempting to integrate southern schools (*FUD* 70–72). But Colonel Shaw emerges finally as the poem's protagonist, seen largely in terms of the way heroic death is memorialized. His predicament bears more than a passing resemblance to the speaker's long dead "uncle Charles," of "Falling Asleep over the Aeneid"—another Union officer and leader of "colored volunteers," buried on that occasion in Concord and with full military honors, attended by "Phillips Brooks and Grant." Colonel Shaw is seen in terms of a culture that is on the verge of utter disappearance. His heroism is of a past order that seems uncomfortable even for an observer who mourns its passing. For this

> Colonel is as lean
> as a compass-needle.
>
> He has an angry wrenlike vigilance,
> a greyhound's gentle tautness;
> he seems to wince at pleasure,
> and suffocate for privacy.
>
> (*FUD* 71)

His wincing at pleasure, his erect, and perhaps narrow moral rigidity ("lean / as a compass-needle") is derived from a culture growing from deeply rooted Puritan beliefs in public probity and Election, out of keeping with a pleasure-seeking and profoundly commercialized contemporary culture. He yearns to escape from history's spotlight. Understanding the value of sacrifice for a higher good, he remains inflexible in its pursuit, and this places him on the margins of contemporary culture.

> He is out of bounds now. He rejoices in man's lovely,
> peculiar power to choose life and die—
> when he leads his black soldiers to death,
> he cannot bend his back.
>
> (*FUD* 71)

Though Colonel Shaw represents an almost oppressive maturity, childhood remains a constant presence throughout the poem, and the gestures and wishes of childhood persist in the adult. The child's awareness is introduced in the second stanza, which generates much of the poem's continuing imagery, imagery persistently identified both with the poem's central observer and with the city's modern urban planners. The child whose "nose crawled like a snail on the glass" of the aquarium parallels the adult who "pressed against the new barbed and galvanized / fence on the Boston

Common." The child's impulse "to burst the bubbles / drifting from the noses of the cowed, compliant fish" suggests a temptation toward violent gesture that is echoed throughout the poem. Of course, fish don't have noses or make bubbles, as the poet surely knew, so this must be a memory, that, like so many of the objects in the poem, has suffered metamorphosis. Though the impulse to violence is later transferred to other figures, we see it first in the speaker. His yearning for "the dark downward and vegetating kingdom / of the fish and reptile" reflects a yearning to reach back through the premoral awareness of early childhood to the amoral awareness of the lower vertebrates (*FUD* 70).

The body of the poem frequently echoes this yearning to escape from cognition and the pain of historical awareness and self-consciousness and responsibility, an escape that the leaders of Boston seem already to have achieved. It might also imply a yearning for the freedom to act on baser instinct, a freedom shared by the lower vertebrates but rejected by Colonel Shaw. The "Parking spaces" that "luxuriate like civic / sandpiles in the heart of Boston" suggest this lingering childishness in the minds of the city's urban planners. But the speaker of the poem is not exempt. When he crouches before his television set to watch the "Negro school-children," he is mimicking his own action as a child peering through the glass of the fish tank; the school children whose faces "rise like balloons" echo the bubbles the child saw in the fish tank and seem just as trapped as the fish (*FUD* 70–72). The child is thus complexly imaged as both aggressor and victim, in a separate world from the adult, yet inexorably linked to adult consciousness.

Dream textures weave in and out of the poem, despite its prevailingly gritty, realistic tone, and dream-logic knits the various strands. The poem's logic resembles the subtle, associational logic of dreams, with its many surrealistic images, its curious doublings and transformations. The "stone statues of the abstract Union Soldier" may be lost in a dream, as "they doze over muskets / and muse through their sideburns," but the central dream-figure is Colonel Shaw himself. When last seen:

> Colonel Shaw
> is riding on his bubble,
> he waits
> for the blessèd break.
> (*FUD* 72)

The bubble he rides survives, with typical dream logic, from the fish tank, and from the faces of the school children who "rise like balloons." Colonel

Shaw yearns to escape the vicarious simulation of life in which he is trapped, to depart a world that has a stable place for him neither in its public environs nor in its collective awareness, and to achieve the "privacy" for which he continually "suffocates." Shaw's final heroism may be the fact that he lingers still, in spite of his yearning to depart.

In his review of *Lord Weary's Castle*, Jarrell noted that Lowell's "poems often use cold as a plain and physically correct symbol for what is constricted and static" in contemporary culture (*P&A* 210). In "For the Union Dead" Lowell uses the temporary displacement of Saint Gaudens's bronze relief of Colonel Shaw and his black regiment in a context awash in parking lots, finned cars, and crass commercialization, to create "a plain and physically correct symbol" for the violent yet barely conscious displacement of mourning in the postmodern world. The washing of Jarrell's ball turret gunner out of his shattered glass turret with a steam hose serves as a parallel and yet more shocking physical and symbolic displacement. The vicarious displacements that occur in a young girl's imagination throughout "First Death in Nova Scotia" reflect a more oblique but no less telling exploration of the lessons cultures indirectly and deviously impart about the need to face death in silence. In Berryman's "Dream Song 29" sorrow is not just displaced but misplaced, since, despite the anguish, fear, and uncertainty that dominate the poem, "nobody is ever missing." Throughout their work these poets were exploring the presence and consequences of postmodern cultural norms that sought to distance or neutralize the terror of death but succeeded only in rendering death unfamiliar. The persistent representation by this midcentury quartet of their culture's will to displace sorrow underlines one of the chief problems of selfhood in the postmodern world.

# 8 A Cycle of Elegies

As I look at my life,
I am afraid
Only that it will change, as I am changing.

Randall Jarrell, "Next Day"

Life by definition breeds on change.

Robert Lowell, "The Nihilist as Hero"

The words won't change again. Sad friend, you cannot change.

Elizabeth Bishop, "North Haven, *In memoriam: Robert Lowell*"

In the chambers of the end we'll meet again
I will say Randall, he'll say Pussycat
and all will be as before
whenas we sought, among the beloved faces,
eminence and were dissatisfied with that
and needed more.

John Berryman, *DS* 90

## "The real real protest"

This study has traced the parallel development of Bishop, Jarrell, Berryman, and Lowell from early childhood through artistic maturity, stressing their ongoing exploration of the individual's experiences of loss, abandonment, powerlessness, grief, and death. By persistently exploring lost worlds, these poets were working counter to midcentury cultural norms that demanded the repression of grief, the plowing under of traumatic experience. The decades-long, four-way conversation amongst these poets about the problem of selfhood in the postmodern world reflected an interactive process of artistic making that answered the poets' need for support and comprehension as they broke new ground. This interactive process helped each to bridge the isolation imposed by subtle but widespread cultural uneasiness with their enterprise and supported each as he or she weathered the exaggerations, misappropriations, incomprehensions, and condescensions imposed by that first generation of interpreters who introduced their work to the reading public.

This concluding chapter will trace the last stages of their ongoing conversation, as the circle's dwindling body of survivors confronted the abrupt and painful passing from the scene of first Jarrell in 1965, then Berryman in 1972, then Lowell in 1977. And it will suggest how the conversation persists among younger generations of voices even after the death of Elizabeth Bishop in 1979.

Despite its presence and persistence, the core preoccupation of this quartet with grief and mourning tends to be overlooked, understated, or localized to a single member even by acute critics. Thus, when Jay Martin remarks in the course of a penetrating essay that "Lowell wrote of death most of his life because he spent his life mourning his early abandonment, a trauma so painful that until just before his death he could deal with it only through mirrors, by writing about the deaths of others," he is clearly right. But when he adds that "Scarcely another poet in the history of literature has been so preoccupied with loss, death, and mourning; few have been so sensitive to the vicissitudes of grief; seldom has a poet taken up elegiac themes so continuously; no other poet, perhaps, has given such anguished expression to his personal encounter with sorrow and mourning,"[1] he is just as clearly wrong. This sensitive, experienced reader overlooks Lowell's frequently remarked influence on Plath, Snodgrass, and Sexton, and obvious parallels with such loss-haunted contemporaries as Roethke, Schwartz, Philip Larkin, and Dylan Thomas, as well as his enduring and profound career-long colloquy on grief and loss with his three closest friends in the art—Jarrell, Bishop, and Berryman. This very preoccupation with grief and loss—in the context of a dominant culture profoundly uncomfortable with such emotions—emerges as a defining characteristic of this midcentury quartet.

Jarrell's prescient 1947 review of Lowell's *Lord Weary's Castle* reads his friend in terms of a "conflict of opposites" centering on "necessity" and "change." Of course, Jarrell knew the text of Lowell's breakthrough book with unusual intimacy, having done much to shape the final draft in a long series of critical editorial letters written from his Army Air Corps training posts. When Jarrell argued in 1947 that *Lord Weary* dramatizes the fate of individuals imprisoned in a "kingdom of necessity," containing "everything that is closed or turned inward, incestuous, that binds or blinds: the Old Law, imperialism, militarism, capitalism, Calvinism, Authority, the

Father" ( 209), he also found powerful, if partially buried or intermittent, counter-forces at work in Lowell's poetry: "struggling within this like leaven, falling into it like light, is everything that is free or open, that grows or is willing to change" (*P&A* 208–9). Lowell notes a similar conflict of opposites in his own 1947 review of Bishop's first book, *North & South*. Here Lowell finds an elusive, yet recurring "symbolic pattern" involving "two opposing factors. . . . The first is something in motion, weary but persisting, almost always failing and on the point of disintegrating, and yet, for the most part, stoically maintained. . . . The second factor is a terminus: rest, sleep, fulfillment or death" (*RLProse* 76–77). The "persisting" attention to "motion" or "change" in Bishop, Jarrell, Berryman, and Lowell suggests that their shared preoccupation with grief, necessity, and loss does not preclude a similarly intense, if sometimes "weary" or "stoically maintained," yearning for survival, recovery, and growth.

The poets themselves were acutely conscious of this conflict of opposites in one another's work. The ambiguous, yet ongoing opposition between "change" and "necessity," "motion" and "terminus" that this foursome discovered in one another's poetry leads toward explicit critique of and effort to alter those binding, incestuous social hierarchies, those blinding psychological imperatives, that made their lives so frustrating and painful. But more often these explorations express less an advocacy for political or cultural change than an unusual "accessibility to experience"—that characteristic Jarrell singles out for praise in his review of Lowell's *Lord Weary*. Specifically, their poems remain accessible to experiences of loss, powerlessness, anxiety, grief, bewilderment, or psychic enclosure—feelings so often marginalized in the dominant cultural discourse of what Lowell aptly termed "the tranquilized Fifties." Their treatment of uncomfortable or unnameable emotional realities is less concerned with the elusive and perhaps illusory promise of specific social remedies, than with the making of compelling and enduring works of art. Hence their poems keep "looking" with urgency and uncertainty—like Bishop's "Sandpiper"—"for something, something, something."

Bishop notes, of her sandpiper, "Poor bird, he is obsessed!" (*EBPoems* 131). There is a similarly obsessional quality in the intent, minute, yet wide-ranging inquiry exhibited in the art of each of these four poets. Their identity as a coherent group within a loss-haunted—though by no means "lost"—generation is in part defined by the remarkable consistency with which, in their work, recovery or cure appears as a tentatively conceived and yearned-for possibility, if never as triumphantly achieved (or transcendently achievable) reality. Thus negotiating the terms of "change," these poets, at their best, avoid rhetorical inflation while lending dramatic currency to core experiences others might choose to repress. Renouncing easy or purely rhetorical "cures" in favor of an intently exploratory aesthetic, these poets opened up a concrete and intuitive inquiry into that complex array of forces most resistant to "change." Their inquiry starts with the premise that those resistant forces—be they familial, cultural, or political, geographical, biological, or psychological—that make real change so difficult are not just exterior to but insidiously within the self.

Given the severe cultural prohibitions these four poets struggled against at midcentury as they labored to create an aesthetic for exploring lost worlds, it is not surprising that they never became wholly conscious of what they were collectively attempting. Still, their published and unpublished interchange teems with intuitive dialogues that bring them eerily close to a full articulation. Thus, after highlighting the exploratory quality of Elizabeth Bishop's 1936 poem "The Man-Moth" (*RLProse* 245) in his 1961 *Paris Review* interview, Robert Lowell goes on to praise the "kind of protest and queerness" he finds in William Carlos Williams and Marianne Moore, concluding of Moore's "terrible, private, and strange revolutionary poetry," that "There isn't the motive to do that now" (*RLProse* 262). Bishop, reading Lowell's interview in Brazil, wrote to her friend asking, "But I wonder—isn't there? Isn't there even more—only it's terribly hard to find the exact and right and surprising enough, or un-surprising enough, point at which to revolt now? The beats have just fallen back on an old corpse-strewn or monument strewn battle-field—the real real protest I suspect is something quite different—(If only I could find it. Klee's picture called FEAR seems close to it, I think.)"[2]

Such radical inquiry into something not quite nameable, but closely identified with an omnipresent fear, may be discovered in even the earliest work of this midcentury quartet. John Berryman's 1942 poem of psychological quest "A Point of Age" notes on setting out that "The desolate childhood smokes on the dead hill," and the poem observes in continuation: "Late, it is late, and it is time to start." Then, as the psychic journey gravitates toward its elusive, ineluctable goal, the poem asserts, in its most memorable line, "We must travel in the direction of our fear" (*JBPoems* 7–8). Six years earlier, in "The Man-Moth," Bishop declares of her own quester into psychical uncertainties, "What the Man-Moth fears most he must do" (*EBPoems* 14). As Charles Thornbury acutely remarks of Berryman, his "dramatic imagination encourages a process of self-inquiry that aims at re-formation and self-definition in which he is willing to be uncertain. It is a drama that allows him to move at will between the predictability of art and the uncertainty of life" ("Introduction," *JBPoems* lviii). In poem after poem, each member of this midcentury quartet looks ambivalently toward "motion" or "change" in poems that are "willing to be uncertain." Each poet dramatizes feelings of displacement and irretrievable loss, stepping with a tightrope walker's uncertain surety along the line dividing art's finalities from life's informalities and fatalities. This pursuit of what one fears most is "stoically maintained" even when on the point of "failing or disintegrating."

Partly through an urge to understand and fully realize themselves, each was engaged in an ongoing process of reading the others. Bishop shared Jarrell's reading of *Lord Weary's Castle*, a point she makes clear in "Some Notes on Robert Lowell," an introduction to the 1962 Brazilian publication of a selection of Lowell's poems (an essay recently tracked down and translated from the Portuguese by George Montiero). Bishop here quotes at length from the very passage detailing Lowell's "conflict of opposites" cited above from Jarrell's review. Bishop explains, moreover, to her Brazilian readers that Lowell's title "comes from the old ballad about a poor stonemason named 'Lambkin' who built a castle for one Lord Weary, but who was deprived of his just payment. In this legend Lowell sees a parable for the modern world—the 'castle'—the crushing superstructure of our civilization."[3] In similar terms, Lowell's *Life Studies* (1959) and later books such as *For the Union Dead* (1964), *Near the Ocean* (1967), *History* (1973), or *Day by Day* (1976) may be read as a "terrible, private and strange revolutionary poetry" that lodges its "real real protest" against an intractable "realm of necessity" discoverable partly in the external world and partly in the self. Bishop, as we have already seen, read *Life Studies* in this way, calling it "heart-breaking, shocking, grotesque and gentle" and comparing its magnifying, objectifying and subjectifying powers to the powers of "a burning glass." In her 1962 "Notes on Robert Lowell," Bishop underlines Lowell's postmodern tendencies, noting for her Brazilian audience that although his artistic "means" may seem traditional, Lowell resembles "our 'action painters'" in that he "expresses, with the same energy and beauty, the problems that any citizen of the United States who is over forty, has already faced and continues to face: the Depression, the War (or Wars), the Affluent Society, the ethics of foreign relations, the Bomb."

In September 1948, just three years after the first atomic bombs were dropped in anger on Japan, and a little more than a year after Jarrell had introduced his two friends to one another at a New York dinner party, Bishop sent a long letter to Lowell from her fog-bound summer lodgings at Stonington on the Maine coast. This letter reveals her own struggles with the darker emotions. "I think you said a while ago that I'd 'laugh you to scorn' over some conversation you and J[arrell] had had about how to protect yourself against solitude and ennui—but indeed I wouldn't. That's just the kind of 'suffering' I'm most at home with and helpless about, I'm afraid, and what with two days of fog and alarmingly low tides, I've really got it bad." Bishop is acknowledging, in this revealing letter to her new friend Lowell, that—despite appearances of calm or self-containment in her work or in her outward demeanor—she has not been able to laugh suffering "to scorn."

Bishop acknowledges a yearning to break free of self-imposed constraints on the expression of grief and anxiety that connects her to her new friends Lowell and Jarrell. "Sometimes I wish I could have a more sensible conversation about this suffering business, anyway. I imagine we actually agree fairly well. It is just that I think it is so inevitable there's no use talking about it, and that in itself it has no value, anyway—as I think Jarrell says in '90 North' or somewhere" (*EBLet* 170). This important passage displays just how conflicted and contradictory were Bishop's feelings about "this suffering business." She yearns to have a "sensible conversation" about suffering, then suggests "there's no use talking about it." She claims both to be "at home" with suffering and to be "helpless" about it. In fact, Bishop seems to be arguing that suffering is so inevitable that one might just as well be quiet about it—except that being quiet remains, of course, impossible, even if expression emerges only through the language of symptoms.

The "fog and alarmingly low tides" of Bishop's Maine coastal village emerge as telling metaphors for her own isolated, depressed, and "helpless" state of mind. And she cites Jarrell's "90 North," arguably his first completely successful early poem, which appeared in the 21 April 1941 *New Republic*, in the same issue as one of Bishop's early triumphs, "Roosters," in support of her view that pain "in itself has no value, anyway." Bishop clearly saw her own private pain implicated in the ending of Jarrell's "90 North," which closes with the lines: "Pain comes from the darkness / And we call it wisdom. It is pain" (*RJPoems* 114). All four of these poets would remain persistently reluctant, throughout their careers, to attach transcendental significance to private suffering, however broadly applicable that private suffering might, at times, appear.

Throughout his career, Jarrell remained keenly attuned to the forces of necessity, while exploring the ambiguous possibilities of change. Thus, Jarrell notes in the early "Children Selecting Books in Libraries" (1941, cited as rev. 1955) that as we read works of the imagination, from Grimm to Proust,

> we live
> By trading another's sorrow for our own; another's
> Impossibilities, still unbelieved in, for our own . . .
> (*RJPoems* 107)

Here "change" amounts to a transitory escape: not Frost's "momentary stay against confusion" but a momentary release from the burdens of selfhood.

> "I am myself still"? For a little while, forget:
> The world's selves cure that short disease, myself,
> And we see bending to us, dewy-eyed, the great
> CHANGE, dear to all things not to themselves endeared.
> (*RJPoems* 107)

In this poem, more explicitly than elsewhere, Jarrell connects the yearning for change to a core deficiency that similarly haunted Bishop, Lowell, and Berryman: a lack of self-love, of self-esteem, stemming, in each poet's case, from unhealed and traumatic experiences of powerlessness, displacement and loss in early childhood. For Jarrell, the sense of loss he suffered from the absence of his father (and beloved paternal grandparents) was intensified by his problematic relationship with a controlling, frequently contemptuous, and possibly abusive mother whom he at once loved, feared, and resented. Jarrell's particular, and keenly felt lack remains a core motivating factor in his recurring, ambivalent yearnings for change.

Jarrell, as did this midcentury quartet, maintained ambivalent feelings about his own individual self as a center of integrity and value. Consequently, change remained for him an open-ended, morally and emotionally charged term whose ambiguous connotations persistently migrate toward opposing, competing, denotative centers. One such rival center is that "great" and fundamental, if elusive, internal change that promises somehow to make "all things not to themselves endeared" more confident, more mature, readier, as Jarrell phrased it in another poem, to take "the chance of life" (*RJPoems* 107, 279). But a rival cluster of meanings for that key word "change" gravitates toward such darker possibilities as loss of vitality, mental disturbance, aging, physical dissolution, or that final change that comes with death.

The romantic poets might aspire to transcend suffering, and the modernists may have raged to give it order, but the poets of this midcentury quartet sought chiefly to survive suffering with selfhood more or less intact, and, if possible, they sought to "change." For these poets the "real real protest" was directed not at any single public injustice or institution, whatever the explicit or implicit references to these in their work, but at something perhaps more terrible and strange and intractable and surprising: the problem of selfhood in the postmodern world. This problem derives at once from life's immemorial fatality and from "the crushing superstructure of our civilization." This crushing superstructure, still under mortgage, magnifies certain aspects of human fatality even as it minimizes others. Hence, their poems travel recurrently in the direction of one's fear, motivated by an ongoing, if tentative and intuitive, search for what Lowell terms, in reference to Bishop, "changes and discovery."

The opposition in their work between a sense of bereavement and a yearning for change reached a peak of intensity in the cycle of elegies the survivors of this midcentury quartet composed in response to the successive passings of their irreplaceable colleagues. In these moving postmodern elegies, as they contemplate the loss of intimate rivals and friends who had been their closest artistic touchstones and foils, the surviving members of this quartet confront the looming reality of their own ultimate loss of self and seek answers to unanswerable questions. This concluding chapter proposes to read this cycle of final elegies in the context of their unfolding personal and artistic relationships, with particular attention to the way a powerful, persistent, yet ambivalent yearning for "change" plays out against their ongoing realization of the necessity of loss in their late work.

## "Tuned Up to the Concert Pitch": Randall Jarrell, 1914–1965

Enrolled in Bishop's "Studies in Modern Poetry" at Harvard University in the spring of 1975, Dana Gioia recalls that though Randall Jarrell "had been dead then for nearly ten years his loss still seemed fresh, for she always spoke of him elegiacally, as if he had died only a few weeks before."[4] Lowell had come away from a brief visit to Jarrell in Greensboro in January 1964 with a sense of his old friend's continuing vitality, writing to Jarrell following this visit, "You stay young, and it's good to think of you, still honest and hopeful and full of brilliant talk and knowledge, able to judge and make."[5] But then, shockingly, on 14 October 1965, Jarrell was struck by a passing car and instantly killed as he walked along a dark roadside, near the state university campus at Chapel Hill, North Carolina. The question of Jarrell's death—was it an accident or a suicide?—remains in dispute, despite a ruling of accidental death on his death certificate, a ruling supported by the coroner and medical examiners. Rumors of Jarrell's suicide grew out of early press reports in the *New York Times* and *Time* hinting at suicide. The coroner and medical examiners based their contrary findings on physical evidence from Jarrell's wounds—all on his left side—and on the pattern of damage to the corresponding (right-hand) side of the vehicle. These suggested, in the words of the coroner, that he was "hit from the side, not the front, or the front wheels of the car" (*RJLet* 520)—and this evidence therefore suggested that Jarrell had not stepped deliberately in front of the car but rather had been sideswiped. If ambiguity remains, it grows in part from the fact that when Jarrell was struck by that passing car he had recently been suffering from acute depression, made worse by badly administered drug therapy at a time when anti-depressant drug treatment was still in its infancy.

When Lowell praised Jarrell for "stay[ing] young" and "still honest and hopeful and full of brilliant talk and knowledge" in January 1964, Jarrell's depression was already beginning. Several months later Jarrell's Greensboro internist prescribed a moderate dose of one of the new antidepressant drugs just then appearing on the market. This dosage had little effect, and when Jarrell later visited a Cincinnati psychiatrist who had impressed him during Jarrell's recent year as Elliston Lecturer on Poetry at the University of Cincinnati, that psychiatrist prescribed a massively increased dosage of the same medication. Soon, Jarrell was exhibiting clear signs of manic behavior, signs noted by friends such as Fred Chappell, his fellow poet and teaching colleague at the Women's College at Greensboro. These manic symptoms escalated, culminating when he spent $3,000 on audio equipment—a small fortune in those days—on a trip to New York City. Shortly thereafter Jarrell wrote a check for $1,500 as a tip to a waitress while making his third trip to Nashville in two weeks to visit his ailing mother. Mary Jarrell reported that, following the episode of the $1,500 tip, his doctors removed him completely from the antidepressant, without the now-standard procedure of slowly tapering the dosage down.[6] This sudden removal from a medication on which he had grown physically dependent sent Jarrell into a dangerously steep depression, during which he was admitted to a Chapel Hill hospital for rest and observation. During this hospital stay Jarrell attempted suicide by slitting his wrists (*RJLet* 500). He survived this attempt, and showed signs of recovery from his depression. Mary Jarrell reports him making hopeful plans for the future. Returning to Hand House at the Medical School of the University of North Carolina, Chapel Hill, with a review copy of Bishop's recently published *Questions of Travel* in his bags, Jarrell was undergoing a course of therapy for his injured wrist when he was struck by that passing car.

Fred Chappell, Jarrell's friend, colleague, and fellow poet at Greensboro—noting that "He suffered from depression" and that he received medication about which, in 1965, "I don't think the side effects were widely known"—concludes with some reason, "I hold the drug treatments of Randall responsible for his death."[7] Whether his death was suicide or the merest accident, it seems unlikely that Jarrell would have found himself walking along that dark roadside were it not for the catastrophic mishandling of his antidepressant medication.

Jarrell's tragic death brought his flourishing career as a poet, critic, novelist, anthologist, children's book author, and teacher to an abrupt close at the age of fifty-one, just months after the appearance of what Lowell and Berryman agreed was his best book of poetry, *The Lost World.* Jarrell's sudden, violent, ambiguous death at the height of his formidable powers shocked, saddened, and disquieted his many friends and admirers in the literary community, especially such long-term friends as Lowell, Bishop, and Berryman. It was the first in the series of sudden fatalities that, over the next fourteen years, slowly depleted the ranks of the midcentury quartet of which he had been so vibrant a member.

Berryman stated in his prose memoir that "Jarrell's death hit me very hard. We were seldom together, but we were friends for a very long time" (*RJ1914* 14). And he noted to Mary Jarrell, in a distraught letter, "We started together, in 1940 [when both appeared in *Five Young American Poets*]. . . . After Roethke's death and MacNeice's I swore never to care any more, but I cried over Randall's. I hope you are being able to console yourself." Berryman confessed not just sorrow in this letter, but also confusion and dismay: "I was stunned by his death, but felt far worse later when a friend passed me the NY Times story saying the troopers called it suicide. He was just not the man to kill himself. He had iron self-confidence, and he was childlike—neither of them qualities leading to suicide." Berryman was himself possessed by suicidal ideation since adolescence, and thus was prone to accepting suicidal motivations in others, yet he had to protest that he found Randall's death, if by suicide, mystifyingly uncharacteristic. Berryman's letter continues, remorseful, and searching desperately for clues: "Did he leave you a note or anything? What in the name of God was wrong, do you know? I have tried to write away my feeling, twice, in Songs . . . but it hasn't helped much. Now I feel bitterly sorry I didn't throw him a postcard to say The Lost World was his very best. What went wrong?"[8]

Bishop, far away in Brazil, first read about Jarrell's death in a *Time* magazine article that quoted the driver whose car killed Jarrell stating that he "appeared to lunge" in the direction of the fatal vehicle, and she felt similarly distraught and puzzled by Jarrell's death. She wrote to Lowell, "I felt awful about Randall. . . . What do you suppose went wrong with him and had he talked to you at all frankly lately or since he was sick? I feel it must have been an accident of an unconscious-suicide kind, a sudden impulse when he was really quite out of his head—because surely it was most unlike him to make some innocent motorist responsible for his death."[9] Like Berryman, Bishop felt that, if it were to be considered suicide—a view considered subject to "reasonable doubt" by the coroner, though such doubts did not appear in these early journalistic accounts—there remained something deeply uncharacteristic in the manner of Jarrell's parting. Gioia's testimony that after "nearly ten years his loss still seemed fresh" indicates that Bishop never fully accepted the loss of a friend she had termed, in a 1955 letter to Jarrell, "the best critic of poetry going," avowing that she could "die in a fairly peaceful frame of mind, any old time" (*EBLet* 312) after Jarrell compared her best poems to the luminescent paintings of Vermeer. Speaking of his 1947 review of her first book, *North & South*, Bishop had written Jarrell from Brazil in 1953 that "that review of yours is the one I hold on to in dark stretches and in a foreign country!" (*EBLet* 284). When Bishop's *Poems* won the 1956 Pulitzer Prize ahead of Jarrell's *Selected Poems*, she admitted to Jarrell that "I was pleased about the Pulitzer business . . . , but I really cannot for the life of me understand why they didn't give it to you. Some of the war poems are surely the best ever written on the subject, honestly—and as far as 'our' wars go, the only ones. But re-reading them I began to think that perhaps that's just why. . . . The war is out of style now and they want to forget it" (*EBLet* 324). Jarrell, however, insisted he was "delighted" (*RJLet* 413) that Bishop won the Pulitzer, stating in his reply that "I like your poetry better than anybody's since the Frost-Stevens-Eliot-Moore generation," a statement backed up by his luminous published reviews.

Jarrell's death deeply troubled, as well, his many admirers at the Women's College at Greensboro, where he was remembered as a solid and widely respected citizen, often charming and generous, sometimes difficult and prickly, always witty and dazzlingly intelligent. His Greensboro friend L. Richardson Preyer, a one-time candidate for governor of North Carolina, recalled that Jarrell "had all the gentler qualities—loyalty, modesty, high courtesy, compassion, regard for the tender places in life," united with the "sterner qualities" of "powerful intellect."[10] Unlike most of his poet friends, Jarrell seldom or never drank—his first wife Mackie recalled that he might occasionally accept a light German white wine because he liked the sweetness. Moreover, while Jarrell was once divorced, the divorce was handled quietly. Though Jarrell had his foibles, his life—unlike the lives of Lowell or Berryman or, in a quieter way, Bishop—remained for its first fifty years untouched by the slightest breath of scandal, a bland fact that the studies by Bawer and Meyers seem peculiarly unable to digest. One student at the Women's College in Greensboro stated flatly after his sudden death, "we loved Randall Jarrell"; another remembered his "innate charm and the very goodness of his heart"; and still another, alluding to Jarrell's teaching of the Tolstoy novella, recalled him as "charming, inspiring, instructive, but most of all, gently, brilliantly master and man."[11] Fred Chappell would relate that "I took over Randall's courses after he died. I took a course he taught called 'Approach to Narrative' and also his 'Modern Poetry'. . . . I taught both of those courses for six or seven years after Randall's death, and the poetry course for maybe ten years after his death. People were still, in their papers and exams, comparing the way I taught the course with the way Randall taught the course—he was that famous a teacher and his teaching methods were that well known. That is amazing . . . that you'd have that kind of a legendary quality about a teacher for so many years."[12]

As an adult, Jarrell, though gentle toward his students, could be, at times, waspish, competitive, or judgmental toward his peers and impatient with the trivialities and necessary subterfuges of social discourse. Berryman's first wife, Eileen Simpson, noted that Randall "had no tolerance for small talk—didn't even know what small talk *was*."[13] Lowell declared that "I have never known anyone who so connected what his friends wrote with their lives, or their lives with what they wrote. This could be trying: whenever we turned out something Randall felt was unworthy or a falling off, there was a coolness in all one's relations with him. You felt that even your choice of neckties wounded him. But he always veered and returned, for he knew as well as anyone that the spark from heaven is beyond man's call and control" (*RLProse* 94).

Moreover, for Jarrell, the chance to share the joyful perception of art, or of a moment of physical grace, almost always brought him out. As another student recalled, Jarrell "was frequently an alarming man, at times so painfully, so infectiously reticent that one could hardly bear to utter a word near him, much less to him. At other times he might be so extravagantly moved by a poem, a piece of music, an unexpected bit of wit, an instant of excellence in ballet or tennis, an animal or bird momentarily seen as never before, that his words, expression, voice, would take off in an arc of astonishment and delight." His tragic death hardly transforms Jarrell's productive career into a life that in Bawer's words was controlled by "pathological excesses." The student just cited termed Jarrell's death "a terrible waste of spirit."[14]

Then why his profound depression, at fifty, after a highly successful life and with no previous history of psychiatric disorder? Jarrell's depression corresponds closely to the outcome Alice Miller predicts in *Drama of the Gifted Child* for a "grandiose personality." According to Miller, "The person who is 'grandiose' is admired everywhere and needs this admiration; indeed, he cannot live without it. He must excel brilliantly in everything he undertakes, which he is surely capable of doing (otherwise he just does not attempt it). He, too, admires himself, for his qualities—his beauty, cleverness, talents—and for his success and achievements. Beware if one of these fails him, for then the catastrophe of a severe depression is imminent."[15] Berryman claims that Jarrell had "iron self-confidence" but there was a layer of fragility, and a need for intensive nurturing from those closest to him, that lay just beneath that facade of self-confidence and self-sufficiency.

Writing with peculiarly detailed, self-analytic candor to Edith Eisler, a woman he had become close to at Salzburg in 1948, when he was thirty-four and beginning to have doubts about his marriage to his first wife, Jarrell drew the following extraordinary self-portrait: "I like the feeling of being taken care of, of having decisions made for me, of being saved bother. I'm quite optimistic, mostly in order to save bother: I accept, dismiss, and forget about bad things that happen as quickly and as well as I can. I guess one great principle of my life is: *O, don't bother, forget about it; I should worry.* (Probably this is because I have a quite emotional nervous temperament, and naturally tend to do the opposite)" (*RJLet* 204–5). It may seem remarkable—and, in a personal sense, tragic—that a writer who declared that strong works of art are "concerned with showing things that are often repressed out of existence,"[16] and whose poetry explores the workings of repression and dramatizes its psychic costs with penetrating honesty, clarity, and intensity, repressed his own deepest feelings by living a life expressly designed to save emotional "bother." The result was an unflagging, if curiously disinterested, quest for external recognition at the price of deliberately repressing ("I accept, dismiss, and forget about bad things that happen as quickly and as well as I can") real sorrows, losses, and disappointments. Of course, a writer's work often warns most insistently against just those subtly self-undermining behaviors that are most characteristic of the writer.

Because Jarrell had "a quite emotional, nervous temperament" and felt he could not afford the "bother" associated with his most intense and painful feelings, he more or less deliberately sacrificed confronting repressed aspects of his own inner life to achieve the freedom to explore the inner lives of others. In contrast, Berryman, whose mother had brought him up in the pseudo-Byronic belief that an artist must suffer and will benefit from "the worst possible ordeal which will not actually kill him,"[17] lived according to an obverse, yet, in retrospect, equally self-undermining mode of psychic economy.

Jarrell's determination to repress emotional bother is confirmed by Eileen Simpson's report of a conversation with Jarrell in Princeton in 1952, where he had recently arrived as a visiting professor. She told her old friend that she was sorry he and Mackie were getting a divorce. "'You needn't be,' he said, as if he were talking about another couple, one he neither liked nor approved of. 'Our interests had changed.' That this coldness was a façade I understood only when we stopped at his house to get a book . . . , and I saw the way he was living. . . . The place was in shocking disorder. On every surface there were plates of half-finished meals (obviously eaten with little appetite), clothes strewn over furniture, stray cats he'd taken in from the streets for company. . . . I . . . realized that Randall was far more depressed than he appeared."[18]

Jarrell's grandiose personality had a strong need to project, to himself and others, an image of rational control over grief, fear, depression, loneliness, and the pain of failure, emotions that in life he chose to dismiss as mere "bother." Only in his poetry would he allow himself the freedom to explore those very forces that, in conscious life, he strove to "repress out of existence." The power of his own explosive feelings of abandonment, anger, and grief can be inferred from the peculiar intensity and thoroughness with which they were repressed in his life, and from their constant, and often magical, reappearance in his art.

Jarrell's quiet, intense, but never wholly acknowledged need for external recognition and applause might seem the obverse of Berryman's overtly grandiose self-dramatizing and self-parodying egocentrism. Nor did Jarrell share Berryman's self-conscious preoccupation with fame. Still, it should come as no surprise that this curiously unworldly man was nonetheless intensely competitive and that no contest was too small. Berryman retells a story, derived from Jean Stafford, in which Jarrell, staying with mutual friends, "played croquet with the children that afternoon and lost." Jarrell was so irked by this defeat that at five the next morning, his hostess noticed him on the croquet field "studying the ground—changing the wickets." Berryman closes his memoir with the observation, "It's a good thing he had a very successful career, as he did, because he was a hard loser. He wasn't a man who liked to lose at all" (*RJ1914* 17). Jarrell's need to win, combined with his quiet, intense craving to be universally admired —on sheer merit—and his unwillingness to compromise his principles in order to please or mollify others, gave his interactions a frequently aggressive edge while underlining a need for external validation characteristic of adults (even apparently independent and self-sufficient ones like Jarrell) who lacked emotional nourishment and validation in childhood. And as external supports began to lose their magic for him, Jarrell became particularly harsh and unforgiving toward his own inevitable process of aging and the comparative limitations of his external recognition as a poet.

The aging woman who looks into her mirror in Jarrell's "The Face" finds herself "Not good any more, not beautiful— / Not even young," the words "not good" moralizing the inevitable changes wreaked by time. And she disavows these changes with the angry "This isn't mine," concluding that:

> If just living can do this,
> Living is more dangerous than anything:
>
> It is terrible to be alive.
>
> (*RJPoems* 23–24)

"The Face," appearing in 1950 when Jarrell himself was just thirty-five, anticipates Jarrell's own despondent response to the aging process as he confronted the end of his first half-century. According to Mary Jarrell, her husband—suffering from severe depression—was admonished by his friend Lucy Hooke at his fiftieth birthday party in May 1964, "Fifty is nothing, Randall. You're making mountains out of molehills." But Jarrell replied ruefully, "When you're depressed there *are* no molehills" (*RJLet* 489).

In "The Woman at the Washington Zoo" (1960), Jarrell would create another woman who feels that "Living is more dangerous than anything," but who nonetheless *yearns* for change and voices a plea for a radical, if impossible, alteration toward a more primal, carnal, and free, if frightening, state of being. This woman who cries "Oh, bars of my own body, open, open!" is trapped by gender and fate in the faceless lower reaches of the national bureaucracy, noting that the animals in the zoo are "beings trapped / As I am trapped but not, themselves, the trap" (*RJPoems* 215). She yearns, as will Lowell in "Waking Early Sunday Morning," to "break loose," both from the bureaucratic hierarchy that circumscribes her professional life and from "this serviceable / Body that no sunlight dyes, no hand suffuses." As in Lowell's poem, this yearning may confront from the start its own impossibility, but that does not diminish the visionary intensity and emotional ambiguity of the closing. This emerges slowly out of the drab quotidian detail of its beginnings, resembling one of Bishop's poems in its drift toward an arresting conclusion. "The Woman at the Washington Zoo" achieves its uncanny, unsettling climax in the woman's concluding apostrophe to a caged scavenger bird.

> Vulture,
> When you come for the white rat that the foxes left,
> Take off the red helmet of your head, the black
> Wings that have shadowed me, and step to me as man:
> To whose hand of power the great lioness
> Stalks, purring. . . .
> You know what I was,
> You see what I am: change me, change me!
> (*RJPoems* 215–16)

Here no "great / CHANGE" is "bending to us dewy-eyed" from a library mural, offering to lift the unhappy child that one was or still might be into a realm of placed, vicarious, and therefore bearable sorrow. Rather, an adult individual who finds little to esteem in herself demands perhaps impossible changes with angry, imperious, visionary force. The woman's voice embodies a yearning to escape conventional moral judgments, such as those that might dismiss a vulture as scabrously inferior, and a still stronger yearning to achieve a state of independent power, to become "the great lioness" who stalks forth (embodying life?) to claim recognition and to acknowledge a complementary power (embodying—or escaping—death?) in another.

Still, these changes represent not an accomplishment but a fictive thing, a dreamlike or visionary yearning: can the vulture really "change me, change me!" as the woman wishes? Read in the context of Jarrell's evolving art and the work of his closest colleagues, "The Woman at the Washington Zoo" characterizes change as both a threat and a felt need. This oppositional intensity appears to arise, as threat and need, from the emotional deprivations Jarrell suffered during what Lowell termed his "lost, raw childhood," causing him to struggle throughout later life with a palpable lack of self-love and self-acceptance that even the great affection and respect his life inspired could not fully assuage.

"Next Day" (1963) looks subtly, compassionately, and ironically at a woman's fear of change, as she voices her confrontation with aging, her anxious embrace of stasis, and her anticipation of death. For a woman who announces, "I am afraid, this morning, of my face," change connotes a more complete self-realization than she has ever known. Contradictorily, yet more immediately and frighteningly, it also represents the immediate loss of youth and the looming inevitability of that most radical change of all, death itself. On the "Next Day" after the funeral of a contemporary and friend, change thus appears, paradoxically, both as the promise the woman most yearns for and the eventuality she most intensely fears and shuns. For change emerges here as that nearly eventless event that surely and inevitably overtakes one, even under an upper-middle-class veneer of health, prosperity, and normalcy, in the form of aging, solitude, and death.

> The dog, the maid,
> And I go through the sure unvarying days
> At home in them. As I look at my life,
> I am afraid
> Only that it will change, as I am changing.
>
> (*RJPoems* 280)

Though she once looked "good enough to eat," this woman, driving home from the supermarket, begins to see and to acknowledge unnerving parallels between her own changed, mirrored faced with its "plain, lined look / Of gray discovery" and the face of her deceased friend whose image hovers gravely at the edge of consciousness.

> And yet I'm afraid, as I was at the funeral
> I went to yesterday.
> My friend's cold made-up face, granite among its flowers,
> Her undressed, operated-on, dressed body
> Were my face and body.
>
> (*RJPoems* 280)

A dead friend's "granite" face, itself "plain," "gray," and "lined," seems, perhaps, ready to successfully resist change—while the colorful flowers that surround it are doomed to rapidly fade. But the dead friend's seeming freedom from change is mere illusion, given her body's inevitable decay. In fact, the friend lying face-up in her open casket has become an object merely, her face "cold" and "made-up," her body "undressed, operated-on," then "dressed" again like a mannequin or a child's doll. In the poem's remorseless logic, to escape the vicissitudes of change, one must die—and thereby undergo the final, ultimate change. Recalling her deceased friend's exclamations on "How young I seem; I *am* exceptional," this woman is forced to recognize that, where aging and death are concerned, "really no one is exceptional, / No one has anything, I'm anybody." And in her imagination she *does* becomes "anybody"—becomes, that is, three figures simultaneously: her now-recently-interred friend; her friend's (and her own) chief mourner, an abstract, impersonal, solitary figure standing beside a grave; and a still-living, upper-middle-class woman driving home from the supermarket with her groceries. As the living woman, she not only confronts the death of her friend, but faces and mourns the losses and limitations she has learned "to overlook" during the course of her own plushly suburban life. Thus, the poem concludes: "I stand beside my grave / Confused with my life, that is commonplace and solitary" (*RJPoems* 280). Mary Jarrell reads "Next Day" aptly, as "a persona mask for Jarrell's own melancholy over growing older and reacting to not one, but two friends' funerals in one month."[19] The peculiar monody Jarrell creates engages in the kind of displacements of and unwilled or unwilling confrontations with sorrow that characterize the postmodern elegy. "Next Day" explores the various ways change can be reconfigured by a woman who only reluctantly acknowledges the reality of loss and death, and who contemplates with equal reluctance any sort of risk or change.

Mary Jarrell recalls that in the spring of 1964, with Jarrell's depression already several months old, "The season of the Pulitzer awards was approaching, and with it Jarrell's fiftieth birthday. This set him reckoning to Mary that all the poets he was ranked with—Shapiro, Lowell, Wilbur, Bishop, and Roethke—had won the Pulitzer Prize before they were fifty" (*RJLet* 489.) Moreover, in 1965 Berryman, whose career had once seemed belated in comparison with Jarrell's, would win a Pulitzer for *77 Dream Songs*. In Jarrell's mind, fame and external success appeared to be failing a person who, however endeared to others, was "not to himself endeared."

Jarrell's competitive streak was particularly apparent when he felt he had to vie for Lowell's attention. Lowell and Berryman each separately recalled in their prose memoirs an earlier get-together between themselves and Jarrell in 1947 at Berryman's Princeton apartment. Though Jarrell and Berryman got on famously as a pair, this particular threesome generated an uncomfortable chemistry. Jarrell was suffering the lingering effects of a bout of food-poisoning from a cocktail party Lowell and Jarrell had attended the previous evening. According to Eileen Simpson "everyone, Cal included, had overindulged—everyone except Randall, who as usual, had drunk not a drop. It seemed hardly fair that the teetotaler should be the one to suffer from a hangover. From the canapès! Cal couldn't imagine anything funnier."[20] And so, as Berryman recalled it, Jarrell walked "up and down my living room, miserable and witty. And very malicious, as he could certainly be, making up a brand-new Lowell poem full of characteristic Lowell properties, Lowell's grandfather and Charon, and the man who did not find this funny at all was Lowell."[21] Eileen eventually "installed him on the couch in the living room with pillows and a comforter," where Jarrell lay while the others dined, "leafing," as Eileen recalled it, "through a book of English ballet photographs," and putting down the English dancers, whom as Lowell notes, "he had never seen." Jarrell disparaged Berryman's taste for English dance, acquired during his Cambridge years, based on what Lowell described as Jarrell's "forty, recent, consecutive nights of New York ballet" (*RLProse* 113). Lowell's memoir omits to mention Jarrell's parodies of Lowell's poems, which Eileen, too, recalled as "wickedly witty . . . , full of sabbaths, sermons, graveyards, ancestors and, not to leave out the religious theme (though it was now out of favor with Cal, the Apostate), the Mother of God,"[22] but Lowell certainly sensed the tension, claiming that "I suffered more than the fighters, and lost authority by trying not to take sides" (*RLProse* 113).

Lowell observed of this occasion in a letter to Berryman after Jarrell's death: "two race-horses, I guess three, and all of us secretly uneasy." As Lowell's letter recalled it, Jarrell developed chills on the Jersey local back to Pennsylvania Station, and "In the sand-colored hard interior of the train home, I remember putting my coat over Randall, who was shivering, and feeling some crisis had passed."[23]

Berryman, even as he was winning for himself a new level of eminence in the mid-1960s, and despite their moments of rivalry, displayed an uncannily intuitive insight into Jarrell's need for public recognition and approval. He understood, as well, that such external forms of validation would inevitably fail to provide sustenance. This point is demonstrated in a remarkable Dream Song from the "Opus Posthumous" section that begins *The Dream Song*'s second and concluding volume, *His Toy, His Dream, His Rest.* Section IV, "Op. posth." posits and dramatizes, in fourteen unsettling and darkly comic songs, Henry's death, burial, judgment, recovery, and subsequent reemergence from the grave:

> digging like mad, Lazarus with a plan
> to get his own back, a plan, a stratagem
> no newsman will unravel.
>
> (*DS* 91)

In the penultimate "Op. posth." Dream Song, just before Henry's dramatic and mysterious scramble back into life, he contemplates his dead friend Jarrell's memory. The ambiguous opening phrase might refer either to Randall or to Henry:

> In the night-reaches dreamed he of better graces,
> of liberations, and beloved faces,
> such as now ere dawn he sings.
>
> (*DS* 90)

Confronted by now-familiar and tormenting dreams of relinquished or unattainable "graces," this song confronts, as well, Berryman's new struggle to accept the death of his old comrade in the arts.

> Let Randall rest, whom your self-torturing
> cannot restore one instant's good to, rest:
> he's left us now.
>
> (*DS* 90)

Berryman received love, as did Jarrell, only conditionally in childhood, in an environment of lingering threat and insecurity. In this poignant and penetrating song, he recognizes that he and Jarrell shared, with unspoken intimacy and commiseration, the fate of those who live in quest of such forms of never-fully-compensatory external validation as the "eminence" that comes with literary achievement.

> In the chambers of the end we'll meet again
> I will say Randall, he'll say Pussycat
> and all will be as before
> whenas we sought, among the beloved faces,
> eminence and were dissatisfied with that
> and needed more.
>
> (*DS* 90)

Even in "the chambers of the end," apparently, one will remain "dissatisfied," one will still need "more," since, for good or ill, "all" in those unearthly chambers "will be as before." In this curiously unchanged afterworld, what will remain includes their friendship, but also their puzzled dissatisfaction with the eminence they sought—and achieved—with such obsessive zeal. For "eminence" as Berryman's own *Love and Fame* would later recognize, cannot answer unmet needs of the abused, unrecognized, or emotionally abandoned child. Neither can "the beloved faces"—the disembodied visages of one's friends and lovers, one's artistic peers, one's "galaxy of grands maîtres," and the great poets of the past. For though these faces may be empowered to confirm eminence in its various forms, they can neither bestow self-love nor show one where to find that "more" one "needed" so urgently.

Bishop, then living in Brazil, was not able attend the memorial at Yale University for Jarrell at which both Lowell and Berryman appeared, but she said, in a prose piece she titled "An Inadequate Tribute," that "Randall Jarrell was difficult, touchy, and oversensitive to criticism. He was also a marvelous conversationalist, brilliantly funny, a fine poet, and the best and most generous critic of poetry I have known. I am proud to remember that, although we could rarely meet, we remained friends for twenty years." (*RJ1914* 20) Bishop's sense of Jarrell's fragility was tied to a unique intensity that set him apart—even when ill he could be uncannily brilliant and incisive—but this level of intensity might in the long run be hard to sustain. "He always seemed more alive than other people, as if constantly tuned up to the concert pitch that most people, including poets, can maintain only for short and fortunate stretches."

Bishop closed her remembrance of Jarrell with a remarkable image summoning up her old friend's intense, and, for Bishop, still lingering presence. "I like to think of him as I saw him once after we had gone swimming together on Cape Cod; wearing only bathing trunks and a very queer straw cap with a big visor, seated on the crest of a high sand dune, writing in a notebook. It was a bright and dazzling day. Randall looked small and rather delicate, but bright and dazzling, too. I felt quite sure that whatever he was writing would be bound to share the characteristics of the day and of the small man writing away so busily in the middle of it all" (*RJ1914* 20–21).

Thus the four-way conversation of this quartet continues even in their prose and verse elegies for one another, which serve to keep the departed member of the quartet imaginatively present by recovering his remembered features or voice. Berryman's "Dream Song" imagines a future conversation with Randall in "the chambers of the end," when "I will say Randall, he'll say Pussycat," and Bishop places him atop that blazing sand dune "writing away busily . . . in the middle of it all." In one of Lowell's unrhymed, elegiac sonnets, the conversation with his friend Jarrell emerges out of a disorienting dream where it becomes impossible to distinguish dream from waking, reason from irrationality, self-imperilment from safety:

> I woke and knew I held a cigarette;
> I looked, there was none, could have been none;
> I slept off years before I woke again,
> palming the floor, shaking the sheets. I saw
> nothing was burning. I awoke, I saw
> I was holding two lighted cigarettes. . . .
>
> (*History* 135)

Penetrating into this unsettled state come the beloved dead, frightening in their strangely revivified humanity, and challenging in their claims upon the world of the living.

> They come this path, old friends, old buffs of death.
> Tonight it's Randall, his spark still fire though humble,
> his gnawed wrist cradled like *Kitten.* "What kept you so long,
> racing the cooling grindstone of your ambition?
> You didn't write, you *re*wrote. . . . But tell me,
> Cal, why did we live? Why do we die?"
>
> (*History* 135)

This poem dramatizes a dream-reunion with the departed Randall, and when Randall speaks, his words are part reproof, containing a series of challenging and perhaps unanswerable questions about the lingering of ambition, the stubborn will to live, and the threat or lure of death. Randall's dream-interrogations hover in the air, echoing the questions asked by the voices of dead Allied bomber crews and their dead civilian victims in Jarrell's "Losses" (1944).

> But the night I died I dreamed that I was dead,
> And the cities said to me: "Why are you dying?
> We are satisfied, if you are; but why did I die?"
>
> (*RJPoems* 146)

Lowell's deliberate, uncanny echoes of Jarrell imply an effort, both as a dramatized, unconscious dreamer and as a consciously writing and rewriting artist, to keep Jarrell's voice—once valued and validating, yet now confrontational and disquieting—alive. Lowell, of course, wrote and rewrote even this poem. Three distinct versions of the poem appear in *Notebook 1967–68*, *Notebook* (1970), and *History* (1973). The last, best version, cited here, in fact replaces the phrase "Surely this life was fast enough" with the more memorable, and accusatory: "You didn't write, you *re*wrote," reflecting, perhaps, Lowell's current anxiety over his obsessive rewriting of his *Notebook* poems, the composition and recomposition of which had preoccupied his creative life for the past half-dozen years.

In Lowell's dream vision, as in Berryman's *Dream Song* elegies for Jarrell, these old friends suggest that as Jarrell passes into the "chambers of the end," he enters an uncanny realm that is neither heaven nor hell, but rather a dreamlike continuation of one's living life. For the surreal realm of death Jarrell fictively inhabits provides no answers to questions about selfhood or art, whereas it preserves ongoing memories of earthly friendship as well as of earthly pain, uncertainty, and loss. As will each surviving poet's own subsequent passing, Randall's death raises more questions. Thus Randall must ask his still living, still writing, still grindingly ambitious friend: "But tell me, / Cal, why did we live? Why do we die?" The Randall who voices this question projects a "willingness to be uncertain" about the most basic questions of human existence that extends even into death. Jarrell had drank next to nothing (until well into his final depression), had lead the life of a stable husband and solid citizen, had displayed a huge capacity for work as teacher, poet, critic, reader, and anthologist, and remained a fine athlete who was just beginning to slow down on the tennis court by 1965. Their shocked reactions to his death confirm that he had seemed to the other members of the quartet the strongest, the sanest, the best disciplined, and hence the safest of the four. If even Randall were vulnerable, then so were they all.

## "Gather ye berries harsh and crude": John Berryman, 1914–1972

On the morning of 7 January 1972, just over six years after Jarrell's too-early death, John Berryman—leaving a dream song draft about a recent, aborted suicide attempt behind in the wastebasket—told his third wife Kate that he was on his way to the University of Minnesota campus to clean out his office. He added, cryptically, "You won't have to worry about me any more."[24] Berryman then caught a city bus to the Washington Avenue Bridge. This broad, imposing auto-and-foot bridge connects the eastern and western halves of the university where these are bisected by a broad ravine. Alighting from his bus at this unsettling declivity, Berryman climbed over the bridge railing, then leapt to his death against the frozen western bank of the Mississippi far below. Berryman, burdened by the enormity of a painful past defined by his father's ambiguous death and the enormity of the "(horrible) *richness*"[25] of his ongoing relationship with his mother, had previously contemplated or attempted suicide on numerous occasions, as early as his days as a student at South Kent School.

Berryman had spent much of his last year quite painfully free of alcohol. His friend William Meredith recalled a poetry festival at Godard College in May 1971 at which Berryman "who would never wear decorations was wearing a rosette: the badge of three months' abstinence, from Alcoholics Anonymous."[26] Alcohol was a drug that, even as it was slowly killing him, served temporarily to mask an apparently unkillable pain. Implicitly reflecting on the difficulty of change, Lowell relates that Berryman explained to him, at their final meeting in New York City "that his doctor had told him one more drunken binge would kill him. Choice? It is blighting to know that this fear was the beginning of eleven months of abstinence . . . half a year of prolific rebirth, then suicide" (*RLProse* 116). In his final year, Berryman seems to have found it impossible to live either with or without alcohol. Moreover, his mother, now in serious ill health, had moved at Berryman's invitation to an apartment directly across the street from Berryman's home. Her son hoped she would there receive better care than she had been experiencing in far away Washington, D.C. But the stress of his mother's presence seemed more than Berryman could endure.

Jarrell's sudden death profoundly shocked and surprised his friends, but Lowell wrote to Bishop that he had expected Berryman's death ever since their last meeting in New York in December 1971. Lowell's prose memoir recalls that he asked his old friend, after a somber midday meal: "'When will I see you again?' meaning in the next few days before I flew to England. John said, 'Cal, I was thinking through lunch that I'll never see you again'" (*RLProse* 116). Two weeks later, Berryman was dead. For his friend Saul Bellow, "At last it must have seemed that he had used up all his resources. . . . What he needed for his art had been supplied by his own person, by his mind, his wit. He drew it out of his vital organs, out of his very skin. At last there was no more. Reinforcements failed to arrived."[27] Eileen Simpson concluded that when Berryman jumped to his death in January 1972, "he did what he'd been rehearsing to do at least as far back as the night of our engagement party."[28]

Bishop produced an elegiac response to Berryman's work three years before his death. Bishop's verse celebration reflects the strong appreciation of his work she had developed in response to *Homage to Mistress Bradstreet* and *The Dream Songs*, an appreciation documented in an important and till now unpublished exchange of letters, beginning with a 1968 fan letter from Bishop in response to the completed *Dream Songs*. In 1962, as large groups of "Dream Songs" by the still not widely known John Berryman were making their first appearances in magazines—and in the process making waves—Bishop wrote to her friend Lowell from Brazil admitting that she found Berryman difficult. But, she continued, "One has the feeling 100 years from now *he* may be all the rage—or a 'discovery'—*hasn't one*?'[29] When the first book-length installment of Berryman's magnum opus appeared two years later, Bishop, on Berryman's list to receive a complementary copy, remarked in an October 1964 letter from Rio to her first biographer, Anne Stevenson, that "I've also been reading carefully in John Berryman's last: 77 DREAM POEMS (sic). He echoes: 'The Wreck of the Deutschland,' Stevens, Cummings, Lowell, a bit, Pound, etc. etc. but it is quite an extraordinary performance, although I think I really understand probably barely half of it." Bishop could be too self-deprecating about her critical ability, but her keenly developed ear for literary quality was put on high alert by Berryman's compelling, original, and difficult art. This prompted her to reveal to Stevenson her profound, if ambivalent, fascination with the work of several of her more overtly self-exploratory contemporaries: "If I were a critic and had a good brain I think I'd like to write a study of 'The School of Anguish'—Lowell (by far the best), Roethke, and Berryman. And then their descendants like Anne Sexton and Seidel, more and more anguish and less and less poetry."[30]

As the years passed, Bishop's admiration for Berryman's capacity to mingle poetry *and* anguish grew. Although these lonely poets never met—Berryman spent his later years teaching in Minneapolis, while Bishop lived mostly in Brazil and Boston—they exchanged a series of letters that make clear their high regard for one another. They had been reading one another appreciatively for three decades, and they had corresponded, infrequently, since the mid-1940s, but Bishop began their interchange in earnest in October 1968, just a year after Lota's suicide with a letter praising Berryman's *Dream Songs*. This prompted a series of cordial, revealing letters between them from 1968 through the early 1970s. Bishop begins, "Dear John: (We haven't met, but I feel I can call you by your first name)" and continues: "I meant to write you a fan letter when the first DREAM

POEMS [sic] came out in 1964, and now I am not sure whether I did or not. Anyway, I admired them enormously. I also liked the Sonnets, and the Short Poems. . . . Now I have HIS TOY, HIS DREAM, HIS REST here, too, and I am awfully pleased. You have found or invented a wonderful form for yourself and it seems capable of including so many things and moods. I happened to see #187 [which refers to Bishop] in a magazine and I was very much amused by it."[31] In this letter Bishop not only acknowledges Berryman as a peer, a fellow inventor of forms. She is also inviting him to become a friend. What was it that drew Bishop so powerfully to a writer whose anguished and grandiosely self-dramatizing gestures might seem so antithetical? To answer this question one must read on through her letter, and the letters and verse tribute that followed.

Here, too, Bishop alludes to an urge to analyze Berryman's work critically. "If I were a critic I'd certainly want to write about you, too, but I don't have much confidence in my powers as a reviewer, so I'd rather abstain from that, and just send you my thanks and congratulations and affectionate regards, personally."[32] She continues, "There is really not much more I can say than this: I like your poetry and Cal's better than any of my contemporaries."[33] And she adds in a postscript "If you ever come this way, please look me up." Berryman's ecstatic reply to this missive, as previously noted, was "Thank you for your lovely letter. . . . There is no one living whose approval I would rather have."[34]

Bishop, depressed and isolated in Brazil following her friend Lota's death, and the impending collapse of her most recent relationship, replied that she found Berryman's "lovely letter . . . the most encouraging thing that has happened in some time."[35] Bishop mentioned in her response, written from Brazil, that "I am going to talk to teachers of English in Belo Horizonte (capital of Minas) next week and you are one of the people I hope to introduce to them." Her letter ends by combining awed artistic appreciation with friendly overture: "'Homage to Mistress Bradstreet' is one of the most amazing feats of the human imagination I know of—there!" And she immediately added, "I expect to return to the USA permanently this year, & hope to meet you sometime."[36] Soon they were making plans to meet and to exchange work in manuscript.[37]

Lowell remarked to an interviewer in 1971 "you write for about fifty friends, twenty of them you've never met."[38] Even after Bishop's increasingly "permanent" move to the States began in 1968, she and Berryman, despite some near misses, never managed to meet. But each counted the other among the intimate circle for whom he or she wrote, one of the small number of peers and colleagues whose example and opinion counted.

In 1969, Bishop would go public with her admiration in a brief but pointed verse tribute titled "Thank-You Note," a poem, appearing in a special *Harvard Advocate* tribute to Berryman, that has excited little critical comment so far. Significantly, Bishop not only told Berryman she liked his and Lowell's poetry "better than any of my contemporaries," but, among the poets of her generation, only Berryman and Lowell were ever to become the objects of published poetic tributes from Bishop. Bishop accomplishes her tribute to Berryman in four deceptively simple lines.

> Mr. Berryman's songs and sonnets say:
> "Gather ye berries harsh and crude while yet ye may."
> Even if they pucker our mouths like choke-cherries,
> Let us be grateful for these thick-bunched berries.
> (*EBPoems* 207)

Bishop's poem looks and sounds like light verse. Of course, this was a mode at which Bishop excelled and into which she could pack an uncanny amount of substance and nuance. In fact, this poem successfully compresses several aspects of the prose critique Bishop lacked the confidence to write into a complex and subtle verse appreciation of a master of "the school of anguish" with whom Bishop knew she had more in common than met the casual eye. The poem repays attentive reading for a sequence of subtle gestures that so shrewd and experienced a reader as Berryman could be counted on to recognize and savor.

Bishop deploys a range of overlapping echoes to place Berryman and herself side by side in common verse traditions, even as she recognizes and celebrates their differences. Referring to Berryman's "songs and sonnets," Bishop quietly alludes to the standard title for those seventeenth century verse collections which she and Berryman had so frequently studied and sought to absorb. Here Bishop recognizes their shared love of seventeenth-century English verse, and its importance as a source of Berryman's own extensive published works, *The Dream Songs* and *Berryman's Sonnets.* Bishop alludes astutely as well to the special importance for Berryman of Milton's "Lycidas," as her opening cunningly mingles the famous first lines of Herrick's carpe diem lyric, "Gather ye Rose-buds while ye may / Old Time is still a flying" with the perhaps still more famous, and far grander, opening trumpet notes of "Lycidas":

> Yet once more, O ye laurels, and once more,
> Ye myrtles brown, with ivy never seer,
> I come to pluck your berries harsh and crude . . .

Thus Bishop's assessment of what "Berryman's songs and sonnets say" places Berryman in two traditions. The lighter, more sensuous Cavalier tradition of Herrick, with its urgent imperative to seize the day is warranted, for example, by the fourth *Dream Song*, with its anguished yet scrumptious celebration of a beautiful, unattainable woman "Filling her compact & delicious body / with chicken páprika." The more austere, sublime tradition of epic Christian tragedy exemplified by Milton is warranted in Berryman's work by his *Homage to Mistress Bradstreet*, his "Op. posth." *Dream Songs*, his extended sequence of elegies to Delmore Schwartz, and many others. These quasi-Miltonic tendencies, which Berryman shared with Lowell, would be confirmed a few years after Bishop's tribute appeared by Berryman's late, remarkable "Eleven Addresses to the Lord," which opens with it supplication to the:

> Master of beauty, craftsman of the snowflake,
> inimitable contriver,
> endower of Earth so gorgeous & different from the boring Moon
> (*JBPoems* 215)

Plucking life's ephemeral berries, even if they are harsh and crude, was an aspect of the elegiac tradition to which both Bishop and Berryman were drawn. Bishop tends to disguise her own indelicacies and crudities in imagery that surrounds them with a context of delicacy or beauty (as in the lines "bright green leaves edged neatly with bird-droppings / like illumination in silver" (*EBPoems* 40));[39] Berryman frequently hides his beauties in a context of harshness, crudity, or indelicacy. Those laurel and myrtle berries from "Lycidas," archaic even in Milton's time, have, of course, been replaced in Bishop's modern "Thank-You Note" with plain, indelicate "choke-cherries." But even these puckery fruit nonetheless elicit our gratitude, coming, as they do in the form of the 385 terrifying and comforting "thick-bunched berries" of Berryman's *Dream Songs*.

Bishop professes, in her 1964 letter to Stevenson, a purely analytical interest in a "School of Anguish," going out of her way to insist on a certain distance between herself and this school she finds at once fascinating and disturbing. "Surely," Bishop continues ambivalently to Stevenson, "never in all the ages has poetry been so personal and confessional—and I don't think it is what I like, really—although I certainly admire Lowell's. —He does manage to make it a bit more universal and less self-pitying—

or is it because I know him and know how courageous he is, etc.? But heaven forbid that I ever try to theorize."[40] Despite her professions of distress or distaste, her doubt about her own (in fact considerable) critical and theoretical powers, and her self-deprecating description of her own writing as "innocuous" (*EBLet* 324), Bishop demonstrates a forceful urge to theorize about this literary phenomenon. Perhaps, just as Blake saw the Puritanic Milton as being "of the Devil's party without knowing it,"[41] Bishop was "of the school of anguish without knowing it"—or at least without acknowledging it.

Bishop's published work is rarely so frank, but it frequently embodies a dramatic struggle between a conscious prohibition against the public exploration of pain or inner turmoil, and a perhaps unconscious imperative to explore these very experiences in poetry, that one elusive medium in which she exercised the greatest power and imaginative authority. Hence Bishop's reference to that "wonderful form" that Berryman had "found or invented" for himself, a form "capable of including so many things and moods" that she admired, and clearly, to a degree, envied. Those poets Bishop thought of as Lowell's mere imitators and artistic inferiors—whose work offered "more and more anguish and less and less poetry"—became the objects of her particular distrust and scorn. But the poets she identified as the school's strongest members, Lowell and Berryman, emerged—by her own private admission—as her favorite contemporaries and the targets of her sole poetic tributes.

Bishop found in the "extraordinary performances" of Lowell and Berryman a skill in artistic making that could shape ordinary human anguish into exploratory art, uncovering mysteries of culture and family, permanence and change, selfhood and survivorship. Bishop acknowledged her private sense of anguish frequently enough in letters to intimates, but she voiced it only covertly and warily in her published work, where it emerges, nonetheless, with all the considerable power of barely voiced latency. Such anguished yet formally capable poets as Lowell and Berryman emerged as her two favorites among her immediate contemporaries because their artistry authorized and exemplified an exploration of anguish in verse that Bishop, too, had long been (more covertly) embarked upon. It now seems clear that Bishop ranks with Berryman, Lowell, and their friend Jarrell as one of the most ingenious, skillful, and in her case, devious proponents of the school of anguish.

Bishop's ambivalent fascination with the school of anguish grew out of a private recognition of kinship based on an ongoing sense of "anxiety and loss" that haunted even her moments of greatest security and fulfillment. Bishop had, from earliest youth, internalized strong taboos against the expression of personal feeling, particularly feelings of mourning, grief, and self-commiseration deemed inappropriate by her late-Puritan culture. But she also bore the lasting scars of early traumas, and her powerful private feelings of "anguish," intensely present and elusively knowable through the language of symptoms and the insistent, ambiguous promptings of memory, demanded expression. Ten years after her death, in his "Overdue Pilgrimage to Nova Scotia," James Merrill mused upon the different image of Bishop that was emerging in "the anguish coming only now to light / In letters like photographs from space,"[42] an image that helps us read her in a different way. Bishop's work, just as Berryman's or Lowell's, is at its most powerful when it is indirectly or even evasively bringing to life hermetic feelings too painful or dangerous to represent directly. As in Berryman's most powerful Dream Songs, the teasing opacity of Bishop's writings at their most telling lead the reader into confrontations with the problematic nature of dreaming, owning, knowing, madness, imprisonment, isolation, and the recognition of and attempt to recover from what Berryman terms "an absolute disappearance of continuity and love." "The Ballad of the Subway Train," "The Man-Moth," "Roosters," "The Prodigal," "Sestina," "First Death in Nova Scotia," "In the Waiting Room," "Crusoe in England," "One Art," "The Country Mouse," and "In the Village" are all examples of such poems and stories.

Bishop, with her affection for "closets, closets and more closets"[43] and her desire to pile on the defenses to protect her privacy, may have required more encouragement toward such confrontations than most, and she found such encouragement in the work of Lowell and Berryman. Jarrell notes the need of the artist "as Cezanne always said, to realize [one's] subject," and he added, significantly, that "some subjects . . . are terribly complicated or partly ambiguous or there are repressed, awful things underneath them."[44] Both Bishop and Jarrell deployed in their lives elaborate mechanisms for repressing feelings that lived on in their unconscious, but they were able to realize these powerfully, if sometimes indirectly, in their art.

Frank Bidart, referring to the anguished occasions in Bishop's life that prompted such poems as "Crusoe in England" or "One Art," observes that, "I think Elizabeth was magnificently inconsistent. On the one hand, she could talk a blue streak about how people shouldn't be writing all these confessional poems, and yet when she had to do it, she did it, and without apology. At a certain level the aesthetic position was quite irrelevant to Elizabeth. I also think she was able to cut off certain parts of her mind in order to make the poem."[45]

One of the most important measures of Bishop's "magnificent inconsistency"—and a mark of her strength as an artist and reader—was her capacity to develop such a keen appreciation for Lowell's commingling of poetry and anguish and her ability to find in Lowell such a close literary friend and ally over the last three decades of her life. Further evidence of this "magnificent inconsistency" was her ability to recognize and celebrate Berryman's extraordinary effort to confront subjects that "are terribly complicated" and "ambiguous," with "repressed, awful things underneath them," and to "realize them truly" in bitter (or sometimes curiously bittersweet) poems whose originality and creative power deserve abiding gratitude and attention.

## Lowell to Berryman: Seven Letters and an Elegy

Lowell, who had known Berryman well for more than twenty-five years, wrote of his death in 1972 with unusual insight, empathy, and intimacy. The growth of that intimacy can be traced in a selection of seven letters (six of them by Lowell) exchanged by these poets over twenty-five years. These letters offer glimpses into the "three forms of responsiveness"—defined by Elliott Carter as "discipleship, companionship, and confrontation"[46]—that entered into their constantly evolving and changing personal and artistic relationship. This dialogue continues, in fictional form, in Lowell's intimate and poignant elegy "For John Berryman," which is addressed directly and intimately to Lowell's departed friend.

The three initial letters in the sequence date from 1948, the second year of their friendship. The first is pure companionship. Lowell on 9 February 1948 is in Washington, D.C., serving as Poetry Consultant to the Library of Congress, and he writes arranging for a visit from Berryman to record readings of his poems for the Library. Thinking of his delightful visit the previous summer with Berryman and his red-headed wife Eileen in Maine, Lowell notes that, "About three weeks ago, I saw a man who looked like you walking with a tall red-headed girl in front of the library; and I said: 'Ah, the Berrymans, there's no one in the world I would want to see more.'"

In a second letter, Lowell writes again to Berryman in March 1948, acknowledging receipt of the latter's first independent volume of poems,

*The Dispossessed.* Apologizing for not having yet given the poems a detailed reading, he insists that, "I do intend to read your new poems with friendly care and be one of the exceptions who does read his friend's work," while offering the general, and largely secondhand, praise that, "Randall & Ransom agree with me that they're a great stylistic development."[47] Lowell's tone recognizes an attitude of discipleship on Berryman's part, but despite his strongly voiced feelings of companionship, Lowell does not quite display the urgency, nor does he offer the specificity of response, that Berryman might have wished for. But, then, *The Dispossessed* is a tricky book for a friendly reader to respond to critically.

In a third letter, dated 30 August 1948, Lowell at last comes to grips with Berryman's promising yet problematic early volume, referring particularly to the "The Nervous Songs," which Jarrell's 17 July review in *The Nation* had singled out for encouraging attention. Jarrell observes that "The style—conscious, dissonant, darting; allusive, always over- or under-satisfying the expectations which it is intelligently exploiting—seems to fit Mr. Berryman's knowledge and sensibility surprisingly well, and ought in the end to produce poetry better than the best of the poems he has so far written in it" (*KA&Co* 152–53). Lowell alludes to this observation in his letter and grows more specifically, and helpfully, critical. He highlights the promise while gently confronting the still-extant problems of "The Nervous Songs," which focus on a wide range of characters, rather than *The Dream Song*'s central subject and invention, Henry. "The new difficult poems seem to me the most wonderful advance that anyone has made. I rather agree with Randall that they exist in bits and passages—so many breaks, anacoloutha etc. that the whole poem usually escapes me." Recognizing the artistic potential of this elusive form for Berryman, Lowell puts his finger on his friend's most urgent need: to find the right material with which to exploit this new, singular, and formidable technique. "You seem to have the equipment to do almost anything now. I think it needs to be docked in some overwhelming and unifying object. Maybe this is stupid criticism."[48] Of course, Lowell's criticism was anything but stupid, as the future would prove.

For even as Lowell was writing this letter, Berryman was finding his first "overwhelming and unifying object" in Anne Bradstreet. Berryman acknowledged that "I made up the Bradstreet stanza in 1948. It's a splendid stanza, it breaks in 3–5, not 4–4."[49] After a long hiatus in which the poem would exist as only its single, opening stanza, "the poem erupted" finally, as Eileen Simpson would later recall it, "in mid-January 1953."[50]

Bradstreet's partly historical, partly fictional life and times, which Bishop rightly termed "one of the most amazing feats of the human imagination I know of," would at last find print in the October 1953 issue of *Partisan Review* in the form of Berryman's unprecedented "Homage," the first of his genuinely grand scale inventions to reach the public. (His long sequence of *Sonnets to Chris*, exploring an illicit 1948 affair, had been suppressed and would not be published, with the name of his paramour altered to Lise, until 1967.)

Berryman would find a still more "overwhelming and unifying object" a few years later—and to far wider recognition and acclaim—in the "plights and gripes" of Henry, the singular protagonist of *The Dream Songs*. As Lowell and Jarrell guessed in 1948, the language of Berryman's *Homage* and *Dream Songs* remains "complicated, nervous and intelligent," and his lines continue to be full of "breaks and anacoloutha"—abrupt changes, within a sentence, to a new syntactical construction inconsistent with the first. Yet in each of these monumental verse-endeavors Berryman located a convincing voice in the process of creating that overwhelming and unifying object in which to "dock" his work. In these second and third letters of 1948, Lowell, just over thirty and three years younger than Berryman, speaks as the senior poet. With his Pulitzer Prize–winning *Lord Weary's Castle* already behind him, Lowell offers advice and encouragement to an aspiring friend, tacitly acknowledging what both then knew: that this friend hasn't quite arrived.

The fourth letter, on the other hand, is from Berryman. Written in 1957, it alludes tactfully to the long lapse since Lowell's last published poems. Lowell's lengthening silence as a poet had grown conspicuous to anyone closely following his career. Alluding to Lowell's prose memoir "91 Revere Street," recently published in the *Partisan Review*, Berryman queries: "Are you writing *verse* ever. The portrait of your father in *PR*'s absorbing." Lowell had in fact produced virtually no verse since the appearance of *The Mills of the Kavanaughs* in 1951—to decidedly ambivalent reviews even from their mutual friend Jarrell. By 1957, Berryman had published *Homage to Mistress Bradstreet:* it appeared first as a succès d'estime in the October 1953 issue of *Partisan Review*, winning him private praise from distinguished poets, but comparatively little public recognition and, after a frustratingly long delay, as a 1956 book, lavishly illustrated with woodcuts by Ben Shahn. Though nominated for the Pulitzer, which Bishop had won in 1956, and Lowell in 1947, *Homage* lost out to Richard Wilbur's *Things of This World*, which also took the National

Book Award. Thus, when Berryman wrote to Lowell in 1957, the latter was still the senior partner, but the two poets were closer to parity.

And Berryman's letter tacitly acknowledges and commiserates over their comparatively long mutual poetic silence. For aside from the belated book publication of *Homage*, Berryman too had published hardly a poem in four years. Still, Berryman mentions, almost shyly, "I . . . set up a new sort of poem two years ago of which I've deep hopes."[51] In fact, though apparently stalled, each of these poets was poised to make a decisive artistic turn, and each was on the verge of his most brilliant and productive phase. Inspired by Bishop's example, and drawing on the prose memoirs of which "91 Revere St." represented just a single episode, Lowell would soon return to verse, at the top of his form, with the poems of *Life Studies.* And the "new sort of poem" that Berryman had "set up" in 1955 would become his *Dream Songs,* the great poem he long knew he had in him and wondered if he would live to write.

In a fifth letter, dated 15 March 1959, Lowell writes to Berryman about "His Thoughts Made Pockets and the Plane Buckt": "Your poems (shall I say it:) have a strange heart-cutting poet maudit and late Elizabethan tragedy quality. . . . I wonder if you need so much twisting, obscurity, archaisms, strange word orders, *&* signs for and, etc.? I guess you do. Surely, here as in the Bradstreet, you have your voice. It vibrates and makes the heart ache."

After Berryman's death, Lowell would admit that he was at first rattled by his friend's mannerisms, though he would soon come to appreciate—and even imitate—the forthcoming *Dream Songs.* But in the same letter, which describes placing a picture of Berryman "among all my other pictures of my best friends," Lowell adds a general comment on the problems of his generation, well before the now famous early deaths of Roethke, Jarrell, Schwartz, and Berryman himself. Noting that he has just visited "Greensboro, where Randall and [I] enjoyed (?) ourselves lamenting the times" Lowell continues, "It seems there's been something curious, twisted and against the grain about the world poets of our generation have had to live in. What troubles you and I, Ted Roethke, Elizabeth Bishop, Delmore, Randall—even Karl Shapiro—have had."[52] Some years later, in his elegy "For John Berryman," this idea would reappear in the lines:

> Yet really we had the same life,
> The generic one
> our generation offered . . .
>
> (*DBD* 27)

The sense of amiable distance implicit in the 1948 letters is beginning to be replaced by an intense level of identification and fellow-feeling.

A sixth letter, from Lowell to Berryman (and dated in Berryman's hand "postm[ark]—22 Sept. [19]68") is full of praise for *His Toy, His Dream, His Rest.* One even detects a note of embarrassment, as if Lowell feels forced to tacitly acknowledge that his *Notebook* betrays Berryman's influence: "I've now read most of the poems, my admiration still rolling up. I'm dumbfounded at how many of the same things we have: rough iambic lines, often pentameter (for me mostly), short sections that are not stanzas; wife, wives, child, old flames, new ones, sex, love, loves, portraits of writer[s] (I have Frost, Jarrell and Williams, too)[,] landscape (I have more of this)[,] portraits of the dead, full middle age, humor, death, etc."[53] By now, each poet had entered "full middle age," each had a Pulitzer under his belt, and Lowell was no longer the senior partner. As was surely clear to both of them, most or all of the characteristics Lowell claims to discover in Berryman's latest book were already present in the earlier *77 Dream Songs* (1964), which predates Lowell's *Notebook* by several years.

This letter may be read as an implicit act of self-confrontation, as Lowell contemplates, "dumbfounded," the evidence of his own discipleship to his old friend and former protégé. Lowell tended to work in parallel with a different member of the midcentury quartet whenever his career was finding a new direction. As he was completing *Lord Weary's Castle* he found a perfect artistic foil in the keen and sympathetic editorial intelligence and judgment of Jarrell, who gave drafts of the poems an intensive and incisive work over in the year before the book's publication. As Lowell approached the writing of *Life Studies*, he drew sustenance from Elizabeth Bishop as a touchstone and guide into a more relaxed and conversational self-exploratory form, as particularly exemplified in her prose memoir "In the Village" and her poem "The Armadillo." As described earlier, Lowell carried a copy of this poem around in his wallet and read aloud and extolled it to anyone who would listen. During his *Notebook* phase, beginning with his 1967 entry into the field and culminating in the simultaneous 1973 publication of three book-length sequences of unrhymed sonnets, *The Dolphin, For Lizzie and Harriet,* and *History,* Lowell was responding most intently to the artistic possibilities of a self-exploratory sequence of brief, semiformal lyrics. These lyrics were full of "wives, child, old flames, new ones, sex, love, loves, portraits of writer[s] . . . , portraits of the dead, full middle age, humor, death"—possibilities vigorously and variously embodied in Berryman's *Dream Songs.*

Finally, in a 10 March 1966 letter that follows the death of their mutual friend Jarrell and reverts to a tone of profound companionship, Lowell begs Berryman to keep well. This is the letter, cited earlier, in which Lowell recalls the tense dinner shared by Jarrell, Lowell, Berryman, and his first wife Eileen in Berryman's Princeton apartment two decades earlier. Lowell reflects on the moment when, alone with Jarrell on the train home, he recognized the latter's fragility underneath his appearance of "iron self-confidence." Lowell's intuition of a connection between Randall's fragility and Berryman's own prompts him to close this letter of shared reminiscence and mourning with a plea to his surviving friend, "Let me beg you to take care of yourself. You must be physically fragile. If anything happened to you, I'd feel the heart of the scene had gone."[54] Far beyond all rivalry, Lowell confronts, with Berryman, in commiserating companionship, the difficulty of change and the more basic issue of survival.

Lowell, like Bishop, never quite recovered from the suddenness and shock of Jarrell's death, and in his Jarrellian elegies he creates for his old friend an edgy, confrontational presence, reflecting perhaps Lowell's own lingering disquiet over this loss. In these poems, which embody a certain guilt at his own persistence in life, and a shock and disbelief in Jarrell's premature departure, Lowell displaces his own dismay and sorrow and enduring doubt onto the voice of Jarrell.

Lowell's elegy "For John Berryman" suggests a different response on Lowell's part, a tone of more comfortable sympathy and identification, as if Berryman's death can be more readily understood and accepted. The note of identification was already struck in a *Notebook* poem Lowell dedicated to Berryman while the latter was still alive:

> I feel I know what you have worked through, you
> know what I have worked through—we are words;
> John, we used the language as if we made it
> (*History* 203)

In a *History* sonnet written after Berryman's death, Lowell reminds himself of the pain of Berryman's life, and closes with the distinctly un-Jeffersonian reflection: "suicide, the unalienable right of man." His final elegy, "For John Berryman," in *Day by Day*, at first reminds us of the distancing element in Berryman's behavior toward the end:

> The last years we only met
> when you were on the road,
> and lit up for reading

your battering *Dream*—
audible, deaf . . .
in another world then as now

(*DBD* 27)

These lines in verse echo Lowell's observation in prose that "As he became more inspired and famous and drunk, more and more John Berryman, he became less good company and more a happening." The discomforts of their later relationship included the fact that, as Lowell's poem acknowledged, "I used to want to live / to avoid your elegy." But, significantly, as Berryman became harder to reach on a personal level, Lowell's sense of quasi-tragic identification with his old friend grew, leading to a tone of direct-address-after-death that is curiously intimate, and that lines up the many parallels between Berryman's life and his own:

first students, then with our own
our galaxy of grands maîtres,
our fifties' fellowships
to Paris, Rome and Florence,
veterans of the Cold War not the War—
all the best of life . . .

(*DBD* 27)

The implicit question seems to be: how could we have gone wrong in this pleasant, encouraging environment? Even enduring the Cold War, anxious work though this was, was not so bad as serving, as did Jarrell, in the War. Yet, as we have seen, Bishop had addressed this very question four decades before in a 1935 notebook, when she reflected on, "My friendly circumstances, my 'good fortune,' surround me so well & safely, & only *I* am wrong, inadequate. It is a situation like one of those solid crystal balls with little silvery objects inside: thick, clear, appropriate glass—only the little object, me, is sadly flawed and shown off as inferior to the setting."[55] Each of these poets, despite the appearance of friendly circumstances and good fortune, still seem one of "*Les Maudit*," one of the order who must struggle with an inner curse no matter how propitious the external setting.

The elegy ends with a tone of intimacy, and a sense of quietness and repose, almost unheard of in Lowell's work, positing, again, a kind of dreamy, continuing, absent-minded, elderly life for the departed Berryman:

Do you wake dazed like me,
and find your lost glasses in a shoe? . . .
To my surprise, John,

I pray to not for you,
think of you not myself,
smile and fall asleep.
(*DBD* 27–28)

The poem is subtitled: "After reading his last *Dream Song*" and the poem has some of that *Dream Song*'s unusual quietness, its acceptance of a weary arrival at a moment of terminus after a stoically maintained series of explorations and psychical adventures.

## "Sad friend, you cannot change": Robert Lowell: 1917–1977

After Berryman's death in 1972, only Bishop and Lowell survived from the original quartet. The years 1972–1977, ending with Lowell's death by a heart attack on 12 September 1997, were eventful and sometimes troubled ones in their relationship. The trouble grew in substantial part out of Bishop's questioning of Lowell's use of Elizabeth Hardwick's letters to him in *The Dolphin*. This disagreement grew not, as has sometimes been assumed, because Bishop disapproved broadly speaking of the self-exploratory urge in Lowell's poetry. As we have seen, she approved far more wholeheartedly of *Life Studies* than did M. L. Rosenthal, the inventor of the term "confessional poetry." Rather, she objected, and clearly felt threatened by, what she considered an invasion of privacy in the publication of excerpts from Hardwick's private letters.

Another aspect of the disquiet in their relationship grew out of Bishop's sense of insecurity in her position at Harvard if Lowell should decide to permanently return there, since Bishop's position had opened with his departure for England. Lowell had acted to secure the position at Harvard for Bishop, and he made it clear that he would never return to Harvard in such a way as to imperil her job. Still, her insecurity about her position left her feeling even more blanketed by Lowell's shadow than she had felt under Roethke's shadow when she taught, earlier, at the University of Seattle. As Frank Bidart recalled it, "now in the early seventies at Harvard, in the heyday of his fame, she felt suffocated." But Bidart adds that "The loyalty, what was obviously love between them was never quite broken; but in the final years it existed in a crucible."[56] Jonathan Galassi, formerly both Lowell's and Bishop's student, recalled a lunch in 1978, the year after Lowell's death, when Bishop brought up Lowell, echoing a complaint that Lowell had earlier made about Berryman. "She said you couldn't talk to him in the last years, that he became a monologue. She felt that Lowell had cut himself off. What also gradually emerged was a sense, hidden under all her modesty, that she had not been appreciated to the extent that she deserved in comparison to her male peers."[57]

Yet while Lowell lived, the crucible of their love and friendship did not preclude humor, and exuberant dialogue was by no means impossible. Lloyd Schwartz recalls a Cambridge birthday party for Lowell hosted by Bidart for which Bishop made fudge, and at which "Elizabeth and Lowell engaged in a hilarious conversation that dominated the whole evening—about who had the worst dental experience. It was one-upsmanship at its most exuberant and teasing. . . . Everyone was in stitches. They were ironic, slightly cynical, willing—even eager—to be self-deprecating, if that made the joke better. They obviously had a tremendous sense of rapport, because even at a time when their relationship was strained, they could still finish each other's punch lines."[58]

Bishop's British friend Ilse Barker recalled that "Elizabeth rang me the morning after Lowell died, four o'clock her time, just to talk. Cal Lowell didn't mean anything to me. It wasn't for my sake. I should imagine she spent the night up emotionally disturbed, calling people."[59] The following spring, Barker was visiting Bishop on the island of North Haven, off the Maine coast, just as Bishop was completing her elegy to her departed friend. Barker remembered that, "We went to the library, where she wanted to look up a reference, a verse or something biblical." Clearly the stanza that Barker has in mind is the poem's third, which describes one of the smaller coastal islands visible from North Haven in terms that are not Biblical but Shakespearean.

> This month, our favorite one is full of flowers:
> Buttercups, Red Clover, Purple Vetch,
> Hawkweed still burning, Daisies Pied, Eyebright,
> the Fragrant Bedstraw's incandescent stars,
> and more, returned to paint the meadow with delight.
>
> (*EBPoems* 188)

Bishop's allusion here, just as her allusions to Herrick and Milton in her "Thank-You Note" to Berryman, seems to define common ground with the intensely learned and bookish Lowell, who tended constantly to see nature both in its own terms and in terms of his extensive and vividly remembered reading. Here Bishop draws specifically on the well-known song that closes *Love's Labour's Lost.* In Shakespeare's song it is "daisies pied and violets blue / And lady-smocks all silver-white / And cuckoo-buds of yellow hue" that serve to "paint the meadows with delight." Shakespeare's list of flowers is mostly different, except for the "Daisies Pied," but arguably no more beautiful than Bishop's. Different too are the birds that sing as spring arrives. For Shakespeare:

> The Cuckoo then, on every tree
> Mocks married men; for thus he sings,
> Cuckoo,
> Cuckoo, cuckoo: O word of fear,
> Unpleasing to a married ear.[60]

Bishop's birds are, of course, native to America and they sing different songs, but these songs are in their own way equally lovely and equally disquieting.

> The Goldfinches are back, or others like them,
> and the White-throated Sparrow's five-note song,
> pleading and pleading, brings tears to the eyes.
> Nature repeats herself, or almost does:
> *repeat, repeat, repeat; revise, revise, revise.*
>
> (*EBPoems* 188)

Barker's memory of Bishop's effort to write the poem underlines Bishop's lingering attachment to her dead friend, whatever their recent differences: "While we were with her, she managed to finish 'North Haven,' the poem for Lowell. She read it to us and walked about with it in her hand. I found it very moving that she felt she could hardly bear it put it down, that it was part of her. She put it beside her plate at dinner. . . . You had that feeling it really was part of her and she liked to have it around with her for a while."[61] The poem begins, as in a traditional pastoral elegy, with its commitment to placing sorrow in a natural setting. And it never leaves that setting. But it resembles the other elegies for quartet members in its tendency to engage in a dialogue with the departed member, first through a recollection of Lowell's own words when on an earlier visit to the island of North Haven he marveled at the clarity of the air and the extent of his vision. Is it Lowell, here, who, in a reversal of their accustomed roles, is acting as a "famous eye."

> *I can make out the rigging of a schooner*
> *a mile off; I can count*
> *the new cones on the spruce. It is so still*
> *the pale bay wears a milky skin, the sky*
> *no clouds, except for one long, carded horse's tale.*
>
> (*EBPoems* 188)

As the poem continues it maintains an ongoing dialogue with the elusive presence of this departed friend whose voice may no longer be heard, only remembered. It is a world that seems solid and continuous, nearly free of the forces of change, for "The islands haven't shifted since last summer," when Lowell was still alive, and the flowers and birds ("or others like them") return with spring. The change that has occurred only appears to "*repeat, repeat, repeat,*" but in fact it has been "revised, revised, revised," like one of the *Notebook* poems that Lowell could never bring himself to leave alone. And that change is the departure of Lowell himself, a revision that Bishop clearly finds it difficult to accept.

> You left North Haven, anchored in its rock,
> afloat in mystic blue . . . And now—you've left
> for good. You can't derange, or re-arrange,
> your poems again. (But the Sparrows can their song.)
> The words won't change again. Sad friend, you cannot change.
> (*EBPoems* 189)

Having entered the realm of death, Lowell has made that final transformation that will not let him change again. Nature can change and revise, but Lowell, and his words, are at last fixed, as immobile as North Haven itself, "anchored in its rock." Yet, in death, Lowell has also found permanence through his published words, a different kind of singing than the "Sparrow's five-note song," but in its own way just as "pleading and pleading" and equally capable of bringing "tears to the eyes."

Frank Lentricchia's 1994 *Modernist Quartet* charts in a sequence of separate chapters the careers of Robert Frost, Ezra Pound, T. S. Eliot, and Wallace Stevens. Only Pound and Eliot amongst this group sustained a lifelong friendship. In most other cases, these poets' personal relationships were decidedly cool. And none wrote the other's elegy.

Bishop, Lowell, Jarrell, and Berryman grew up as poets under different circumstances, and their careers reflect significantly closer relations. Bishop's elegy for Lowell, for example, expresses the decades of intimacy and artistic interchange, of discipleship, companionship, and confrontation, that marked this indispensable friendship and artistic alliance. Over the course of the midcentury decades, beginning first with the quartet's remarkably parallel childhood experiences, extending through their first tentative interactions in the mid-1930s, and on into the firm if unofficial establishment of the circle in the 1940s, these four poets would continue to develop in significant relation to one another. Together they would evolve one of the most influential and artistically successful, but least recognized, branches of postmodern American poetry. Their aesthetic would be marked by its flexible, exploratory approach to form and by a self-exploratory approach to content that places the physically or psychologically imperiled individual in a context of symbolically significant cultural markers. It would be marked as well by its invention and persistent exploitation of various modes of postmodern narrative. They would extend the dramatic and psychologically telling use of personae in new directions, exploiting post-Freudian insights into individual human psychology and deploying a keen awareness of cultural change in the postmodern world to probe deep into the individual psyche, with particular sensitivity to the importance of childhood losses and traumas. They would discover new ways of handling traditional stanza forms (Bishop's sestinas, Berryman's Dream Song sestets) as a medium of psychological revelation. They would develop a new mode of dramatic narrative involving an individual speaker moving through multiple layers of time and consciousness. And they would invent a new mode of postmodern elegy, which they would tune up to such an extraordinary pitch that they would ultimately become their own best elegists.

These poets never quite found the "great change" they yearned for. Yet, through an extensive and courageous act of interactive making that spanned the middle decades of the twentieth century, they achieved an unsettling and uncannily active form of permanence. The active permanence of their work had to be imagined and then made after "a long, often backbreaking search for an inclusive style." Through their imagination, arduous self-training, intrepid persistence, and insistence on excellence, they created an emotionally telling aesthetic whose potentialities remain active in the work of a wide array of contemporary poets. Through a closer study of this aesthetic, we may yet arrive at a deeper understanding of their art and a greater responsiveness to the problems of selfhood in the postmodern world.

# Notes

## Introduction

1. This book will draw frequently on the unusually extensive manuscript record these four poets left behind, a record of letters, workbooks, drafts, and journals that now resides in numerous library archives. Lowell's papers are to be found chiefly at Harvard University's Houghton Library and (from 1970 on) at the University of Texas at Austin's Ransom Library; Jarrell's papers reside in the Special Collections Division, Jackson Library, University of North Carolina at Greensboro and at the New York Public Library's Berg Collection; Bishop's are chiefly at the Rare Books and Manuscripts Division, Vassar College Library; and Berryman's at the Manuscripts Division, University of Minnesota Libraries. Further caches of important papers, documenting their relations with mentors like John Crowe Ransom, Allen Tate, Marianne Moore, Mark Van Dorn, R. P. Blackmur, Robert Penn Warren, and William Carlos Williams, among others, are spread among manuscript libraries across the United States, including those at Yale, Princeton, Vanderbilt, and Washington Universities, and at the Rosenbach Museum in Philadelphia. Moreover, significant Bishop manuscripts, including completed but previously unpublished poems, are turning up with some regularity in Brazil, where Bishop lived and worked for nearly two decades. And an extensive archive devoted to Bishop and her mother's family has been cataloged and is now preserved at Acadia University in Wolfsville, Novia Scotia, near Bishop's childhood home in Great Village. See Sandra Barry, *Elizabeth Bishop: An Archival Guide to Her Life in Nova Scotia* (Hantsport, Nova Scotia: Lancelot Press, 1996).

2. Frank Lentricchia's *Modernist Quartet* (New York: Cambridge Univ. Press, 1994), for example, devotes most of its length to separate chapters on Frost, Eliot, Pound, and Stevens. The sense of kinship was far more pervasive, and the dialogue more extensive and lasting, in this midcentury quartet than in Lentricchia's modernist quartet.

3. See, for example, Jeffery Meyers, *Manic Power: Robert Lowell and His Circle* (New York: Arbor House, 1987).

4. Elliott Carter, liner notes, *String Quartets Nos. 1 & 2* (New York: Nonesuch Records, n.d.), sound recording.

## 1 Midcentury Quartet

1. Elizabeth Bishop to Robert Lowell, 23 February 1966, bMS Am 1905 (62)–(264), Houghton Library, Harvard University.

2. David Kalstone so describes Bishop in *Five Temperaments* (New York: Oxford Univ. Press, 1977), 12.

3. Robert Lowell, "On Freedom in Poetry," in *Naked Poetry: Recent American Poetry in Open Forms*, ed. Stephen Berg and Robert Mezey (New York: Bobbs-Merrill, 1969), 124.

4. Elizabeth Bishop, "It All Depends," in *Mid-Century American Poets*, ed. John Ciardi (New York: Twayne, 1950), 267.

5. Elizabeth Bishop to Robert Lowell [1961], bMS Am 1905, Houghton Library, Harvard University.

6. John Berryman to Randall Jarrell, 9 Dec., 1962, John Berryman Papers, Manuscripts Division, University of Minnesota Libraries.

7. Berryman to Mary Jarrell, 30 October [1965], Special Collections Division, Jackson Library, University of North Carolina at Greensboro.

8. Paul Hoover, "Introduction," *Postmodern American Poetry* (New York: W. W. Norton, 1994), xxv.

9. Ibid.

10. Donald Allen and George F. Butterick, eds., *The Postmoderns: The New American Poetry Revised* (New York: Grove, 1982), 11.

11. John Ashbery, "The Complete Poems," *New York Times Book Review*, 1 June 1969, 8.

12. Hoover, "Introduction," xxv.

13. Michael Palmer, "An Interview with Michael Palmer," *Contemporary Literature* 30.1 (1989): 10. Cited from Mutlu Konuk Blasing, "Rethinking Models of Literary Change: The Case of James Merrill," *American Literary History* (summer 1990): 300–301. James Longenbach's *Modern Poetry after Modernism* (New York: Oxford, 1997) appeared after this book went to press. Longenbach and I agree in casting doubt on an aesthetic of "breakthrough" as a uniquely defining principle or governing mythos of postmodernism, but Longenbach views such an aesthetic of breakthrough in a negative light, whereas I am inclined to view such an aesthetic more neutrally. The mythos of breakthrough is central and necessary for certain important and entirely valid branches of postmodern poetry but by no means necessary for others. These tend to stress an aesthetic of exploration rather than breakthrough. On the other hand, breakthroughs may occur even for these exploratory postmodernisms as a spontaneous (and generally welcome) consequence of their exploratory efforts. When Longenbach reads Lowell as preoccupied with an aesthetics of breakthrough and thereafter pits Bishop against Lowell to the latter's discredit, we obviously differ. The evidence seems clear that Lowell, like Bishop, was less concerned with achieving aesthetic breakthroughs than with the ongoing problem of making particular poems. And in the work leading to *Life Studies*, often claimed as Lowell's decisive "breakthrough," Lowell freely acknowledged that he was working under the direct influence of Bishop. Hence Lowell's acute and generous remark in a letter to Bishop that "really I've just broken through to where you've always been." Unfortunately, despite the frequent critical freshness of his approach, Longenbach's insistence on using Bishop to denigrate Lowell leads him to perpetuate existing literary-historical paradigms that my research requires me to question.

14. For a similar view, see Peter Bürger, *Theory of the Avant-Garde*, trans. Michael Shaw (Minneapolis: Univ. of Minnesota Press, 1984).

15. Fredric Jameson, "The Cultural Logic of Late Capitalism" (1984), *in Postmodernism or, The Cultural Logic of Late Capitalism* (Durham: Duke Univ. Press, 1991), 16.

16. Elizabeth Bishop, "Algumas notas sobre Robert Lowell" (Some Notes on Robert Lowell), in Robert Lowell, *Quatro Poemas* (Rio de Janeiro: 1962), trans. George Montiero, *Elizabeth Bishop Bulletin* (summer 1998).

17. John Crowe Ransom, "Constellation of Five Young Poets," *Kenyon Review* 3 (1941): 377–79. Quoted from Suzanne Ferguson, ed., *Critical Essays on Randall Jarrell* (Boston: G. K. Hall, 1983), 15. This first literary use of the term "postmodernist," which passed unremarked for many years, was brought to my attention by Richard Flynn. Jarrell has often been given credit for coining the term in "Land of Unlikeness," his 1947 review of Lowell's *Lord Weary's Castle*.

18. Stephen Best and Douglas Kellner, *Postmodern Theory: Critical Interrogations* (New York: Guilford Press, 1991), 2.

19. Blasing, "Rethinking Models of Literary Change," 304.

20. Jameson, "Cultural Logic," 15.

21. Elizabeth Bishop, dust jacket blurb to Robert Lowell, *Life Studies* (New York: Farrar, Straus & Cudahy), 1959.

22. Stanley Kunitz, "Talk with Robert Lowell," *New York Times Book Review*, 4 October 1964, 34–38.

23. John Plotz et al., "An Interview with John Berryman," *Harvard Advocate* (spring 1969): 4–9. Quoted from Harry Thomas, ed., *Berryman's Understanding: Reflections on the Poetry of John Berryman* (Boston: Northeastern Univ. Press, 1988), 6.

24. A(lfred) Alvarez, "A Talk with Robert Lowell," *Encounter* 24 (Feb. 1965): 39–43. Quoted from Jeffery Meyers, *Lowell: Interviews and Memoirs* (Ann Arbor: Univ. of Michigan Press, 1988), 101.

25. Brett C. Millier and Jay Parini, eds., *Columbia History of American Poetry* (New York: Columbia Univ. Press, 1993).

26. In his 1964 interview with Stanley Kunitz, Lowell states, "The poets who mostly directly influenced me . . . were Allen Tate, Elizabeth Bishop, and William Carlos Williams. An unlikely combination! . . . but you can see that Bishop is a sort of bridge between Tate's formalism and William's informal art." Kunitz, "Talk with Robert Lowell," 34–38.

27. David Kalstone, *Becoming a Poet: Elizabeth Bishop with Marianne Moore and Robert Lowell*, ed. Robert Hemenway (New York: Farrar, Straus & Giroux, 1989), ix.

28. Robert Wilson, "Peter Taylor Remembers Robert Lowell," in *Conversations with Peter Taylor*, ed. Hubert H. McAlexander (Jackson: Univ. of Mississippi Press, 1987), 39.

29. Elizabeth Bishop to Robert Lowell, 23 February 1966, bMS Am 1905, Houghton Library, Harvard University.

30. Letter to Anne Stevenson, *Elizabeth Bishop* (New York: Twayne, 1966), 66.

31. Theodore Roethke, *On the Poet and His Craft: Selected Prose*, ed. Ralph J. Mills, Jr. (Seattle: Univ. of Washington Press, 1965), 160.

32. Theodore Roethke, *Collected Poems* (Garden City, N.Y.: Doubleday, 1965), 61.

33. Ian Hamilton, *Robert Lowell: A Biography* (New York, Random House, 1982), 335.

34. Ibid., 337.

35. Elizabeth Bishop to Robert Lowell, [13] April 1960, bMS Am 1905, Houghton Library, Harvard University.

36. Roethke, *Collected Poems*, 239.

37. See Bruce Bawer, "Schwartz, the Paradigm," in *The Middle Generation: The Lives and Poetry of Delmore Schwartz, Randall Jarrell, John Berryman, and Robert Lowell* (Hamden, Conn.: Archon Books, 1986), 68–79.

38. Carter, liner notes, *String Quartets Nos. 1 & 2*.

39. Peter Stitt, "The Art of Poetry: An Interview with John Berryman," *Paris Review* 53 (winter 1972). Quoted from Thomas, *Berryman's Understanding*, 21.

40. James E. B. Breslin, *From Modern to Contemporary* (Chicago: Univ. of Chicago Press, 1984), 3–4.

41. One could argue for a shift toward an emerging postmodern style, and in particular a sense of embattled personalism, in several of the late modernist works just cited—especially Pound's *Pisan Cantos*, Eliot's *Four Quartets*, some of Stevens's more self-exploratory late lyrics, and such late Williams sequences as "Of Asphodel, That Greeny Flower."

42. Jean-François Lyotard, *The Postmodern Condition*, trans. Geoff Bennington and Brian Massumi (Minneapolis: Univ. of Minnesota Press, 1984), 60.

43. Madan Sarup, *An Introductory Guide to Post-Structuralism and Postmodernism, 2d ed.* (Athens: Univ. of Georgia Press, 1993), 153–54.

44. Jameson, "Cultural Logic," xxii.

45. Randall Jarrell to John Berryman, [dated in Berryman's hand, 12 Feb. 48], Manuscripts Division, University of Minnesota Libraries.

46. Brett C. Millier, *Elizabeth Bishop: Life and the Memory of It* (Berkeley: Univ. of California Press, 1993), 186.

47. John McCormick, "Falling Asleep over Grillparzer," *Poetry* 81 (Jan. 1953). Quoted from Meyers, *Lowell: Interviews*, 30.

48. Fredrick Seidel, "The Art of Poetry: Robert Lowell," *Paris Review* 7 (winter-spring 1961); Jane Howard, "Applause for a Prize Poet," *Life* 58 (19 February 1965). Cited from Meyers, *Lowell: Interviews*, 67, 95.

49. Elizabeth Bishop to Robert Lowell, quoted from Charles Thornbury's "Introduction" to John Berryman, *Collected Poems, 1937–1971* (New York: Farrar, Straus & Giroux), xvii.

50. Dana Gioia, "Studying with Miss Bishop," *New Yorker*, 15 September 1986, 150. Cited from George Montiero, ed., *Conversations with Elizabeth Bishop* (Jackson: Univ. Press of Mississippi, 1996), 147–48.

51. Elizabeth Bishop to John Berryman, 14 October 1968, Manuscripts Division, University of Minnesota Libraries.

52. Lloyd Schwartz and Ilse Barker in Gary Fountain and Peter Brazeau's *Remembering Elizabeth Bishop: An Oral Biography* (Amherst: Univ. of Massachusetts Press, 1994), 340, 344.

## 2 The Confessional Paradigm Revisited

1. M. L. Rosenthal, *The New Poets: American and British Poetry Since World War II* (New York: Oxford Univ. Press, 1967), 25.

2. Stitt, "Art of Poetry," 21.

3. Joel Conarroe, ed., *Eight American Poets: An Anthology* (New York: Random House, 1994), 109.

4. Stitt, "Art of Poetry," 29.

5. Ibid., 31.

6. For further discussion of how a "process of life and a process of art" relate to Berryman's aesthetic, see Thornbury, "Introduction," *JBPoems*, especially lviii.

7. Adrienne Rich, "Mr. Bones, He Lives," *The Nation*, 25 May 1964, 538.

8. Ibid., 538.

9. John Berryman to Adrienne Rich, [dated "Washington, Friday 14." and addressed "Dear Adrienne Rich, and I mean *dear*."], Carbon in Manuscripts Division, University of Minnesota Libraries.

10. M. L. Rosenthal, "Poetry as Confession," *The Nation*, 19 September 1959, 154.

11. Rosenthal, *New Poets*, 26.

12. Alicia Ostriker, *Stealing the Language: The Emergence of Women's Poetry in America* (Boston: Beacon Press, 1986), 7, 54. Ostriker comments more positively on the autobiographical turn of *Geography III*, Bishop's last book.

13. Betsy Erkkila, *The Wicked Sisters: Women Poets, Literary History and Discord* (New York: Oxford Univ. Press, 1992), 150.

14. Breslin, *From Modern to Contemporary*, 3–4.

15. Alan Williamson, *Introspection and Contemporary Poetry* (Cambridge: Harvard Univ. Press, 1984), 2.

16. M. L. Rosenthal, *The Modern Poets* (New York: Oxford Univ. Press, 1960), 253–55.

17. For an account of Bishop's recent elevation to the status of major poet, see Thomas Travisano, "The Elizabeth Bishop Phenomenon," *New Literary History* (autumn 1995): 905–30, later collected in Margaret Dickie and Travisano, eds., *Gendered Modernisms: American Women Poets and Their Readers* (Philadelphia: Univ. of Pennsylvania Press, 1996), 220–44.

18. Adrienne Rich, "The Eye of the Outsider: The Poetry of Elizabeth Bishop," *Boston Review* 8 (April 1983): 16.

19. Ibid., 17.

20. Elizabeth Bishop to John Berryman, 14 October 1968, Manuscripts Division, University of Minnesota Libraries.

21. Elizabeth Bishop to Anne Stevenson, [dated "Rio, October 27th, 1964"], Rare Books Department, Washington University Library.

22. Elizabeth Bishop to Robert Lowell, April 1960, bMS Am 1905, Houghton Library, Harvard University.

23. Elizabeth Bishop to Robert Lowell, 15 June 1961, bMS Am 1905, Houghton Library, Harvard University.

24. Richard Wilbur in Fountain and Brazeau, *Remembering Elizabeth Bishop*, 108.

25. Robert Lowell to Elizabeth Bishop, 10 June 1957, Rare Books and Manuscripts, Vassar College Library.

26. See Thomas Travisano, *Elizabeth Bishop: Her Artistic Development* (Charlottesville: Univ. Press of Virginia, 1988), 151–56.

27. Diane Wood Middlebrook, "What Was Confessional Poetry?" *Columbia History of American Poetry*, 636.

28. Robert Lowell to Elizabeth Bishop, 20 April 1958, Rare Books and Manuscripts, Vassar College Library. Quoted from Travisano, *Elizabeth Bishop*, 153.

29. Beatriz Schiller, "Poetry Born out of Suffering," *Conversations with Bishop*, 76.

30. Stitt, "Art of Poetry," 21.

31. John Haffenden, *The Life of John Berryman* (New York: Ark Paperbacks, an imprint of Routledge & Kegan Paul, 1982), 2.

32. Williamson, *Introspection and Contemporary Poetry*, 7.

33. Harold Bloom, "Introduction," *Elizabeth Bishop: Modern Critical Views* (New York: Chelsea House, 1985), 1–3.

34. Harold Bloom, "Introduction," *Robert Lowell: Modern Critical Views* (New York: Chelsea House, 1987), 1.

35. Ibid.

36. Ibid., 2

37. Richard Flynn, *Randall Jarrell and the Lost World of Childhood* (Athens: Univ. of Georgia Press, 1990), 140.

38. James Longenbach, "Elizabeth Bishop and the Story of Postmodernism," *Southern Review* (summer 1992): 483–84. This interpretation appears, slightly reworded, in Longenbach's *Modern Poetry after Modernism*, 18.

39. Steven Gould Axelrod, "Lowell's Living Name: An Introduction," *Robert Lowell: Essays on the Poetry*, ed. Axelrod and Helen Deese (New York: Cambridge Univ. Press, 1986), 6.

40. Wilson, "Taylor Remembers Lowell," 39.

41. John Keegan, *The Second World War* (New York: Viking, 1989), 426.

42. Rich, "Mr. Bones, He Lives," 538.

43. Elizabeth Bishop, dust jacket blurb for Robert Lowell's *Life Studies* (New York: Farrar, Straus and Cudahy, 1959).

44. Ibid.

45. James Merrill, "A Class Day Talk," in *Recitative: Prose*, ed. J. D. McClatchy (San Francisco: North Point Press, 1986), 163.

46. Jane Howard, "Applause for a Prize Poet," 94.

47. Merrill, "An Interview with Donald Sheehan," *Recitative*, 24–25.

48. I would like to thank Charles Thornbury for drawing my attention to this Dream Song.

49. Haffenden, *Life of Berryman*, 55–56.

50. Homer, *The Iliad*, trans. Robert Fagles (New York: Viking, 1990), 77.

51. Haffenden, *Life of Berryman*, 56.

52. Stitt, "Art of Poetry," 21.

53. Rosenthal, "Poetry as Confession," 154.

54. Alice Miller, *The Drama of the Gifted Child*, trans. Ruth Ward (New York: Basic Books, 1981), 90.

55. Meyers, *Manic Power*, 13.

56. Flynn, *Randall Jarrell*, 136.

57. Adrienne Rich, "Living with Henry," *Harvard Advocate* 103 (spring 1969). Quoted from Thomas, *Berryman's Understanding*, 127.

58. Fred Chappell, "The Indivisible Presence of Randall Jarrell," *North Carolina Literary Review* 1 (summer 1992): 26.

59. Bawer, "Schwartz, the Paradigm," 4.

60. Rosenthal, "Poetry as Confession," 154.

61. Randall Jarrell, "Robert Lowell's Poetry" in *Mid-Century American Poets*, 165.

62. Kunitz, "Talk with Robert Lowell," 89.

63. Philip Booth, "Summers in Castine: Contact Prints, 1955–1965," quoted from Meyers, *Lowell: Interviews*, 200.

64. Kunitz, "Talk with Lowell," 85.

65. The phrase is Robert Pinsky's, in a prose memorial to Bishop, "Elizabeth Bishop, 1911–1979," *Elizabeth Bishop and Her Art* (Ann Arbor: Univ. of Michigan Press, 1983), 257.

## 3 Expulsion from Paradise

1. The best treatment of childhood's importance for a member of this generation is Flynn's *Randall Jarrell and the Lost World of Childhood.*

2. Sigmund Freud, *History of the Psychoanalytic Movement* (New York: Collier Books, 1963), 49.

3. Sigmund Freud, "Five Lectures In Psychoanalysis," in *The Complete Psychological Works of Sigmund Freud*, vol. 11, ed. James Strachey (London: Hogarth Press, 1955), 41.

4. "The Development of Anne Frank" was completed in 1967 and published for the first time among Berryman's collected essays, *The Freedom of the Poet* (New York: Farrar, Straus & Giroux, 1976), 91–106.

5. Irv Broughton, ed., "Allen Tate," interview, *The Writer's Mind*, vol. 1 (Fayetteville: Univ. of Arkansas Press, 1989), 38.

6. Miller, *Drama of the Gifted Child*, 74.

7. John Bowlby, "Violence in the Family," *A Secure Base: Parent-Child Attachment and Healthy Human Development* (New York: Basic Books, 1988), 78–79.

8. John Haffenden, *John Berryman: A Critical Commentary* (New York: New York Univ. Press, 1980), 81.

9. Lloyd Schwartz, dust jacket blurb in Fountain and Brazeau, *Remembering Elizabeth Bishop*.

10. Ibid.

11. Ibid.

12. Bishop to Anne Stevenson, "Answers to your questions of March 6th - [1964]," quoted from Thomas Travisano, "Emerging Genius: Elizabeth Bishop, 1927–1930," *Gettysburg Review* (winter 1992): 34.

13. Millier, *Elizabeth Bishop*, 20.

14. Dr. Richard Famularo, "What Are the Symptoms, Causes, and Treatments of Childhood Post-traumatic Stress Disorder?" *Harvard Mental Health Letter* 13 (Jan. 1997): 8.

15. Bishop's "Ballad of the Subway Train" was discovered by Gary Fountain. The present author arranged for its republication and provided an introduction, Thomas Travisano, "Heavenly Dragons: A Newly Discovered Poem by Elizabeth Bishop," *Western Humanities Review* (spring 1991): 26–33.

16. Elizabeth Bishop, "The Ballad of the Subway Train," *Western Humanities Review* 45 (spring 1991): 25–26.

17. Bishop, letter to Lowell, 11 July 1951, bMS Am 1905, Houghton Library, Harvard University, quoted from Jeredith Merrin, "Elizabeth Bishop: Gaity, Gayness and Change," in Marilyn May Lombardi, ed., *Elizabeth Bishop: Geography of Gender* (Charlottesville: Univ. Press of Virginia, 1993), 168.

18. Miller, *Drama of the Gifted Child*, 68–69.

19. Fountain and Brazeau, *Remembering Elizabeth Bishop*, 29–30.

20. Ibid., 28.

21. Ibid., 29–30.

22. Miller, *Drama of the Gifted Child*, 54.

23. Famularo, "Post-traumatic Stress Disorder," 8.

24. Fountain and Brazeau, *Remembering Elizabeth Bishop*, 29.

25. Bishop to Anne Stevenson, [March 1964], Rare Books Department, Washington University Library. Quoted from Millier, *Elizabeth Bishop*, 39.

26. Bowlby, *Secure Base*, 79.

27. Fountain and Brazeau, *Remembering Elizabeth Bishop*, 330.

28. Elizabeth Bishop, "The Past," Rare Books and Manuscripts, Vassar College Library.

29. Elizabeth Bishop, notebook, "E. Bishop, 1934, 1935, 1936, 1937," Rare Books and Manuscripts, Vassar College Library.

30. Schiller, "Poetry Born out of Suffering," 76.

31. Octavio Paz, *World Literature Today* (winter 1977): 16.

32. Bishop, 1978 interview with Alexandra Johnson, "Geography of Imagination," quoted from *Conversations with Elizabeth Bishop*, 99.

33. Helen Vendler, "Lowell in the Classroom," *Harvard Advocate* 113 (Nov. 1979), quoted from Meyers, *Lowell: Interviews*, 291–92.

34. William Wordsworth, *Selected Poems and Prefaces* (Boston: Houghton Mifflin, 1965), 186.

35. Henry David Thoreau, *Walden; or Life in the Woods* (New York: Signet, 1960), 71.

36. Alfred Kazin, "Randall: His Kingdom," in Lowell, Peter Taylor, and Robert Penn Warren, eds., *Randall Jarrell: 1914–1965* (New York: Farrar, Straus & Giroux, 1967), 89.

37. M. H. Abrams, *Natural Supernaturalism* (New York: Norton, 1971), 382.

38. See Philippe Ariès, *Centuries of the Child: A Social History of Family Life* (New York: Vintage, 1962); Jean Jacques Rousseau, *Émile* (New York: Dutton, 1911), 5.

39. Eileen Simpson, *Poets in Their Youth: A Memoir* (New York: Vintage, 1983).

40. Mary Jarrell, "The Group of Two," in *Randall Jarrell, 1914–1965*, 284–85.

41. Randall Jarrell to Amy Breyer, November 1942. Quoted from Stuart Wright, *Randall Jarrell: A Descriptive Bibliography* (Charlottesville: Univ. Press of Virginia, 1986), 227.

42. Mary Jarrell, interview by author, Greensboro, North Carolina, 18 October 1994.

43. Ibid.

44. Flynn, *Randall Jarrell*, 18. See Flynn pp. 18–21 for a discussion of the cited poems.

45. Mary Jarrell interview, 18 October 1994.

46. "Jarrell: 'Poetry . . . An Extreme State of Realization," *Greensboro Sun* (March-April 1977), 12.

47. Karl Shapiro, "The Death of Randall Jarrell," in *Randall Jarrell: 1914–1965*, 223.

48. Robert Lowell to Elizabeth Bishop, 24 October 1956, bMS Am 1905, Houghton Library, Harvard University.

49. Mary Jarrell, "The Group of Two," in *Randall Jarrell: 1914–1965*, 286.

50. Johnson, "Geography," in *Conversations*, 98.

51. E. E. Cummings, "In Just," *E. E. Cummings: A Selection of Poems* (New York: Harcourt, Brace, 1965), 25.

52. Lowell, "Randall Jarrell," in *Randall Jarrell, 1914–1965*, 178.

53. Helen Vendler, "Robert Lowell's Last Days and Last Poems," in Meyers, *Lowell: Interviews*, 302.

54. Paul Mariani, *Dream Song: The Life of John Berryman* (New York: Morrow, 1990), 12.

55. Simpson, *Poets*, 59.

56. Haffenden, *Life of Berryman*, 30.

57. Simpson, *Poets*, 61.

58. Berryman, Manuscripts Division, University of Minnesota Libraries. Quoted from Haffenden, *Life of Berryman*, 32.

59. Simpson, *Poets*, 63.

60. Stitt, "Art of Poetry," 31.

61. Simpson, *Poets*, 41.

62. Sigmund Freud, *Beyond the Pleasure Principle*, vol. 18 of *The Complete Psychological Works of Sigmund Freud*, ed. James Strachey (London: Hogarth Press, 1955), 37.

63. This poem, which Berryman did not include in later collections and omitted from *JBPoems*, is quoted from Haffenden, *Life of Berryman*, 139.

64. See Paul Mariani, *Lost Puritan: A Life of Robert Lowell* (New York: Norton, 1994), 27, and Lowell's "Unwanted" (*DBD* 122).

## 4 Points of the Compass

1. A(lfred) Alvarez, "Robert Lowell in Conversation," Meyers, *Lowell: Interviews*, 82.

2. *We Dream of Honour: John Berryman's Letters to His Mother*, ed. Richard J. Kelly (New York: W. W. Norton, 1988), 29.

3. Simpson, *Poets*, 23, 28.

4. Elizabeth Bishop to Anne Stevenson, "Answers to your questions of March 6th - [1964]," quoted from Travisano, "Emerging Genius," 34.

5. A list documented by an insurance inventory of his pre-college library; see appendix to Flynn, *Randall Jarrell* for this extraordinary list of books Jarrell lost in a fire when he was 18.

6. Jarrell, "Shakespeare Versus Ibsen," *Hume-Fogg Echo* (March 1930): 16.

7. Jarrell, "Libraries," Berg Collection, unpublished lecture, c. 1960, New York Public Library. In this lecture Jarrell states "The library seems to me—all exaggeration apart—the primary, essential medium for the dissemination of culture."

8. Mark Van Doren to John Berryman, 18 August 1936, Manuscripts Division, University of Minnesota Libraries.

9. John Berryman, *We Dream of Honour*, 112.

10. Haffenden, *Life of Berryman*, 76.

11. Allen Tate to John Berryman, 20 September 1936, Manuscripts Division, University of Minnesota Libraries.

12. John Berryman to Milt Halliday, 16 March 1937, Manuscripts Division, University of Minnesota Libraries. Quoted from E. M. Halliday, *John Berryman and the Thirties: A Memoir* (Amherst: Univ. of Massachusetts Press, 1987), 136.

13. Stitt, "Art of Poetry," cited from Haffenden, *Life of Berryman*, 90.

14. Kelly, ed., *We Dream of Honour*, 112.

15. Mary Jarrell in *Randall Jarrell's Letters*, 6, cites the number of manuscripts submitted as "478." Mark Van Doren to John Berryman, 8 September 1936, Manuscripts Division, University of Minnesota Libraries.

16. Allen Tate to John Berryman, 20 September 1936, Manuscripts Division, University of Minnesota Libraries.

17. Mark Van Doren to John Berryman, 8 September 1936, Manuscripts Division, University of Minnesota Libraries.

18. John Berryman to Allen Tate, 11 October 1936, Princeton University Library.

19. See Stuart Wright, *Randall Jarrell: A Descriptive Bibliography*, 1929–1983 (Charlottesville: Univ. Press of Virginia, 1986), 217–20.

20. Jarrell, newly discharged by the Army Air Corps, was taking over the duties of Margaret Marshall as *The Nation*'s Literary Editor while Marshall took a year's leave of absence—the only important editorship any of these poets would ever hold. Editing the new writing of the age, a crucial activity for the generation of Eliot, Pound, Moore, Ransom, and Tate, was less crucial for this generation because a range of venues was already open to them. As Jarrell collected congratulations for his temporary editorship of *The Nation*, Berryman was also receiving accolades because Tate had offered to pass on to his young protégé the editorship of the *Sewanee Review*. But Berryman decided to turn this editing job down in favor of continuing to teach under an annual contract at Princeton. Ultimately, this quartet chose not to devote their energies to editorial work.

21. Robert Penn Warren to John Berryman, 7 October 1936, Yale University Library.

22. John Berryman, Journal IV, 10 November 1937.

23. Kelly, ed., *We Dream of Honour*, 80.
24. Kelly, "Introduction." *We Dream of Honour*, 5.
25. Stitt, "Art of Poetry," 44.
26. Kelly, "Introduction." *We Dream of Honour*, 6.
27. Meyers, *Lowell: Interviews*, 296.
28. Kelly, ed., *We Dream of Honour*, 111.
29. Kelly, ed., *We Dream of Honour*, 111–12.
30. Miller, *Drama of the Gifted Child*, 28.
31. Notes taken in 1970, quoted in Haffenden, *Life of Berryman*, 30.
32. Miller, *Drama of the Gifted Child*, 28.
33. Ibid.
34. Kelly, "Introduction." *We Dream of Honour*, 6.
35. Ibid., 93.
36. Ibid., 94.
37. Robert Lowell to Elizabeth Bishop, 3 December 1957, Rare Books and Manuscripts, Vassar College Library. Quoted from Thomas Travisano, *Elizabeth Bishop: Her Artistic Development* (Charlottesville: Univ. Press of Virginia, 1988), 153.
38. *Southern Review* editors Warren and Brooks did not like Jarrell's prize-winning poem, "Orestes at Tauris," as much as did contest judges Tate and Van Doren. In fact, they chose not to print it, excusing themselves on the basis of the poem's length—oddly so, given that the prize was for a long poem. *Southern Review* instead published in its autumn 1937 issue a spread of eight shorter Jarrell poems. "Orestes" would finally appear in the winter 1943 issue of *Kenyon Review*.
39. Simpson, *Poets*, 121.
40. John Crowe Ransom, "The Rugged Way of Genius," in *Randall Jarrell: 1914–1965*, 155.
41. Allen Tate, "Young Randall," *Randall Jarrell: 1914–1965*, 231.
42. Ibid.
43. Ibid.
44. Undated tape recording of Ransom and Jarrell, Special Collections Division, Jackson Library, University of North Carolina at Greensboro.
45. Alvarez, "Talk with Lowell," in Meyers, *Lowell: Interviews*, 106.
46. Ransom, *Alumni News* (University of Greensboro), spring 1966, 8.
47. Ibid.
48. Ransom, "The Rugged Way," *Randall Jarrell: 1914–1965*, 155.
49. Alma Graham, "The Students Remember," *Alumni News* (University of Greensboro), spring 1966, 21.
50. June Cope Bencivenni, "The Students Remember," *Alumni News* (University of Greensboro), spring 1966, 19.
51. Robert Penn Warren, "University Tribute," *Alumni News* (University of Greensboro), spring 1966, 23.
52. Ibid.
53. Peter Taylor, "Randall Jarrell," in *Randall Jarrell: 1914–1965*, 242–43.
54. Flynn, *Randall Jarrell*, 57.
55. Ibid., 58–59.
56. Mary Jarrell to the author, 19 July 1986.

57. Marianne Moore to Elizabeth Bishop, 28 August 1936, Rare Books and Manuscripts, Vassar College Library, quoted from Millier, *Elizabeth Bishop*, 106.

58. John Berryman to Elizabeth Bishop, 22 December 1969, Rare Books and Manuscripts, Vassar College Library.

59. Marianne Moore, "Archaically New," in *Trial Balances*, ed. Ann Winslow (New York: MacMillan, 1935) p. 82. Reprinted in *Elizabeth Bishop and Her Art*, ed. Lloyd Schwartz and Sybil P. Estess (Ann Arbor: Univ. of Michigan Press, 1983) 175.

60. Elizabeth Bishop to John Berryman, 18 January 1970, Manuscripts Division, University of Minnesota Libraries

61. Berryman and Bishop may have met fleetingly at the crowded party staged at the Gotham Book Mart in November 1948 honoring Edith and Osbert Sitwell. Bishop had not planned to attend, but Marianne Moore "was firm. 'We must be *polite* to the Sitwells,' she said" (*EBProse* 150). Berryman—like Bishop excessively shy in his early years—disappeared when the famous *Life Magazine* photo was snapped. More than twenty years later, Berryman would conclude his 22 December 1969 letter to Bishop, "May we meet some time and talk. Merry Christmas." Unfortunately, this meeting never took place.

62. Elizabeth Bishop to Frani Blough (Muser), 7 February 1938, quoted from Millier, *Elizabeth Bishop*, 116.

63. Fountain and Brazeau, *Remembering Elizabeth Bishop*, 68.

64. Millier, *Elizabeth Bishop*, 112.

65. Simpson, *Poets*, 61.

66. Draft of letter, Marianne Moore to Elizabeth Bishop, 10 February 1938, Rosenbach Museum and Library. Quoted from Millier, *Elizabeth Bishop*, 137.

67. Bishop would write to Robert Giroux with characteristic self-deprecation after profiles of herself and Rukeyser appeared in the same 1978 issue of the *Vassar Quarterly*: "Her life is one heroic saga of fighting for the underdog: going to jail, writing about silicosis, picketing alone in Korea, also thinking very deeply about POETRY and motherhood. In comparison I sound about like Billie Burke." Elizabeth Bishop to Robert Giroux, *EBLet* 632.

68. Millier, *Elizabeth Bishop*, 134.

69. Fredrick Siedel, "The Art of Poetry: Robert Lowell," Meyers, *Lowell: Interviews*, 55–56.

70. Charlotte Lowell to Robert Lowell, n.d. but early August 1936. Cited from Mariani, *Lost Puritan*, 55.

71. Ransom, *Alumni News*, 8.

72. Kunitz, "Talk with Lowell," 86.

73. Robert Lowell, Sr., to Evans Dick, 23 December 1936. Cited from Mariani, *Lost Puritan*, 56.

74. Jahan Ramazani, *Poetry of Mourning: The Modern Elegy from Hardy to Heany* (Chicago: Univ. of Chicago Press, 1994), 227.

75. Ransom, *Alumni News*, 8.

76. Elizabeth Bishop to Robert Lowell, 15 June 1961, bMS Am 1905, Houghton Library, Harvard University.

77. Elizabeth Bishop to Robert Lowell, 23 January 1962, bMS Am 1905, Houghton Library, Harvard University.

78. Mary Jarrell interview, 18 October 1994. Letter from Mary Jarrell to the author.

79. James Merrill, *A Different Person: A Memoir* (New York: Knopf, 1993), 141–42.

80. On 26 April 1957 Elizabeth Bishop wrote to Robert Lowell, "This letter is partly to ask you to do something for him, or me—and it may be foolish of me; you may have already done it many times, for all I know, but anyway—In conversation with Marianne this morning I said I'd like to nominate Randall for the [National] Institute [of Arts and Letters] and she immediately said she'd be one of the 2nds. So I sent off the form, suggesting you as the other 2nd. . . .—well, not that any of it signifies much, but my idea is that it would be nice to have one's friends in so that those dinners, etc., might be fun in our old age. But probably Randall has made many enemies!—(I shld. hope so—) I did go to the dinner and it was something—it reminded me of a large and particularly painful family Thanksgiving dinner." bMS Am 1905, Houghton Library, Harvard University.

## 5 The Problem of Selfhood in the Postmodern World

1. Ransom, "Constellation," 377–79.

2. William H. Pritchard, *Randall Jarrell: A Literary Life* (New York: Farrar, Straus & Giroux, 1990), 94.

3. See Randall Jarrell, "Levels and Opposites: Structure in Poetry," *Georgia Review* (winter 1996): 697–713, and my introduction, "Randall Jarrell's Poetics: A Rediscovered Milestone," *Georgia Review* (winter 1996): 691–96.

4. Robert Lowell to Elizabeth Bishop, 25 October 1957, bMS Am 1905, Houghton Library, Harvard University.

5. Randall Jarrell, "Answers to Questions," in *Mid-Century American Poetry*, ed. John Ciardi (New York: Twayne Publishers, 1950), 183.

6. Bruce Michelson, "Randall Jarrell and Robert Lowell: The Making of *Lord Weary's Castle*," *Contemporary Literature* (winter 1985). Quoted from *Robert Lowell: Modern Critical Views*, ed. Harold Bloom (New York: Chelsea House, 1987), 139.

7. "Jarrell: 'Poetry . . . An Extreme State of Realization," *Greensboro Sun* (March-April 1977), 12.

8. For further detail see Pritchard, *Randall Jarrell*, 97–99.

9. James McCorkle, *The Still Performance: Writing, Self, and Interconnection in Five Postmodern American Poets* (Charlottesville: Univ. Press of Virginia, 1989), 40. McCorkle sees this opening as evidence that Bishop "further dislodges the authority of art."

10. Langdon Hammer, "The New Elizabeth Bishop," *Yale Review* (winter 1993): 137.

11. Bishop, "It All Depends," in *Mid-Century American Poets*, ed. Ciardi, 267.

12. *Ibid.*

13. Ashley Brown, "An Interview with Elizabeth Bishop," *Shenandoah* 17 (winter 1966): 13.

14. *Ibid.*, 296.

15. Breslin, *From Modern to Contemporary*, 298.

16. Jan B. Gordon, "Days and Distances: The Cartographic Imagination of Elizabeth Bishop," *Salmagundi* 22–23 (1973): 60.

17. William Carlos Williams, "Preface," *Paterson, Book I* (New York: New Directions, 1946).

18. Wallace Stevens, "The Man with the Blue Guitar," *Collected Poems* (New York: Knopf, 1954), 165.

19. Ezra Pound, *The Cantos* (New York: New Directions, 1972), 796.

20. John Berryman to Allen Tate, Oct. 11, 1936, Firestone Library, Princeton University.

21. Simpson, *Poets*, 112.

22. Ibid., 107.

23. Berryman, "On Poetry and the Age," in *Jarrell, 1914–1965*, 10.

24. John Haines, "Further Reflections on Line and Poetic Voice," in *A Field Guide to Contemporary Poetry and Poetics*, ed. Stuart Friebert and David Young (New York: Longman, 1980), 71.

25. Mariani, *Dream Song*, 75.

26. Vendler, "Lowell in the Classroom," 22–26, 28–29, quoted from Meyers, *Lowell: Interviews*, 289.

27. Simpson, *Poets*, 6.

28. Mariani, *Dream Song*, 90.

29. Robert Pinsky, *The Situation of Poetry* (Princeton: Princeton Univ. Press, 1976), 24–25.

30. For a discussion of Bishop's subtle exploitation of breachs of good taste, see Thomas Travisano, "'The Flicker of Impudence': Delicacy and Indelicacy in the Art of Elizabeth Bishop," in *Geography of Gender* (Charlottesville: Univ. Press of Virginia, 1993)

31. Actually, in his original review of *Mills of the Kavanaughs* in *Partisan Review* in 1951, Jarrell wrote that "Falling Asleep over the Aeneid" is "almost as good" as "Mother Marie Therese." However, when he reprinted the essay in *Poetry and the Age* in 1953, Jarrell reversed his preference, a fact pointed out to the author by Steven Gould Axelrod.

32. Simpson, *Poets*, 115.

33. Kelly, ed., *We Dream of Honour*, 223–24.

34. Simpson, *Poets*, 130.

35. Ibid., 132.

36. Samuel Johnson, "Life of Milton," *The Lives of the English Poets*, vol. 1 (Philadelphia: J. B. Lippincott, 1866), 167–68.

37. Ezra Pound, "The Hard and Soft in French Poetry," *Literary Essays*, ed. T. S. Eliot (New York: New Directions, 1935), 287.

38. Eliot, *Selected Essays* (New York: Harcourt Brace, 1950), 268

39. W. H. Auden, "Robert Frost," in *The Dyer's Hand* (New York, 1963), 340–1.

40. Simpson, *Poets*, 132–33.

41. Samuel Taylor Coleridge, *Inquiring Spirit: A Coleridge Reader* (New York: Minerva Press, 1951), 165.

42. John Crowe Ransom, "A Poem Nearly Anonymous," *The World's Body* (Baton Rouge: Louisiana State Univ. Press, 1938), 1.

43. Ibid., 27–28.

44. Robert Lowell to Peter Taylor, [n.d., but 1941], Vanderbilt University Library.

## 6 Exploring Lost Worlds

1. "Jarrell: 'Poetry . . . An Extreme State of Realization," *Greensboro Sun* (March-April 1977), 12.

2. Berryman, unpublished notebook, Manuscripts Division, University of Minnesota Libraries.

3. Lowell's review of 77 *Dream Songs* is slightly misquoted by Berryman. Lowell calls *Homage* "the most resourceful historical poem in our language" (*RLProse* 106).

4. Peter Stitt, "Art of Poetry," 24.

5. Kalstone, *Becoming a Poet*, 187–88.

6. Robert Lowell to Elizabeth Bishop, 20 April 1958, Rare Books and Manuscripts, Vassar College Library. Quoted from Travisano, *Elizabeth Bishop*, 153.

7. Alvarez, "Robert Lowell in Conversation," in Meyers, *Lowell: Interviews*, 80–81.

8. Gioia, "Studying with Miss Bishop," *Conversations*, 150.

## 7 Displacing Sorrow

1. Jahan Ramazani, *Yeats and the Poetry of Death* (Yale Univ. Press: New Haven, 1990), 8.

2. Ibid., 9.

3. Jarrell, "Levels and Opposites: Structure in Poetry," 705.

4. Ellen Zetzel Lambert, *Placing Sorrow, A Study of the Pastoral Elegy Tradition from Theocritus to Milton* (Chapel Hill: Univ. of North Carolina Press, 1976), xxv.

5. Pritchard, *Randall Jarrell*, 119–20.

6. Lambert, *Placing Sorrow*, xv.

7. Jarrell, "Structure in Poetry," unpublished lecture, Berg Collection, New York Public Library.

8. Ariès, *Hour of Our Death*, 6.

9. Ibid.,15.

10. Ibid.

11. G. W. Pigman, *Grief and English Renaissance Elegy* (New York: Cambridge Univ. Press, 1985), 5

12. Ariès, *Hour of Our Death*, 28.

13. Pigman, *Grief*, 4.

## 8 A Cycle of Elegies

1. Jay Martin, "Grief and Nothingness: Loss and Mourning in Lowell's Poetry," in Axelrod and Deese, eds., *Robert Lowell: Essays on the Poetry*, 30–31.

2. Elizabeth Bishop to Robert Lowell, 25 June 1961, in bMS Am 1905, Houghton Library, Harvard University. Quoted from Victoria Harrison, *Elizabeth Bishop's Poetics of Intimacy* (New York: Cambridge Univ. Press, 1993), 30.

3. Elizabeth Bishop, "Algumas notas sobre Robert Lowell" (Some Notes on Robert Lowell), in Robert Lowell, *Quatro Poemas* (Rio de Janeiro: 1962), trans. George Montiero. *Elizabeth Bishop Bulletin* (summer 1998).

4. Dana Gioia, "Studying with Miss Bishop" New Yorker, 15 September 1986, 90–101. Cited from George Montiero, ed., *Conversations with Elizabeth Bishop* (Jackson: Univ. Press of Mississippi, 1996), 147–48.

5. Quoted from *RJLet* 487.

6. Mary Jarrellinterview, October 18, 1994.

7. Irv Broughton, "Fred Chappell," *The Writer's Mind: Interviews with American Authors*, vol. 3 (Fayetteville: Univ. of Arkansas Press, 1990), 112.

8. Berryman to Mary Jarrell, 30 October [1965], Berg Collection, New York Public Library.

9. Elizabeth Bishop to Robert Lowell, 18 November 1965, bMS Am 1905, Houghton Library, Harvard University.

10. L. Richardson Preyer, "A Gentle Power," in *The Alumni News*, spring 1966: 15.

11. Heather Ross Miller, Dr. Ineko Kondo, and Pamela Paff, "The Students Remember," in *Alumni News*, 16–18.

12. Broughton, ed., "Fred Chappell," 112.

13. Simpson, *Poets*, 111.

14. Jean Farley White, "The Students Remember," *Alumni News*, 16.

15. Miller, *Drama of the Gifted Child*, 60.

16. "Jarrell: 'Poetry . . . An Extreme State of Realization," *Greensboro Sun* (March-April 1977), 12.

17. Stitt, "Art of Poetry," 44.

18. Simpson, *Poets*, 240.

19. Mary Jarrell, "Foreword," *The Lost World:* Twenty Years After. *The Lost World* (New York: MacMillan, revised ed. 1985), xiv.

20. Simpson, *Poets*, 147.

21. Berryman, "Randall Jarrell," *Randall Jarrell: 1914–1965*, 15.

22. Simpson, *Poets*, 148.

23. Robert Lowell to John Berryman, 10 March 1966, Manuscripts Division, University of Minnesota Libraries.

24. Haffenden, *Life of Berryman*, 419.

25. Ibid., 56.

26. William Matthews, "In Loving Memory of the Late Author of *The Dream Songs*," in *Berryman's Understanding*, 83.

27. Saul Bellow, "John Berryman," foreword to Berryman's *Recovery* (New York: Farrar, Straus & Giroux, 1973), xiv.

28. Simpson, *Poets*, 252.

29. Elizabeth Bishop to Robert Lowell, quoted from Thornbury, "Introduction," in *JBPoems* xvii.

30. Elizabeth Bishop to Anne Stevenson, letter dated "Rio, October 27th, 1964," Rare Books Department, Rare Books Department, Washington University Library.

31. Elizabeth Bishop to John Berryman, 14 October 1968, Manuscripts Division, University of Minnesota Libraries.

32. Elizabeth Bishop to John Berryman, 14 October 1968, Manuscripts Division, University of Minnesota Libraries.

33. Elizabeth Bishop to John Berryman, 14 October 1968, Manuscripts Division, University of Minnesota Libraries.

34. John Berryman to Elizabeth Bishop, 22 Dec. 1969, Rare Books and Manuscripts, Vassar College Library.

35. Elizabeth Bishop to John Berryman, 18 January 1970, Manuscripts Division, University of Minnesota Libraries.

36. John Berryman to Elizabeth Bishop, February 1970, Vassar College Library.

37. Elizabeth Bishop to John Berryman, 18 January 1970, Manuscripts Division, University of Minnesota Libraries.

38. Dudley Young, "Talk with Robert Lowell," *Lowell: Interviews*, 148.

39. See Thomas Travisano, "'The Flicker of Impudence': Delicacy and Indelicacy in the Art of Elizabeth Bishop," in Lombardi, ed., *Geography of Gender*, pp. 111–25.

40. Elizabeth Bishop to Anne Stevenson, "Rio, October 27th, 1964," Rare Books Department, Washington University Library.

41. William Blake, "The Marriage of Heaven and Hell," *The Poetry and Prose of William Blake*, ed. David V. Erdman (Garden City, New York: Doubleday, 1965), 35.

42. James Merrill, "Overdue Pilgrimage to Nova Scotia," *A Scattering of Salts* (New York: Knopf, 1995), 88.

43. Fountain and Brazeau, *Remembering Elizabeth Bishop*, 330.

44. "Jarrell: 'Poetry . . . An Extreme State of Realization," *Greensboro Sun* (March–April 1977).

45. Fountain and Brazeau, *Remembering Elizabeth Bishop*, 333.

46. Elliott Carter, liner notes, *String Quartets Nos. 1 & 2*.

47. Robert Lowell to John Berryman, [March 1948], Manuscripts Division, University of Minnesota Libraries.

48. Robert Lowell to John Berryman. 30 August [1948], Manuscripts Division, University of Minnesota Libraries.

49. Plotz et al., "Interview with John Berryman," 12.

50. Simpson, *Poets*, 224.

51. John Berryman to Robert Lowell, 1957, bMS Am 1905, Houghton Library, Harvard University.

52. Robert Lowell to John Berryman [15 March 1959], Manuscripts Division, University of Minnesota Libraries.

53. Robert Lowell to John Berryman, 22 September 1968, Manuscripts Division, University of Minnesota Libraries.

54. Robert Lowell to John Berryman, 10 March 1966, Manuscripts Division, University of Minnesota Libraries.

55. Elizabeth Bishop, notebook, "E. Bishop, 1934, 1935, 1936, 1937," Rare Books and Manuscripts, Vassar College Library.

56. Fountain and Brazeau, *Remembering Elizabeth Bishop*, 272.
57. Ibid., 341.
58. Ibid., 341–42.
59. Ibid., 341.
60. William Shakespeare, *Love's Labour's Lost*, in *The Complete Penguin Shakespeare*, ed. Alfred Harbage (Baltimore: Penguin, 1969), 209.
61. Fountain and Brazeau, *Remembering Elizabeth Bishop*, 344.

# Index